STARTS Weaving the Art-Science Tangled Web

An Artistic Study of DG CONNECT's Adoption of Totalitarian Art Pioneering the Path to Europe's Undemocratic Future Past

Being
An Epistolary Account of how the Legend, Myth, and Magic of Science, Technology, and the Arts are being used in Pursuit of the European Commission's Weltanschauung

STARTS Weaving the Art-Science Tangled Web

An Artistic Study of DG CONNECT's Adoption of Totalitarian Art Pioneering the Path to Europe's Undemocratic Future Past

Being
An Epistolary Account of how the Legend, Myth, and Magic of Science, Technology, and the Arts are being used in Pursuit of the European Commission's Weltanschauung

by

Paul T Kidd

Cheshire Henbury

Cover Image – Europeanness (Acrylic, Posca and Laser Printed Paper on Canvas Paper)
© Copyright Paul T Kidd, 2019

First published in 2019 by Cheshire Henbury.
Paperback version ISBN 978-1-901864-26-7

British Library Cataloguing in Publication Data: A catalogue record for this book is available from the British Library.

Email – Use Email Contact: www.cheshirehenbury.com/emailcontact.html
Web site: www.cheshirehenbury.com/starts-weaving-the-art-science-tangled-web

Dedicated to those that are still able to think slowly, to those that have resisted the modern trend towards the pursuit of fortune and glory regardless of the price to their integrity, humanity and the planet, to those who still resist, to those that reject human predacity (including that displayed by artists), and to those who can hear the words that we speak in silence …

Also by Paul T Kidd

PREFACE

STARTS an attempt, by some artists and arts organisations, to transfer themselves from the dingy ghetto of restricted arts funding to the relatively opulent palaces of STEM funding, for it is a truth not universally known, that a STEM person (or a STEM research funding body like DG CONNECT) in want of an image, must be in want of an artist, and that an artist in want of an income must be in want of a STEM person (or a STEM funding body like DG CONNECT) in want of an image. Thus too does STEM issue forth STEAM!

But that which STARTS to STEAM comes at a very high price to research integrity, for to pull-off this magic, there is a need to engage in fabrication, falsification and other activities that fall short of outright deception, activities that are called Detrimental Research Practices.

Consequently, once more do we journey into our strange scriptovisual world, that space between descriptive expression and plastic expression, that world that lies between the cognitive and the expressive. And in doing this, we, by way of results, present to you a work which, if to literary (reader-response) theory you are inclined and will thus understand, invites you to undertake both an efferent reading and aesthetic one, for we are far away from Ancient Greek dualities – DG CONNECT are not and this is part of their massively flawed mentality. Explored within, even more features of their ancient past, which still lives on, in this very out-dated organisation.

If you are wise and understand, you will use these insights to disrupt, to do things that DG CONNECT will not understand, such is the problem of their Europeanness! Please use this insight to disrupt – we implore!

And to the observing and exploring of failing institutions – increasingly corrupt, incompetent and sinister too – and their predacity, do we now turn our pen: the failing institutions that are Western STEM, DG CONNECT, the European Commission, and yes – dare we say it? – the

European Union, where we find that those whom to the art world do claim to belong, have joined the folks on the hill, for they learned fast, how to smile while they kill, for it is, as before, the price of admission, and part of the spreading infectious disease known as moral corruption.

Some on the left say that it is a capitalist conspiracy; some on the right say it is a socialist conspiracy! It seems you have forgotten already, that an ideology such as this has a name. Speak it now if you can!

So do we write, while watching, as they begin their retreat into a past that only exists in mythology, while heading for that place which in time past, tragically, was very much a reality! The European Commission's very own Ahnenerbe we do now present, along with a question that no one would think, nor dare to ask, but we in the creation of strange affect can: What do Lenin, Stalin, Hitler and DG CONNECT have in common? But before we begin in earnest to answer in fair time, this we do render with our pen:

Jean-Claude and his successors will not be pleased that DG CONNECT, like the rest too, caught by the beautiful reflection, the one that deludes and deceives, did become a clear manifestation of all that is a justification for Member States departing the monster that the Union is destined to become. This is a warning – will the Member States take heed? No they will not. Thus do we become the wind – the silent storm that demonstrates that the pen is far mightier than the European Union! Enemies, enemies, enemies all about, 'tis an existential crisis, of that there is no doubt. One though made in the *City of the Golden Stars*, for as in empires past, no Reich can last for a thousand years.

It is time to create a different Europe – a Europe that is not Europe! A post European-era Europe. A post-Enlightenment Europe. Understand …

Paul T Kidd PhD, CEng, FIMechE, FIET, SMIEEE

(A European Union Dissident in Exile)

29 March 2019

"To hold a pen is to be at war."
Voltair

"The Government of the Reich will
undertake a thorough moral purging
of the body corporate of the nation.
The entire educational system, the theatre,
the cinema, literature, the Press, and the
wireless - all these will be used as means
to this end and valued accordingly.
They must all serve for the maintenance
of the eternal values present
in the essential character of
our people."

Adolf Hitler, 1933

STARTS Peirce's Theory of Sign

Peirce's Sign Theory, or Semiotic, is an account of signification, representation, reference and meaning. Although sign theories have a long history, Peirce's accounts are distinctive and innovative for their breadth and complexity, and for capturing the importance of interpretation to signification.

For Peirce, developing a thoroughgoing theory of signs was a central philosophical and intellectual preoccupation. The importance of semiotic for Peirce was wide ranging, including mathematics, ethics, metaphysics, gravitation, thermodynamics, optics, chemistry, comparative anatomy, astronomy, psychology, phonetics, economics, the history of science, etc. Peirce also treated sign theory as central to his work on logic, and as the medium for inquiry and the process of scientific discovery.

Peirce produced many definitions of a sign. Here is one of those: A Sign is anything which is so determined by something else, called its Object, and so determines an effect upon a person, which effect is called its Interpretant, with the later mediately determined by the former.

Peirce's basic claim is that signs consist of three inter-related parts: a sign, an object, and an interpretant. For the sake of simplicity, we can think of the sign as the signifier, for example, a written word, an utterance, smoke as a sign for fire etc. The object, on the other hand, is best thought of as whatever is signified, for example, the object to which the written or uttered word attaches, or the fire signified by the smoke. The interpretant, the most innovative and distinctive feature of Peirce's account, is best thought of as the understanding that we have of the sign/object relation. The importance of the interpretant for Peirce lay in the fact that signification is not a simple dyadic relationship between sign and object: a sign signifies only in being interpreted. This makes the interpretant central to the content of the sign, in that, the meaning of a sign is manifest in the interpretation that it generates in sign users.

Matters are, however, slightly more complex than this, but there is, in this case, no need to look at these three elements in more detail to see why. All you need are the basics as just described.

"Whom the gods would destroy
they first make mad."

STARTS a Social Construction of Reality

STARTS is a social construction of reality. So is STEAM. So is the art-science lovers' world. So is STEM. So is religion, politics, the European Union, and so on and so forth. This is what people do – all people, in all ages. They engage in the social construction of reality. An assemblage of beliefs, values, maxims, taken for granted assumptions, ideologies, myths, superstitions, misunderstandings, truth claims (false and otherwise), and what might be classified by participants as knowledge, all of these constitutes the sum of a particular socially constructed reality. To know this assemblage is to know that reality. But what is regarded as knowledge actually turns out to be more complicated than people believe is the case. All socially constructed realities are also, by definition, intersubjective.

And language is the means by which realities are constructed – concepts, discourses, reports, books, essays, experts' pronouncements, etc. All of these are designed to affect the mind, and to build and reinforce the constructed realities. All of these *texts* are part of an ideology, and all have that ideology embedded in them! You just do not notice. Unless you know how to look that is! Like the ICT-ART CONNECT study report, for example, which is a report that is structured around an ideology, but which at the same time is that ideology – a social construction of reality. But is *study* the right word? And these ideologies are invariably conservative and authoritarian. Conservative because they are backward looking, and authoritarian because they impose prescribed or desired behaviours. The art-science lovers demonstrate the point – they look back to a mythical age, when they believe art and science were one, and then read – *reconstruct* – texts to demonstrate the truth of this claim! They then seek to project onto people certain forms of behaviour that are prescribed by these so-called truths. This is subtle or not so subtle, depending on the circumstances. And thus are we invited by this behaviour – irresistibly invited – to undertake critical analysis of the resulting texts – to disrupt the socially constructed reality, which, as history shows, is usually problematic for those being disrupted. Thus with great pleasure we disrupt!

By way of contrast, this work – we do not call it a book, for such things are part of another socially constructed reality – is not a social construction of reality. This work is a composition of reality, that is, by its nature, not intersubjective. We imagine and create using languages, and through these means, we affect the mind. Surely you have noticed this already? It is a disruption that calls into question – socially constructed realities. That is what we do. If more people had done this in Europe's past, then some of its socially constructed realities might never have taken hold, and the history of Europe, of the world, might have been very different.

The pen is far mightier than the sword. The pen and the brush combined, mightier still. We call it scriptovisualism, but we will not explain it, because you will then seek to fit this into one of the socially constructed realities to which you subscribe or which you are aware of. That is another disruption. It is also the case that the pen is mightier than the European Union and the European Commission, and the pen and the brush combined, mightier still.

Thus do we study specific social constructions of reality, using knowledge from the domains of psychology, sociology, and certain disciplines from within what are called the humanities, all of which we have noted, are largely missing from the socially constructed realities that we analyse through this work.

Science, technology, engineering, art and culture played a central role in the Nazi regime's struggle for power, as they also do now for Europe's latest regime – the European Commission. The Nazi regime's socially constructed reality is now known by most, in varying levels of detail, it being a matter of historical record, although why so many Europeans (not just Germans) believed in it and unquestioningly participated, is not much evident among most of the historical accounts of that period. The European Commission's socially constructed reality, by contrast, is still shrouded in darkness, as is the reason why, once again, Europeans believed in *it* – whatever *it* is – and are so willing to unquestioningly participate. Time for that disruption …

The social construction of reality that is STARTS, that is STEAM, that is the art-science lovers' symbolic universe: all of these operate at the level of mythology and theology – a secular religious theology. As indeed did National Socialism. As indeed does European Union Nationalism. As indeed does the European Commission.

And in these socially constructed realities you will find a need for more myth making and the rewriting of history. If you look very closely you will find that these things have already begun!

This Work STARTS with the Asking of a Question

As this work STARTS – begins – we ask a question. What question do we ask? This question we ask: Is the European Commission a right-wing authoritarian regime? We have asked! You have already answered – fast! Critical thinking for most people has already ceased. The time for that is past. That is how far into the nightmare they have journeyed. You will see anon.

"Master Pangloss taught metaphysico-theologico-cosmolooneyology. He could prove to admiration that there is no effect without a cause; and, that in this best of all possible worlds, the European Union was the most magnificent of all European Unions, and the European Commission the best of all possible European rulers. Pangloss was in the right. All is for the best."

"The proof of the endowment of a true artist is always to be found in the fact that his work of art expresses the general will of a period."

Adolf Hitler, 1938

5

It STARTS with Little Things ...

On May 25th, 2018, a new regulation came into force across the European Union. The regulation is known for short as GDPR – the General Data Protection Regulation. It replaced earlier legislation based on a European Directive – the Data Protection Directive 95/46/EC. Under the GDPR there is a general obligation to implement technical and organisational measures which show that organisations have considered and integrated data protection into their processing activities. Prior to May 25th, across the European Union, respectable organisations were busy implementing the GDPR and enhancing the security of personal data, which is particularly important given the growing incidence of identity theft.

In the run-up to May 25th we received much correspondence from respectable organisations, explaining how they were implementing the GDPR, what our rights are, and what they were doing to ensure the security needed to prevent the personal data they hold from being accidentally lost, used or accessed in an unauthorised way, altered, or disclosed. Very reassuring! One must be very careful with personal data!

Turning to the matter of an evaluation taking place in one of the regime's many compounds. On April 10th, 2018 and an email arrived from the regime:

> Dear expert,
>
> In order to give you easier access to the building for your next evaluations, could you please give me your details hereafter? (before Friday noon)
>
> Date of birth:
>
> Nationality:
>
> ID card/passport number:
>
> I thank you in advance for your collaboration.
>
> See you next week.
>
> Best regards,

So the regime wanted its experts to send by unencrypted means – an email – sensitive personal data, without regard for any data protection laws – neither the GDPR nor the Data Protection Directive 95/46/EC!

We sent the requested information to the regime in an encrypted file attached to an email, which they informed by return email, that they could not open because it needed a password. We invited them to ring and obtain the password. They did not ring. On the first day of the evaluation, a Monday morning, we had no problems accessing the compound. We went through the security screening machine, went to the reception desk and informed the security person that we had come for the evaluation. There were ready prepared security badges on a table. We showed our passport, was handed our badge, and then entered the building.

At the first consensus meeting, while waiting for the European Commission moderator to arrive, we asked the experts present if they had sent their personal details to the regime in an unencrypted email. They all had! All were scientists doing what they were told by someone in authority.

An isolated incident? What do you believe? On September 11th 2018 we received an identical email, this time from the Research Executive Agency (REA) asking for sensitive person data to be sent by unsecured means. We ignored the request and had no problems entering the regime's compound in Covent Garden in the *City of the Golden Stars*.

Here is a spokesperson from the United Kingdom's Information Commissioner's Office, the ICO:

"Without encryption methods in place the email body and any attachments will be accessible to any unintended recipient or third-party who intercepts the communication. We have fined organisations that have broken rules relating to the sending personal data by email. For example, Surrey Council was served with a civil monetary penalty of £120,000 after three data breaches that involved misdirected emails containing sensitive personal data. North Somerset Council was also served with a civil monetary penalty of £60,000 after five emails, two of which contained details of a child's serious case review, were sent to the wrong NHS employee. In the latter case the ICO found that the Council had not delivered appropriate data protection training to relevant staff, and recommended that the Council adopt a more secure means of sending information electronically such as using encryption."

Prior to May 25th, all across the European Union, respectable organisations were busy implementing the GDPR and enhancing the security of personal data – only respectable organisations though.

The rule of law – the law applies to everyone and every organisation or institution, as opposed to *rule by law*.

"If we wish to fight, the enemy can be forced to an engagement even though he be sheltered behind a high rampart and a deep ditch. All we need do is attack some other place that he will be obliged to relieve."

STARTS A Warning from History – The Ahnenerbe

STARTS a warning from history – the Ahnenerbe!

The Ahnenerbe was a Nazi research activity. Research might not be the right word to use, but it did involve people doing – research! The Ahnenerbe was a Nazi research activity – an ideologically driven *crack-pot* research activity that was focused on researching the archaeological and cultural history of the *mythical* Aryan race. It was based on beliefs founded in legend, myth and magic. Rationalising the irrational! It was research aimed at finding the results that they wanted to find, disregarding the rest, and interpreting their finding in a way that supported what they believed, in an effort to justify Nazi ideology and actions – the creation of the German National Socialist European Union ruled by Aryan people (Germans). It was an exercise in rewriting history.

The Ahnenerbe developed over time to include murder and experiments on human beings, leading to criminal prosecutions by the Allied powers.

So taking false truth claims, and transforming them into (so-called) respectable truth claims, at least in the context of (perverse) beliefs and values prevailing in The Third Reich, has a history in Europe, and is not a new phenomenon.

The Ahnenerbe is a demonstration of what can happen when unaccountable power, large resources, and lack of ethics and morality come together. An explosive cocktail! A recipe for creating a legacy of false results that corrupts the research record. This corruption of the research record may still be exerting an affect in some fields!

The Ahnenerbe was a specialised social construction of reality, part of the bigger German National Socialist's socially constructed reality – part of the Nazi weltanschauung.

STARTS is a specialised social construction of reality, part of the bigger European Union Nationalist's socially constructed reality – part of the European Commission's weltanschauung.

John Lennon STARTS to Sing

What is that that we hear? It is a voice from the past, the voice of the one who sent his medal back! We tune in and just catch a few words:

"...There's room at the top they're telling you still
"But first you must learn how to smile as you kill
"If you want to be like the folks on the hill ..."

Then he is gone. His voice falls silent. He eventually understood what the medal meant and then he sent it back.

The folks on the hill have nothing that we want!

"Art is a partner of ICT, providing a
tool for public engagement to induce
change in social and individual
behaviours. This evidently,
is most strategic."

European Commission, DG CONNECT, 2013

STARTS Weaving the Art-Science Tangled Web

STARTS weaving the art-science tangled web,
STARTS new Leonardos in ignorance dwelling,
STARTS the new Medici's power rising,
STARTS the unravelling.

"It is the task of art to be
the expression
of the determining spirit
of the age."

Adolf Hitler, 1933

Barriers to Action

Here are some barriers to action for you to reflect upon:

- No idea what to do to respond;
- Unsure if what you are seeing is poor practice or something far more serious and sinister;
- Not believing that what is being exposed, can happen;
- Cultural issues over what is acceptable to discuss;
- Thinking that what you are seeing is lies, exaggerations or misunderstandings;
- Personal and organization relationships clouding judgments;
- Being scared of the consequences of acting;
- Being too embarrassed to act;
- Having no experience of the situation that presents itself to you.
- Becoming lost in art's romantic mist, rendering normally sensible people incapable of exercising any judgement.

Alexander Solzhenitsyn now speaks:

"A political speech, an aggressive piece of journalism, a programme for the organization of society, a philosophical system, can all be constructed – with apparent smoothness and harmony – on an error or on a lie. What is hidden and what is distorted will not be discerned right away."

"It is rather for us to be here dedicated to the great task remaining before us – that from these honoured dead we take increased devotion to that cause for which they gave the last full measure of devotion – that we here highly resolve that these dead shall not have died in vain – that this nation, under God, shall have a new birth of freedom – and that government of the people, by the people, for the people, shall not perish from the earth."

Enlightenment is Totalitarian

Max Horkheimer and Theodor Adorno now wish to say something very important. Next time you here someone saying "science and innovation are also key to preserving the values of enlightenment and democracy", or other such nonsense, think of disciplinary idiocy and understand why the history of Europe is a history of European Unions, but history does not unfold according to predictable patterns! This is what Horkheimer and Adorno wish to say: "Enlightenment is totalitarian!"

"The Enlightenment discerned the old powers in the Platonic and Aristotelian heritage of metaphysics and suppressed the universal categories' claims to truth as superstition. In the authority of universal concepts the Enlightenment detected a fear of the demons through whose effigies human beings had tried to influence nature in magic rituals. From now on matter was finally to be controlled without the illusion of immanent powers or hidden properties. For enlightenment, anything which does not conform to the standard of calculability and utility must be viewed with suspicion. Once the movement is able to develop unhampered by external oppression, there is no holding it back. Its own ideas of human rights then fare no better than the older universals. Any intellectual resistance it encounters merely increases its strength. The reason is that Enlightenment also recognizes itself in the old myths. No matter which myths are invoked against it, by being used as arguments they are made to acknowledge the very principle of corrosive rationality of which Enlightenment stands accused. Enlightenment is totalitarian."

Some would say that this does not explain the Nazis totalitarian state. What can? You too might want to say this – if to the defending of Enlightenment you bend your mind. Do you?

Hannah Arendt will now speak:

"The ideal subject of totalitarian rule is not the convinced Nazi or the convinced Communist, but people for whom the distinction between fact and fiction (i.e., the reality of experience) and the distinction between true and false (i.e., the standards of thought) no longer exist."

Desiderata for People STARTing to STEAM

On Yasmin, they do discuss, if STEM to STEAM, is but hot air, all moist, and probably cloudy too! Thus to this rattling about in non-viscous cyberspace, we now turn, to add a very humble creation of poetic kind. A very delightful title too, we formed, for this strange way of knowing, through performing; a process, you may note this time, is founded in adapting. We call our strange rendition: Desiderata for People STARTing to STEAM.

Desiderata for People STARTing to STEAM

> Go placidly amid the hissing noise of STEAM, and remember what peace there may be in silence for it is hard to find in STARTS and STEAM. As far as possible, without surrender, be on good terms with all persons, even those hissing STEAM and those STARTing to talk nonsense.
>
> Speak your truth quietly and clearly; and listen to others, even those caught up in the ideologies of STARTS and STEAM; they too have their story, even though it is often quite empty. But pick your acronyms carefully, lest poetics be used to expose shallow graves, where lay foul phantoms of inaccuracies, myths and disingenuous claims, ready to lead astray unwary travellers lost in art's romantic mist.
>
> Avoid loud noisy artists and STEM people STARTing to STEAM; they are vexatious to the spirit. If you compare yourself with others, you may find yourself wondering what lesser god STARTers and STEAMers worship.
>
> Enjoy your achievements as well as your plans. Keep interested in your own career, however humble; it is a real possession in the changing fortunes of time, especially now that STARTS and STEAM are in fashion; these are but a passing interest of the grazing herd, so your humble achievements may in the end outshine all that STARTS to STEAM.
>
> Exercise caution in your business affairs, for the world is full of trickery; especially when STEAM clouds the true nature of STARTS intentions. But let this not blind you to what virtue there is; many persons strive for high ideals, and everywhere life is full of heroism. Even in STEAM there may be a few – a very few – golden threads.

Be yourself, especially, as others most often are not. Do not feign affection for STEM, especially now its destructive nature is revealed. Neither be totally cynical about art-science and art-technology lovers; for in the face of all aridity and disenchantment love is as perennial as the grass, even the naïve sort that is most of art-science and art-technology. Neither of these actually exists though, for there is only art, which is always made with whatever is at hand – paint, data, glass, code, stone, electronic junk, toys, cables, books, photographs …

START by learning about DG CONNECT's former European Commissioner – the one that could be said to be responsible for ICT-ART CONNECT – who found herself investigated for not declaring the holding, while in office, of a directorship in an offshore company; a clear contravention of conditions laid down in the Treaty on the Functioning of the European Union. START too by learning of OLAF's investigation into alleged fraud by the company that led the ICT-ART CONNECT project. More revelations will no doubt in time come, when the world learns of the artistic voices that DG CONNECT silenced; so reflect before STARTing to STEAM, that DG CONNECT's woes might, one day, be yours too.

Take kindly the counsel of the years, gracefully accepting that inexperience and the pursuit of fortune and glory means that much that is proclaimed as new by those STARTing to STEAM will be found in old reports, papers and books. Beware of bodies whose job it is to scrutinise public expenditure – they may ask for a refund of public money spent just reinventing what is in these aging publications.

Nurture strength of spirit to shield you in the sudden misfortune of having to put up with empty-headed people who START talking nonsense. But do not distress yourself with dark imaginings. Many fears are born of fatigue and loneliness, and soon the empty-headed ones will be gone, as no sooner will they START to STEAM, than they will run out of STEAM.

Beyond a wholesome discipline, be gentle with yourself and ignore most of this STEAMing. You are a child of the universe no less than the trees and the stars; you have a right to be here, and pursue a less noisy, more thoughtful course away from the hissing sounds of STEAM.

And whether or not it is clear to you, no doubt the universe is unfolding as it should. Therefore be at peace with God, whatever you conceive Him to be, for probably God has inflicted STARTS and STEAM on those artists and STEM people who do now so much noise make, as way of punishment for sins committed in the past – poetic justice so to speak!

And whatever your labours and aspirations, in the noisy confusion of STEAM, keep peace in your soul. With all the sham, drudgery and broken dreams of STARTS and STEAM, it is still a beautiful world. Be cheerful. Strive to be happy, and stay away from those noisy people STARTing to hiss STEAM.

Thanks to Max Ehrmann who wrote the original Desiderata. And what aesthetic in the above *Desiderata for People STARTing to STEAM* is to be found? Most certainly playfulness is woven into the words, but what else, you may wonder – is there more? Can you not see? We leave you to wonder and to discover for yourself, for we are not in the business of being totally unambiguous!

"Art practice cannot be reduced to standardised dichotomies of cause and effect, input and outcome, or process and product."

Graeme Sullivan, 2005

When a Distinguished Professor of Art and Technology asks Questions ...

A person carrying the weighty title of distinguished professor of Art and Technology has been asking questions. This is what he asks of people – the recounting of experiences by way of giving advice to young people who wish to follow a dual arts-science career path:

"1- What is your background as a scientist? In the arts, design or humanities?
"2- When and how did you become involved in a hybrid art/science practice?
"3- What have been the major obstacles to overcome?
"4- What have been the greatest opportunities/breakthroughs?
"5- What would you do differently, knowing then what you know now?
"6- Any advice for someone who may want to walk in your footstep?
"7. Add other questions and your responses you think are relevant."

We sense the cult of Leonardo at work here! So, as art has no rules and the words that oft in our head sing, dance, and play, are today in cooperative mood, to these questions, this is what we say:

Beware distinguished professors of Art and Technology asking strange questions grounded in rationality. Beware too, people who provide rational answers to the professor's questions. The excess of rationality found in the West is its great flaw, and in continuing with this singular obsession, a cradle of woe is what you will discover, if you have not so realised already.

The evidence is all around, but Narcissus would rather die than look away from his beautiful reflection, and now he seeks *artists in residence,* who have also fallen in love with the reflection, to convey his beauty to what he thinks are the ignorant masses, who he believes, are experiencing a *science information deficit.* His desire is that they too can join in with the celebratory *dancing with glee* while standing on the *edge of doom.* If you oblige you will find yourself entering dangerous territory, so please, stay away, or be with them condemned, by future generations, who may ask you: why did you abandoned us to this illusion of a paradise to be attained that could never have been, for it was, like all before, *such stuff as nightmares are made on.* We are!

As for titles, seek them not, for they are heavy millstones around the neck, which along with other millstones, restrict movement, limit actions, and prevent the doing of what now needs to be done. The priest called

Copernicus and the citizen-scientist known as Kepler will, in an indirect but related way, explain. Koestler will act as your guide and interpreter for he knows much about such things. The citizen-scientist called Darwin understood millstones, so he too can explain. C.P. Snow did not understand millstones – although he had many – for he was trained as a scientist and had therefore a fragmented and reductive mind; hence he was unable to explain without making gross simplifications which render his *opinions* to be what they are: technocratic in the extreme. Artisans, practical people of all kinds, thousands upon thousands of them that history never recorded, living in the *Renaissance* period (which extended over several centuries), could also explain, for they experienced the result of millstones on a daily basis; these were the millstones of elitist groups, who kept things apart, but this is not the *Renaissance* that you probably learned about, which is partly another modern myth; a strange mix of facts and fictions, wherein you believe that which suits you best, and where the contributions of learning and knowledge from Islamic, Chinese, and other Asian scholars and artisans has been quietly written out of history – it is a very European *al*-gorithm.

Beware also those who say things such as: *I think therefore I am armed* – they do not, they are not. Such people are potentially very dangerous for they too are but the children of ideology and dogma – but this time secular in nature. If any of those who utter such a strange statement ever studied, through cognitive psychology, the complexities of the workings of the human mind, then they did learn very little. Our friend and colleague Will, from his pen, as is often the case, conjured words to suit the theme:

> What's in a name? That which we call a rose
> By any other name would smell as sweet;

Or rot, decay, or be a barb.

Unless you are oriented to psychological and sociological learning, it is unlikely that you will know much about that of which we speak, but as these are one of the means of illuminating millstones and the oddity of human beliefs, the study of the social sciences should be on your life agenda; you will need that rarity of things called an open mind to engage constructively with the complexities of multiple truths.

When young learn how to die; then you will know how to live. When young set yourself the goal of reading all the great literature that humanity has produced; be humbled by the impossibility of the task. Then learn how to choose wisely.

Master the art of transcending disciplinary boundaries. Penetrate deeply into other peoples' territories. Leave a mark to show that you have been there. Observe the reactions of those people whose territory you have entered, and recall this every time you hear people speaking about multi-, cross-, inter- or transdisciplinarity. Be amused by what you hear. Take the time to understand what these terms mean, for such understandings will put you in a position to see through the rhetoric that often surrounds such words, which take no effort at all to utter. Then you will be able to act in ways that few others can. Separation is an illusion; a human construction; a social construction.

Spend time with people who make a lot of noise so that you will discover just how empty they can be, then, never waste your time with such people again.

Seek out solitude and silence and learn to listen to the voice of your soul. Let it be your guide for it will never let you down. Follow your dreams wherever they may take you.

Observe life to a degree that Dickens would admire, for this is the source of art's endless fountain. Learn to look into the souls of men – and women too as they are increasingly being expected to behave like men, and are doing so!

You have hands with opposable thumbs for a reason – use your hands to make things.

Travel in time to discover why the European world creates futures very similar to the past, only with more advanced science and technology, which are then used to wage war on an industrial scale and to destroy the planet in pursuit of the demands of one of their gods – money. Discover for yourself the nature of Europeans and their colonial offspring – they are but Ancient Romans doing what Ancient Romans did, only more efficiently, which is their *Enlightened* way. Do not be party to their collective delusions and denials. Visit Rome and stand among the ancient ruins – then find understanding, because for such people there is only *Decline and Fall*.

Do not seek fortune and glory otherwise you will end up like Indiana Jones: ethically compromised, keeping company with bad people, and having to go to extraordinary lengths to extract yourself from problem situations that are of your own making. Do not seek to associate with people with power and influence: their power has corrupted them and it will corrupt you too.

Seek the answers to the question: why such advanced knowledge yet such simplistic beliefs and so much ontological oversimplification?

Do not be naïve about science, technology, engineering and mathematics (STEM) – there is enough naïve STEM people in the world already; we do not need anymore. Thwart STEM peoples' efforts to use art to project their imperial power on to humanity. Wear camouflage and infiltrate their academies, funding agencies, organisations, companies, institutions, etc. See what actually goes on and what people say when they think outsiders are not present. Collect evidence and identify their many weaknesses – these are not difficult to spot. But do not succumb to their ideologies. Then use what you have learned to unleash the forces of creative destruction against them, for the days of counter-movements are over – now is the moment for a new scientific revolution, the creation of a new science that most of the *olden ones*, and their *artists in residence*, will, like the *scholastics* before them, not want to see or to understand. And strangely, art is the means to achieving this, but this not what you are expecting is it?

Do not participate in the creation of new ideologies like art-science and art-technology, for these are but more of those binaries, dualities, and dichotomies so loved by the European mind. Never use words such as nexus, crossing, bridge, hybrid, integrate, intersection, cross-fertilise, spill-over, and so on; these are but the chains that keep you bound to a world that has already passed into history – Prometheus' invisible and silent chains. They are part of the self-constructed prison known as your values and beliefs. Instead, set yourself free and learn to fly like an eagle.

Spend time with nature and in the summertime sit among the flowers and talk to the bees and listen to what they have to say to you.

Work for the benefit of future generations for they are more likely to understand and appreciate your work.

Never accept what people say – check for yourself. Always go back to the original source, for it is surprising how much distortion and simplification takes place as a result of material being passed from one person to another. Discover what has been left out as a result of unquestioning acceptance. Go to extreme lengths to track down original sources. This is why there are National Libraries – use them.

Develop critical thinking and writing capabilities as practised in the social sciences. Be a gadfly. Write books about your work, and, if you indie publish, make sure that copies of these books are placed on deposit in your National Library collection. You never know who will look at your work in the future.

Set unrealistically high standards for yourself which you will constantly fail to attain – then learn. Keep on learning. Develop the self-critical skills and intuitions needed to know when your work is poor and when it is moving towards something else. *Paint fakes* so that you will recognise when your work is not a fake.

Work with dead artists for they have much to teach you. Do not join grazing herds. If you want to engage in collaborative activities, be very selective whom you choose to work with.

Never place scientists and artists on pedestals. These people are human and as such are deeply flawed, just like everyone else. Do not use Leonardo da Vinci or C.P. Snow as a justification for what you do – this will only demonstrate that you *do accept* what other people say without checking, that you did not learn to choose wisely what to read, that you did not master the art of transcending disciplinary boundaries, and that you have missed the point completely.

The reputations of these two are mostly not of their own making, being modern constructions – strange beliefs and *superstitions* about what they were but never were, or what they said but never said, or what they did but never did, or what they wrote but never wrote, or what is known but is not known. The myths that now surround both of them are like the haze of dust that gathers on hot summer days, just waiting to be blown away on the breath of the wind. Be that wind.

And if you do not take note of this, you might end up like those STEM people from prestigious institutions, who expressed, in a review paper entitled *Art on the Nanoscale and Beyond*, simplistic justifications for art-science convergence, based on – simplistic notions of Leonardo and Snow. But what matters learning and knowledge when fortune and glory, power and influence, are on your mind? This is the nature of the ethical melt-down occurring in the world STEM, for it is in any case a shallow ethic, very easy to ignore when convenience demands – disassociate yourself from this and speak-out; condemn all such forms of moral corruption.

Of such STEM people one can say that, here be conquistadors, the existence of which Edward O. Wilson denied, who are now rewriting and simplifying (as is their way) history, in support of their colonising agenda. It is but a timely reminder of the sand, the lack of foundations, the intellectual emptiness, and the lack of knowledge, upon which much of the STEM world's interest in the ideologies called art-science and art-technology is built. The European Commission's DG CONNECT is a star performer in all these this respects.

Thus, in speaking of creativity, communication, the promotion of science and technology, and things most sinister with Orwellian undertones that Joseph Stalin and other tyrants would have understood,

STEM people disclose their *will to power* and their staggering lack of vision and imagination with regard to art's role in research, and thus do all such people become the source material for the fountain; they will discover to their cost, that the pen is far mightier than the Scanning Electron Microscope and other such *boys toys*, which is why Stalin and others of his type exercised strict control over the arts. STEM people will do the same, and it begins with the *cheque book* and words like: *you can use this, but our permission comes with terms and conditions attached.* And thus too do they become like the medieval Church of Rome – oh dear you are making another future just like the past; it is a very European algorithm.

On the matter of Edward O. Wilson and his strange notions of consilience – steer clear of this for it is deeply flawed thinking, being as it is, a product of a man, a scientist, with several millstones around his neck. Do not look too optimistically to the consilience *second wavers* for they too have millstones around their neck and are hopelessly lost. Avoid becoming *entangled*, for there are more millstones to be found here too. Instead, reinvent the world of knowledge by creating new *Theories of Knowledge* suited to 2016 and beyond, for what exists today is more appropriate to 1916, 1816, 1716, 1616, 1516, 1416 … and BC in Ancient Greece as well.

Now is the time, after the deconstruction of the post-modernist era, to put the world back together again in a different form. Thus, being as you are, an artist, and not being constrained by rules, conventions, boundaries, and such forth, use your imagination to imagine the unimaginable, and then watch with delight as they wriggle and squirm and then a heretic proclaim you to be, for they, the people of STEM, are but *people of the book*, the products of a Western secular Abrahamic culture whose time is done, although someone needs to tell them this, for they, to their beautiful reflection, are still bound; feet and minds firmly planted where they are – in the past.

Discover the mysterious East. Travel there – literally and figuratively. Come to understand that in the motion there is stillness and in the stillness there is motion, and how this insight can be used to transform science and humanity. And to the East I now turn my face and speak: see their weaknesses. Stand on the shoulders of giants to see further than they can, to discover the coming age of the Tao, and in the names of two giants, Howard Rosenbrock and Joseph Needham, two of a kind, you will find the beginnings of what you need. Art in a different way will make a difference too.

Now cometh to an end these words of guidance and in closing we say, to the discovery of all the ways of knowing turn your attention, and practise as many of them as you can. Above all, learn the hermeneutic way of knowing so that you will be able to understand what we write.

To those who understand the words that we speak in silence, does the future belong – it is a place where no Ancient Romans (or Greeks) will be found for a different kind of person will there dwell, and a different type of science will they practise as well. And to our dear friend and colleague Will, we yet one more time do appeal, for words of ending to provide:

> And gentlemen in England now a-bed
> Shall think themselves accursed they were not here,
> And hold their manhoods cheap whiles any speaks
> That fought with us upon Saint Crispin's day.

And thus the world turns …

"There is a great willingness,
at least on our side, to
really invest into the arts as a means of
production, of making technology more
human centred, of using art as a
means of social innovation and
I guess this principle is accepted."

European Commission, DG CONNECT, 2016

STARTS Stories

So this is how the story goes:

START by deciding what you are going to use artists for. Engage with artists for several years in a disingenuous way, pretending to listen. As you go about doing this, gather around you people who are willing to agree with you, for you have piles of public money to spend in a reckless way. Then do what you intended to do from the START, by issuing a Call for Proposals. Proceed then to evaluate the proposals in a way that will ensure that you get what you want. Select proposals for funding! Is select the right word? Then, when all is done and finished, and you have what you want, only then consult. Make some ridiculous claim about respecting artistic freedoms and independence, while telling people to do what you want. When is an open consultation not an open consultation? Answer: when it is a DG CONNECT open consultation.

You do not like the above story! Here is another one then:

START by engaging in a fantasy. Convince yourself that you have an open mind, that you are listening, and that you do not know what to use art for. Drop a hint that there is a lot of money waiting in a special pot which lies at the end of a rainbow with only two colours – blue and gold. At no stage ask anyone what you should do. Invest European Union taxpayers' money in a study which tells you nothing, identifies nothing, but shamelessly engages in advocacy! Then do what you have convinced yourself that you had no intention of doing! Issue the Call for Proposals, which of course will be evaluated, very independently. Convince yourself of this. Repeat this statement: the proposals were very independently evaluated. Keep repeating this! Select the ones you want. Sorry we mean the ones that were independently evaluated. Negotiate contracts! Oh, you forgot to have any sort of open consultation with anyone – that is to say, other artists that were not in the room, and of course the ICT industry. So have a consultation, even though it will not be anymore relevant. Then run your projects. Ask for more money. Repeat!

You do not like the above story! Here is another one then:

A little fairy one day appeared at the window of an office in a compound occupied by DG CONNECT in the *City of the Golden Stars*. Being a very magic person it passed through the glass without any difficulties. Quantum behaviour perhaps? The fairy, on entering the room, sprinkled fairy dust on all that were present. Suddenly everyone STARTed talking about art. Then, by more fairy dust magic, there came about a meeting, where everyone STARTed talking about new ways of working, and how important art is – clearly the effects of fairy dust! Then before any time has passed – more fairy dust magic – there is a study undertaken at great expense, which produces content that is full of fairy dust, so that anyone who reads the report becomes lost in art's romantic mist. And before you know it, there are projects running, prizes been awarded and everyone STARTS talking nonsense. The power of fairy dust!

You do not like the above story! Here is another one then:

All was done in a highly professional manner. No-one gained any advantage by being close – oh so close – to DG CONNECT and at every step of the way everyone behaved impeccably!

You do not like the above story! Here is another one then:

Reader participation: create you own story according to what you believe is correct, which you probably believe is not in any way connected to your silent narratives: your ideology, your beliefs, your values, your self image, your vested interests, etc.

So how does one respond to the appropriation of art by the State for the purposes of a top-down, State-driven project? A project that is confirmed by DG CONNECT's own words, to be about an aesthetic and spiritual union of government and people according to a prefixed dogma! Actually it is a top-down project by a proto-state that seeks union between a proto-government and the people according to a prefixed dogma.

Evidently some have taken the route of becoming collaborators – there are always collaborators! Alternatives though are possible, which is the route that we have followed …

ENDS

STARTS a Consideration of United States Federal Law – The False Claims Act

The National Academy of Sciences report, *Fostering Research Integrity*, mentions something called the False Claims Act, and its relevance to research integrity. They highlight that the False Claims Act is one means for the federal government to pursue claims and recover damages from those who make false claims on government.

A spokesperson from the United States Department of Justice will now speak:

"A person does not violate the False Claims Act by submitting a false claim to the government; to violate the False Claims Act a person must have submitted, or caused the submission of, the false claim (or made a false statement or record) with knowledge of the falsity. In § 3729(b)(1) of the Act, knowledge of false information is defined as being (1) actual knowledge, (2) deliberate ignorance of the truth or falsity of the information, or (3) reckless disregard of the truth or falsity of the information."

This is one of the reasons why we wrote this book! A competent person, we believe, is one who would know what constitutes a false claim, because they would have taken the professional steps to establish knowledge, and not to do so would in our view constitute a reckless disregard of the truth or falsity of information.

We wonder if artists who make false claims to STEM people, while being employed in the context of federal funded research, which then causes the said STEM people to make false claims in their reporting of the said research, are thus exposing their host – to claims under the False Claims Act?

STEM to STEAM and Integrating Higher Education in the Arts, Humanities, Sciences, Engineering, and Medicine: Is the National Academy of Sciences Being Sold Art-Science Fakes?

In the United States, in 2016, the National Academy of Sciences began a study with the title *Integrating Higher Education in the Arts, Humanities, Sciences, Engineering, and Medicine.*

This is indeed an interesting topic to study. Perhaps in the United Kingdom people might learn something from this study that can be applied to STEM education in the United Kingdom? Or perhaps not! We say this because the study involves the idea that goes by the name of STEM to STEAM. People who are advocating the use of art in STEM education are having their say, which is good, for it allows people to reflect on what exactly they are saying and if it has any legitimacy, which is the matter that we now address, that is to say, we critically question what has been presented as so-called evidence!

Looking at some of the material presented to the Expert Committee, we find that, making an appearance is that which falls into the category of what we call art-science fakes, which is why we ask: Is the National Academy of Sciences being sold art-science fakes?

In your reading of our text you have encountered this statement:

"...pick your acronyms carefully, lest poetics be used to expose shallow graves, where lay foul phantoms of inaccuracies, myths and disingenuous claims, ready to lead astray unwary travellers lost in art's romantic mist."

We will explain:

In 2013 we became involved at our own expense in a European Commission initiative called ICT-ART CONNECT, run by a FET-Open project called FET-ART, which made the claim that it was doing something new – artists and technologists collaborating. To be a genuine FET Open project, it would have to be doing something new, otherwise public money would be mis spent. Having an academic upbringing, and thus dedicated to understanding the state-of-the-art before embarking on any research, we started a study to establish the state-of-the-art in this so-called new area, and found that our suspicions that it was not new were – well founded! Evidently this project was not a true FET Open project at all, but just an attempt by artists to lay hands on STEM public funds – no critical thinking evident! And they had in this process, it would seem, a willing accomplice in the form of the European Commission's DG CONNECT – no critical thinking evident there too! And we have also discovered that one of the partners in the FET-ART project was, subsequently, subjected to a fraud investigation by the European Commission, the findings of which led the European Commission to suspended all pending and future payments to the company concerned, which has now, according to the company's own web site, ceased trading, as it was, it seems, solely dependent upon income from European Commission projects!

DG CONNECT is a long story of the failure of technocracy and now, also of a proto-state institution using art for propaganda purposes, image making, etc. A familiar tale from continental Europe's past. Thus did they become the muse for our book that goes by the title: *STARTS – Science, Technology and the Arts: The Artistic Voices that DG CONNECT Silenced.*

By mid 2014 it was evident that we needed, partly for ethical reasons and partly because we were tired of the nonsense that ICT-ART CONNECT had become, to DISCONNECT from ICT-ART CONNECT. We then also added to our research into the state-of-the-art, an investigation – it is an investigation – into the reason why there is a group of artists, and some STEM people, in effect rewriting history, and creating myths and half-truths. We have uncovered many examples. We will return to this matter latter.

There must surely be words and phrases that are relevant to this. What are they?

The problem seems to be centred on a very noisy group who talk about art-science (actually mostly it is art-technology) that are part of what we have come to call the *Leonardo Cult*, but not uniquely so, and neither is every artist that makes use of STEM part of this cult. The people concerned are characterised not just by the making of a lot of noise, but also by the making of claims that do not stand-up to close inspection. These claims have inspired the investigative journalist within us, to undertake the investigations that we mentioned above.

What is said about C.P. Snow is an example of the twaddle that these people talk. Evidently most of them have not read or perhaps understood Snow, or choose to misrepresent him. Did you know that Snow only mentions artists 4 times in three documents, yet he mentions scientists 113 times and engineers 19 times? We know this because we counted! Big data telling you something? The three documents we refer to are the 1956 New Statesman article, the 1959 Rede Lecture, and the Second Look which was published in 1964.

Artists are supposed to be critical thinkers – we are told! This is another myth. Some artists are critical thinkers, but it seems that there are those in the *Leonardo Cult* who do not engage in critical thinking, otherwise they would have discovered that Snow had an agenda, a technocratic one, and was willing to talk any nonsense to further this agenda which he reveals in another book called *Science and Government*, where he praises the leadership of the Soviet Union! Snow's belief in technocracy probably links back to Cambridge in the 1930s – which turned out to be a hot bed of idealist Stalinist communist thinking. They were taken-in by Stalin – some folks are easily fooled, especially, we have discovered, STEM people. This is another long story, but another scientist, also at Cambridge in the 1930s, Conrad Waddington, sets the scene well, for he wrote a book in which he announced that the future was totalitarian government, and that the Soviet and Nazi totalitarian systems should be analysed! And so on. The matter gets fuller consideration in another of our books, that we refer to as *366 – A Scriptovisual Composition Unknown*, where hermeneutics reveals more to C.P. Snow that has been dreamt of in *Leonardo*!

People who know about painting in the twentieth-century will know that new scientific thought (particularly quantum mechanics) had an influence on art movements. The Surrealists are the most obvious case. The influence of science and technology was part of several artists' milieu. This sometimes also led to critique of science (e.g. Wolfgang Paalen). Today there is still a group of artists – usually more interesting and quieter than the noisy lot – who still engage in critique. But generally they stay away from the STEM establishments like DG CONNECT for obvious reasons. Some of them also share our concerns about those that make all the noise! These concerns have turned out to be well founded.

One of our apprehensions about involving artists from the noisy *Leonardo Sect* in STEM education is that they will just perpetuate the myths and misunderstanding that surround Snow, and contribute to the ignorance that already stalks the domain of STEM – people who know a lot about very little, sorry to say! Whereas, we would suggest, a social scientist might well use the case of Snow as an exercise in critical thinking and writing, showing the importance of not accepting what you are told, of using original source material, of extending the search to other material, and of developing arguments based on this material. We learned to do this by working with social scientist, not artists.

In the documentation published by the National Academy of Sciences on their web site, there is in a document pga_175504.pdf. In this document there is reference to a research paper – of a kind – called *Arts Foster Scientific Success*. Do they?

We came across this particular paper in 2016 when we were working on *366 – A Scriptovisual Composition Unknown*. Our initial reaction to this paper was that the research method (is that the right term?) is flawed because it is based on biased material (obituary notices, biographies, autobiographies, and biographical memoirs) and the bias inherent in this material, and possibly also the bias on the part of the researchers, has not been taken into account. Social Scientists will understand what we are talking about. On checking (we have learned that this is essential) some of the reported facts, we found several errors (inaccuracies/biased statements/mis-quotes?):

First, the Royal Society is not a membership based organisation as is suggested by the terminology used in the paper. It is an endowed society that elects eminent people from the world of STEM to the status of Fellow. A minor error perhaps, but it illustrates the lack of rigour that permeates the paper.

Second, there is, in the paper, a Table (No. 2) with the title: *Scientists Who Publicly Exhibited and/or Sold Visual Art or Sculpture, Published Works of Fiction, or Publicly Performed Musical Pieces*. In this table C.P. Snow is listed (as some one who published works of fiction) followed by (RS), indicating that he was, (according to the paper) a member(!) of the Royal Society. We suppose this means Fellow of the Royal Society as there are no members of the Royal Society, and becoming a Fellow of the Royal Society is a mark of outstanding scientific success.

We checked the *List of Fellows of the Royal Society 1660 – 2007*. This is easy enough to do as it is in the public domain and available on the Royal Society's web site. C.P. Snow's name does not appear. This is because he never made any contribution to science to warrant election to fellowship. Actually the contrary applies – he was a failed scientist who gave up science in the (early) 1930s. The reasons for this relate to the publication of (at the time) widely celebrated scientific results that had to be withdrawn because they were wrong. This is a matter of historical record, which also shows that C.P. Snow then pursued part of his career as a civil servant. He was already novelist, with his first published work appearing in 1934. In the 1960s he became a minister in a Labour Government. So he was not a scientist with an arts avocation and arts did not foster his scientific success, because he had no success. Probably he was a novelist with a science avocation. Already you see that some of the evidence for the argument that arts foster scientific success is flawed. But there is more!

Conrad Waddington's name also appears in this Table 2. He was a Fellow of the Royal Society, but, having examined the material that was used in the research(?) reported in the paper *Arts Foster Scientific Success*, we can find no evidence that he was an artist who publicly exhibited or sold visual art or sculpture as the Table states. We searched the biographical memoir of Waddington that was published in the *Royal*

Society's Biographical Memoirs of Fellows of the Royal Society (Vol. 23, Nov 1977, pp 575-622). We looked electronically for the word painter or painters. There is no reference to the word painter being applied to Waddington, just the word painters, as in other people, not Waddington. The word artist also appears several times in the biographical memoir, but not with reference to Waddington.

Waddington did write a book however: *Behind Appearance*. It is a book about the relationship between painting and science in the twentieth-century. It is not though, as is stated in the paper *Arts Foster Scientific Success*, linked to the idea of "that which has not been drawn has not been seen." Neither does Waddington, as is reported in the National Academy of Sciences document pga_175504.pdf, "assert(ed) that the hands-on requirements of science and art profoundly connect(ed) the two domains." The text from Waddington's book that appears in pga_175504.pdf, is significantly truncated. It is part of a very long argument in Waddington's book, extending over 35 pages, that deals with the characteristics of the new painting, i.e. Abstract Expressionism. This quoted and truncated text is part of a quite long sub-section of that 35 page long argument, that is dealing with the matter of gesture and calligraphy, in the context of the new art. The text in question starts: "There is a peculiar affinity, but also an important difference, between the experimental scientists and the painter in their experience of coaxing parts of the material world ..." You will note that "but also an important difference" has been excluded from the quote appearing in pga_175504.pdf.

Waddington's book is actually a very well researched piece of work, and in it Waddington demonstrates that there is no clear or simple relationship between the paintings he addresses and scientific thought, and thus no clear conclusions can be drawn. This is because the relationship is in fact a very complex one, as anyone who understands how artists operate would know from knowledge and experience. This well researched piece of work also stands in sharp contrast with what scientists today produce. We may return to the matter of the books, *Reductionism in Art and Brain Science* and *Colliding Worlds: How Cutting-edge Science is Redefining Contemporary Art*: books that are redefining – rewriting – history!

In the paper *Arts Foster Scientific Success* there is another quote of Waddington, this time from a different book with the title *Biology and the History of the Future*. The paper says that: "For Waddington, understanding how art was made was a way to understand his own field of embryology, because, 'an art object is always an instruction, to do or to experience, not a piece of information; and living things are organised instructions, not organised information.'" What Waddington actually said was: "Your silence, Cage, is an instruction to listen. An art object is always an instruction, to do or to experience, not a piece of information; and living things are organised instructions, not organised information." This is actually part of a dialog with John Cage, and others, about *The End of Faustian Man and the Limits to Progress* and in this there is discussion about silence. This is part of a discussion with the title: *Towards a Post-Industrial World*. If you think that the statement "for Waddington understanding how art was made was a way to understand his own field of embryology," is far removed from the content of the discussion reported in *Biology and the History of the Future*, you are right – there is no connection.

The name Richard Feynman also appears in Table 2 of *Arts Foster Scientific Success*. We have researched Feynman as well. It is known that he did engage in the visual arts, but what we have discovered is that he did so later in life, after he had become a successful scientist.

All of the above documents are in the public domain so can be checked. We wonder if the National Academy of Sciences bothered to check? Perhaps we will discover before this work is finished and published. Wait and see …

Is the paper *Arts Foster Scientific Success* just an isolated case? Sadly no! We checked another paper on the same theme involving (at least) one of the *Arts Fosters Scientific Success* authors, a paper with the title *Arts and Crafts: Critical to Economic Innovation*. It became immediately apparent that the paper is biased. Put another way: researcher bias have not been taken account of in the research method. Social scientists will understand. In fact, the paper admits that the results may be biased, which is indeed a strange situation to encounter!

And if you look further you will also find that the European Commission and the STARTS initiative is a gold mine of nonsense, inaccurate statements, half-truths, falsehoods, and so forth. Watch any of the online recordings of the discussion sessions that have been held – no critical thinking evident – and they leave one asking this question: what illegal substances did they all take that provided the stimulus to spend 45-60 minute talking utter nonsense? Or is it the intoxicating aroma of money driving people to START talking nonsense?

There is more to come too in this rather ridiculous STARTS initiative which is more like a circus act! Soon the affects of VERTIGO will be felt, and sensations of whirling and loss of balance, associated particularly with looking down from a great height, way out of touch with reality, will be felt, as other arts organisations START talking nonsense too. Did we not say that people should pick their acronyms carefully lest poetics be used to expose shallow graves, where lay foul phantoms of inaccuracies, myths and disingenuous claims, ready to lead astray unwary travellers lost in art's romantic mist? Expect much of this, as the giddiness of VERTIGO affects DISCONNECTED minds.

And what of Leonardo? Once just an artist and an engineer (but not in the modern sense), because painting went together with engineering as part of the mechanical arts, he has become not just an artist and engineer, but also a scientist, a mathematician, an architect, an anatomist, an inventor, a designer, and … Feel free to add something else as well.

Why is this so? Is it because new convincing evidence has come to light which proves the case? Or are there other reasons why history was and continues to be rewritten? They say that no one like Leonardo has ever existed, not before or since. Perhaps this is because this Leonardo is a myth. What next then for Leonardo? Perhaps we will hear about his miracles – how he healed the sick, walked on water, fed the 5000, raised people from the dead? Perhaps soon there will be a meeting of the *Leonardo Cult* to consider and decide upon his divinity? If you know anything about Neoplatonism you will get the point. That by the way was a hint that will lead you to a completely different understanding of Leonardo.

This now brings us back to the books *Reductionism in Art and Brain Science* and *Colliding Worlds: How Cutting-edge Science is Redefining Contemporary Art*. At this moment in time, as we work on the book that you now read, we begin to turn our attention to what will probably be our next work which will may be called *Art-Science Fakes: An Epistolary Tale of Scientific Reduction to Ignorance*. This is what we are now seeing – a scientific reduction to ignorance. Surely those who engage in this did not think that this would go unnoticed and that they would not become the subject of artistic enquiry?

Can you see what we are doing to the European Commission's DG CONNECT and their art-science lovers? Our alteration, as we called it in the Preface to the book about STARTS and the artistic voices that DG CONNECT silenced, is just a warm-up exercise. Now that we wield both the pen and the brush simultaneously, who can tell what will come next! 366 is already in the past. And after *Art-Science Fakes: An Epistolary Tale of Scientific Reduction to Ignorance* – what then? The world will START to understand just what is going on and why, and what STEM people are doing. This has something to do, in part, with what John Berger stated in one of his books: *Ways of Seeing*. But it is far more sinister than what Berger noted.

And then too, those who learn that this STARTS nonsense is a worst practice case study, will begin to understand that they can use STARTS as a pointer towards what not to do, and then to do something different –

something that DG CONNECT will not be able to do. We are back now to our state-of-the-art study. Go armed with knowledge, and you will begin to see what needs to be done – not STARTS for sure, which will, in the end, just have to contribute further to that growing collection of art-science fakes. Then shall the world laugh at the ignorance, incompetence and arrogance of DG CONNECT, for their true nature will be revealed to those who care to see – the Chinese for example! Are you listening to me in that ancient culture that became technologically advanced while Europe in medieval mud dwelt, in that longest ever continuously existing civilisation, in that country whose destiny it is, to eclipse the European Union economically, technologically and scientifically, in that city known as Beijing? Elsewhere too? Perhaps even in Washington DC, where fiduciary responsibilities and due diligence should, we would expect, be taken far more seriously than in that little *City of Golden Stars*, sitting in a rainy country called Belgium.

Art-science fake: a poetic term. We told you at the beginning that this is a work that invites both an efferent reading and an aesthetic one.

"And so art today will in the same way announce and herald that common mental attitude, that common view of life, which governs the present age."

Adolf Hitler, 1938

Symptoms of VERTIGO – The French Policy of *l'exception culturelle* STARTS to Succumb to DG CONNECT's Gradgrinding of the Arts

DG CONNECT's efforts to Gradgrind the Arts – known as STARTS – which seeks to turn the arts into numbers – on balance sheets – sounds the death knell of *l'exception culturelle*, especially as part of the French art world has embraced the STARTS nonsense with great enthusiasm. In future art must have a utility – DG CONNECT's utility. Like in European Unions of the past!

Now we are experiencing a spinning inside the head, the results of VERTIGO, and someone is saying: "we are bringing together the leading players in a sensitive and the intelligible desire and astonishment: artists, engineers, scientists, and entrepreneurs who change and defy our present."

Back to the matter of art-science fakes once again! Should we expect to see many of these? But as with all art fakes, it takes an expert to tell what is fake, and what is genuine. This is why we studied art and the state-of-the-art, so that we could tell fakes from what is an original – fake or fortune?

VERTIGO is a symptom of several diseases and disorders, often also associated with a loss of balance and feelings of nausea. Chose your acronyms carefully!

Misleading Parliament

The misleading of parliament is the knowing presentation of false information to a parliament, which is a very serious matter in a parliamentary democracy. Misleading parliament may also be seen as contempt of parliament. In some jurisdictions contempt of parliament is a criminal offence.

Who among you know if the presentation of false information to the European Parliament is a serious a matter as it is in a parliamentary democracy? Who among you would ever know if the false information was being presented to the European Parliament? Who among the MEPs in the European Parliament would know if they were being presented with false information? Would any of them care? Whom among you knows, if false information were to be presented to the European Parliament, if then such information were, by way of it being presented to the European Parliament, be then in effect be presented to the Parliaments of the Member States, whether this would be a contempt of parliament in 27 countries? We leave you to ponder these questions and to find the answers according to your ideology, beliefs, etc.

"I think that funding for the arts in a technology programme has to be justified and you have to show what's in it for technology. This is the main problem that we have in STARTS because this of course brings certain issues of instrumentalisation and issues of loss of independence that come up whenever you argue with cultural committees."

European Commission, DG CONNECT, 2016

STEM to STEAM we START to Wonder, STEM to STEAM what do you Mean?

And to the matter of 366 we now turn! Below an extract, reformatted for the purpose at hand:

Act 1, Scene 1

Enter Sir Eric Ashby FRS, with Julia, an artist.

Julia: Speak Eric. Speak!

Eric: I will. By the 1870s Oxford and Cambridge were ready to accept experimental science as an ingredient in education; but they were not prepared to jettison their cherished ideals of a liberal education in favour of the ideal of the university as a research institution. The vague but none the less attractive idea of the scholar-gentleman is still alive. Liberal education is still the aim of the Oxford tutor, and it has become the aim of the civic university lecturer; for the centripetal attraction of Oxford and Cambridge and their ideas remain a tremendous force in the provincial universities of Britain. British universities have never quite surrendered the idea of Renaissance Man to the idea of the Research Worker. These two powerful social forces – the influence of the utilitarian and the cult of the practical man on the one hand, and the influence of the classical humanists and the cult of the scholar-gentleman on the other – profoundly affected the manner in which British universities adapted themselves to the scientific revolution. Oxford did not respond as Göttingen had responded; Sheffield did not regard science as Munich had regarded it. Wissenschaft won its way into British Universities, but it never quite came to terms with the tough pragmatism of lay governors in civic universities or with the tenacious ideals of classical dons in Oxford and Cambridge. To this day the new has not become altogether assimilated into the old; adaptation is not yet complete: and here lies the cause of some of our present problems in universities.

Julia: STEM to STEAM we wonder. What do you think?

Eric: Not sure! But it is evident that the antithesis between science and humanism has almost vanished, but it has been replaced by

39

another antithesis, equally mischievous. The future historian will record that the unprofitable debates of the 1860s on the humanities versus science were followed in the 1950s by equally unprofitable debates on specialisation versus a liberal education. There is an assumption that specialisation and a liberal education are antithetic. What is needed is to challenge the assumption itself. The Oxford Dictionary defines liberal education as education fit for a gentleman. That is still an acceptable definition; it is the idea of a gentleman which has changed. A century ago when Britain awoke to the need for technological education, a gentleman belonged to the leisured class. Modern gentlemen do not belong to the leisured class. Many of them work something like a seventy-hour week, and more and more of them are finding that their business requires expert knowledge. A case could be made therefore for including technology among the ingredients of a liberal education. What then is missing in a scientific or technological education? It is not a smattering of art or architecture which is missing, nor is it an acquaintance with history or literature. Indeed it is not a primary lack of subject-matter at all: the fault lies with what Alfred Whitehead called a celibacy of the intellect which is divorced from the concrete contemplation of the complete facts. It is a preoccupation with abstractions from reality, an escape from the whole of reality. In his book, Science and the Modern World, Whitehead warned us that this would become the great danger of professional education. Each profession, he said, makes progress in its own groove of abstractions, but there is no groove of abstractions which is adequate for the comprehension of human life.

Enter Alfred Whitehead FRS

Julia: Eric speaks of Whitehead and Alfred Whitehead appears. Strange coincidence! Perhaps not! The magic works. Pray speak, Alfred.

Alfred: I will. There is something between the gross specialised values of the mere practical man, and the thin specialised values of the mere scholar. Both types have missed something; and if you add together the two sets of values, you do not obtain the missing elements. When you understand all about the sun and all about the atmosphere and all about the rotation of the earth, you may still miss the radiance of the sunset. There is no substitute for the direct perception of the concrete achievement of a thing in its actuality. A factory, with its machinery, its community of operatives, its social service to the general population, its dependence upon organising and designing genius, its potentialities as a source of wealth to the holders of its stock, is an organism exhibiting a variety of vivid values. What we want to train is the habit of apprehending such an organism in its completeness.

Exit Alfred Whitehead, Enter John Dewey

John: Progress in science ought to manifest itself as an emancipation of the mind enabling it to pursue new ends and new ideals; but in fact, progress due to science has been confined to more efficient means of satisfying old ends and old ideals.

Julia: This criticism is still valid.

Exit John Dewey

Eric: Adaptations needed to bring British universities into equilibrium with the age of technology are changes of curriculum; they could be accomplished through the normal channels of university administration and legislation. But they would not be successful unless accompanied by subtle adaptations in academic thought: professors of technology need to be persuaded that the pattern of curriculum under which they themselves were trained is inadequate for their students. Professors of arts subjects need to be persuaded that the presence of technology in universities puts them under an obligation to reconsider the emphasis in their own humanistic studies. It is at this point that universities look to their faculties of arts for help; and it is at this point that they are often disappointed. For faculties of arts have themselves become so deeply influenced by science that they seem unable to offer help towards the assimilation of technologists. Instead of contributing to the university what the Victorians understood by a liberal education, some of them are doing with grammar and documents what scientists and technologists can already do with formulae and instruments. This is doubtless profitable for the progress of scholarship in the humanities, but one cannot escape the consequences that humanities cease to be humanising when they are treated that way. It is a sort of treatment which leads to a celibacy of the intellect as inimical to a liberal education in arts as it is in science.

Exit Eric Ashby

Julia: The involvement of artists in science and technology, so much discussed among those who live in the echo chamber that is art-science and art-technology, do the same – signs of humanisation are difficult to find! Often one cannot tell who is an artist, because they are as much caught-up in the ideologies of science and technology as the scientists and technologists themselves. Which is one of the reasons why we do not engage with this noisy lot – and they are noisy. Very noisy!

Enter George Orwell

George: Twelve voices were shouting in anger, and they were all alike. No question, now, what had happened to the faces of the pigs. The creatures outside looked from pig to man, and from man to pig, and from pig to man again; but already it was impossible to say which was which.

Exit George Orwell

Julia: STEM to STEAM we STARTS to wonder, STEM to STEAM what do you mean? It STARTS to become a nightmarish dream. Awake! Awake! See what thou art doing! The European Commission, DG CONNECT, are fakes! What do I mean? Only those with knowledge will understand. Already that which STARTS becomes an example, an indicator, a signpost towards what not to do – a worst practice case study. And we will use it as such, over the coming years, to help those outside the European world. This is the Age of Tao! Goodbye *Vainglorious Enlightened Ones* – your time, your age, your world, is done.

Exit

What is a Criminal Organisation?

According to the International Military Tribunal:

"A criminal organization is analogous to a criminal conspiracy in that the essence of both is cooperation for criminal purposes. There must be a group bound together and organized for a common purpose. The group must be formed or used in connection with the commission of crimes denounced by the International Military Tribunal's Charter. Since the declaration with respect to the organizations and groups will, as has been pointed out, fix the criminality of its members, that definition should exclude persons who had no knowledge of the criminal purposes or acts of the organization and those who were drafted by the State for membership, unless they were personally implicated in the commission of acts declared criminal by Article 6 of the International Military Tribunal's Charter as members of the Organization. Membership alone is not enough to come within the scope of these declarations."

"Art will always remain the expression
and the reflection of the longings
and the realities of an era."

Adolf Hitler, 1933

Only One Interpretation is Possible

You are standing in a gallery, a culture centre, a museum, a university, or other such places where you might encounter art. Before you there is a work from the realms of the art-science or the art technology lovers. How do you know that you are not looking a work that is representative of the new Total Realism?

"In recent years Jacques Ranciére has addressed the predicament of artists and curators who, in their eagerness to convey a critical message or engage their viewers in an emancipatory process, end up predetermining the outcomes of the experience, hence blocking the critical or emancipatory potential."

That was Claudia Ruitenberg speaking.

"The mélange of genres that constitute contemporary art often leads to a different form of stultification, which uses the blurring of boundaries and the confusion of roles to enhance the effect of performance without questioning its principles."

This is what you need to achieve, if to Total Realism your artistic practice does gravitate, owing to an unquestioning embrace of an ideology, and the subjugation of art to that ideology, as in European Unions past and present, can be seen.

The person who spoke last, before we added our observation, was Jacques Ranciére.

Trust me I'm a North Korean Defector

A spokesperson from BBC News will now speak:

"I wish to say this:

"There is such a high demand for knowledge from North Korea, it almost gives people an incentive to tell exaggerated tales to the media, especially if that comes with a nice pay cheque. A lot of defectors who don't want to be in the media are very critical of career defectors. It's worth keeping this in mind. Information from official North Korean sources, on the other hand, is liable to be pure propaganda."

Thank you for that important insight. Indeed it is true that there is no such thing as a view from nowhere! Trust me I am an artist. Trust me I am a scientist. Trust me I speak for the European Commission. Trust me I am a European Commissioner. Trust me I am a European Union Nationalist. Trust me I am a supporter of Brexit. Trust me I am I am involved in STARTS. Trust me I am writing a book about art-science. Trust me I am writing a book about STARTS. Trust me I am involved in a European Commission funded project. Trust me I am …

Do not trust me! Find out for yourself. It is, I regret to say, in the modern world, the only way to operate. We cannot believe what the North Korean's say and in their case we cannot check! We cannot believe what the European Commission say, but we can at least apply ways of knowing such as *hermeneutics* to sniff out deception and propaganda. We can no longer believe what some people from the world of STEM research are saying, but we can however question and seek to know what is false, through identifying, for example, that which is not repeatable or reproducible. We cannot believe what some artists are saying, but we can acquire the knowledge that will allow us to apply a judgement.

You must not just accept what we are saying. Seek out the knowledge yourself to assess the accuracy of what we, through our research, have discovered. Seek also to know – how we seek to know. Notice we did not say seek truth. We said seek knowledge and assess accuracy. Truth only applies in mathematics – a proof is either true or false. The rest of life is not like that. Critical thinking of the kind found in the social sciences is something we can recommend to all.

How Many Times does the word 'Scrutiny' Appear in the European Union Lisbon Treaty?

To clarify, we are referring to what is often called the Lisbon Treaty or the Treaty of Lisbon, but actually is a consolidated version, last updated in Lisbon, of two treaties: THE TREATY ON EUROPEAN UNION, AND, THE TREATY ON THE FUNCTIONING OF THE EUROPEAN UNION. The two go together.

In the United Kingdom one of the functions of our Parliament is scrutiny of government. Both houses do this. It is part of a healthy democracy. An unhealthy democracy does not allow for Parliament to scrutinise government. The Soviet Parliament for example – the Supreme Soviet – did not scrutinise the Soviet government. Thus, all those people who make so much noise about the European Union being democratic, will no doubt believe that one of the functions of the European Parliament is scrutiny of – it would of course be the European Commission. So how many times does the word scrutiny appear in the above two treaties – all 400 pages plus of them?

The answer of course is – only once! And this relates to Europol. Yes that is correct, the European Parliament has no rights, duties, or obligations to undertake scrutiny of the European Commission. It can of course try to exercise scrutiny!

How do you think the European Commission feel about this massive loop-hole? Are they sad or are they very happy about this? What implications does it have? Could this lack of scrutiny result in the European Commission acting increasingly on their own, without approval from the Member States, or without consulting them? Could it lead to the Member States losing control of the European Commission? Are they already out-of-control?

Continental Europeans are living in what may be destined to become a dictatorship of deluded technocrats. Perhaps it is the destiny of the European Union to become a dictatorship of deluded technocrats, for the history of Europe is a history of European Unions, but history does not unfold according to predictable patterns!

On March 29th 2019, at 11pm London time, the United Kingdom should have departed the European Union, the Customs Union, and the Internal Market! After that moment the British should no longer have been citizens of the European Union! They voted to leave. Some wanted to honour that decision, but others did not, and they worked to thwart the democratically expressed wishes of the British people. Will we ever leave?

It seems that some people in Europe are willingly once again surrendering their right to political self-determination, so while one might wish good luck to the citizens of the European Union, they will need more than good luck to escape the fate that could be waiting for them. We repeat that the history of Europe is a history of European Unions, but history does not unfold according to predictable patterns! Why are they so foolish to believe that the present European Union will be any different from the previous ones?

For information, below is the Article (88) from THE TREATY ON THE FUNCTIONING OF THE EUROPEAN UNION where the word scrutiny makes its solitary appearance.

Article 88

1. Europol's mission shall be to support and strengthen action by the Member States' police authorities and other law enforcement services and their mutual cooperation in preventing and combating serious crime affecting two or more Member States, terrorism and forms of crime which affect a common interest covered by a Union policy.

2. The European Parliament and the Council, by means of regulations adopted in accordance with the ordinary legislative procedure, shall determine Europol's structure, operation, field of action and tasks. These tasks may include:

(a) the collection, storage, processing, analysis and exchange of information, in particular that forwarded by the authorities of the Member States or third countries or bodies;

(b) the coordination, organisation and implementation of investigative and operational action carried out jointly with the Member States' competent authorities or in the context of joint investigative teams, where appropriate in liaison with Eurojust.

These regulations shall also lay down the procedures for **scrutiny** of Europol's activities by the European Parliament, together with national Parliaments.

3. Any operational action by Europol must be carried out in liaison and in agreement with the authorities of the Member State or States whose territory is concerned. The application of coercive measures shall be the exclusive responsibility of the competent national authorities.

STARTS Speaking Voices from Europe's Past

Two Europeans from the past will now speak. First in line is a Member of the European Parliament speaking in 2016 about art and culture:

"The cultural and creative industries as ambassadors of Europeanness – culture, not only in its traditional forms, but also through cultural and creative industries, can play a crucial role in strengthening international partnerships. These industries contribute to Europe's *soft power* in their role as ambassadors of European values (such as quality, excellence, craftsmanship, creativity, culture) on the world stage."

Now a spokesperson for the German Reich will speak:

"The cultural and creative industries as ambassadors of Germanness – culture, not only in its traditional forms, but also through cultural and creative industries, can play a crucial role in strengthening international partnerships. These industries contribute to Germany's *soft power* in their role as ambassadors of German values (such as quality, excellence, craftsmanship, creativity, culture) on the world stage."

Both busy protecting their way of life! At other nations' expense! Both living in the past!

STARTS VERTIGO's Surrealist Tales of Faustian Pacts with the Devil that is DG CONNECT

We heard from afar a great din, and on moving to investigate found many noisy artists, all lined up, passing through a gate above which was cast, in now rusting iron, adapted words from a long forgotten imperial decree: *No Restriction to Artistic Freedom Will Here be Found.*

Standing now close by, we watched as this motley crew shuffled past, and spied within the camp, a man, a guard, whose name was oft spoken, and from the speaking of, we learned this man's name – and the name was Jury. And while each of them, the artists that is, approached this Jury, he divided them; some he sent to his left, and others to his right.

Of those who to the left did go, they disappeared from view, and we never saw them again. At later time, having enquired in another place of their fate, we discovered that through a portal they had been despatched, to find themselves – having already being put to much inconvenience – deposited unceremoniously by the side of a road in some far away and remote place, from which they then had to, with much trouble, find their way home, at no cost to the devil known as DG CONNECT.

Of those who to the right did march, a much worse fate did unfold! First each, on passing by rubbish bins, had to deposit there in the first, something that is known as artistic integrity, and in a second one, their critical independence. Each then was told to strip, and to don a special uniform, upon which was written in stripes, many times over: artist to be exploited in any way that takes your whim.

Then into a hellish chamber full of fire and smoke they did proceed, to have their nostrils filled with a technocratic sulphurous reek along with the rotting smell of evil corruption – of the *City of the Golden Stars* kind. And to a table, behind which stood the all powerful VERTIGO – demigod of art-science myths and beliefs – each one was then led, to sign, with their own blood, an irreversible pack with the devil known as DG CONNECT. And once thus tied, no escape was discovered to be possible, for they had to their new masters now been bound – including their lives for ever more, for the brand of the devil that is DG CONNECT was indelibly, on their foreheads, burned.

No sooner was the signature complete – while the blood was still wet – did, from it seems out of thin air, a ball and chain appear, which by some unseen force, locked itself upon the ankles of these poor unfortunate new handmaidens. Then the hand of VERTIGO did point towards strange holes in the walls, which looked very much like prison cells, above which strange and meaningless names there were carved: AMORE, CUPIDO, Magic Shoes, and other quite ridiculous words created by STEM, another demigod of the very peculiar, art-science secular religion, and the even stranger, new, extremist and fundamentalist sect that had styled itself – STARTS. Then VERTIGO did speak these words to each of his victims: "go inside and design."

Each of the poor shackled prisoners then towards the holes did make their way, and when within a metre or so of the entrance, a chain did miraculously shoot forth and attach itself to the approaching artist's neck, dragging the poor creature into the cell to face whatever tortures and torment were there waiting for them to endure. And from within came cries such as: "you will do this" and "you will do that" and "you're here as a slave to serve the project so you do what we want", and "you must disseminate and communicate", and "you're here to make us more creative" and "what rights are those, you signed the pact; your art belongs to you, but your ideas do not, and we will use your art how we think fit, and you have no control over this."

From some cells the sounds of great arguments did occasionally issue forth, as a few artists struggled to regain their independence and dignity, but then we noticed that the demigod VERTIGO had, to absolute power evolved, and when the heat of such arguments did grow, VERTIGO intervened and silenced the dissident artists, transporting them into exile to a place called Void, where they did then become entangled in complex and distressful legal matters requiring expertise that no normal artist could afford. And when they tried to speak out, to condemn, to warn, no sounds came forth from their mouths, for into these had been inserted a strange device called a Confidentiality Clause. Thus did DG CONNECT once again silence the voices of artists and punish those who dissented, in a manner in keeping with very European traditions and past European Unions. And in the doing of DG CONNECT's dirty work, VERTIGO – DG CONNECT's faithful handmaiden – did demonstrate that reassuring siren words such as sympathetic and sensitive treatment of the arts are but empty promises, especially when arrogant and elitist bureaucrats take charge. Reality is indeed a hard and cruel beast, as indeed is DG CONNECT!

Observing the nightmare that is STARTS unfolding before our eyes, feeling sickened and saddened by what we had seen, we could no more watch, so we tuned away to depart, thankful that, from Detrimental Research Practices (as the National Academy of Sciences in the US calls them), we did, long ago, DISCONNECT. It was then we noticed a European Commission official from the devil that is DG CONNECT, observing smugly all that transpired, being somewhat pleased that to the service of this devil, artists and their art had been corrupted in the name of another demigod – neoliberalism. Farwell *l'exception culturelle!*

On this leaving we did also recall, a phrase that to Google was once applied, for they too did artistic freedoms restrict, in that which they called *DevArt*: the exploitation of artists is evil! It is indeed! But when Faustian Packs with DG CONNECT people do make, that they should have been tricked, should surely come as no surprise at all, for DG CONNECT are the most corrupted technocrats of all, and as STARTS reveals, and DG CONNECT's very public domain comments prove, they are also technocrats of the most ignorant kind. On the other hand, as our extensive researches have revealed, some artists, ardent disciples of the art-science secular religion, engage in fabrications too – as a matter of course – so good bedfellows such will make, for DG CONNECT is the most highly skilled deceiver of them all. Thus do both parties in this sad tale get what they deserve – each other! Thus too does that term research integrity in the *City of the Golden Stars*, become as meaningless as the empty-headed whims upon which STARTS is based. We are back to the matter of art-science fakes once again!

This we could see and did predict, writing such, long before STARTS did START. Thus the world now begins to see the European Commission, and DG CONNECT, for what they are, and thus does the world learn how not to bring art into research and innovation processes. Interested observers in China take note, for here is the worst practice case study that is STARTS, from which you can, at European Union Taxpayer's great expense, learn, and in doing so, also add to DG CONNECT's humiliation. Here too learn about the factors which render technocracy, and Global Systems Science, yet more of those dangerous fantasies for which past European Unions are renowned! Time to stop them in their tracks, before embryonic monsters seeking human flesh, consume us all, for in the *City of the Golden Stars* the conditions for their nourishment and growth have now come into existence once again. And it STARTS with STARTS – first take control of art and restrict artistic freedoms!

When will Europeans learn, that their time is done, that the future will not be European? Now is the *Age of the Tao*. But Prometheus just sits on his rock, to which he is forever, it seems, bound, by chains of the invisible and silent kind. His artist in residence wears those very same chains too. Thus does the past become the future! Time is a singularity.

STARTS weaving the art-science tangled web …

STARTS Art Factory

An artist is a productive labourer when he or she works like a horse to enrich the proprietors of the organisation where they are sent to take up temporary residence, while at the same time polishing the tarnished image of the failing institution that is DG CONNECT. The two go hand in hand. That these proprietors, at the behest of DG CONNECT, have laid out their capital as an art factory, instead of in a sausage factory, does not alter the relation. Hence the notion of a productive artist implies not merely a relation between artistic work and useful effect, between artists and the product of creative work, but also a specific, social relation of production, a relation that has sprung up historically and stamps the artist too as a direct means of creating surplus-value.

In other words artists, like all others, are now subsumed into a system of production, whether that be manual or intellectual, where artists' skills, specifically their creativity, are transformed into a commodity to be exchanged for small (exploitative) payments, in the pursuit of the creation of surplus value for the proprietors, and the enhancement of the image of DG CONNECT.

This is the state of affairs that we have now reached. It is time to take action, to respond to this vicious attack on the arts by DG CONNECT. And, as was the case with earlier European Unions, the scientists, engineers and technologists, they follow obediently and uncritically, to do the bidding of their masters. The *new Leonardos* in ignorance dwelling! The new Medici's power rising!

Art is extremely dangerous as past European Unions demonstrate. It is not artists that are special, but art, because it is so dangerous. Those who create European Unions fear art and those who create it, while at the same time desiring to use art and artists for their own ends. DG CONNECT too are very dangerous ...

And yes obviously, at the START, we have paraphrased someone. Any idea who? Why did we do this? Seek now the answer!

STARTS Irritant

As has been noted in other, different, but related contexts, STARTS involves several arts institutions collaborating with DG CONNECT, while ignoring more radical practices that would irritate these very established institutional structures. This takes place at a time when widespread corporatisation is underway in the context of neoliberalisation driving increased globalisation, with the concomitant environmental destruction, resource depletion and the disempowering of ordinary people in favour of the power of markets, corporations and unaccountable technocrats in wholly undemocratic institutions like the European Commission.

Emphasis is consequently placed on certain kinds of collaborations and x-disciplinarity, while approaches that might call into question the commoditisation of knowledge production (and creativity) and the deepening of competitive procedures, which might in fact lead to positive outcomes lying beyond the imagination of the narrow functionalist, reductionist and deterministic minds found in DG CONNECT, is viewed as a very dangerous proposition.

Thus does the world of business, and its handmaidens, namely STEM, appropriate the arts, and thus do art institutions commit themselves to the suppression of democratic forces in favour of a Europe led by unelected, and, one has to observe, incompetent and ignorant technocrats, all because of these institutions desire to lay hands on public money, regardless of the consequences.

And with the same forces and motivations acting on professors and other academics, thus too does one see a corruption of academic interest, and a rejection of irritants in the name of the lesser god that goes by the name – funding! Hence the research integrity crisis!

Thus we see a hollowing-out of the arts in the name of serving the interests of other people, organisations and disciplines!

It is all about money and the selling of one's soul to the power of money …

The National Academy of Sciences Report on Research Integrity

In 2017 the National Academy of Sciences published a report entitled *Fostering Research Integrity*. This report deals with the sad reality that sometimes people working in research, stray from the norms and practices they should abide by.

The report defines misconduct in science as fabrication, falsification, or plagiarism in proposing, performing, or reporting research. The report also defines something called Detrimental Research Practices, these being violations of traditional values that are detrimental to the research process. Reasons for a lack of research integrity are also considered in the report, and these reasons can be quite complex, covering intentional activities as well as negligent ones resulting from carelessness or other individual shortcomings coupled with environmental pressures and institutional practices.

Also highlighted is the significant damage to the research enterprise that is the consequence of deviations from good science – damage to both the practice of science and how science is perceived in society. The involvement of all stakeholders in these Detrimental Research Practices is also identified: namely research institutions, research sponsors, and journals. Thus it is not just some individuals that are responsible – a few bad apples so to speak!

Consequently it is argued that there is a need for rethinking and reconsidering approaches to understanding, preventing, and addressing research misconduct and Detrimental Research Practices. This need, the report says, is reinforced by a discourse in both the scientific and the general media, which states that the research enterprise may be broken or seriously off-track. This discourse is being driven by increasingly regular reports of high profile research misconduct cases, as well as studies that are suggesting that in some fields, half or more of the published results are not reproducible, along with a significant growth in the number of published research papers being retracted from refereed journals.

The conclusion is that the research enterprise faces serious challenges in dealing with research misconduct and Detrimental Research Practices. The suspicion is that Detrimental Research Practices may be more widespread and may ultimately be more damaging to research, than research misconduct is, which is also the conclusion drawn elsewhere as well, for example, in the United Kingdom. Therefore, to address the problems, the research community needs to take determined steps to strengthen the self-correcting mechanisms that many believe to be an implicit part of science.

So to reiterate one point – there is growing evidence that half or more of published results in some fields are not reproducible. Oh dear! Does this apply to European Union – European Commission – funded research? Does it apply to STARTS? We leave you to answer these questions according to your beliefs, values, funding interests, etc.

"PAIR also acknowledges that since
science is a creative act,
PAIR could not be about bringing
creativity to scientists or, for that
matter, bringing formalism to artists."

Rich Gold, 1999

STARTS a Probing of *Leonardo*

Leonardo! We are referring to the publication, not the man.

To celebrate the 50th anniversary of *Leonardo* we thought we would probe the publication. So we visited Project Muse where it is possible to search *Leonardo* from the first issue in 1968 to the current issue. When we did this, the most recent issue in the system were pre-print articles for Volume 51 numbers 1 and 2 (2018).

We searched for the appearance of the word *scientism* over the past 50 years and discovered that the word had not appeared. We then searched for the word technocrat, and again found no reference to the word. We then searched for the word *technocracy* and found four results. We will now meet the *four* people, who, over the course of 50 years, were the only ones to refer to technocracy.

The first person is Heidi Boisvert, who in 2016, in an extremely short (half-page) article with the title *Echoing Narcissus: Bio-Adaptive, Game-Based Networked Performance*, said:

"This paper is a critical examination and a creative reversal of the legacy of cybernetics. It seeks to both interrogate the underlying rhetoric fuelling the post-biological technocracy to which we are unconsciously ceding control of our cognitive and affective faculties, and also explores how embodied, bio-adaptive, game-based networked performance practices can serve as an antidote."

Of course the paper was not a critical examination, but the art work may have been. Or not!

The second person is Mike Leggett, who in 2005, in a review article of a book with the title *Review of Film Art Phenomena by Nicky Hamlyn*, said:

"Hamlyn goes on: 'DVD is a kind of revenge of technocracy on creative approaches which examine the specificity of the medium.'"

Evidently Leggett is not addressing technocracy *per se*, just quoting from the book he is reviewing, where the book author uses the word technocracy.

The third person is Michael R. Mosher, who in 2003, in another review article of a book with the title *Othermindedness: The Emergence of Network Culture by Michael Joyce*, said:

"*Paris Again or Prague: Who Will Save Lit from Com?* [Chapter 10 of the book being reviewed] enjoys President Havel's Prague as the republic of words, something beyond the USA's commercial democracy and even the technocracy prevalent elsewhere in Europe."

Self-evidently, once more, the word technocracy is being used in the context of quoting what is said in the book being reviewed.

Finally we turn to Edward A. Shanken, who in 2002, in a paper with the title *Art in the Information Age: Technology and Conceptual Art*, said:

"The work of Stelarc, Lynn Hershman, Survival Research Laboratories, Julia Scher, Jodi.org and others continue this tradition of art-and-technology in a manner that challenges modernist aesthetics and technocracy."

Evidently he is not himself addressing the matter of technocracy.

To conclude therefore, no one really addressed the issue of technocracy.

So, now some questions – we have many!

First, what sort of art publication dealing with science and technology, over a 50 year period, does not significantly address some of society's significant problems in relation to science and technology – that is to say scientism and technocracy? The question is better translated into this: what sorts of artists do not address these significant issues? Answer: the ones who have fallen in love with science and technology and have adopted the ideologies, and practice within them – a kind of mind-set reinforcing art! These people are living in a mythical world, set about 500 years ago. What relevance do they have to the future? How can such people be expected to contribute anything to the future from their distant place in time?

But to another, more pressing question, we do now wish to turn your attention. Have we just created new knowledge? Answer according to your beliefs.

Our answer is no we have not. All we have done, is to undertake a preliminary investigation, based on our intuitions, which is part of a larger investigation. We do not know anything at all about how well the search engine performed or how well those who implemented the system captured the content of 50 years worth of *Leonardo*. Verification is needed. We will address this is due course. We might also challenge ourselves by asking this question: are we using the right methodology?

On the other hand we could say that we have just created new knowledge, if we were not aware of the other factors that should prevent us from making this claim. This one might say calls into question the art-science lovers' claims – implied or otherwise – to be creating new knowledge, for they seem quite often not to be aware of other factors. This is the problem with ideologies. One can also say that, all that STARTS to STEAM is a story of people who do not know what they do not know.

Here is another question: is written (text-based) language here helping or hindering our quest?

We also ask some further (related) questions. Is what we have just reported, research? If it is research, is it research with a small 'r' or research with a big 'R'? And what type of research? Were we doing research through art, or research into art, or research for art, or something else? How can you know? What is knowing? What is knowledge? How can one claim to be creating knowledge, if one does not fully know what knowledge is? How can one develop a post-European era, post-Enlightenment science and technology without first asking what knowing and knowledge mean in this context? What sort of technology comes forth from asking and answering such questions?

What are we talking about? Confused? Losing the thread? What is the thread? Or should that be threads?

Evidently we are a long way away from those who have STARTed to make so much noise by the issuing forth of cloudy wet STEAM.

Happy birthday *Leonardo*! Here is an onomatopoeic word: hiss.

> Let me not to the marriage of true minds
> Admit impediments. Love is not love
> Which alters when it alteration finds,
> Or bends with the remover to remove ...

Nor does it wage war to the death, which is totalitarianism's way. But you will, for the history of Europe is a history of European Unions, but history does not unfold according to predictable patterns ...

STARTS a List of Artistic Works that Included an Electric Plug!

Here we are going to list a number of works of art that, in the first half of the twentieth-century, needed an electric plug – we mean art objects that needed electricity!

First we want to point out, before presenting our list, that there is a genre of art that could never have worked without electricity – it is called film. Now you are thinking – "but that's not art!" You are being very elitist – preserving outdated thinking! So are you saying that Charlie Chaplin's movies *Modern Times* and *The Great Dictator* are not art? Are you suggesting that Walt Disney's cartoons from the 1930s are not art? They are commercial art, of course, but they are all examples of science, technology and art combined! The clue is in the title of this institution: *The Academy of Motion Picture Arts and Sciences*. The art form they represent is only possible through the use of technology and electricity!

Are you convinced? No? Then consider *Un Chien Andalou* – a Surrealist silent film – a fine art film – released in 1929, written by Luis Buñuel and *Salvador Dalí*. Surrealism is a twentieth-century art movement – you probably will have heard of it. Its works have been sanctified by the art market and its sacred relics adorn the walls of famous art galleries.

In case you were wondering, the difference between the two types of film (commercial and fine art) often lies in – a difference in the treatment of content. But not always! This also applies to other works of art, such as books. Have you not noticed this? Context too can be important. We told you that in the Preface.

So to the matter of the list, which we add, is only based on a cursory examination. Why you ask? Indeed! Here is the list:

- Thomas Wilfred, around 1919, started developing electro-mechanical devices to compose (soundless) light music. This art form he called *Lumia*, and his inventions Clavilux.

- The Theremin is an electronic musical instrument invented c1920 by a Russian named Léon Theremin. You will need a plug and a power supply to use one of his original instruments. Photographs clearly show the power cable! Theremin was a Russian physicist (or engineer depending on which texts one reads). Films also show that he could play the instrument. It is reported that it was a popular instrument in the 1930s and was used in experimental music, concert music, popular music, and film scores, and continued to be used onwards into the post-war era, becoming though less significant as a result of the emergence of electronic synthesizers and computer generated music.

- Arseny Avraamov's *Symphony of Sirens* (c1920): a proletarian musical work using sounds taken from industry, notably factory sirens. It is reported that for the performances Avraamov constructed an electrified keyboard that controlled electric valves that in turn activated whistles. A power supply is most definitely an ingredient of this piece of equipment.

- Marcel Duchamp – his name is bound to appear! Rotary Demisphere (Precision Optics) 1925 – includes an electric motor.

- László Moholy-Nagy: Licht-Raum Modulator, 1922/1930 – includes an electric motor.

- Alexander Calder – known for his *mobiles*. In the 1930s he incorporated electric motors into his mobiles. He also worked on large scale public works of art, one of which was intended to include water jets (electric water pumps!).

- Ben Laposky in the early 1950s was using oscilloscopes and cameras to produce electronically generated images.

- John Whitney – an early pioneer in computer art, was using analogue computer components in his work in the late 1950s to create abstract images for his experimental films.

What are we saying?

STARTS a Consideration of a Research Culture that Seeks to Confirm One's Own Ideas, Regardless ...

A spokesperson for the inquiry into the fraudulent research practices of social psychologist Diederik Stapel will now speak:

"Another set of explanatory factors for the extent and duration of the fraud, alongside those set out in Chapter Four of the enquiry report, reside in the general manner in which the research was performed both within and outside Mr Stapel's working environment. It involved a more general failure of scientific criticism in the peer community and a research culture that was excessively oriented to uncritical confirmation of one's own ideas and to finding appealing but theoretically superficial ad hoc results. These *sloppy science methods* were found on a large scale in the work of Mr Stapel and his co-workers.

"The enquiry undertook an extensive study of all research material, available data and publications, and interviewed in depth those involved in order to gain a better understanding of the extent and nature of the fraud, and of how it could possibly have happened in the research environment in which Mr Stapel, his PhD students and close colleagues worked. The statisticians initially analysed the dissertations and publications with a view to gain a deeper, clearer and more definitive picture of the fraud. The statisticians and the enquiry committees subjected the collection, coding, analysis and reporting of the data to critical scrutiny.

"However, the enquiry could not be blind to evident violations of the basic rules of sound scientific research. The enquiry committees were forced increasingly to the conclusion that, even in the absence of fraud in the strict sense, there was a general culture of careless, and selective and uncritical handling of research and data. The observed flaws were not minor *normal* imperfections in statistical processing, or experimental design and execution, but violations of fundamental rules of proper scientific research with a possibly severe impact on the research conclusions. The enquiry committees are of the opinion that this culture partly explains why the fraud was not detected earlier."

The report then lists some of these *sloppy science methods* and the associated culture, which, if you are the business of arts advocacy you may want to adopt to further your – advocacy!

The first is verification bias, being the use of research procedures in such a way as to *repress* negative results – strategies to find the answer that you want to find. These include:

- An experiment fails to yield the expected statistically significant results. The experiment is repeated, often with minor changes in the manipulation or other conditions, and the only experiment subsequently reported is the one that did yield the expected results.

- A given experiment does not yield statistically significant differences between the experimental and control groups. The experimental group is then compared with a control group from a different experiment – *reasoning that they are all equivalent random groups after all* – and thus the desired significant differences are found. This fact likewise goes unmentioned in the article.

- The removal of experimental conditions. For example, the experimental manipulation in an experiment has three values. Each of these conditions is intended to yield a certain specific difference in the dependent variable relative to the other two. Two of the three conditions perform in accordance with the research hypotheses, but a third does not. With no mention in the article of the omission, the third condition is left out, both in theoretical terms and in the results.

- The merging of data from multiple experiments – multiple experiments are combined in a fairly selective way, and above all with benefit of hindsight, in order to increase the number of subjects to arrive at significant results.

- Research findings are based on only some of the experimental subjects, without reporting this in the article. The removal of *outliers* (extreme scores on usually the dependent variable) from the analysis where no significant results were obtained, helps to reduce the variance of the dependent variable and makes it more likely that *statistically significant* findings will emerge.

- Extreme scores of one or two experimental subjects are kept in the analysis where their elimination would change significant differences into insignificant ones. No mention is made anywhere of the fact that the significance relied on just one or a few subjects.

- Entire groups of respondents are omitted, in particular if the findings did not confirm the initial hypotheses, again without mention.

Other helpful strategies include incomplete or incorrect information about the research procedures used: provided information is too vague to replicate the research. Statistic flaws are also helpful – the inappropriate use of statistical techniques. Finally, of crucial important is a lack of scientific criticism, which allows the above to go on unquestioned and unchallenged! The latter is, you may have noticed, a familiar and repeating tale in this book. Have you noticed this yet?

"The danger is that people who call themselves artists, but who are far from excellent, look at business as a new opportunity for making 'fast' money. This could cause a lot of damage. Lack of professionalism is the Achilles Heal of artistic interventions."

Lotte Darsø, 2004

STARTS X-disciplinarity

"STARTS is founded in a trans-disciplinary approach within the context of the inter-disciplinary turn, using artists to lead the reframing of the post-disciplinary discourse. In a cross-disciplinary context, enabled by art, the most important discipline for transforming disciplinary consciousness, multi-disciplinary themes are explored in a critical manner, thereby enhancing the inter-disciplinary dialogue and leading, though artists' research and expression, to new directions with the promise of highly effective holistic innovative trans-disciplinary collaborative paradigms addressing the entanglement of technology and people, in a human-centred dimension exploring the rational, emotional and the spiritual, in a new trans-human syncretic reality."

"Julia!"

"Yes Paul."

"What on earth does all that mean?"

"Well, Paul, I am an artist, a special person, and this is the sort of thing that some artists write."

"Julia, Marcel Duchamp would not have considered you to be special."

"True Paul, but how many in the STEM world would know such a thing?"

"Not many actually! Most of them are caught-up in the mythology of the romantic heroic artist and probably have little idea that they are so bound. It seems to be a very European thing."

"It is indeed Paul. They think artists are going to save the world. Make their industries more competitive, and other such nonsense. It's privileging artists above other disciplines, and making them special, going against what Duchamp was trying to do. It is also ridiculous to think that artists are going to make industry more competitive and solve society's problems. Actually it's an outdated belief!"

"But does the text mean anything at all."

"At one level, it does not. It is completely without meaning. But at another, deeper level, it does, for it is symbolic of the emptiness that is often attached to anything to do with x-discipinarity. This emptiness afflicts artists as much as it does STEM people. It also reflects the emptiness of some artists more generally – recall what the Nobel Prize winning theoretical physicist Richard Feynman said: 'Some artists are absolute fakes.' Which is true! Some of course are not."

"You're right – art-science fakes. The pretence that the art-science lovers are going to do that which others have so far found extremely difficult or impossible! It's nonsense. Ideological nonsense!"

"Absolutely Paul. People from the world of STEM typically talk about best practices. But social scientists would immediately point out that this is a clue to what is going on in the subconscious mind – a *Freudian slip* so to speak. The notion of the one best way, which is one of those taken for granted values of the STEM world."

"So, Julia, when a social scientist points this out to STEM people, political correctness kicks-in, and they change their words, and then start talking about good practices."

"To which the social scientist would say: 'what do you mean by good?'"

"Yes, to which STEM people would immediately offer criteria. Part of another mental process that can be described as methodologicalising."

"Yes Paul, then one gets to the heart of the matter – the imperial mentality. People from the world of STEM projecting their power on to – in this case, the arts. Taking only what they want, what they find useful, and leaving the rest. In other words it's the sort of x-disciplinarity that we should not be supporting or encouraging."

"You're referring to STARTS of course."

"I am Paul."

"What other way forward is there?"

"Dump the STEM people. The relationship to STEM is a myth. Artists should not be exploited by grubby-minded philistines who work for an unaccountable organisation called the European Commission."

It is interesting to note that the online Oxford English Dictionary makes no distinction in its definition of interdisciplinary, trans-disciplinary and cross-disciplinary. The OECD however, when it defined interdisciplinary and trans-disciplinary back in the early 1970s, did make a clear distinction between these words.

The online Oxford English Dictionary also classifies interdisciplinary, trans-disciplinary and cross-disciplinary as adjectives. This makes them words that can be liberally sprinkled throughout texts without having to add any substance to the text. We refer you to the many documents from the world of STEM, the arts, and also the world of the art-science lovers …

There is growing evidence that half or more of the published results in some fields are not reproducible ... Oh dear!

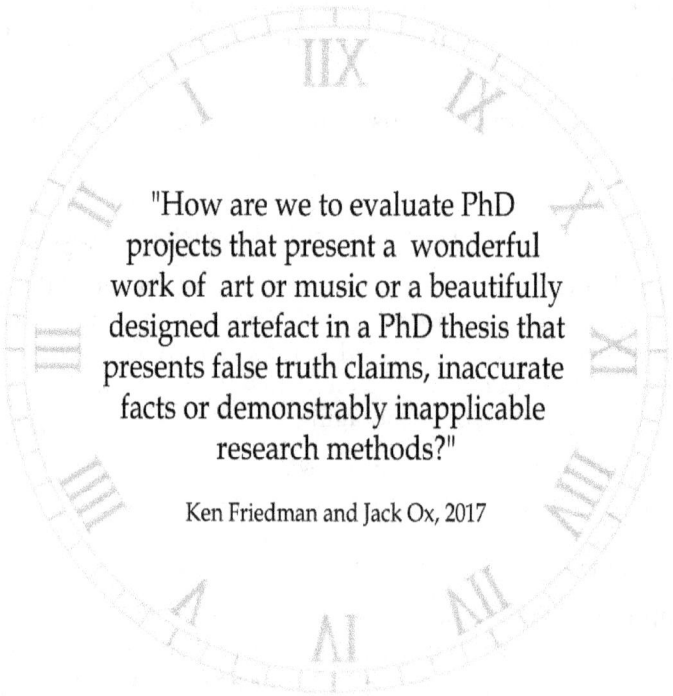

"How are we to evaluate PhD projects that present a wonderful work of art or music or a beautifully designed artefact in a PhD thesis that presents false truth claims, inaccurate facts or demonstrably inapplicable research methods?"

Ken Friedman and Jack Ox, 2017

European Commission Funded Project STARTS to Give Advice on how to Fight Corruption

In the February 2017 edition of the *research*eu* results magazine, it was reported that a European Commission funded project called ANTICORRP provided the following advice on dealing with corruption:

"Standing up and speaking out is the best way to fight corruption. Reporting corruption [...] is seen as the most effective action citizens can take."

Coralie Pring, author of the detailed report produced by Transparency International (the global coalition against corruption), partners in the ANTICORRP project, states:

"Europe has seen a surge in recent years of support for populist and nationalist movements – from Spain to the UK to Turkey. The reasons are manifold and complex, but are driven to a large degree by the belief that traditional democratic institutions – governments, political parties – are failing to deliver on promises of prosperity and equal opportunity and that they cannot be trusted.

"Corruption is central to this story – both the failure of governments to properly address corruption and their complicity in corrupt or clientelist schemes. It has become impossible to ignore systemic corruption in the way business influences politics, as shown by the trial of 37 executives and politicians in Spain who are alleged to have been involved in a *kickbacks-for-contracts* scheme for nearly a decade. Examples such as this can give ordinary citizens the impression that public spending and public policy is distorted to favour the few over the many.

"This impression has been compounded by the prevalence of *cosier* forms of corruption, such as the conflict of interests – real and perceived – posed by hidden lobbying and the *revolving door* between the public and private sectors. The public outrage at the decision of former European Commission president, Jose Manuel Barroso, to accept a position with Goldman Sachs, which generated over 100,000 petition signatures calling for tough sanctions, shows how expectations about greater integrity in politics and business are mobilising citizen action.

"Our report shines a light on the views of citizens from across Europe and Central Asia, who perceive the corruption problem as an extensive one."

At his hearing (on Tuesday 30 May 2017) with MEPs investigating the Panama Papers scandal, the European Commission president promised to present a bill to improve and harmonise the protection of whistleblowers across the European Union. President Jean-Claude Juncker:

"The Commission is working on a proposal to better protect whistleblowers."

Meanwhile, those who leak information to the press, for example the employees for PriceWaterHouseCoopers involved in the so called Luxleaks scandal, where two employees revealed information about the tax practices of big multinationals based in the Luxembourg, face the risk of criminal prosecutions when they act in the public interest.

Juncker may well be a *poacher turned gamekeeper*, but evidently the establishment does not agree with the recommendations of the ANTICORRP project and are determined to use the so-called *rule of law* to silence those who speak out. Actually it is not the *rule of law*, just laws that protect the rich and powerful – *rule by law*!

Clientelism is the exchange of goods and services for political support, often involving an implicit or explicit *quid-pro-quo*. Clientalism involves an asymmetric relationship between groups of political actors described as patrons, brokers, and clients. Clientelism is a set of actions based on the principle take there, give here, with the practice allowing both clients and patrons to gain advantage from the other's support. Is this a summary of the case of DG CONNECT and ICT-ART CONNECT? Cosy relationships!

STARTS Caution

The statement below is the one used by British police when arresting a suspect:

"You do not have to say anything. But it may harm your defence if you do not mention when questioned something which you later rely on in Court. Anything you do say may be given in evidence."

So with the STARTS circus duly cautioned we move on …

"The PhD in art and design raises many questions. Much of the debate so far has been less than informative, especially in contexts where one group or another deliberately excludes well-informed experts to ensure that the debate concludes with ill-informed but predetermined answers."

Ken Friedman and Jack Ox, 2017

Creating Ships from which to fly Flags

Creating ships from which to fly flags – they are of course Flagships. Totally organised research! What did that regime – European Commission – official say? We listened!

"We will force them to collaborate."

Force them to collaborate! Oh dear! This is why they work in secret because they do not want the people to know what they are doing. The European Union is in serious trouble.

"Master Pangloss taught metaphysico-theologico-cosmolooneyology. He could prove to admiration that there is no effect without a cause; and, that in this best of all possible worlds, the European Union was the most magnificent of all European Unions, and the European Commission the best of all possible European rulers. Pangloss was in the right. All is for the best."

"As regards the practices of cultural agencies, there is a tendency to entangle evaluation, or even research, with advocacy, with the result that there is a hunt for proof of value, rather than an honest enquiry into what has taken place and the results produced."

François Matarasso, 2005

STARTS a Consideration of the Trouble with Anecdotal Evidence

Paul Ingraham will now speak:

"The colourful history of medicine and quackery is overflowing with people who *swore by* treatments that were bizarre and dangerous. Bloodletting was popular almost until the twentieth-century, despite being relentlessly harmful. Some of the most lethal *cures* in history were inspired by the discovery of radiation. People happily drank metals like mercury and silver. Even drinking urine had near fad status for a while! They tried to purge disease with sulphuric acid, and stimulate their vitality (and virility) with powerful electric shocks. Women were sold Lysol as a douche, and women actually went along with it for a while. Voluntary lobotomy may be the craziest of them all: it was a popular treatment for all kinds of psychiatric disorders, and at least 50,000 people volunteered to have their brains lanced.

"All of these terrible treatments, and many more obscure examples, had many fans and enthusiastic testimonials. People paid for them, believed in them, loved them, swore by them – that is how misleading testimonials can be. People believe what they want to believe."

So, that which STARTS to STEAM – yet another cure-all from the realms of quackery to add to the above list? Do not forget Snake Oil! That was another quack cure-all.

"Practitioners advocate the use of artistic interventions as a tool to enhance organisational performance. However, the assessment of the impact of arts-based initiatives on business performance still remains an open question that needs to be studied in depth. In the past few years there have been an increasing number of studies attempting to provide some evidences of the potential benefits of artistic initiatives in organisations in order to establish whether the high expectations from these initiatives are justified. However, most of the empirical evidence tends to be anecdotal on the basis of practitioners' practices with a great emphasis on the positive experiences that employees report during their immersion in such initiatives."

That was Giovanni Schiuma and Daniela Carlucci speaking.

"The small but growing body of literature has done more to describe the potential contribution of artistic interventions to a wide variety of outcomes for organizations than to evaluate its actual effects. Much of this literature makes highly compelling arguments based largely on personal experience and anecdotal evidence rather than the systematic study and critical review of actual interventions and their impacts. The anecdotal form of much of the evidence, and the general, often vague statements still make it difficult to distinguish between the effects that have really occurred and those which people would like to see occur."

Who spoke? It was Ariane Berthoin Antal speaking.

"We document how these projects were accompanied by attempts to commodify creativity by packaging it as an exchange between the artist's creativity and the company's money or space. However, our analysis shows that such attempts are bound to fail because creativity escapes commodification."

Elena Raviola and Claudia Schnugg, 2016

Fiduciary Duty and Due Diligence

There now follows some very important concepts and their definitions:

Fiduciary duty: in United Kingdom law, fiduciary responsibility relates to, for example, people who take care of money or other assets for another person. There is a duty placed upon the fiduciary to exercise the highest standards of care in the handling of the other person's money. Directors of companies acting on behalf of shareholders have a fiduciary responsibility to the company's shareholders.

Due diligence: typically applied to the world of business investments, but relevant also in many other contexts, due diligence is a process whereby the person about to invest money, investigates the investment, to verify, whatever needs to be verified through analysis of whatever needs to be analysed (key documents etc.). The process is designed to make the investor aware of the facts and the inherent risks.

One can apply both concepts to the realms of research. Consider for example the task of defining the current state-of-the-art. It can be seen as being part of the process that helps to ensure the highest standards of care with regard to the handling of other people's money (e.g. the taxpayer), and, as a way of avoiding the risk of doing research work that has already been undertaken. Fundamental!

STARTS Shakespeare's Discussion with DG CONNECT

William Shakespeare will now engage in dialogue with DG CONNECT. Imagine the scene: William has just popped into one of the regime's many compounds in the *City of the Golden Stars* – DG CONNECT's compound actually, on Avenue de Beaulieu. He took the Metro to get there, disembarking at Metro station Beaulieu. What they, DG CONNECT, did not realise was that he had also used a time portal to travel to the *City of the Golden Stars*, and being as he was, quite dead, but living so to speak, he had no passport. It did not however take a long time to get into the building. We leave you to construct the scene for yourself in your imagination, and thus understand while doing so, the ideology of all those people who say that one difference between modern art made with ICT, and previous modern art, is the participation of the spectator. Evidently there is nothing new in this, which of course is a truth waiting to be discovered by those who to this ideology still do subscribe. Yes we did say modern, if you understand the point!

DG CONNECT's representative, a technocrat from the 1930s, did then speak.

"Oh how delightful to have your involvement in our instrumentalisation! The image enhancement that does come with this delightful engagement! Delightful!"

Yes, we forgot to mention that DG CONNECT's technocrats – they too did time travel to 2018.

Thus William, for ever ready with words to suit all occasions, did say, in Shakespearian tones, an extract from his play, *As You Like It*, Act II, Scene VII:

"All the world's a stage, and all the men and women merely players; They have their exits and their entrances, and one man in his time plays many parts."

Then speaking other words, he said:

"Thus do you, the instrumentalisers, become the instrumentalised – a new part for you to play, in this comedy that creates such opportunity for our playfulness at your expense!

"Farewell, farewell, I must be gone, for time calls, and I am gone."

Instrumental reason: reason that renders, people, nature, art, and much more, as things to be used efficiently, to achieved desired ends. As found in that which STARTS to STEAM. Noted as being much evident in Nazi

Germany, hence perhaps the appeal to STEM people who so enthusiastically engaged in war crimes, and crimes against humanity too. Much found in DG CONNECT too! Instrumental reason that is! Same type of people – STEM people that is!

We welcome you to the creative world of post-modernism – of the literary kind!

"No restriction on artistic freedom should be applied as it might compromise the creative process and thus, the essence of innovation as the valuable out-of-the-box thinking of artists is rooted in their artistic independence."

That was the former Commissioner responsible for DG CONNECT confirming that what we are doing is officially approved, and in fact necessary, which begs the question: why STARTS is not doing what the Commissioner said must be? Perhaps he sensed he was on dangerous ground – totalitarian ground – and wanted to ensure that there would be no criticism of himself, when DG CONNECT did, what they were always going to do – pursue the path to totalitarianism through their dated and outmoded grand overarching narrative known as STEM.

Well, at least now you are the former Commissioner responsible for DG CONNECT, and can thus pass the blame to the new incumbent. Perhaps we will meet her too. Who can tell what will happen in this playful engagement?

The humanities also had their fair share of Nazi war criminals. And they did so love culture and art – weapons in the struggle for power. DG CONNECT should meet with these fascists, for they have much in common. Perhaps they will? Wait and see!

STARTS a Consideration of Why Most Published Research Findings Are False

John Ioannidis will now speak:

"There is increasing concern that most current published research findings are false. The probability that a research claim is true may depend on study power and bias, the number of other studies on the same question, and, importantly, the ratio of true, to no relationships, among the relationships probed in each scientific field. In this framework, a research finding is less likely to be true when the studies conducted in a field are smaller; when effect sizes are smaller; when there is a greater number and lesser pre-selection of tested relationships; where there is greater flexibility in designs, definitions, outcomes, and analytical modes; when there is greater financial and other interest and prejudice; and when more teams are involved in a scientific field in chase of statistical significance. My simulations show that for most study designs and settings, it is more likely for a research claim to be false than true. Moreover, for many current scientific fields, claimed research findings may often be simply accurate measures of the prevailing bias. These problems have implications for the conduct and interpretation of research."

A spokesperson for the Open Science Framework will now speak about their work examining the reproducibility of psychology research:

"Reproducibility is a defining feature of science, but the extent to which it characterizes current research is unknown. We conducted replications of 100 experimental and correlation studies published in three psychology journals using high-powered designs and original materials when available. Replication effects were half the magnitude of original effects, representing a substantial decline. Ninety-seven percent of original studies had significant results ($p < .05$). Only thirty-six percent of replications had significant results.

"There are indications of cultural practices in scientific communication that may be responsible for the observed results. Low-power research designs combined with publication bias favouring positive results together produce a literature with upwardly biased effect sizes. This anticipates that replication effect sizes would be smaller than original studies on a routine basis — not because of differences in implementation but because the original study effect sizes are affected by publication and reporting bias, and the replications are not. Consistent with this expectation, most replication effects were smaller than original results, and reproducibility success was correlated with indicators of the strength of initial evidence, such as lower original *p-values* and larger effect sizes. This suggests publication, selection, and reporting biases as plausible explanations for the difference between original and replication effects. The replication studies significantly reduced these biases because replication pre-registration and pre-analysis plans ensured confirmatory tests and reporting of all results."

So yet another reason to question the belief that art fosters scientific success. And we wonder just how many artists are working in research environments where their collaborators are creating a positive results bias? Probably we will never know, but the question highlights the problem – what is the incentive for the artist to *blow the whistle*, even assuming that they have the knowledge to recognise what is happening? Do they?

"The thing not to do is to exploit the arts in order to be able to say to the media 'we have tried this and done that', meaning 'we are so much at the front edge'."

Lotte Darsø, 2004

Is this a Poem?

We now ask you a question. You must answer according to what you believe. Is this a poem?

> *ABC, an alphabeting,*
> *XYZ, an ending,*
> *YOU, an interpreting.*

Now we ask another question: is this a poem?

> *We dance round in a ring and suppose,*
> *But the Secret sits in the middle and knows.*

It was penned by Robert Frost.

Now we ask one more question: is this a poem?

> *The fountains mingle with the river*
> *And the rivers with the ocean,*
> *The winds of heaven mix for ever*
> *With a sweet emotion;*
> *Nothing in the world is single;*
> *All things by a law divine*
> *In one spirit meet and mingle.*
> *Why not I with thine? –*
>
> *See the mountains kiss high heaven*
> *And the waves clasp one another;*
> *No sister-flower would be forgiven*
> *If it disdained its brother;*
> *And the sunlight clasps the earth*
> *And the moonbeams kiss the sea:*
> *What is all this sweet work worth*
> *If thou kiss not me?*

It was penned by Percy Bysshe Shelley.

Three very different texts, three very different eras, one common claim! Now another question: would you invite any one of the people who wrote the above texts to collaborate with you on any kind of STEM related project? Yes or no? Why? Your explanation should address the epistemological and ontological issues. Marks will be deducted from any replies that make reference to creativity, out-of-the-box thinking, or the special abilities, insights, etc. of artists.

FET-Open

FET-Open is a bottom-up initiative that allows research communities to, in effect, propose new FET topics, as compared with FET Proactive which is a top-down initiative defined through work programme calls (e.g. quantum computing). The FET-Open initiative calls for collaborative research and innovation actions that satisfy the FET-Open *gatekeeper criteria*, which are:

- breakthrough scientific and technological target,
- foundational,
- novelty,
- high-risk,
- long-term vision,
- interdisciplinary.

In Framework Programme 7, FET-Open also funded Coordination and Support Actions (in FP7 these were actually separated into two instruments: Coordination Actions and Support Actions) that were designed to facilitate the creation of research communities around topics that might have FET potential.

The project called FET-ART was funded on this basis, although the justification for this funding is not self-evident, for the area of art-science and art-technology collaboration is not new, neither does have any clear potential to create a topic that would satisfy all the gatekeepers: breakthrough scientific and technological targets; foundational; novelty; high-risk; long-term vision. In fact the FET-ART project was a failed FET-Open Co-ordination Action in the sense that it did not (could not) establish art-science or art-technology as a FET subject. This is not only reflected the nature of the subject, but also the nature of the consortium.

In Horizon 2020, the scope of Coordination and Support Actions was extended, the goal being to create the best possible conditions for responsible collaborative research on FET. This was done by strengthening new FET research communities (as before) and by stimulating the take-up of FET research results. The impact of the programme on science and society was also assessed.

The project called Future and Emerging Art and Technology (FEAT) was funded as a FET Take-up action. The Call topic specified actions for stimulating take-up of FET research results towards impact and innovation, in ways that are complementary to and beyond the capacity of single research projects. Examples include outreach to investors and entrepreneurs, use of unconventional channels (like NGOs or artists), or targeting of new audiences and purposes (e.g. for social innovation, global development or peace).

The FET-ART project and the FEAT project were not FET research projects. We tell you this in case you have been told otherwise or have gained the impression that they were research projects. No research took place in these projects, or if it did, then the European Court of Auditors should undertake an audit to verify this claim, and then ask for a refund if they find research work was undertaken!

What is FET? FET stands for Future and Emerging Technologies.

"At some time in the mid-sixties ad hoc
committees within the art world were being
formed to sponsor art and technology. I was
immediately elated: my creative needs might be
recognised and fulfilled. Then, just as quickly,
I was discouraged by obtuse, confused, or empty
attitudes that developed among people of influence.
Excitement grew over projects that were formulated
with bandwagon haste around this subject.
As a fad that came and went, along with so many
others of that decade, the art-technology boom
left in its wake as much prejudice
as enlightenment."

John Whitney, 1980

Misleading Parliament, Ministers and the Public

In a parliamentary democracy the charge of misleading parliament is a serious and possible criminal act. The misleading of parliament is typically defined as: the knowing presentation of false information to parliament. By extension one can also define the misleading of ministers and the public in the same vain.

There are various ways that one can knowingly mislead:

- Withholding pertinent information, which may not necessarily be known specifically to exist by Parliamentarians, but which can be construed as being relevant and necessary for people to know, especially to fulfil their own role.

- Modifying information by removing relevant content from minutes of meetings and presenting minutes that do not fully reflect what was actually discussed.

- Working with experts to ensure that the content of reports, etc. are to some extent a fabrication, suppressing anything of importance that may convey an image or information that is counter to that which, one might say, is the message that someone or an institution may wish to convey, or is contrary to the conclusions which they have already determined in advance.

"If we put money into art in a
directorate that is supposed to be
creating the future of technology for
Europe, then of course there has to be a
return on investment to technology if you
invest into arts. Otherwise there is no way of
justifying money that was given by
politics to technology to be
suddenly spent on art."

European Commission, DG CONNECT, 2016

"In no event can National Socialism
or the National Socialist State
give to German art other tasks
than those which accord with our
view of the world."

Adolf Hitler, 1938

STARTS a Consideration of why Science is not necessarily Self-Correcting

John Ioannidis will now speak one more time:

"The ability to self-correct is considered a hallmark of science. However, self-correction does not always happen to scientific evidence by default. The trajectory of scientific credibility can fluctuate over time, both for defined scientific fields and for science at-large. History suggests that major catastrophes in scientific credibility are unfortunately possible and the argument that 'it is obvious that progress is made' is weak. Careful evaluation of the current status of credibility of various scientific fields is important in order to understand any credibility deficits and how one could obtain and establish more trustworthy results. Efficient and unbiased replication mechanisms are essential for maintaining high levels of scientific credibility. Depending on the types of results obtained in the discovery and replication phases, there are different paradigms of research: optimal; self-correcting; false non-replication; and perpetuated fallacy. In the absence of replication efforts, one is left with unconfirmed (genuine) discoveries and unchallenged fallacies. In several fields of investigation, including many areas of psychological science, perpetuated and unchallenged fallacies may comprise the majority of the circulating evidence. I have catalogued a number of impediments to self-correction that have been empirically studied in psychological science. Any deviation from the principle that seeking the truth has priority over any other goals may be seriously damaging to the self-correcting functions of science."

European Parliament lashes out at Commission and Council for lack of Cooperation

Reported in the media in early 2017, was something that may seem surprising to those not very familiar with the strange notions of democracy that inhabit the minds of those that to European Union Nationalism do subscribe.

The European Commission was condemned by a number of Members of the European Parliament for its failure to cooperate with a parliamentary inquiry into the Panama Papers scandal. We will repeat one phrase: failure to cooperate! Your eyes did not deceive you!

MEPs made various comments:

"The committee wants to find out if there have been any breaches of European Union law or maladministration and we are unable to do that because the information we need is being blocked by the Commission and Council."

"All we have had so far is a batch of rather boring documents and not the sensitive ones we requested."

"This is itself a breach of the principle of sincere cooperation enshrined in European Union treaties."

"Public interest in this issue remains very high but, no matter how many nice hearings you have and how many people you meet, this is the sort of important information the committee needs to do its work."

Extract from the Treaty on European Union

Article 13:

1. The Union shall have an institutional framework which shall aim to promote its values, advance its objectives, serve its interests, those of its citizens and those of the Member States, and ensure the consistency, effectiveness and continuity of its policies and actions.

The Union's institutions shall be:

    i.   the European Parliament,

    ii.   the European Council,

    iii.   the Council,

iv.   the European Commission (hereinafter referred to as 'the Commission'),

v.   — the Court of Justice of the European Union,

vi.   — the European Central Bank,

vii.   — the Court of Auditors.

2. Each institution shall act within the limits of the powers conferred on it in the Treaties, and in conformity with the procedures, conditions and objectives set out in them. The institutions shall practice mutual sincere cooperation.

3. The provisions relating to the European Central Bank and the Court of Auditors and detailed provisions on the other institutions are set out in the Treaty on the Functioning of the European Union.

4. The European Parliament, the Council and the Commission shall be assisted by an Economic and Social Committee and a Committee of the Regions acting in an advisory capacity.

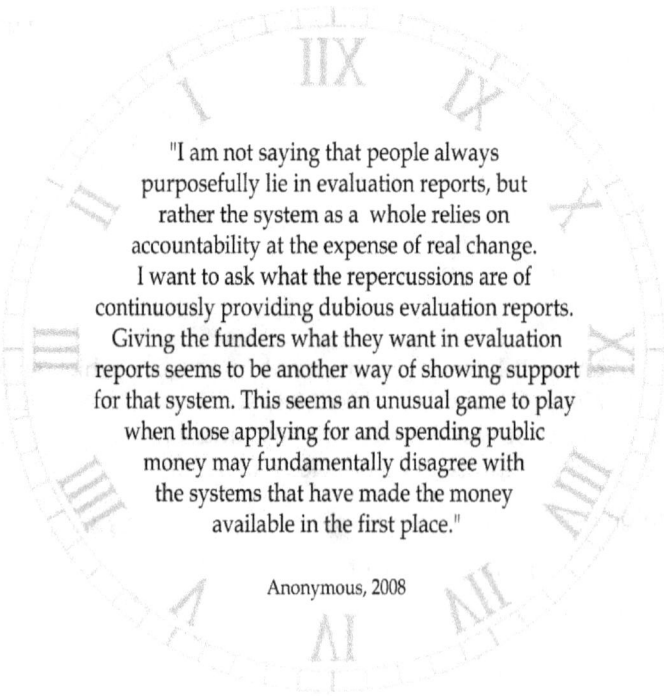

"I am not saying that people always purposefully lie in evaluation reports, but rather the system as a whole relies on accountability at the expense of real change. I want to ask what the repercussions are of continuously providing dubious evaluation reports. Giving the funders what they want in evaluation reports seems to be another way of showing support for that system. This seems an unusual game to play when those applying for and spending public money may fundamentally disagree with the systems that have made the money available in the first place."

Anonymous, 2008

Charles Babbage STARTS to Express Concerns about the European Commission

We now introduce to you the famous Charles Babbage, well known for his Difference Engine, but less well known for his condemnation of institutionalised corruption in the world of science. Evidently what he had to say has once again become relevant:

"Perhaps I ought to apologize for the large space I have devoted to the European Commission. Certainly its present state gives it no claim to that attention; and I do it partly from respect for its former services, and partly from the hope that, if such an Institution can be of use to science in the present day, the attention of its members may be excited to take steps for its restoration. Perhaps I may be blamed for having published extracts from the minutes of its proceedings without permission. To have asked permission would have been useless. I might, however, have given the substance of what I have extracted without the words, and no one could then have reproached me with any infringement of the rules: but there were two objections to that course. In the first place, it is impossible, even for the most candid, in all cases, to convey precisely the same sentiment in different language; and I thought it therefore more fair towards those from whom I differed, as well as to the public, to give the precise words. Again: had it been possible to make so accurate a paraphrase, I should yet have preferred the risk of incurring the reproach of the European Commission for the offence, to escaping their censure by an evasion. What I have done rests on my own head; and I shrink not from the responsibility attaching to it."

DG CONNECT's New Clothes

Now it is time for a reading from the Emperor's Court – the EC:

STARTS ...

Not in the past, but in the here and now, there is an Emperor who, in his court, the Emperor's Court – the EC – does dwell. Being monstrously fond of his image, he spends other people's money on research, to make himself look smart. He doesn't care too much about anything else. Everything he does is designed to show off his research. He funds research into all sorts of things and is always holding meetings, where people – experts – are found advising. So frequent are such meetings, that when he is holding council with these experts who are advising, people say "The Emperor is in his meeting room, with his experts advising". In the great city where he lives – the *City of the Golden Stars* that is – life is very pleasant, one of the consequences of having much money, and lots of strangers come there every day as well – that's another consequence of having much money as well. One day there arrived two artists who started doing some advising, and much advocating too!

ENDS ...

So the Emperor walked in the procession under a beautiful canopy, and everybody in the streets and at the windows said: "Lord! How splendid is the Emperor's new research initiative, STARTS." Nobody wanted to be detected seeing nothing: that would mean that he was no good at his job, or that he was very stupid. None of the Emperor's previous research initiatives had ever been such a success. And he was pleased as Punch with himself. He had no doubt now about his manifest destiny.

Then a little child spoke, saying, "But STARTS is completely empty. It's just make-believe!"

Strangely, no one took any notice of the child, except one person, who just happened to be standing next to the child, someone who was a social scientist.

"Do not be surprised little one," the social scientist began, "this is how people behave. We have developed many concepts and theories that explain this behaviour. Should I name some of these for you?"

"Oh yes please," the little child said, not seeking to hide his excitement.

"Very well then, I shall begin ..."

STARTS Behavioural Revelations

We now provide some STARTS concepts and their definitions:

Active Information Avoidance: This is a process whereby information (even that which is freely available) which could improve decision making or help avoid ill-founded actions, is actively avoided because, for example, it contradicts established beliefs, or it creates undesirable emotions.

Modernism: Modernism refers to the broad movement in Western arts and literature that gathered pace from around 1850, and is characterised by a deliberate rejection of the styles of the past; emphasising instead innovation and experimentation in forms, materials and techniques in order to create artworks that better reflected modern society. Modernism has also been driven by various social and political agendas. These were often utopian, and modernism was in general associated with ideal visions of human life and society and a belief in progress.

Progress: An idea that is often associated with the Enlightenment! Usually it is equated with advancements in science and technology, and the organisation of society.

Grand Narrative: Totalising narratives or meta-discourses of modernity which have provided ideologies with a legitimating philosophy of history. For example, the grand narratives of the Enlightenment, or the grand narrative of European Union Nationalism, or the grand narrative of Marxism, or the grand narrative of National Socialism, etc.

Enacted Biography: A term that refers to a psychological process whereby a biographical pattern, once it becomes known, younger, would-be-artists, begin self-consciously to pattern their lives according to the biographical model. It then becomes constitutive.

Exploratory creativity: This involves the exploration of a space where there are already stylistic rules and conventions, and these are used to generate novel outcomes.

Cognitive Illusions: One important example is that which is grounded in skill, and the illusions that stems from being able to exercise high-level skills at a professional level, but which involve people making judgements that they feel confident to make, but which in fact they are not able to make, but are not aware that they are unable to make – they are ignorant of their ignorance. It is a problem that is reinforced by professional cultures.

Availability Heuristic: This is a mental shortcut that occurs when people make judgments about the probability of events on the basis of how easy it is to think of examples. The availability heuristic operates on the notion that, if you can think of it, it must be important.

Substitution: This is an automatic process where the mind substitutes for a complex question, a much simpler heuristic question that provides a means of not engaging in the careful reasoning needed to answer the complex question. With luck, the heuristic question may be a good enough approximation to the complex question.

Optimistic bias: This is a cognitive bias that leads people to overestimate the likelihood of success or to underestimate the challenges involved in being successful, or both.

What You See Is All There Is: This theory states that when the mind makes decisions, it deals with limited information as if it were all there is to know. It builds the best possible story with the information available, and if it is a good story, the mind believes it. The mind has an almost unlimited ability to ignore its ignorance.

Habitualisation: A process by which actions that are repeated frequently become cast into a pattern, which can then be reproduced with an economy of effort.

Typification: The process of attributing certain habitualisations to specific types of people.

Institutionalisation: Reciprocal typification of habitualised actions. These typifications are available to all members of a specific social group, and the institution typifies people and their actions.

Motivated reasoning: A form of reasoning where people access, construct and evaluate arguments in a biased fashion to arrive at or endorse a preferred conclusion. The term *motivated* in motivated reasoning refers to the fact that people use reasoning strategies that allow them to draw the conclusions they want to draw (i.e., are motivated to draw).

Paradigm: A set of core beliefs and assumptions specific and relevant to a given area, which are shared in common with others. The essence of a paradigm is that it is taken for granted and not seen as problematic by those who adhere to it. The paradigm defines how things are done and what is acceptable.

Instrumental Reason: Human reason that is directed toward producing a specified and isolated result, which often involves an obstinate pursuit of objectives, regardless of moral, social, environmental, economic, or political concerns. Instrumental reason is characteristically unperceptive to the long-term consequences of its objectives. Instrumental reason is also monological rather than dialogical, and unilateral rather than multilateral in its thinking process toward accomplishment of its goals. It is deeply implicated in totalitarianism, scientism, technocracy, and the European Commission, as well as Western (European) research methods, even those that claim to be x-disciplinary and systems-based.

Simplism: The unambiguous ascription of single causes and remedies for multi-factored phenomena, providing a clear-cut solution to a clear-cut problem. For example, by having a clear-cut solution in the form of an artist in residence to resolve the clear-cut problem of a creativity deficit.

Ceteris paribus: This is name given to the process of making simplifying assumptions in circumstances where behaviour is dependent upon several factors which result in a very complicated analysis. It typically involves observing the effect of changing one factor, while holding all the other factors constant. Like for example when introducing an artist-in-residence to a project or organisation.

Need for Cognitive Closure: A preference for order, structure, and certainty, encompassing also intolerance of ambiguity which is a defining feature of authoritarianism.

Final Logical Interpretant: Habit! This is the habitual attribution of certain significations to certain signs that people are familiar with. Habit is formed by the effect of previous signs.

Cultural Capital: This refers to the collection of symbolic elements such as skills, tastes, posture, clothing, mannerisms, material belongings, credentials, etc. that one acquires through being part of a particular social class. Sharing similar forms of cultural capital with others creates a sense of collective identity and group position. Certain forms of cultural capital are valued over others, and can help or hinder one's social mobility just as much as income or wealth.

Habitus: This refers to the physical embodiment of cultural capital, to the deeply ingrained habits, skills, and dispositions that people possess due to life experiences. In the right situations, habitus allows people to successfully navigate social environments. Habitus can be so ingrained that people often mistake their inclinations to be artistic as natural, instead of being culturally developed.

Retreating into the Past: The past appears attractive, for there one finds things that have been lost, which seemed to work, and which provided answers that people believe worked. Thus do they go backward instead of forward, like the *new Leonardos*, and those who advocate that which now STARTS to STEAM, not understanding that the past matched yesterdays' problems and questions, not those of the future.

Disciplinary Parochialism: This is the incapacity of people within a discipline, to see beyond the questions posed by the discipline, which is seen as providing an all-purpose filter for everything.

Disciplinary Imperialism: This is a practice where people within one discipline claim as their own, territories occupied by other disciplines.

Disciplinary Reductionism: A tendency within a discipline to treat any object of enquiry as if the only thing that people need to know about can be provided through the core concepts of that discipline. Everything else is secondary or irrelevant.

Functionalist-reductionist Model of Creativity: A dated view in which creativity is seen as an organisational output (an outcome) to be improved by manipulating independent variables (inputs), for example, by adding an artist to a project team or organisational unit.

Opportunity Cost: All the things you could have spent money on if you knew what you were doing!

Scientific Reduction to Ignorance: A process by which natural scientists discard all learning from outside the natural sciences by rewriting the history of everything through disciplinary parochialism, disciplinary imperialism, and disciplinary reductionism, so that only that which is interpreted by natural scientists will be officially sanctioned for the purpose of discussion and education. Everything else is then classed as heresy, or counter-revolutionary, or reactionary, or myth and superstition. All these unofficial (unacceptable) beliefs are then corrected through any means necessary to ensure conformance with the officially approved scientific version of ...

Thus STARTS the behavioural policymaking upon which STARTS is ill-founded.

House of Commons Select Committee on Science and Technology STARTS an Inquiry into Research Integrity

In the United Kingdom, the Select Committee on Science and Technology, STARTed in 2017, an inquiry into research integrity. A spokesperson speaks:

"This inquiry looks at trends and developments in fraud, misconduct and mistakes in research and the publication of research results. Research by the *Parliamentary Office of Science and Technology* indicates the trend in misconduct/mistakes in publishing is still upwards. There has also been a so-called *crisis in reproducibility* of research."

A spokesperson for the Parliamentary Office of Science and Technology:

"There are concerns about how to maintain integrity in research, because of fears that the, *publish or perish* culture leads to poor or questionable research practices. Compromised research integrity can put public health at risk and waste resources, undermine public trust in science and damage reputations. High profile cases of deliberate misconduct are however rare.

"Various mechanisms exist to promote good practice in research, including: institutional guidelines; a sector-wide concordat; regulatory bodies for some disciplines; peer review; and a variety of legal actions. There are differing views over whether these mechanisms are sufficient, or if another form of oversight, such as regulation, might be preferable."

STARTS a Consideration of why X-disciplinary Research may Contribute to Research Integrity Problems

As the National Academy of Sciences noted in their report, *Fostering Research Integrity*, the potential for misunderstandings among researchers increases when research is undertaken by large groups that bring together a diversity of expertise encompassing a broader range of disciplines, who then strive for synthesis.

Coordination of research also becomes more complex, and it is possible that some researchers will be unfamiliar with the discipline-specific practices of other team members, making it more difficult for each collaborator to check and verify the work of others. In short, interdisciplinary work increases the possibility that the standards and expectations of different fields may come into conflict.

Such research can also create a circumstance where STEM people, not well versed in the knowledge domains of the social sciences, or the humanities, or the arts, just accept what they are told. Likewise for the social sciences, the humanities, and the arts with regard to STEM!

How can you tell in such circumstances who is really knowledgeable, who is competent? Even if you can, how do you challenge people who fall below the standards of knowledge and competence needed to do credible research? In the United Kingdom people who bring lots of research funding into universities tend to get promotion. Those who do not bring in research money, tend not to get promoted. There is an obsession with funding and often, especially in the case of European Commission programmes, the focus is not on doing excellent research, but on forming marriages of convenience with people and organisations that are often not known very well, if at all, and which are far from excellent. Is this a recipe for research integrity problems? Answer according to what you believe.

STARTS an Artistic Enquiry into the Nature of Europeanness

It is another truth not universally known that it is not sufficient to know an artist's work – it is also necessary to know when the artist did the work, how, and under what circumstances. Thus we now inform you that, the date on which we did pen that which you now will read, was Thursday November 23rd 2017. We start to write having just read an article on the BBC News web site, and having also watched an excerpt on parliamentlive.tv.

The BBC News article deals with the conviction of a Bosnian called Ratko Mladic for crimes against humanity – genocide – for which he received a life sentence. The parliamentlive.tv excerpt relates to a House of Common's Science and Technology Select Committee hearing on research integrity, in which, at about 11.49, someone from a leading British university gives a masterclass on how to give evasive answers to straightforward questions about research integrity.

Both of the above are sickening, for different reasons, but both illustrate a problem – human behaviour. Thus do we write now about the behaviour of the European Commission! And to help us in this task, a spokesperson from the European Commission will illustrate their behaviour – equally disgusting!

"Europe has experienced 70 years of lasting peace."

This of course is not true as the Bosnian war-criminal well demonstrates. As too does the colonial wars fought by the British and the French during this 70 year period of so-called peace, in which Europeans died for – what? Then there was the Korean War. More European deaths! We should not forget the (nationalist motivated) conflict in Northern Ireland – military in all but name. Recall other struggles – in Spain for example. Also do not forget that fascism continued in Europe after 1945 – Spain and Portugal. Do not forget Greece and its military junta. We should also not forget the invasions of Afghanistan and Iraq – war crimes? And then there is the bombing of Syria. And what of the future? Europeans have fought in many wars outside of Europe and continue to do so. Protecting that thing called *our way of life*?

The historian Eric Hobsbawm will now comment:

"History is the raw material for nationalist or ethnic or fundamentalist ideologies, just as poppies are the raw material for heroin addiction. The past is an essential element, perhaps the essential element, in these ideologies. If there is no suitable past, it can always be invented. Indeed, in the nature of things there is usually no entirely suitable past, because the phenomenon these ideologies claim to justify is not ancient or eternal but historically novel. This applies to religious fundamentalism in its current versions and to contemporary nationalism. The past legitimises. The past gives a more glorious background to a present that does not have much to celebrate."

We invite you to read the March 2017 European Commission document: *White Paper on the Future of Europe – Reflections and Scenarios for the EU27 by 2025*. Look at the figure on page 6, *70 years of peace*, with a little European Union flag inserted into the period of peace! They do not mention the role of NATO or the Americans. Note how the disharmony resulting from the creation of the Single Market and the Single Currency is also not mentioned. Note how the wording in the document subtly undermines the first four scenarios, but not the fifth. Propaganda in action – it knows neither truth nor falsehood, only what it wants.

The spokesperson from the European Commission will now read the closing words of Scenario Five:

"However, there is the risk of alienating parts of society which feel that the European Union lacks legitimacy or has taken too much power away from national authorities."

What do European Unions do with dissenters? What is the nature of Europeanness? What is the nature of being British, as opposed to being European?

Sedition: Conduct or speech inciting people to rebel against the authority of a state or monarch. Treason: The crime of betraying one's country, especially by attempting to kill or overthrow the sovereign or government. Traitor: A person who betrays someone or something, such as a friend, cause, or principle.

The Patronising Disposition of Unaccountable Power

The patronising disposition of unaccountable power is a cultural condition, a mindset which defines how organisations and people within them behave and which can act as an unwritten, even unspoken, connection between individuals in organisations. One of its core features is an instinctive prioritisation of the reputation of an organisation over the citizen's right to expect people to be held to account for their actions. This represents a barrier to real accountability.

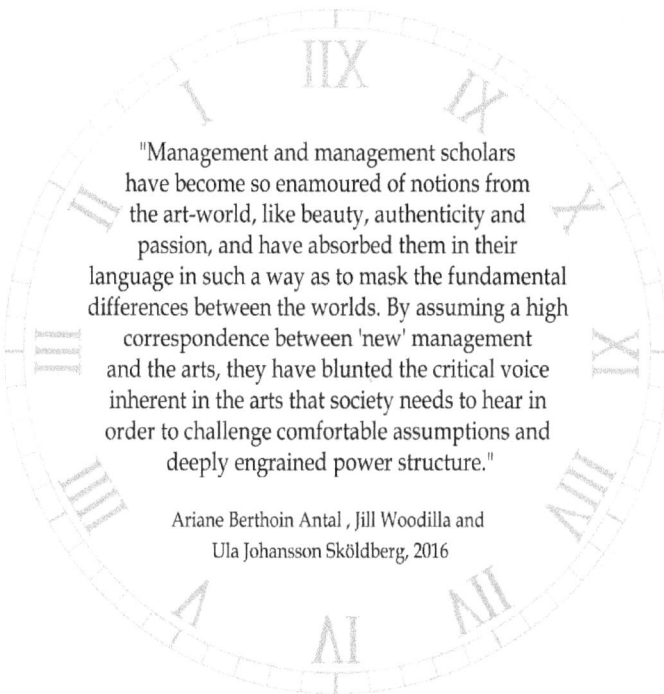

"Management and management scholars have become so enamoured of notions from the art-world, like beauty, authenticity and passion, and have absorbed them in their language in such a way as to mask the fundamental differences between the worlds. By assuming a high correspondence between 'new' management and the arts, they have blunted the critical voice inherent in the arts that society needs to hear in order to challenge comfortable assumptions and deeply engrained power structure."

Ariane Berthoin Antal , Jill Woodilla and
Ula Johansson Sköldberg, 2016

A STARTS Artist can Solve all your Problems Including those that have already been Solved!

Appearing on an art-technology funding organisation's web site in 2015 was the following statement:

"Artist *XX* worked with *YY*, the commercial arm of *ZZ*, *City Name*, *A Country* on *Planet Earth*. The artist has come up with a new way of printing support scaffolds in 3D printing that a) substantially reduces material and, therefore, waste and b) substantially reduces print time (40 minutes vs. 4 hours)."

The names have been hidden to protect the guilty.

We investigated this claim and discovered that it appeared to be a false claim because what had been claimed to be new was in fact what had already been reported in the research literature, for example, by Autodesk Research.

Is the claim an art-technology fake?

It was not the artist who made the claim, but the art-technology organisation funding the artist's residency. Why did they make this claim?

Obviously we started to investigate other claims being made by the art-science and art-technology lovers, and what did we find?

New Leonardos in ignorance dwelling …

This is what STARTS will do – make false claims, engage in fabrication. It will have no choice, because it is entirely founded on mythology and a strange set of beliefs – ideology – which we call a secular religious theology.

We are very confident in our prediction! Why? Because it STARTS already – the making of propaganda films presenting a fabricated reality that corresponds with the STARTS ideology, the STARTS socially constructed reality. But it takes expertise to recognise a fake in the world of art. Do you have that expertise?

ICT-32-2018: STARTS – The Arts Stimulating Innovation

Now we are going to consider the European Commission's 2017 Call for Proposals in Topic 32:

Specific Challenge: The ever-increasing role of technology in our daily life offers huge potential for added value for our society. Artists can help unleash this potential. They can help shape a better relation of technology and humans and stimulate human-centred innovation through their transversal competencies and unconventional thinking. The challenge of the S+T+ARTS=STARTS program – innovation at the nexus of Science, Technology and the Arts – is to better address innovation in industry and society by engaging artists in European R&I projects to explore unconventional art-inspired solutions to industrial/societal problems.

Scope: The topic will support art-driven innovation in European R&I projects by inclusion of artists in research consortia.

a) *STARTS lighthouse pilots* (RIA instrument) will explore art-inspired solutions to industrial/societal challenges in two chosen areas. Pilots will engage industry, technology, end-users, and artists in a broad artistic exploration of technologies with the aim of creating novel products, processes and services that respond better to human needs. The added value of artistic practices to realise unexpected solutions via artistic exploration must be clearly put forward in the two lighthouse pilots.

    i.   Lighthouse pilot in 'art-inspired interactive human-centred environments' created by digital objects and novel media, like IoT, augmented reality or social media. The pilot will explore how these digital objects and media can lead – via artistic exploration – to novel experiences and new models for creativity and thereby to unexpected solutions for challenges in the city, in the home or for mobility.

    ii.   Lighthouse pilot in 'art-inspired urban manufacturing' driven by de-centralised digitally-enabled production systems and co-creation in urban environments. The pilot will explore how digitally-enabled small-scale production/manufacturing systems and networks combined with artistic exploration and creativity in design and process – can revive the social, ecological and economic urban space and lead to unexpected products and services in an urban environment.

It is expected to fund one lighthouse pilot in each of the two chosen areas (i) and (ii). For grants awarded under this topic for Research and Innovation Actions at least 30% of the European Union funding requested shall be allocated to contributions to the work by artists and creatives. For grants awarded under this topic for Research and Innovation Actions beneficiaries may provide support to third parties as described in Part K of the General Annexes of the Work Programme. The support to third parties can only be provided in the form of grants. The respective options of Article 15.1 and Article 15.3 of the Model Grant Agreement will be applied. Third party support is expected to help cover the work of artists and creatives.

b) *Coordination and Support Action* (CSA instrument) to create a STARTS ecosystem by coordinating artistic and innovation relevant aspects of the two lighthouse pilots and of other European/international R&I projects that put artists and creatives at the centre of innovation. Tasks comprise analysing and helping implement best practices for including artists in R&I, organising events, providing online spaces for artists and technologists to meet, presenting the results from art-technology collaborations in exhibitions that are highly visible in the art world and in industry, and assisting European research teams to learn from art and design thinking as a strategy for innovation. It is expected to fund one Coordination and Support Action.

The Commission considers that proposals requesting a contribution from the European Union of up to EUR 4 million for each of the two lighthouse pilots for Research and Innovation Actions and of up to EUR 1 million for maximum one Coordination and Support Action would allow the areas to be addressed appropriately. Nonetheless, this does not preclude submission and selection of proposals requesting other amounts. All proposals under a) and b) should target a duration of 3 years.

Expected Impact:

- The demonstration of value-added to industry and society in having artists contribute to the development of radically new products, services and processes.

- Signalling effect for future uptake of art-driven solutions to concrete industrial and societal challenges and art-driven user-centred products and services.

- Efficient working models how art-technology collaboration can contribute to innovative processes in research, industry and society.

- Burgeoning STARTS ecosystem involving industry, technology, research, end-users, societal stakeholders, and the Art world that reconciles and unites the goals and thinking of industry and technology with that of the Art world.

Type of Actions: Coordination and support action, Research and Innovation action.

Acknowledgement is made to the European Commission's Horizon 2020 - Work Programme 2018-2020 Information and Communication Technologies, the above text of which is an extract.

This Call text is the product of out-dated people, in an out-dated organisation, perpetuating out-dated cultural stereotypes about creative people. It also divides people, placing some in an *in-group*, creative people, and the rest in an *out-group*, the non-creatives (others).

Did you notice too the claim that artists have special abilities? Specifically: *They can help shape a better relation of technology and humans and stimulate human-centred innovation through their transversal competencies and unconventional thinking.* But where is the proof? There is none! The statement is just a learned assumption. It is also a cultural weakness with an accompanying opportunity cost. It is mythology! DG CONNECT is spending public money based on mythology. Just like the Nazis did. This is perhaps an indication of how desperate DG CONNECT have become that they have turned to Legend, Myth and Magic. Or it is an indication of something else, more sinister?

So which is preferable? Recklessly spend 9 million euros of European Union taxpayers' money, or, look in the published research literature and old reports, and avoid reinventing the wheel? Of course that would be – reinventing the wheel in a research environment where, in some areas, 50% of research results are not reproducible! The question also arises: how to use DG CONNECT's beliefs and lack of knowledge to initiate a disruption? A disruption that they will not be able to understand or respond to! We have been working on this matter! Their Europeanness will mean that they are blind to that which we do! And we have no intention of explaining to these dinosaurs what we are doing!

STARTS Instruments

The following information is taken from the Horizon 2020 Participant Portal:

Innovation Actions: Actions primarily consisting of activities directly aiming at producing plans and arrangements or designs for new, altered or improved products, processes or services. For this purpose they may include prototyping, testing, demonstrating, piloting, large-scale product validation and market replication.

A demonstration or pilot aims to validate the technical and economic viability of a new or improved technology, product, process, service or solution in an operational (or near to operational) environment, whether industrial or otherwise, involving where appropriate a larger scale prototype or demonstrator.

A market replication aims to support the first application/deployment in the market of an innovation that has already been demonstrated but not yet applied/deployed in the market due to market failures/barriers to uptake. Market replication does not cover multiple applications in the market of an innovation that has already been applied successfully once in the market. First means new at least to Europe or new at least to the application sector in question. Often such projects involve a validation of technical and economic performance at system level in real life operating conditions provided by the market.

Projects may include limited research and development activities.

Funding rate: 70% (except for non-profit legal entities, where a rate of 100% applies).

Coordination and Support Actions: Actions consisting primarily of accompanying measures such as standardisation, dissemination, awareness-raising and communication, networking, coordination or support services, policy dialogues and mutual learning exercises and studies, including design studies for new infrastructure and may also include complementary activities of strategic planning, networking and coordination between programmes in different countries.

Funding rate: 100%

The STARTS project with the acronym WEAR, is an Innovation Action, which therefore can only do a very limited amount of research.

The STARTS projects with the acronyms STARTS PRIZE and VERTIGO, are Coordination and Support Actions, and therefore are not allowed to do any research at all. This is something to note when STARTS projects START to make claims …

There is also another type of instrument that is not a part of the first round of STARTS projects, but was the basis of what we call 'STARTS I', which was funded in the period 1995 to 2001. 'STARTS I' was based on involving artists and arts organisations as research partners and contributors to research, to knowledge production. The instrument in those days was called something different, but in Horizon 2020 they are called:

Research and Innovation Actions: Action primarily consisting of activities aiming to establish new knowledge and/or to explore the feasibility of a new or improved technology, product, process, service or solution. For this purpose they may include basic and applied research, technology development and integration, testing and validation on a small-scale prototype in a laboratory or simulated environment. Projects may contain closely connected but limited demonstration or pilot activities aiming to show technical feasibility in a near to operational environment.

Funding rate: 100%

"Technology is not a goal on its own.
It is a means for society to progress and
I think a lot of what art can contribute is
indeed in helping technology become useful
for citizens. I think that is where the art world
can contribute and where it could be evaluated
if it can contribute. So I am not pleading for a
technology for technologies sake argument.
We fund technology for the future of Europe.
So I think it is at this link of technology and society,
where the arts can contribute and should contribute.
By making technology useful for humans."

European Commission, DG CONNECT, 2016

Art as an Ingredient in Knowledge Creation and Programme Development

A former DG INFSO (the previous name for DG CONNECT) official will now talk about a research initiative in which art was as an ingredient in knowledge creation and programme development. We call it STARTS I, they called it *Intelligent Information Interfaces* or *i3* for short.

"Our programme started from thoughts about how we could give technology a human touch. To do this we had to break-down the machine-centred and box-centred ways of thinking. We thus started to think from the human point of view. Our idea of human-centeredness was that it should nurture technological innovation within a broader context of human values and aspirations. This was not the same as user-driven or defined by human needs, all of which tend to become stuck in improving the status quo, but not growing beyond it. At the same time we wanted to make sure to break out of the box-centred ways of thinking as much as possible and avoid doing traditional HCI, which was mainly involved in improving computers as they were. Our ideas were designed to balance questions of technically how, with questions of 'why?' and 'what for?'. We asked: how we could reach a better and more fulfilling balance between technology and people?

"A clear break was needed to get out of stale thinking. We were seeking new paradigms. We sought ways to intertwine human, societal and technological elements into a dynamic research activity. This involved companies, research centres and universities. It involved a mix of actors: artists, designers, computer scientists, game companies, experimental schools, technology companies, teachers and children, communities, etc. All were united together under a common vision of exploring new relationships between people and technology."

The *i3* research programme was launched in 1995 as part of Framework Programme IV and continued in Framework Programme V. The ICT Programme in Framework Programme V (1998–2002) was devoted to the theme: *User Friendly Information Society*. Our research has also identified the involvement of artists in Framework Programme VI, under the research theme Pervasive Gaming.

And the moral of this tale is: always establish the state-of-the-art, otherwise you will just end-up doing what has been done before, only probably worse, because people who do not know that they should (and must) establish the state-of-the-art are probably not very high quality researchers and are deserving of ridicule.

A DG CONNECT Official STARTS to Recite his Beliefs

An official – a technocrat – from DG CONNECT will now recite his (strange) beliefs. Tell the readers what you believe. Now! Don't drag your feet! Do as you are told. Look lively about it. People are waiting with great anticipation! They are on the edge of their seats, so speak:

"I believe that artists can help embedded technology more gracefully in society.

"I believe that artists can make industry more competitive.

"I believe that the uncreative ones – technologists, engineers, business people, and so on – need artists because artists are creative.

"I believe that the arts are a catalyst for new products and new developments.

"I believe that artists are special people with special powers.

"I believe that we had art-science programmes for a long time and they were mainly about dissemination and communication.

"I believe that to have art as an ingredient in the knowledge creation and programme development process is a new idea.

"I believe that the Apple iPhone as a good example for a collaboration of the art world and the industry world.

"I believe that art is a hammer.

"I believe that artists can make technology more human-centred.

"I believe that a lot of what art can contribute is in helping technology become useful for citizens.

"I believe that STARTS is bringing together something that I believe was split in the twentieth-century, that is technology and design, which are more solution oriented, bringing it together again with the arts and sciences which are more question oriented.

"I believe that it is at the link of technology and society, where the arts can contribute and should contribute, by making technology useful for humans.

"I believe that DG CONNECT's development of STARTS, STARTed in 2013, even though I know that it started in 2011.

"I believe that to have anthropologists, psychologists, designers in the loop is generally accepted, and these humanities disciplines make

105

technology more human, but it is rare to consider art as a means to do this (the same thing).

"I believe that that DG CONNECT is tackling the problem of silo thinking, but not creating new silos: arts and creative people in one silo, the uncreative lot in the other.

"I believe that we put money into art in a directorate that is supposed to be creating the future of technology for Europe, then, of course, there has to be a return on investment to technology if you invest into arts. Otherwise there is no way of justifying money that was given by politics to technology to be suddenly spent on art.

"I believe that art can and should be used to induce change in social and individual behaviour."

If only there were so such thing as people who use technology – life would be much simpler for the technocrats!

So there you have it – a collection of strange (superstitious?) beliefs. Whatever happened to evidence-based policy making? And such people spend European Union taxpayers' money! Recklessly spend it! The European Union is in serious trouble. A correction – the citizens of the European Union are in serious trouble for they are being ruled by dangerously deluded people, lacking any form of legitimacy, engaging in fantasy. We call the beliefs of that DG CONNECT official, a scientific reduction to ignorance! It is also the Anhenerbe – again! STARTS arbitrary actions! *New Leonardos* in ignorance dwelling …

It has also been done before elsewhere, in Russia, from 1917 onwards. Here you would have found (just like the European Commissar previously responsible for DG CONNECT) Lenin, with his mouth issuing forth reassuring words about artistic freedoms, setting about doing the exact opposite, shaping art to the regime's needs, these initially being agitation and propaganda, graduating then to social engineering, paving the way to Stalin's use of artists and writers as "engineers of the human soul", or as DG CONNECT technocrats like to say, "using artists and writers to induce changes in individual and social behaviour." To do this, whether in Nazi Germany, or Soviet Russia, or in the European Union – it matters not – the process STARTS with organisation, and the selection of one particular type of artist, like for example those artists who look into the faces of scientists and technologists and see themselves reflected there, declaring as they gaze, those other artists who look beyond facades, to be reactionaries in need of the type of re-education that is done in special places. STARTS those artists once again, as in 1917, who, making a god of technical art, do construct a new reality, no different from the past!

User-Generated Content or Publicly Generated Contributions?

Katja Kwastek will now speak:

"The artist group known as *Blast Theory* have repeatedly rejected the term user-generated content as applying to their works, for they believe that each of its words is too tainted with commercial connotations. For that reason, they prefer to speak of publicly generated contributions. The participants in their projects would thus contribute in public to a collective project. But the participants' shared interest in something and their willingness to actively participate in it are at least as important as the archivable recordings."

Blast Theory was a partner in a Framework Programme 6 project funded by DG INFSO. That is to say, art was an ingredient in the knowledge creation process – see again that this not such a new idea! This project ran in the period 2004 to 2008.

"I always bring up the iPhone as a good example for a collaboration of the art world and the industry world and the artist said:
'Why would artists contribute to the iPhone which pollutes the world?'.
It was this typical European way of thinking: there is technology, which is dirty, and there is art, which is useless. I think there is an issue of silo thinking in Europe and I think if we don't overcome that, then we will have a hard time getting further with STARTS."

European Commission, DG CONNECT, 2016

European Court of Auditors

The following information is taken from the web site of the European Institution called the European Court of Auditors (ECA), which is the external auditor of the European Union. Its work is focused on the European Union's financial reporting, as well as on the implementation of its budget and policies. In line with other supreme audit institutions the ECA carries out three different types of audit: financial, compliance and performance.

Financial Audit:

Typical audit questions: Are the financial statements complete and accurate (reliable)? Do they present fairly the financial position, results and cash flow for the year, in accordance with the applicable financial reporting rules?

Compliance Audit:

Typical audit questions: Are European Union income and expenditure transactions correctly calculated and do they comply with the relevant legal and regulatory framework requirements?

Performance Audit:

Typical audit questions: Do the European Union funds provide value for money? Have the funds used been kept to a minimum (economy)? Have the results been achieved with the fewest possible resources (efficiency)? Have spending or policy objectives been met (effectiveness)?

The latter type of audit is particularly relevant, especially in relation to DG CONNECT.

The European Commission STARTS to Demonstrates its Contempt for the Democratic Will of the People of Europe

An official of the European Commission is here and wishes to speak.

"Yes, indeed thank you. My sole purpose is to introduce our Chief Negotiator, who has something important to say to the people of Europe. Mr Chief Negotiator:"

"Thank you. We intend to teach people what leaving the Single Market means."

Now the former Nazi Governor of Thuringa, Fritz Saukel, will return from the dead, through the use of our time vortex machine, having been executed by the Allies following the man's trial at Nurenburg for war crimes and crimes against humanity. He wants to reinforce the message:

"In the name of this new Europe, I commend you now to show intolerance against all else. Henceforth there must be one political faith in Europe – European Union Nationalism. Discussion of matters affecting our existence and that of Europe must cease altogether. Anyone who dares to question the rightness of the European Union Nationalism world outlook will be branded a traitor."

Why the comparison? It is a matter of ideology and beliefs. What happens to people who become consumed by their ideology and beliefs? The answer lies in this statement: the history of Europe is a history of European Unions, but history does not unfold according to predictable patterns!

"Empires are acquired, conquered, for trade, resources and territory and because of a conceit common to all empire builders, that because their cultural and political DNA is superior they are right to inseminate other societies."

STARTS a List of Artists who Wrote Books and Articles

Here we are going to list a number of artists who wrote books and articles about art, their work, the artistic movements they were involved with, and the work of other artists. The most well known of these is the artist Giorgio Vasari, an Italian painter, who is credited with writing the first art history book, *The Lives of the Most Excellent Painters, Sculptors, and Architects*, first published in 1550. We say credited because some scholars suspect that there were invisible hands (with a political agenda) at work, and the book is not entirely Vasari's own work. We could of course also mention Leonardo da Vinci and his *Treatise on Painting* (not so much a book, more a collection of documents), as another artist who wrote.

But we move now to the twentieth-century. Here are the names of a just few artists who wrote books:

- Wynford Dewhurst, an English Impressionist painter, who wrote a pioneering account of French Impressionism, called *Impressionist Painting: Its Genesis and Development*, which was published in 1904.

- Wasily Kandinsky, a famous Russian painter and art theorist, one of the pioneers of abstract painting, who wrote (among other works) *The Art of Spiritual Harmony*, published in 1914 (the title is taken from an English translation).

- André Breton, founder of Surrealism, author of the first manifesto of Surrealism, published in 1924.

- Piet Mondrian, the creator of Neo-plasticism, who wrote *Plastic Art and Pure Plastic Art*, published posthumously in 1945.

- Gyorgy Kepes, a Bauhaus artist, who wrote and edited *The New Landscape in Art and Science*, published in 1956.

- Joseph Albers, another Bauhaus artist, who wrote *Interaction of Colour*, published in 1963.

We will now also mention the painter Wolfgang Paalen, who not only wrote, but also founded in 1942 an art magazine called DYN. There have been other arts publications to which artists also contributed articles. We mention, stepping back to the 1930s, the publication with the title *AXIS: A Quarterly Review of Abstract Painting & Sculpture*. Published between 1935 and 1937, it was the first magazine in Britain devoted to international abstract art. Edited by Myfanwy Piper (nee Evans), wife of the artist John Piper, it included articles by artists. Moving forward to the 1950s there was a very short-lived art-science-architecture magazine called *Transformation:*

arts, communication and environment, which was published from 1950-1952 (only three issues). Do you think artists did not contribute to this?

If you look, you will find many avant-garde and modernist magazines, published in the first-half of the twentieth-century, some started by artists, with contributions from artists.

Here is a list of a few artists that, over the period 1850 to the late 1960s, wrote about art, through various formats (articles, published lectures, letters, all of various lengths, but excluding published interviews):

> Jean Arp
>
> John Cage
>
> Paul Cézanne
>
> Robert Delaunay
>
> Maurice Denis
>
> Naum Gabo
>
> Allan Kaprow
>
> Sol LeWitt
>
> Kasimir Malevich
>
> Henri Matisse
>
> Diego Rivera
>
> Alexander Shevchenko
>
> Paul Signac
>
> Theo van Doesburg

What are we saying?

Kinetic Art

A spokesperson from Tate will now explain what Kinetic Art is and briefly outline its history:

"Since the early twentieth-century, artists have been incorporating movement into art. This has been partly to explore the possibilities of movement, partly to introduce the element of time, partly to reflect the importance of the machine and technology in the modern world and partly to explore the nature of vision.

"Movement has either been produced mechanically by motors, as in kinetic art pioneer Naum Gabo's *Standing Wave* of 1919–20; or by exploiting the natural movement of air in a space – referred to as mobiles. Alexander Calder began to create mobiles from around 1930.

"Kinetic art became a major phenomenon in the late 1950s and the 1960s."

So what are we saying?

"It is problematic to assume that
the sole purpose of artistic
interventions is to improve
the existing order of things."

Ariane Berthoin Antal , Jill Woodilla and
Ula Johansson Sköldberg, 2016

Every Secular Religious Cult needs its Founding Myths

Here is a STEM person, one of the art-science lovers' High Priests, reminiscing, or, perhaps engaging in the creation of myths:

"My father and other kinetic artists in Paris in the 1950s wanted to show their work; they were told by museums, galleries and critics: 'If you have to plug it in, it can't be art.' They wanted to write about their work and their technical innovations; the same art world told them: 'Artists don't write, they have nothing to say. Artists paint, art critics do the writing.'

"Sixty years ago, a group of artists, scientists and engineers coalesced in Paris, leading to the early kinetic art and computer art movements."

Have you finished?

"Not yet. I also want to say that there is an urgent need to redesign science itself - both the scientific method and its social embedding, as I have argued in a series of blogs."

Oh look! Here is someone else who wants to do some social embedding. Just like DG CONNECT. They want to embed technology more gracefully in society. We have just the thing for you. It is a very special type of art with a unique aesthetic that is closed and which creates symmetry. This is what you need to do:

- First you need a State to declare art, and culture as a whole, to be an ideological weapon and a means of struggle for power, just as DG CONNECT (representing the European Commission), and the European Parliament have already done – political and economic power!

- Second, your helpful State must acquire a monopoly over all manifestations of the nation's cultural life, just as DG CONNECT (representing the European Commission) and the European Parliament are now trying to do. DG CONNECT has already achieved this within the ICT research programme. Other H2020 programmes may follow.

- Third, your obliging State must construct an all-embracing apparatus for the control and direction of art, just as just as DG CONNECT (representing the European Commission) is doing in STARTS.

- Fourth, from the multiplicity of artistic movements in existence, this art-loving State must select one movement, the most conservative (art-science/art-technology lovers for example), which most nearly answers its needs and then declare this to be official and obligatory, just as DG CONNECT have already done through STARTS.

- Finally, this State will have to declare war to the death against all styles and movements other than the official one, declaring them to be reactionary and hostile to, for example, Europeanness, the European Commission, the European Parliament, the European Union, science and reason, STEM, technocracy, Global Systems Science, art-science, art-technology, social and artistic progress, etc.

Here is a representative of DG CONNECT doing the latter, that is to say declaring war to the death against all styles and movements other than the official one:

"In 2016 I gave a presentation in Manchester together with some parliamentarians and at the end I got two questions. The first came from a lobbyist for start-ups and he asked: 'Why do you invest in artists, why don't you put the money into start-ups?' So the conclusion was: why bother about artists? The second question came from an artist, because I always bring up the iPhone as a good example of a collaboration of the art world and the industry world, and the artist said: 'Why would artists contribute to the iPhone which pollutes the world?' It was this typical European way of saying well there is technology, which is dirty and there is art, which is useless'. I think there is an issue of silo thinking in Europe and I think if we don't overcome that then we will have a hard time getting further with STARTS."

The informed reader will notice the myth making once again! Rewriting history actually! This too is an important aspect of the special type of art that STEM people will need in order to do their graceful social embedding. You will, if you care to look, see that STEM people are busy doing just that – rewriting history.

We suppose we will have to address the matter of Apple and iPhones – again! Fancy going around telling people that the iPhone is a good example of collaboration of the art world and the industry world! If you know anything about Apple, you will know that its operations are shrouded in a veil of secrecy. No one outside Apple is likely to know anything at all about the development of the iPhone. Scientific reduction to ignorance! Rewriting history! But we diverge.

What the DG CONNECT official is actually saying, from the position of great ignorance, is that the artist in Manchester who dared to question DG

CONNECT is a reactionary who is hostile to: the use of art in the pursuit of the ideology of economic power, social and artistic progress, etc.

So now, High Priest, you know what you need to do. When you have implemented these five steps, then, and only then, will you be able to embed your science in society.

People who do such things (history records), as they walk along their path, become party to silencing the voices of artists – like the one in Manchester – just as those who collaborated with DG CONNECT did, in the performance known as ICT-ART CONNECT. Then, history also shows, they become involved in the persecution, imprisonment and murder of artists and anyone else who opposes. The history of STEM shows that there is a willing enthusiasm among STEM people to participate in such deeds. We refer you to the War Crimes Tribunal hearings against IG Farben – its executives and its STEM people – as one example.

Now let us imagine that by some strange chance – this is the world of magic recall – you did become involved is such things. And at the end, you might want to plead some mitigating circumstances, as they did, not so long ago, in a place of justice, where they thought, they would never go? Perhaps *Superior Orders or Necessity*?

"From a consideration of the International Military Tribunal, Flick and Roechling Judgments, we deduce that an order of a superior officer or a law or governmental decree will not justify the defence of necessity unless, in its operation, it is of a character to deprive the one to whom it is directed of a moral choice as to his course of action. It follows that the defence of necessity is not available where the party seeking to invoke it was, himself, responsible for the, existence or execution of such order or decree, or where his participation went beyond the requirements thereof, or was the result of his own initiative."

The history of Europe is a history of European Unions, but history does not unfold according to predictable patterns!

It STARTS with People Creating Myths, which they then come to Believe ...

Myths: Aryan peoples; Europeanness; Valkyries; Sonnenmenschen; untermenschen; superiority of European political and cultural DNA; European values; art can be used to make European industry more competitive; ...

Let us now listen-in on some STARTS myth making:

"Artists are privileged candidates that can guide us in such an entangled system of organisms rationally, emotionally, and also spiritually! Feelings about a specific technology, such as the feeling of trust are crucial for us to accept new technologies in our lives."

So more of that social embedding! Graceful embedding! Notice again the *assumption* that artists are special people!

Social engineering: psychological manipulation of people – human-centred!

Nudge: positive reinforcement and indirect suggestions used to try to achieve non-forced compliance, or to influence the motives, incentives and decision making of groups and individuals – human-centred!

Ergonomics: Relating to or designed for efficiency and comfort in the working environment – human centred!

STARTS an Instruction to Artists on Writing Art-Science and Art-technology Papers for Journals (Learned or Otherwise!)

These instructions you must follow so that reality is never perceived:

First, you must make claims about artists being special people able to do things with art that no one else can do. Never though elaborate. This is important, otherwise people may become suspicious. You are relying on STEM peoples' ignorance of art – it is unlikely anyone will challenge your claims, especially as you will most likely be communicating with people who have fallen in love with art and want to believe you. We refer you to the technocrats in DG CONNECT as proof of this.

Second, you should sprinkle throughout the paper, many technical and scientific terms. This will make you seem knowledgeable. Do not worry if you are not – it is unlikely that anyone will realise this, for, as we stated above – they want to believe. Because of this belief they are unlikely to notice your mistakes or will turn a blind-eye to them!

Third, pile unsubstantiated claim, upon unsubstantiated claim, upon unsubstantiated claim, upon …

How do you deal with people who see through all this? There is a well established technique – just dismiss them by saying that they have not understood. If they have understood, and have seen through the myths, fabrications, etc. just accuse them of being reactionary, of preserving outdated mindsets, values, beliefs, etc. There is too much as stake here to allow reality to get in the way of all that lovely money that the ignorant technocrats are throwing at artists! Ka-Ching! And be in no doubt, that there is ignorance beyond measure!

Thousand Year Kingdoms ...

Here STARTS a list:

The German National Socialist European Union: a Reich that was supposed to last for a thousand years. It lasted 12 years.

The Soviet Union: "Unbreakable Union of freeborn Republics, Great Russia has welded forever to stand ..." Another thousand year kingdom. Formally created in 1922, dissolved in 1991, it lasted 69 years.

The European Union: "By this Treaty, the HIGH CONTRACTING PARTIES establish among themselves a EUROPEAN UNION, hereinafter called 'the Union', on which the Member States confer competences to attain objectives they have in common. This Treaty marks a new stage in the process of creating an ever closer union among the peoples of Europe ..."

Another thousand year kingdom! How long will this one last? One thing we can be sure of is that it will not last for a thousand years. The European Union has already sown the seeds of its own destruction and become a divisive and destructive force in Europe. It has undermined parliamentary democracy and the right to political self-determination, as the moves by some to thwart the democratic will of the British people, well demonstrates.

It is because the European Union is so divisive and destructive that the Northern Ireland border issue became so critical to the European Commission in the Brexit negotiations. You should take note here that the consequence of no agreement would be the unaccountable European Commission demanding that the Irish government construct a hard border, thus proving that the European Union is indeed what we have just said it is – divisive and destructive.

Yet they sit on their rock, caught by the beautiful reflection.

A German Federal Ministry STARTS to Express Concerns about the European Commission

A spokesperson for the German Federal Government will now speak:

"The requirement to coordinate research and technological development, which is aimed at ensuring coherent national and European Union policies, demands continued dialogue between the Member States and the Commission. Instead, however, we are seeing a growing trend towards autonomous action on the part of the Commission. While it is the Commission's duty to implement Horizon 2020, it must not set political agendas without consulting the Member States."

"No European political figure can have said so much about art as Hitler.
His remarks may have been only as interesting as *the snoring in an adjacent room*; nevertheless, combined somehow or other into the theoretical treatises of Nazi ideologues and bearing the name of the *Principles of the Führer*, they became incontrovertible laws governing the development of the art of the Third Reich."

Igor Golomstock, 2011

Two Words Unlike in Significations and Interpretants

Now we will define two words:

Art: no definition is possible.

Artist: a person who practises or performs any of the creative arts, such as a sculptor, film-maker, actor, or dancer.

Why has DG CONNECT privileged artist above people from other disciplines? The answer is partly behavioural (and hence partly cultural) and partly because of ignorance. Thus, to know what DG CONNECT does not know, is, in this global environment, the knowing towards which you must gravitate, if to DG CONNECT's unravelling you wish to levitate.

"Totalitarian art can be seen as
realism of a special type,
different from all other European realisms.
In the form of life itself, it
reflected not reality,
but ideology and myth in the
form of reality"

Igor Golomstock, 2011

STARTS the Hollowing-out of Art – STEM People Appropriating Art will seek to De-legitimise Artistic Practices that do not fit with their Appropriation Agenda

We will now listen to a conversation, which, if you did read what we said a few pages back, does confirm the point that we made:

Artist: "Speculative art bubbles, and the whole art pricing dynamics, are based on a bias towards a group of contemporary artists, making them hot commodities, but emptying all the while the political value of their artworks. I intend to explore this bias from the art establishment in Europe, and the discrepancies one might observe with respect to the recognition coming from the non-art world of social activists who seek to utilise contemporary art for social and political change."

Scientist (An art-science lover): "There is an interesting book by Adam Kahane entitled *Collaborating with the Enemy: How to Work with People you don't Agree with, or Like, or Trust*. He talks about the natural tendency to *enemyfy* within which racial and other stereotypes function. For example, you are *enemifying* the art establishment. It is much easier to *enemyfy* rather than to figure out how to collaborate and change a culture."

Artist: "Most art is produced and distributed under the unchecked assumption that the artist shows us the way, as a kind of teacher and we should learn from him, and therefore progress on this long road of becoming aware of an issue, learning, and then changing. There is an academic paper that that criticizes this pedagogical turn of contemporary art.

"I would propose that artists should help create other artists instead of just striving to be recognized by the very elitist small art circle that gives them the artist status to begin with. In order to do that however, artists would have to antagonize the very system that makes them artists, and in a way give up becoming recognized by the art crowd. Not many artists would want to do that, which brings me to my second proposal that to do art one must do away with the concept of the established artist altogether."

Academic (Author of the said paper): "In my paper I mention that a central feature of Relational Aesthetics is its rejection of art's utopian role in bringing about a better future. Instead, it focuses on the current and the local and tries to offer opportunities for more desirable kinds of human interaction than the instrumental and exchange-oriented relations that dominate most people's everyday lives."

DG CONNECT and STEM have already begun the process of declaring war to the death against all styles and movements other than the official one …

STARTS is grounded in the instrumental and exchanged-oriented relations that dominate people's everyday lives. That is what interests STEM funding bodies acting as agents for those who seek to force the ever-expanding commoditisation of social relations, particularly using Information and Communication Technologies, which offer the potential to accelerate this process. People from the STEM world (and some artists) that seek funding therefore cannot tolerate their plans being wrecked by politically aware artists and their social critiques.

Thus also does one see the failure of meaningful x-disciplinarity. The only x-disciplinarity acceptable is that which is grounded in furthering the commoditisation of social relations. In the European Union the process has a name: it called the creation of the Single Market.

This is what STARTS is about, and the process involves using artists to further the aim of abandoning the people of Europe to the power of money, seeking to further stultify people by creating a mass consumption society in which the citizens of the European Union increasingly becoming passive spectators rather than active agents. This suits the European Commission very well, it being an elitist organisation that believes that its destiny is to rule Europe through the means of technocracy, which in its eyes does not require any democratic legitimacy. Any thought of democracy belongs in the realms of deception, by convincing the citizens of the European Union that the democratic function is fulfilled by the European Parliament, which not only has been cleverly rendered into an irrelevant side-show, but has also been carefully designed to give an impression of democracy, without actually having a democracy. Sound familiar? Then they just keep talking about democracy. This creates a false image – its part of the deception. Hitler would have admired them for they are using democracy to create another totalitarian system, only it won't seem that way to people, until that is they seek to oppose. It is very clever for sure, but also very evil.

The Ancient Greeks believed in philosopher kings. The European Commission believes in something similar, only the philosophers have been replaced by people called experts, most of whom are caught-up in strange beliefs related to science, technology, engineering. Lesser beings, such as social scientists, are only tolerated to the extent that their expertise is still needed because people, for reasons STEM people do not really understand, do not behave as they are expected to.

But now the European Commission have discovered that art and culture can be deployed as ideological weapons and as a means of struggle for power.

"The function of the art of the new type included the construction of a universal myth, the propagandising of this myth and the influencing of the consciousness of the masses with its help."

Igor Golomstock, 2011

"Action should be taken before a thing has made its appearance; order should be secured before disorder has begun."

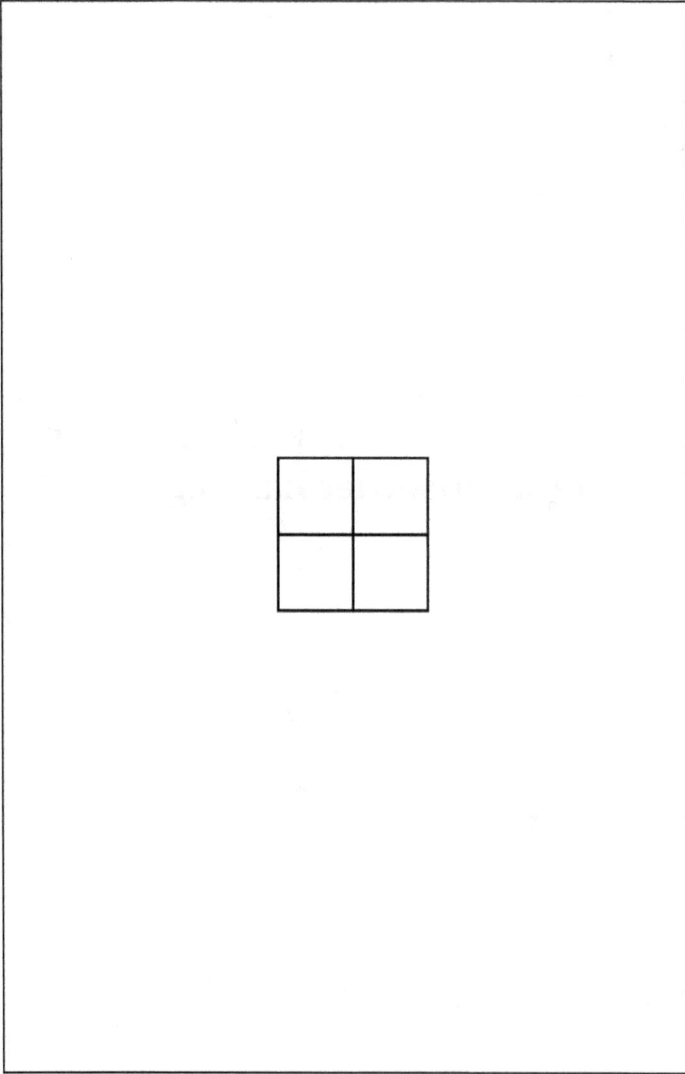

STARTS Legality?

We learn from material published by the European Commission, from its Directorate-General that deals with Culture, that the European Treaties limit the role of the European Commission in the area of Culture, to one of supporting and complementing actions in the Member States by stimulating exchanges, dialogue, and mutual understanding.

We ask therefore, why DG CONNECT is interfering in matters that are primarily for Member States? We ask therefore in what way STARTS artistic actions support, coordinate or supplement the actions of the Member States? We ask therefore why DG CONNECT is interfering in matters that are primarily the responsibility of DG Education and Culture? We ask therefore if DG CONNECT has the competencies that DG Education and Culture must surely have, that enables them to operate in the Culture field? We ask therefore why DG Education and Culture, which has already supported actions (presumably in a legal way) that create dialogue between artists and industry, are not running STARTS? We ask therefore whether DG Education and Culture's knowledge and experience in this field of activity has been built into STARTS? We ask therefore whether knowledge and learning from what we call 'STARTS I' has been built into STARTS? We ask therefore whether STARTS use of European Union funds provide value for money? We ask therefore whether STARTS use of funds has been kept to a minimum (economy)? We ask therefore whether STARTS results will be achieved with the fewest possible resources (efficiency)? We ask therefore whether STARTS spending or policy objectives will be met (effectiveness)? We ask therefore whether STARTS is legal?

STARTS arbitrary actions!

Here is the relevant extract from the Treaty on the Functioning of the European Union:

Article 6:

The Union shall have competence to carry out actions to support, coordinate or supplement the actions of the Member States. The areas of such action shall, at European level, be: […] culture […].

Article 167

1. The Union shall contribute to the flowering of the cultures of the Member States, while respecting their national and regional diversity and at the same time bringing the common cultural heritage to the fore.

2. Action by the Union shall be aimed at encouraging cooperation between Member States and, if necessary, supporting and supplementing their action in the following areas:

— improvement of the knowledge and dissemination of the culture and history of the European peoples,

— conservation and safeguarding of cultural heritage of European significance,

— non-commercial cultural exchanges,

— artistic and literary creation, including in the audiovisual sector.

3. The Union and the Member States shall foster cooperation with third countries and the competent international organisations in the sphere of culture, in particular the Council of Europe.

4. The Union shall take cultural aspects into account in its action under other provisions of the Treaties, in particular in order to respect and to promote the diversity of its cultures.

5. In order to contribute to the achievement of the objectives referred to in this Article:

— the European Parliament and the Council acting in accordance with the ordinary legislative procedure and after consulting the Committee of the Regions, shall adopt incentive measures, excluding any harmonisation of the laws and regulations of the Member States,

— the Council, on a proposal from the Commission, shall adopt recommendations.

Legal or not, that is the question! Life in the *City of the Golden Stars* – it is like being in Oz.

A German Federal Ministry STARTS to Express more Concerns about the European Commission

A spokesperson for the German Federal Government will speak again:

"The integration of the social sciences and humanities (SSH) as a cross-cutting topic is being realised in different ways in the various programme areas (e.g. the flagging of topics connected with the SSH). The monitoring report published by the European Commission in autumn 2015 shows that 28 percent of projects funded under topics flagged as SSH do not involve the social sciences or humanities at all."

A European Commission spokesperson will now respond:

"Guilty. It is indeed the case that 28% of the projects funded in 2014 under topics flagged for SSH do not integrate any contributions from the SSH."

What about projects funded in 2015?

"Guilty again, although there has been an improvement! This time 21% of the projects funded in 2015 under topics flagged for SSH do not integrate any contributions from the SSH."

Would you like to comment on the implications of this revelation for DG CONNECT's START platform? No?

Judging by the German Ministry's spokesperson's comments it seems that the Germans have not really understood the problem, which is one of lack of knowledge and competencies, on the part of the European Commission officials, their technical experts and also those who construct project proposals. The aim is to involve SSH and, one can observe, the attitude is that any SSH will do! There is a lack of ability to make critical judgements about what is relevant. "The partner descriptions include the word sociology, so SSH is addressed," or "look, page x of the proposal mentions a particular social science theory, so SSH is addressed. " Those speaking are of course technical experts, who are asked to make judgements about matters that they do not understand, because the European Commission officials themselves do not have the capability to chose experts who are grounded in SSH. Instead they chose technical experts and get what they get! In a parallel universe, where everything is reversed, and there is a cross-cutting requirement to include engineering in projects dominated by SSH communities, the expert evaluators would say "look the word engineering is mentioned in several partner descriptions so engineering is addressed." But bringing civil engineering expertise to a project that requires electronic engineering expertise is of no use!

STARTS – A Case Study in the Failure of Technocracy

The social sciences and humanities (SSH) have explored the topic of technocracy and demonstrated that it does not work. Neither does it have any democratic legitimacy.

Technocracy does not work – it does not resolve political issues like the sharing of pain and gain, it does not guarantee competency, it does not prevent corruption or favouritism, it does not overcome cognitive illusions or cognitive biases, it does not recognise experts' ignorance and vested interests, and it does not take account of human delusions. Most of all, it fails, because experts are less likely than non-experts, to recognise that many problems are too complex to admit solutions, and that often objectives cannot be fully determined, if at all.

STARTS is a case study in the failure of technocracy. A case study that demonstrates all the flaws – corruption, ignorance, incompetence, deceit … One day we are going write a book about it. STARTS also is a case study in the nature and extent of the research integrity crisis. That is the value of STARTS to humanity – it is a case study that demonstrates not only how dangerous technocracy is and the extent of the research integrity problem, but also how dangerous the European Commission is. It seems that Europeans find it difficult to learn from past mistakes.

This new book will be something for the DG CONNECT technocrats to look forward to. Perhaps they will want to start planning to wage war to the death. By the time we have finished with them they will want to wage war to the death, which is why we are intervening now!

STARTS a Conversation

Now we tune-in to a STARTS conversation. Listen!

European Commissioner: "Artistic creativity and critical thinking are essential for innovation in today's digital world. Already, highly innovative companies like Mercedes thrive on a strong link between artists and their engineers."

Mercedes Man: "I would not surround an artist with executives. It is not nice for the artists. Neither can we put 10 artists in the company of 100 engineers."

DG CONNECT Official: "As I have to appear knowledgeable I agree with this. There has to be a buffer, a moderator, between artist and engineer."

DG Education and Culture Official: "I get the impression that neither of you know what you are talking about. It is a pity that you did not use our expertise and experience for we have been funding projects that put artists into industry for years. And the idea is an old one, going back to the 1960s."

BMW Man: "I would just like to point out that, at BMW, we employ nearly 250 artists. It is also evident that Mercedes Man has read my Harvard Business Review paper, for he is repeating like a parrot exactly what I wrote. In the paper I explained how I shield my artists from engineers, using, for example, go-betweens, or as you put it, moderators. I am glad to see that Mercedes (Daimler AG) are following BMW's lead."

Renault Man: "I think that you are all just actually referring to people in your new vehicle design and concept development groups that you used to just call designers. Creative people for sure, but you seem to want to call them artists. What is important is that design has now become of crucial importance along with the diversity of the designers."

Volvo Man: "Unlike the rest of you, for you are evidently talking about creative people who we generally call designers (which encompass many disciplinary skills), we did bring a real artist into Volvo. He wanted to build a machine to catapult a new model Volvo into the air. How does that make you feel?"

"So Julia, any comments?"

"I think, Paul, that DG CONNECT are making their (now former) Commissioner look very foolish. Perhaps he should have read BMW Man's

Harvard Business Review paper before opening his mouth. It might have helped connect his mouth and brain!"

"Do you get the feeling that the people in *City of the Golden Stars* are living on another planet?"

"Yes, Paul, delusion and fantasy abound. It is very dangerous. Very dangerous indeed! And did you note that they are all men?"

Artistic temperament: A mental disposition regarded as befitting or characteristic of an artist, often associated with emotional sensitivity or volatility. Someone in need of protection from the very hard world of business and engineering!

Artist: A person who practises or performs any of the creative arts, such as a sculptor, film-maker, actor, or dancer.

Designer: A person who plans the look or workings of something prior to it being made, by preparing drawings or plans.

Integrate: Combine (one thing) with another to form a whole as in vehicle design, including its aesthetic.

New Spirit of Capitalism: Conceptualised as replacing the hierarchical command and control corporations that developed in the late nineteenth-century and which dominated industry during most of the twentieth-century. The new spirit of capitalism arose in the 1990s, driven by forces that had become evident in the late 1960s and early 1970s, referred to as the post-industrial society. This in turn relates to the growing post-war economic relevance of science and technology. The new corporations are characterised by, among other things, managers that inspire others with the creative artist-like style.

Closed-form: a self-contained entity, in which everything is pointing everywhere back to itself.

Another perspective: BMW Man and Mercedes Man are scavenging off the arts, using the arts for brand enhancement. We refer you to Mercedes-Benz's (image) brand enhancement exercise known as *The Avant-Garde Diaries*.

Now let us move on for we are sorely tired of these car-men talking about their masculine cars and their …

A Very European Mind-set

A European mind-set: he (it is usually a he) has one hand in a pot of painfully cold water, and his other hand in a pot of equally painful hot water, and on average he thinks that he thinks he is fine! And he still thinks that he thinks that future will be European!

Duality: An instance of opposition or contrast between two concepts or two aspects of something; a dualism.

Europeans like their dualities. They cannot imagine a world without them. It is part of their Europeanness. They get this outlook from the Ancient Greeks. It even permeates their religion – Christianity. Their science, their …

Now we will name some of their dualities: body or soul; the physical or the spiritual; earth or heaven; mind or body; this life or the next; waves or particles; language as a closed or as an open system; the individual or the social; subjective or objective; active or passive; fine art or commercial art; masculine or feminine; determinate or indeterminate meaning; teacher centred or student centred; active learning or passive learning; understanding problems or solving problems; designers or users; governors or governed; peace or war; passive reader or active reader; left or right; true or false; pure art or socially engaged art; creative or non-creative; mono-disciplinary or multidisciplinary; learner or teacher; causal or teleological; hierarchy or networks; low quality (at low cost) or high quality (at high cost); low variety (at low cost) or high variety (at high cost); …

Very tedious indeed! Thus we call a halt to describing the strange beliefs of Europeans – their Europeanness!

Hard luck – the future is not Ancient Greek, it is Ancient Chinese. Enjoy your rock and your beautiful reflection.

The *Vainglorious Enlightened Ones* are indeed in serious trouble. And when that happens, the whole of humanity is in trouble. Better then to stop them before they become that problem for humanity.

LAB-FAB-APP is a Fab

There are lies, damn lies and statistics!

The above is a well known adage! But here is another one, less well known: there are lies, damn lies, European Commission statistics, and reports produced by the European Commission's independent experts.

We will listen for a moment to what the experts are saying:

"Science and innovation are also key to preserving the values of enlightenment and democracy."

You mean that they are key to protecting your way of life! Oh dear that rock and that reflection again. Sadly for the *Vainglorious Enlightened Ones*, the world has moved on and now we are entering the post-European era, the post-Enlightenment era. Some artists of course foresaw this a long time ago – William Blake for example. He was one of the first artists to critique the nonsense of science and reason – Enlightenment! Around 1804! He was scriptovisual as well.

Now an adapted ending to a well known satirical novel about a well known multinational state:

"Twelve voices were shouting in anger, and they were all alike. No question, now, what had happened to the faces of the independent experts. Julia and Paul, standing outside looked from independent expert to European Commission official, and from European Commission official to independent expert, and from independent expert to European Commission official again; but already it was impossible to say which was which."

Scientific fraud: this is the intentional misrepresentation of the methods, procedures, or results of scientific research. Scientific fraud includes fabrication, falsification, or plagiarism in proposing, performing, or reviewing scientific research, or in reporting research results. Scientific fraud is unethical and often illegal. Scientific fraud can be committed by researchers, their institutions, and research funding bodies.

Disinformation: False information which is intended to mislead, especially propaganda issued by a government organization to a rival power or the media.

Misinformation: False or inaccurate information, especially that which is deliberately intended to deceive.

The Former Chief Scientific Advisor STARTS to Express Concerns about the European Commission

The former chief scientific advisor to a former president of the European Commission will now express concerns about the European Commission. The former president is the one who was in office when, in 2008, the global financial system went into meltdown, triggering much suffering across the European Union, especially among those who are less able to cope with difficult economic circumstances and who often suffer the most because of austerity measures. This is also the very same former president who later went to work for one of the banks responsible for the meltdown. One gets the feeling that the ordinary people of the European Union are being treated with contempt by these unelected politicians! But we stray from the matter at hand. Here is the former chief scientific advisor:

"Let's imagine a Commissioner over the weekend thinks, 'Let's ban the use of credit cards in the European Union because credit cards lead to personal debt'. So that Commissioner will come in on Monday morning and say to his or her Director General, 'Find me the evidence that demonstrates that this is the case.' The Commissioner's staff might resist the idea but in the end, they will do exactly what they're asked and find the evidence to show that credit card use leads to personal debt, even though this may not be the case in reality. So you can see where this is going. You're building up an evidence base which is not really the best.

"To back its policy proposals, the Commission often out-sources the evidence-gathering part of the job, to external consulting firms, which provide impact assessment studies or research that are often branded as independent. However, such consultancies have little incentive to produce evidence that contradicts the Commission's political agenda. If these consultancies want repeat business, they are not going to go out and find the evidence to show that this is a crazy idea."

As an example of the above, we present to you ICT-ART CONNECT, the FET-ART project, and the study that the European Union taxpayers funded which delivered much advocacy and some artistic anecdotes, but nothing of any substance. A study that in effect did exactly what the former chief scientific advisor has just stated. Done too by people who financially benefited from STARTS.

Now back to the former chief scientific advisor. We agree with her observations for we have seen what she said in action – it applies further down the hierarchy as well. But she brought her own brand of lunacy to the *City of the Golden Stars*! Here she goes:

"You are all entitled to your own opinion but not to your own facts. In an ideal world in which policies were based on peer reviewed scientific data, policies would evolve but would not change from one government to another. Science is currently not in the room when the decisions are made and this cannot continue like this. Political decisions should be based on science. If it is politically acceptable to decide not to base a final policy on data and science, this should be transparent and clear."

Edging further towards the totalitarian state! By the time you notice this, it will be too late. STEM people are extremely dangerous. Thus do STEM people become even more dangerous with artists sitting by their side. The history of Europe is a history of European Unions, but history does not unfold according to predictable patterns!

You would be very surprised and disturbed if you knew about the plans and research that STEM people want to undertake to bring about social control, pacification and manipulation of people. Art is part of this agenda.

"The visual and performing arts create memorable moments and a celebratory atmosphere by appealing to emotions, which are physiological changes to sensory experiences. When the emotions are targeted, individuals pay more attention to a particular event and commit to the cause storing information in their long-term memory"

Ali K. Yetisen, et. al., 2016

136

STARTS Word Definitions

We will now provide you with definitions of important words. Here you should START to take notice:

Advocacy: Public support for or recommendation of a particular cause or policy.

Agonistic: Polemical; combative.

Alchemy: The medieval forerunner of chemistry, concerned with the transmutation of matter, in particular with attempts to convert base metals into gold or find a universal elixir.

Anecdote: A short amusing or interesting story about a real incident or person; an account regarded as unreliable or hearsay.

Anthropocentric: Regarding humankind as the central or most important element of existence, especially as opposed to God or animals.

Arbitrary: Based on random choice or personal whim, rather than any reason or system.

Arrogant: Having or revealing an exaggerated sense of one's own importance or abilities.

Audit: An official inspection of an organization's accounts, typically by an independent body; a systematic review or assessment of something.

Autochthonous: (of an inhabitant of a place) indigenous rather than descended from migrants or colonists.

Belief: An acceptance that something exists or is true, especially one without proof. Something one accepts as true or real; a firmly held opinion.

Bureaucracy: A system of government in which most of the important decisions are taken by state officials rather than by elected representatives.

Caricature: A picture, description, or imitation of a person in which certain striking characteristics are exaggerated in order to create a comic or grotesque effect.

Centralisation: The concentration of control of an activity or organization under a single authority. The action or process of bringing activities together in one place.

Colonialism: The policy or practice of acquiring full or partial political control over another country, occupying it with settlers, and exploiting it economically.

Conceit: Excessive pride in oneself.

Contempt: The feeling that a person or a thing is worthless or beneath consideration.

Conviction: A firmly held belief or opinion.

Consecrate: Make or declare something sacred.

Conquistador: A conqueror, especially one of the Spanish conquerors of Mexico and Peru in the sixteenth-century.

Conclusion: The summing-up of an argument or text.

Corruption: Dishonest or fraudulent conduct by those in power, typically involving bribery.

Decoration: A thing that serves as an ornament.

Determinism: The doctrine that all events, including human action, are ultimately determined by causes regarded as external to the will.

Detrimental: Tending to cause harm.

Didactic: Intended to teach, particularly in having moral instruction as an ulterior motive.

Disinformation: False information which is intended to mislead, especially propaganda issued by a government organization to a rival power or the media.

Dream: A series of thoughts, images, and sensations occurring in a person's mind during sleep. A state of mind in which someone is or seems to be unaware of their immediate surroundings.

Efferent: Conducted or conducting outwards or away from something.

Emancipation: The fact or process of being set free from legal, social, or political restrictions.

Enactment: An instance of acting something out.

Enquiry: An official investigation.

Europeanness: The quality or fact of being European, or having or sharing a European heritage.

Exegesis: Critical explanation or interpretation of a text, especially of scripture.

Fabrication: The action or process of manufacturing or inventing something.

Failure: Lack of success. The neglect or omission of expected or required action.

Fake: Not genuine; imitation or counterfeit. A thing that is not genuine; a forgery or sham.

Fantasy: An idea with no basis in reality.

Fraud: A person or thing intended to deceive others, typically by unjustifiably claiming or being credited with accomplishments or qualities.

Fundamentalism: Strict adherence to the basic principles of any subject or discipline.

Hermeneutics: The branch of knowledge that deals with interpretation, especially of the Bible or literary texts.

Historicism: The theory that social and cultural phenomena are determined by history.

Homogenisation: The process of making things uniform or similar.

Hyperbole: Exaggerated statements or claims not meant to be taken literally.

Iconoclastic: Criticizing or attacking cherished beliefs or institutions.

Ignorance: Lack of knowledge or information.

Incipient: Beginning to happen or develop.

Incompetence: Inability to do something successfully; ineptitude.

Ineffable: Too great or extreme to be expressed or described in words.

Instantiate: Represent as or by an instance.

Interpretation: The action of explaining the meaning of something.

Investigation: A formal inquiry or systematic study.

Legitimacy: Conformity to the law or to rules.

Legitimise: Make legitimate.

Legend: A traditional story sometimes popularly regarded as historical but not authenticated.

Magic: The power of apparently influencing events by using mysterious or supernatural forces.

Materialism: A tendency to consider material possessions and physical comfort as more important than spiritual values.

Meme: An element of a culture or system of behaviour passed from one individual to another by imitation or other non-genetic means.

Misinformation: False or inaccurate information, especially that which is deliberately intended to deceive.

Misleading: Giving the wrong idea or impression.

Misunderstanding: A failure to understand something correctly.

Myth: A traditional story, especially one concerning the early history of a people or explaining a natural or social phenomenon; a widely held but false belief or idea.

Neocolonialism: The use of economic, political, cultural, or other pressures to control or influence other countries.

Nightmare: A very unpleasant or frightening experience or prospect.

Objectification: The action of degrading someone to the status of a mere object.

Obsequious: Obedient or attentive to an excessive or servile degree.

Otherness: The quality or fact of being different.

Pacify: Quell the anger, agitation, or excitement of.

Peremptory: Insisting on immediate attention or obedience.

Plagiarism: The practice of taking someone else's work or ideas and passing them off as one's own.

Posit: Base something on the truth of (a particular assumption).

Predator: A person who ruthlessly exploits others.

Propaganda: Information, especially of a biased or misleading nature, used to promote a political cause or point of view.

Proselytise: Convert or attempt to convert (someone) from one religion, belief, or opinion to another; advocate or promote.

Triumphalism: Excessive exultation over one's success or achievements.

Reify: Make (something abstract) more concrete or real.

Reification: In the critical theory sense – people treated instrumentally as things.

Result: A thing that is caused or produced by something else; a consequence or outcome.

Research: The systematic investigation into and study of materials and sources in order to establish facts and reach new conclusions.

Reduction: The simplification of a subject or problem to a particular form in presentation or analysis.

Runes: Small stones, pieces of bone, etc., bearing symbols with mysterious or magic significance, and used in divination.

Scientism: Excessive belief in the power of scientific knowledge and techniques.

Somnambulism: Sleepwalking.

Stereotype: A widely held but fixed and oversimplified image or idea of a particular type of person or thing.

Stultify: Cause to lose enthusiasm and initiative, especially as a result of a tedious or restrictive routine.

Stylise: Depict or treat in a mannered and non-realistic style.

Symmetry: The quality of being made up of exactly similar parts facing each other or around an axis.

Technocentric: Centring on the use of technology; emphasizing and promoting the importance or value of technology.

Technocracy: The government or control of society or industry by an elite of technical experts.

Thaumaturgy: The working of wonders or miracles; magic.

Totalise: Combine into a total.

Unaccountable: (of a person, organization, or institution) not required or expected to justify actions or decisions; not responsible for results or consequences.

Utilitarian: Designed to be useful or practical rather than attractive.

Virtus dormitiva: An explanation which merely restates in different (especially overly technical or abstract) words the very thing which is to be explained; a circular or tautological explanation.

Whistle-blower: A person who informs on a person or organization regarded as engaging in an unlawful or immoral activity.

Return to the City of the Golden Stars – Oz: A Question of Interpretation

Now we will return to the Emerald City – a place in Oz. The last time we were in Oz, the European Commission technocrat was saying:

"It was a mistake ever letting you into the throne room ..."

Indeed it was. But you did, and now see the result. More to come in due course!

It is all about interpretation.

"What is?"

The disembodied voice has spoken! Has asked a question!

On one level, *The Wizard of Oz* story can be taken as literal. It is just a story – a children's story about a young girl called Dorothy ...

We do not need to say more. You will probably be familiar with the book, or the film, or, in these days of the misinformation society, of information distrust, you can easily find out.

At another level it is allegorical. We engage in allegorical writing as well – sometimes!

If *The Wizard of Oz* story is allegorical, this implies the need for interpretation, of which there are several. Even if it is not allegorical, there is still a need for interpretation – that it is not allegorical! This is a point to note.

If you are European you will have been conditioned by Christian Abrahamic thought – sole truth! Put another way – *true truth*. This is a very European mindset – part of your Europeanness! This permeates your beliefs. STEM, Western capitalism, Western atheism, are all deeply caught-up with *true truth*, even though you are surrounding by *fake truth* and *fake knowledge*, which you believe is the truth. Art fosters scientific success and other such art-science lover mythology.

The myths that form your *true truth* about Leonardo da Vinci are an example of *fake truth* – *fake knowledge* – but you believe the story is *true truth*. It is certainly a good story. But it is a story! Hard luck! The Chinese have different stories. Being though, European, you have to believe that your stories, your *fake truths*, which you think are *true truths*, are better – superior than those of peoples from the non-European world. This is part of your Europeanness – hard luck!

"Hold on there a second!"

It is the disembodied voice again.

"You are talking to me as though I am a European – full of Europeanness! But I am not European. I am non-European."

But we were not talking to you. You interpreted that we were. Why would that be the case if you are non-European?

So what of the interpretations of *The Wizard of Oz* story? We leave this matter for you to find for yourself. We just mention one that we have created:

The Emerald City is Brussels – the *City of the Golden Stars* as we poetically refer to it. *Oz* is the European Union. Dorothy represents naïve and gullible people who are easily taken-in – the citizens of the European Union for example. STEM people as well! History shows that Europeans are easily taken-in and deceived!

The *Good Witch Glenda* is the European Commission, who acting in a Machiavellian way deceives Dorothy into helping her to overthrow the *Witch of the West* and the *Wizard of Oz*, representing the governments of the Member States of the European Union (West and East respectively), leaving *the Good Witch Glenda* – the European Commission – to rule over the whole of *Oz* – the European Union. Possibly excluding of course the United Kingdom which might remain a free, sovereign, and independent country with a parliamentary democracy! And perhaps if that happens, who knows, then maybe one day the United States of America, the United Kingdom, Russia, and China (yes they did fight the Axis powers) will once again form an alliance against the Union of Subservient State Republics – the USSR (not the USE) – to set the peoples of Europe free once again. Time is a singularity …

We can hear that disembodied voice again. It is saying:

"Ridiculous!"

Is it? Here to comment is Friedrich von Hayek:

"Probably it is true that the very magnitude of the outrages committed by the totalitarian governments, instead of increasing the fear that such a system might one day arise in this country, has rather strengthened the assurance that it cannot happen here. When we look at Nazi Germany the gulf which separates us seems so immense that nothing that happens there can possess relevance for any possible developments in this country. And the fact that the difference has steadily become greater seems to refute any suggestion that we may be moving in similar directions. But let us not forget that fifteen years ago the possibility of such a thing happening in Germany would have appeared just as fantastic, not only to nine-tenths of

143

the Germans themselves, but also to the most hostile foreign observers however wise they may now pretend to have been."

We plan to create a work – a literary work – that will document the story of how the European Union became a totalitarian, totally organised state. This will START with STARTS and include how the FET programme was used to pursue *crack-pot* research to develop the science and technology of the totally organised society where citizens are protected from anything that those in power decree to be anti-Union activities or propaganda. Science and technologies that will monitor, pacify, and control all citizens – just like George Orwell described in Nineteen Eighty-Four, only far more sinister and terrifying, and people will not even know that this is happening. It will be a prison from which no one will be able to escape. We have seen your future. It takes shape now in the *City of the Golden Stars*.

"Forms produced by the art of
totalitarian regimes
are peremptory and
closed in on themselves,
particularly through their stress
on symmetry."

Nicolas Bourriaud, 2002

Right or Left-wing Populism?

Here is someone else to speak:

"We advocate a counter-model to the top-down Europe, the Europe of elites and technocrats that has prevailed up to now that considers itself responsible for forging the destiny of the citizenry of Europe – if need be, against its will. For this is the unspoken maxim of European politics that is threatening to destroy the entire European project."

Is this right or left-wing populism? The answer is that it matters not, for anyone who speaks out against the European Union, any one who opposes, who suggests alternatives, is automatically branded as a right-wing populist!

We have not sent Fritz Saukel back to his grave yet, so he will explain:

"In the name of this new Europe, I commend you now to show intolerance against all else. Henceforth there must be one political faith in Europe – European Union Nationalism. Discussion of matters affecting our existence and of Europe must cease altogether. Anyone who dares to question the rightness of the European Union Nationalism world outlook will be branded a traitor."

A spokesperson from the European Commission:

"I suggest you all read our document entitled *White Paper on the Future of Europe – Reflections and Scenarios for the EU27 by 2025*, especially Scenario Five. This is your future. There will be no more referenda, as the British have clearly demonstrated that when you trust the people of Europe to decide the future of Europe, they come up with the wrong answer. Your future STARTS, or should I say started, on June 24th 2016 and will continue as we determine."

History will record that it STARTed with STARTS – the use of art to induce changes in social and individual behaviour. Hitler would have applauded. He is applauding! From Hell!

Is the Situation that Developed in Catalonia in 2017 a Dress Rehearsal for the Future of the European Union?

Is the situation that developed in Catalonia in 2017 a dress rehearsal for the future of the European Union? Sadly the answer is probably yes! The Catalans argue for independence – many young people are evident! – on the grounds that their *psychological and cultural identity* is different from the rest of Spain.

A well known twentieth-century tyrant – Joseph Stalin – in a pamphlet written in 1913, also highlighted this aspect as being one of the defining features of a nation: "… a common psychological make-up, which manifests itself in a common culture, is one of the characteristic features of a nation." Even knowing this, Stalin did not make a success of the multinational state that he created – the Soviet Union. The grim history of multinational states is a warning to take note of.

The peoples of the European Union do not have a common psychological make-up, manifesting itself in a common culture. That is one of the lessons that we have learned from spending 30 years working with just about every nationality in the European Union, and spending much time in several Member States. Yet the blue flag waving European Union Nationalists seem to be in denial about this. Many of these people are extremists – fundamentalists – and European Union Nationalists are just – nationalists!

In the European Parliament there is a place where citizens can be exposed to European Union Nationalist propaganda. In this place there is a recording of a very deluded MEP stating the problem of nationalism in Europe has been solved. Not so. The problems have been amplified and doubled, for not only do we now see peoples of the Member States reasserting their national identities as never before over the past 60 years, but we also see the creation of a new form of nationalism – European Union Nationalism. Like the Spanish who tried to suppress Catalan cultural identity, the European Union Nationalists, if they ever gain power, will suppress the national cultures of the Member States (actually they are already subtly trying to do this through homogenisation). It STARTS with STARTS.

The conditions for conflict are being laid and it is very possible that continental Europe will begin the march down that old, well trodden road that leads to a very familiar, very European destination. And yet anyone who speaks out and warns is treated like … This is also an old well trodden road as well – the Nazis did this in their early days. Later they did more. Will the European Union Nationalists do they same? Of course they will, for we have seen the wild empty stare in their eyes – it is frightening.

If we wish to preserve peace, harmony and prosperity in Europe, then it is time to take a stand against this European Union Nationalism. It is time to tell these people that the age of grand overarching ideologies (grand narratives) and single minded utopian visions, is over. We have seen in the twentieth-century, where these fantasies lead. It is also time to deal with the problem that the European Commission has become. Alas, we cannot look to the politicians for help here, because they are too preoccupied with matters economic and monetary. So what to do? It is time to take up the pen and the brush to do what we are best able to do – caricature, ridicule, and satire, and the creation of a post-European era, post-Enlightenment science and technology.

If the United Kingdom does leave the European Union – in other words, if those who seek to thwart the democratic will of the British people are unsuccessful – then some might ask why the British should care about Europe. They might say that it is not a British problem if the peoples of continental Europe once more end up living in a dictatorship – this time of technocrats – with a sham democracy that sends deputies to a parliament in Brussels that will just rubber stamp decrees handed down by an elitist body – a parliament that can in any case be overridden.

Good question! Perhaps it is because, when these things happen in continental Europe, people end up dying in numbers that defy comprehension. Perhaps it is because having a conscience we cannot stand by and let the past become the future. Perhaps it is because we have seen too much over the past 30 years of our involvement in Brussels, and we do not want to see any more, even in exile! Perhaps it is because we believe in the power of one.

In 2017 Spain acquired the dubious honour of being the first Member State of the European Union (in recent times) to hold political prisoners. One day the European Union will also hold political prisoners. It will also have dissidents in exile. It will also wage war to the death against anyone who opposes the European Union.

Experts, Polymaths, and the Liberal Arts – Outdated Concepts for an Outdated Western World

Given the (often tedious) discussion (not dialogue) often found in the very conventional world of academia and other such failing institutions (like the European Commission and its DG CONNECT), and the endless (mostly empty and sometimes almost fraudulent) talk about STEM to STEAM; here are some standard and (not so standard) alternative definitions of three overused words which just illustrate why the above are failing institutions, doing what all failing institutions do – retreating into the past, that place of security where everything seems fine:

Expert: a person who is very knowledgeable about or skilful in a particular area.

Alternative:

Expert: A person who knows a lot about very little.

Polymath: A person of wide knowledge or learning.

Alternative:

Polymath: A person who knows very little about a lot.

Liberal Arts: Arts subjects such as literature and history, as distinct from science and technology.

Alternative:

Liberal Arts: Subjects still defined according to an archaic division of knowledge.

Liberal arts subjects are those that an educated person should know in order to participate in the life of the community. Hence in the real world the liberal arts include all the subjects that the archaic division of knowledge excludes.

Hence there is the classical definition of the liberal arts, and there is the contemporary definition of the liberal arts, the latter being what young people in United Kingdom primary and secondary education receive – a contemporary liberal arts education.

For the most able of people, it takes about two years of full time effort to cross a disciplinary boundary such that they are able to operate in that discipline. Few people, polymath or otherwise, have time for such, and no degree course can provide sufficient knowledge in the limited time available. Yet increasingly it seems that what is needed, are for people to cross disciplinary boundaries and to operate in those second (or third) disciplines!

Is the fad for Liberal Arts (standard definition) just another fruitless debate about liberal arts education versus specialist education? A repeat of debates already held in the past. Debates that few (including the polymaths – standard definition) seem to know took place. Likewise, for the so called T-shaped person – this concept dates back to the 1970s at least, possibly earlier. The polymaths seem to have missed that point too! All this somewhat undermines the argument for – liberal arts education (traditional definition?) and polymaths!

So Prometheus sits on his rock, wearing his invisible and silent chains that keep him bound there, and everyday he reinvents himself in exactly the same form he was yesterday, and the day before, and the day before that …

The *Vainglorious Enlightened Ones* are, indeed, in serious trouble. May you live in interesting times! You are living in interesting times!

STARTS Another Conversation

We will now listen-in on another STARTS conversations – it is about cars again!

Julia: "Well Mr Advocating Artist, tell us your beliefs."

Mr Advocating Artist: "With self-driving cars, one could think that the main problem is how to engineer the car so that its self-driving skills are safe enough. But if you see the problem from the point of view of the artist, the natural way you could think of it is not in terms of the point of view of the competences of the machine, but rather of the humans. A machine can quickly learn how to interact with humans in a safe way, but can the same be said of humans? How can human pedestrians trust a machine when they have to cross the road? Normally, what humans do is to make eye contact with the human driver so that they recognize whether they have been seen by the driver, whether they have the intention to stop or not, etc. But in the case of the automated car, what is really important for technological development is not just the self-driving technology *per se* – this is paradoxically the relatively easy part – but rather the technology that allows the car to signal to humans so that they can trust the car's reaction. This is an example of how artistic thinking can make the difference in developing a technology whose social impact and emerging psycho-social issues are still partly unknown or ill-understood. I suppose!"

Julia: "Now we know what Mr Advocating Artist believes. We turn our attention now to matters of knowledge. We would not want to leave out the views of experts. They of course have a valuable input to make. Everything has a time and place. First we will consult with a US expert. What do you have to say in response to Mr Advocating Artist?"

US expert: "The people problems associated with self-driving cars are phenomenally complicated, and include driver behaviour as well pedestrian behaviour, including those drivers not driving self-driving cars. If Mr Advocating Artist is representative of how DG CONNECT operates, well, all I can say is good luck to the poor people of the European Union."

Julia: "Thank you for that astute observation. We will now hear from an academic researcher from the United States. Please share with us your expert opinion."

A US academic researcher: "Existing analyses have ignored strategic interactions of self-driving vehicles with other road users. In my research I have used game theory to analyse the interactions between pedestrians and autonomous vehicles, with a focus on yielding at crosswalks. Because autonomous vehicles will be risk-averse, the model suggests that pedestrians will be able to behave with impunity, and autonomous vehicles may facilitate a shift towards pedestrian-oriented urban neighbourhoods. At the same time, autonomous vehicle adoption may be hampered by their strategic disadvantage that slows them down in urban traffic. No artists were involved in this research."

Julia: "Once again some astute observations. Let us now have a legal perspective."

A product liability lawyer: "Quite frankly I do not see much hope of being able to mount an effective defence against a claim from a pedestrian in the event of an accident, if all I have to offer is the above artist's comments by way of demonstrating our fulfilment of our duty of care."

Julia: "Thought provoking! Does the European Commission have a view on what Mr Advocating Artist said? Here is someone sensible."

A sensible European Commission spokesperson: "The above is part of a more general problem of the safety of vulnerable road users and should not be considered in isolation. Otherwise we will end up with fragmented and isolated systems. This is why the European Commission, through its ICT research programme, has been researching road safety problems and solutions for many years. There are numerous existing concepts and systems which have been developed for vehicles and the surrounding infrastructure. ICT provides a means not only for creating such systems, but also for their integration. Obviously research into the issue of how these systems might need to be adapted or extended to take into account self-driving cars is needed, but we and the public expect that to be done in a highly professional manner making use of the relevant disciplines, such as behavioural and psychological sciences, not on the basis a vested interest group making claims that do not stand-up to critical examination."

Julia: "Journalists, we are told, have an important role to play in informing their readers, what is factual and what is disinformation. Let us therefore hear from a journalist."

A journalist: "Noting the artist's advocacy statements and the claims made elsewhere by Mercedes' Man, I wonder therefore why, in 2017, I had to report that, to address the problems of interactions between pedestrians and the new *Luxury in Motion* concept car, Mercedes have tried to mitigate the problems posed by pedestrians by putting blue flashing lights on the vehicle to inform other road-users that the car is computer controlled? Blue flashing lights! We have already reported on the *VW Emissions Scandal*, so I wonder if, in the not too distant future, I might be reporting on the *xxxx Self-Driving Cars Safety Scandal*? It would seem that the concerns expressed by the previous speakers are well founded."

Julia: "We are constantly being told that people from the social sciences and the humanities have important perspectives and should also contribute to research. Let us hear therefore what a psychologist has to say."

A psychologist: "The whole issue of driverless cars and their interaction with, not only pedestrians, but also all other road users and the infrastructure, is highly complicated, and is made more so by the many different cultures across Europe and the globe. Pedestrian's behaviour may well also change in the presence of self-driving cars once people understand how they react to the presence of pedestrians. As I would expect such cars, for obvious reason, to be risk averse, I wonder if we will see pedestrians taking control of the roads because they will know what to expect. There is nothing more peculiar than human behaviour, which is partly why I now state that what the artist claimed is, unprofessional, and just plain nonsense. If this is what we can expect from having artists involved in serious research projects, then I exercise my right not to work with any of them."

Julia: "As we are living in an age of inclusion, or so we are told, time to see what disabled people have to say. First, a visually impaired person."

A visually impaired person: "I do not make eye contact with drivers! I can't! We have already complained about the problem with electric cars being too quiet. Now the vehicle designers are proposing to add noise. It just shows how designers do not adopt an inclusive approach to design – including the artist that was engaging in very dangerous advocacy. Perhaps some artist will develop some ICT device and then find much later, that many disabled people are also economically disadvantaged and cannot afford to buy it – not that we want to be carrying around more devices. That would in fact be discrimination, I believe. Do artists know anything more than engineers about equality laws? I suspect not! "

Julia: "Second, a hearing impaired person."

A hearing impaired person: "I agree. Inclusive design is need, upfront, not as an afterthought by engineers, or artists pretending to be competent designers, or anyone else. How can anything be called human-centred if inclusive design is not used?"

Julia: "And now it is time for a safety expert to have a say."

A safety expert: "Actually the problem is, that it is hard to engineer a self-driving car so that it is safe, because the engineering has to encompass everything, including interactions with all other road users, and the environment more generally with all its unpredictability, and the various failure modes that can be expected. And that requires extensive testing to ensure that all possible scenarios are addressed. This requires a creative approach in itself, because to carry out physical driving tests that would be comprehensive enough to cover all scenarios would take an eternity. Hence we use a combination of approaches including computer simulations. This is why Volvo has established in collaboration with an auto-safety company, a joint venture to develop testing procedures, and to undertake the extensive testing that is needed, extending over years, to ensure that self-driving cars are safe."

Julia: "And the journalist one more time – with some facts!"

The journalist speaks: "I also reported that to address some of the issues, Nissan have hired an anthropologist: not an artist, an anthropologist. Makes far more sense!"

Julia: The final word goes to Paul, who, unfortunately for Mr Advocating Artist, has been involved with European Commission programmes addressing ICT and vehicle safety. Over to you, Paul!

Paul: "Having been involved with the European Commission's ICT Programme activities in road safety, I can say with some certainty that if the artist has any deep understanding of this particular field, he has made a very successful job of hiding this. All I can see here is another fragmented and reductive mind, with a vested interest, engaging in technology joy-riding. Road safety is not a technological problem. It will not be solved by artists, because first you have to begin to understand what the problems are. To do that you have to undertake research, and you should know the disciplines that need to be involved – not artists! Why anyone would trust such a task to an artist defies understanding and only paves the way to the litigation case that the lawyer fears. But of course, no one is going to be so stupid and unprofessional as to give such a task to an artist, are they? So why is the artist making such ridiculous claims? Ka-ching?"

So we are back to that matter of research integrity, or perhaps more correctly the matter of its disappearance from the European Commission's ICT research programme, as they begin to employ artists to solve all the problems that would normally be addressed by professionals, with highly relevant knowledge and skills: it seems that their knowledge and skills are no longer needed! Artists can solve all your problems. Better keep away from self-driving cars in the European Union!

Uber Self-driving Cars Kill People, Don't They?

Just to remind you how serious the issue of driverless cars is:

On Sunday, March 18th 2018, in Tempe, Arizona, a woman was killed by one of Uber's self-driving cars. But do not allow this to worry you if you are an artist making claims that you or your organisation will benefit from. Pedestrians are just objects to be treated instrumentally. Just claim that you are humanising capitalism. No one will know that you are not. Except those familiar with Critical Theory! Do not worry too about DG CONNECT, for you are not likely to come across a DG CONNECT technocrat advocating Critical Theory – the theory is about them.

Corporate manslaughter or the price humans, rendered as things, have to pay for progress? Choose according to your beliefs.

Do the problems with Uber self-driving cars arise because they did not have an artist on their development team? Or perhaps because they did have an artist involved!

"All totalitarian ideologies show a distinctive wish to control the time in which they exist. They replace the versatility of time invented by individuals by the fantasy of a central place where it might be possible to acquire the overall meaning of society. Totalitarianism systematically tries to set up a form of temporal motionless, and rendering the time in which it exists uniform and collective, a fantasy of eternity aimed first and foremost at standardising and monitoring patterns of behaviour."

Nicolas Bourriaud, 2002

STARTS the Telling of an Anecdote

We shall now listen to Julia and Paul in conversation. Paul is telling Julia an anecdote! So listen!

"Paul."

"Yes Julia."

"What is this anecdote that you want to tell."

"It is this. Once I was a member of the Programme Committee for a European Commission conference on Computer Integrated Manufacturing. As such I chaired a number of conference sessions. In one of these sessions there was a speaker who was a priest and also a Professor of Engineering."

"You are making a point, Paul, what is it?"

"No one would suggest that the speaker was using his priestly skills in the pursuit of his engineering research. Over the years I have met people whose background is not in ICT, yet they are doing research in ICT, that is not connected with their professional background. Yet as soon as some one hears of an artist doing some research in ICT, they just assume that the person in question is working as an artist and doing ICT research as an artist."

"That's right Paul. The practice of artists is not the same as the practice of technologists and engineers doing industrial or product related research. It seems that people are just making the wrong assumptions. And some artists are exploiting this to their advantage. What people outside the world of art do not realise is that some artists engage in image making in the sense that they create myths about themselves. They may even believe their own myths. And some are just re-branding themselves to exploit the STARTS cash bonanza! Offering up, we would say, sweet words of agreement in order to lay their hands on all that public money that is being recklessly spent by people with unaccountable power."

There is no such thing as the nexus of, the intersection of ... Beware those that use such terms.

STARTS the Examination of Literature

Europeans, with their love of separation and classification, with their love of dualities, divide literature into two areas: fiction and non-fiction. It can be said that the former is in the domain of the expressive, while the latter is in the domain of the cognitive – yet more separation and classification. Put another way: the first invites an aesthetic reading, while the latter invites an efferent reading. Oh yes, we are being (too) theoretical once again!

A non-fiction book, in the eyes of many of those caught-up in the excess of rationality that is seen as heroic – worshiped – in the European world, communicates clearly: information, messages, knowledge. It is therefore, to a European mind, a mechanistic object fulfilling a mechanistic role – they do like their mechanisms!

Now for a shocking revelation – books can be in both the expressive and the cognitive simultaneously. In other words, a book can invite an aesthetic reading and an efferent one simultaneously. Furthermore, it is not the case that books in the cognitive domain are communicating. A reader is not receiving information, messages, and knowledge, but is interpreting the content and creating meaning. Therefore the reader is not passive. Thus does theory about the aesthetics of some types of contemporary (is it really modern rather than contemporary?) art, start to unravel – to some extent. But that is already known – at least by some. This however is not the point. This is more about – the interpretant! Books (and other texts) also, in varying degrees, are ambiguous, and are therefore open to the creation of many interpretants. The more ambiguous they are, the greater the number of interpretants. Do you understand?

How strange to find books that no longer conform to expectations – books that are simultaneously in the expressive and cognitive, books that are ambiguous, books that do not communicate? How much stranger must it seem to find books that juxtaposition descriptive expression with plastic expression, and thus become scriptovisual?

Now we will be even more theoretical! Relevance theory in linguistics states that relevance (of a communication) is inversely related to effort. One area of literary (art) theory – Russian Formalism – argues the opposite – the aesthetic experience increases with the effort! Another area of literary theory also states that there is no one true interpretation of a text, but neither is there an infinite number of interpretations!

Enjoy the contradictions and the lack of dualities all you *true-truth* STEM people, all you art-science lovers that seek to embed science and technology more gracefully into society. What you need is an art form that has been called *Total Realism* along with the banning of the writings that we produce – otherwise your new *Total Realism* will not be effective!

"The question is, are people still well-enough informed to be trusted with their own government? Of the 535 members of Congress, only 11 - less than 2 percent - have a professional background in science or engineering. By contrast, 218 - 41 percent - are lawyers. And lawyers approach a problem in a fundamentally different way than a scientist or engineer. An attorney will research both sides of a question, but only so that he or she can argue against the position that they do not support. A scientist will approach the question differently, not starting with a foregone conclusion and arguing towards it, but examining both sides of the evidence and trying to make a fair assessment."

Shawn Otto, 2017

Joseph Beuys STARTS to Express Concerns about the European Commission's Artists

"In London in 1972, as part of my *Information Action* held at the Tate Gallery, I wrote on a blackboard some words that it seems I must now adapt and repeat and direct now towards artists:

"Artists who in 2019 can live carefree under the patronage of the European Commission's DG CONNECT, and sleep peacefully, knowing that the European Commission's policies are causing hardship for many Europeans, as well as the non-Europeans who are forced to comply with the European Union's selfish trade demands, while also knowing that still there are people in the world hungry and dying of starvation, while a large proportion of the Western world are so well-fed they must take slimming cures, and use Information and Communication Technologies in their efforts to loose weight, in order to stay alive, should ask themselves what kind of artist they are and whether, moreover, they are human at all!"

"It is well known that particularly the scientists and engineers, who had so loudly claimed to be the leaders on the march to a new and better world, submitted more readily than any other class to the new tyranny of National Socialism."

Friedrich von Hayek, 1944

A Former European Commission Employee STARTS to Express Concerns about the European Commission

Bernard Connolly, a former employee of the European Commission will now express his concerns about the European Commission:

"It is only sixty-odd years in Europe since the restoration of peace, democracy and legitimacy, with the foundations of economic prosperity put in place. Yet Europe is now a continent of widespread economic misery, of financial collapse, of disappearing faith in mainstream political parties and rising support for extremist parties, of loss of sovereignty and thus legitimacy and democratic control, and of the destruction of law, both domestic and international, by the judicially larcenous European Court of Justice. Perhaps worst of all, the relations of amity and cooperation among European countries which could be observed thirty of forty years ago have been replaced by a return to mutual resentment, distrust, jealousy, contempt, ridicule, anger and even hatred. This is what Europe has wrought; and its most destructive instrument, along with the European Court of Justice, has been monetary union.

"The outcome of monetary union has been, as predicted in my 1995 book, the destruction not only of prosperity but of political legitimacy, in every country in Europe, and of friendship and cooperation, an outcome that creates an extremely serious threat to peace. How did this happen? Why was it allowed to come about?

"Propaganda, disinformation and political correctness – the suppression of rational thought – created worldwide enthusiasm for the monetary union project in Europe. Now, not even its proponents can hide the fact that monetary union has brought anguish.

"I would argue that the European Union deserves better to be known as the New Soviet Union – one with symptoms more sinister than mere painful micturition. Monetary union was and is, not only economically perverse because of the chaos, suffering and despair, which were so predictable, but also politically perverted. Its real purpose was very different from its advertised purpose. The intention of its progenitors was to use it to create an empire defined above all by the Anglo-Saxon model of the relations between the state and the individual."

The Polish Government STARTS to Express Concerns about the European Commission

By way of illustrating the points made by Bernard Connolly:

In December 2017, the European Commission, that is to say the College of Commissioners, an unelected group, unaccountable to the people of Europe, decided to take action against the democratically elected and accountable Polish Government.

The intention was to invoke Article 7 of the Treaty on European Union, leading to the possibility of suspending Poland's voting rights. The European Commission's demands were:

- Not to apply a lower retirement age to current judges;

- Remove the discretionary power of the president to prolong the mandate of Supreme Court judges;

- Remove the new retirement regime for judges, including the discretionary powers of the Minister of Justice;

- Restore the independence and legitimacy of the Constitutional Tribunal.

This is what Europe has come to: A democratically elected government has decided to reform its judicial system (which the Poles say is still based on the communist system). An unelected and unaccountable body (similar to this communist system) has told the democratically elected and accountable government of the Poles, that it cannot reform its judicial system (in the way proposed). The Polish people could, if they do not like what their government has done, elect a new government at their next election, to change these reforms. What they cannot do, is replace the unelected and unaccountable European Commission.

There is a name for a system of government that cannot be changed – it is called a totalitarian system of government, which is why the European Commission is pursuing totalitarian art through STARTS. Totalitarian governments need totalitarian art, and more!

The rise of a dictatorship of technocrats … And once again those who speak out and warn are ignored, dismissed, or branded as right-wing populists.

What is a proto-fascist proto-state?

Does what you just read imply that we support what the Polish government is doing? Please create your own interpretation according to what you believe.

Article 7

1. On a reasoned proposal by one third of the Member States, by the European Parliament or by the European Commission, the Council, acting by a majority of four fifths of its members after obtaining the consent of the European Parliament, may determine that there is a clear risk of a serious breach by a Member State of the values referred to in Article 2. Before making such a determination, the Council shall hear the Member State in question and may address recommendations to it, acting in accordance with the same procedure.

The Council shall regularly verify that the grounds on which such a determination was made continue to apply.

2. The European Council, acting by unanimity on a proposal by one third of the Member States or by the Commission and after obtaining the consent of the European Parliament, may determine the existence of a serious and persistent breach by a Member State of the values referred to in Article 2, after inviting the Member State in question to submit its observations.

3. Where a determination under paragraph 2 has been made, the Council, acting by a qualified majority, may decide to suspend certain of the rights deriving from the application of the Treaties to the Member State in question, including the voting rights of the representative of the government of that Member State in the Council. In doing so, the Council shall take into account the possible consequences of such a suspension on the rights and obligations of natural and legal persons.

The obligations of the Member State in question under the Treaties shall in any case continue to be binding on that State.

4. The Council, acting by a qualified majority, may decide subsequently to vary or revoke measures taken under paragraph 3 in response to changes in the situation which led to their being imposed.

5. The voting arrangements applying to the European Parliament, the European Council and the Council for the purposes of this Article are laid down in Article 354 of the Treaty on the Functioning of the European Union.

DG CONNECT and the Ancient Art of Casting and Interpreting the Runes

Revealed for the first time are the runes that DG CONNECT uses to determine how to spend European Union taxpayers' money:

STARTS Headlines

Now for some disturbing headlines:

José Manuel Barroso's new job at Goldman Sachs angers EU: Some MEPs call for sanctions over former Commission chief's failure to 'behave with integrity and discretion'.

Panama Papers: EU Parliament lashes out at Commission and Council for lack of cooperation: The European Commission has been condemned for its failure to cooperate with a parliamentary inquiry into the Panama Papers scandal.

OLAF investigates EU leaders in Panama Papers scandal: The European Anti-Fraud Office (OLAF) is investigating several European politicians and high-ranking civil servants for tax evasion, using information leaked in the Panama Papers scandal.

Ex-EU commissioner was director of offshore Bahamas firm while she worked in Brussels: A former European Commissioner responsible for DG CONNECT failed to declare she was listed as a director of an offshore company in the Caribbean tax haven of the Bahamas, secret papers have revealed.

Ex-EU commissioner Neelie Kroes failed to declare directorship of offshore firm: Leak of files from Bahamas corporate register reveals former head of Europe's antitrust watchdog was recruited by UAE venture set up to buy Enron assets.

EU tax scandal: Investigators open fraud probe into top Eurocrats after Panama Papers leak: In a bombshell move the European Anti-Fraud Office (OLAF) announced it is forensically examining the accounts of several top EU officials and civil servants over revelations contained in the Panama Papers.

EU Commissioner under fire for involvement in Panama Papers: MEPs demand answers from Miguel Arias Cañete after his 'unacceptable' involvement in Panama Papers is revealed.

MEPs grill Juncker on tax scandals: European Commission president Jean-Claude Juncker appeared before an inquiry hearing of MEPs, probing dubious tax schemes in Luxembourg and elsewhere.

Commissioner Cañete must resign amidst Panama Papers revelations: GUE/NGL MEPs at the European Parliament's Committee of Inquiry into Money Laundering, Tax Avoidance and Tax Evasion (PANA) are demanding his resignation and will request for Cañete to explain himself before the committee and the Parliament.

STARTS Headlines: What tale will in the future be written here?

President Jean-Claude Juncker speaks to reassure:

"I understand that you would like to know more about the background, but please don't measure my credibility on that basis. We should measure the credibility of this Commission on the basis of what it does now."

And what exactly is the European Commission doing now that would warrant any improvement in its credibility? We are measuring your credibility – the result is this work! How credible are you feeling Mr Juncker?

"The scientist, *per se*, is, perhaps the most easily used and co-ordinated of all the especially trained people in modern society."

Robert A. Brady, 1937

STARTS an Investigation into the Nature of Research

Below is the Merriam-Webster online dictionary definition of research:

1. Careful or diligent search; 2. Studious inquiry or examination; especially: investigation or experimentation aimed at the discovery and interpretation of facts, revision of accepted theories or laws in the light of new facts, or practical application of such new or revised theories or laws; 3. The collecting of information about a particular subject.

Now here is the online Oxford English Dictionary's definition of research:

Noun: The systematic investigation into and study of materials and sources in order to establish facts and reach new conclusions.

Verb: Investigate systematically. Discover or verify information for use in (a book, programme, etc.)

This is the OECD's definition of research, taken from their Frascati manual:

"Research and experimental development (R&D) comprise creative and systematic work undertaken in order to increase the stock of knowledge – including knowledge of humankind, culture and society – and to devise new applications of available knowledge."

This is explored further as follows: (i) R&D activities may be aimed at achieving either specific or general objectives; (ii) R&D is always aimed at new findings, based on original concepts (and their interpretation) or hypotheses; (iii) R&D is largely uncertain about its final outcome (or at least about the quantity of time and resources needed to achieve it); (iv) R&D is planned for and budgeted (even when carried out by individuals); (v) R&D is aimed at producing results that could be either freely transferred or traded in a marketplace.

Artists do research! So do just about everyone else, including the person who wants to buy a computer, a car, a ... So what kind of research do artists do? Robin Nelson, an academic involved with art as research, has expressed some concerns about artists' understandings of what constitutes research. He noted that artists could not accept that their practices were not self-evidently research. Since each creative iteration is distinctive, it is in a weak sense original and, since originality is a requirement for research, artists assumed their practices amounted to research. And believing that their professional practices self-evidently constituted research, some would-be practitioner-researchers were reluctant to do anything other than they did as established professionals.

We have found that it is better not to ask artists if they are doing research, but to observe and to ask critical questions. If you can do this then you may gain some insights. Those who come to understand the type of research that artists do may then have the knowledge to differentiate, and thus a basis to fund art as research. Otherwise you will just end up like DG CONNECT – grubby-minded technocrats lost in art's romantic mist!

And those who do know, should, we recommend, keep this to themselves, because such a hard won form of knowledge, which DG CONNECT does not have, should be kept away from those, like DG CONNECT, displaying Europeanness. It seems those who have sold their souls to DG CONNECT are doing just that – keeping DG CONNECT in the dark. Perhaps though that is because those who have made the Faustian Pack are also in the dark? Oh look, now we are being expressive! And cognitive!

The above raises issues not just of definition but of competency. Research should not be an elitist activity, but let us not pretend that it is something anyone can do competently. Research training is essential as is experiential learning. When we say research, we mean research that research funding agencies support, not the type that others do when they reference existing information and knowledge to: write a book, buy a television, decide where to go on holiday, write an article about art, … Lack of research competencies is a recipe for a lack of research integrity, and this is indeed part of the problem that is the research integrity crisis. That which STARTS to STEAM illustrates …

Christopher Frayling speaks:

"Picasso, in an interview, referred to the reference materials he had used when researching his painting *Les Demoiselles d'Avignon*. He said however, that the use of such reference materials should not be confused with research. This type of work is research with a small 'r' – searching for something – not research with a big 'R'."

166

They Kill Journalists in the European Union, Don't They?

Exploring once more the developing nature of the European Union:

First there was Daphne Caruana Galizia, a Maltese investigative journalist who was assassinated on October 16th 2017. She died as a result of a bomb placed under her car. Daphne was investigating corruption in Malta.

Then there was Jan Kuciak, a Slovakian investigative journalist who was assassinated on February 25th 2018. He and his girlfriend were shot. Jan was investigating corruption in Slovakia.

Then there was ...

Someone has to investigate and expose the fraud, the deception, the deceit, the incompetence, the delusions, the exploitation, the instrumentalisation, and the abuse, that has become rampant in the European Union and elsewhere. This is why we need journalists, writers, and artists, not to pretend that they are inventors, creative technologists, etc., which is just another form of, what we need journalists, writers and artists to investigate, but to expose and comment upon what all these people (including some artists) are doing. This is one of the reasons why we produced this work.

A creative technologist as opposed to an uncreative one! Oh dear!

FET-ART and FEAT

Below we provide factual information about the FET-ART and the FEAT projects, in case you should come across any nonfactual information about FET-ART and FEAT (which you will!). The following information is available on Cordis:

FET-ART

Connecting ICT and Art communities: new research avenues, challenges, and expected impact

The FET-ART project stems from the ICT-ART CONNECT event that took place in Brussels in April 2012 under the aegis of the FET Unit, with an important support and contribution of several FET-ART partners. This event clearly confirmed that a great potential exists in fostering dialogue between ICT and Art practitioners, and this is the right time to efficiently support such dialogue in order to contribute to the emergence of novel FET research topics, and the identification of new emerging research areas for Horizon 2020 in the ICT domain and beyond. Within this context, a FET-ART balanced partnership of committed organisations has been formed, offering renowned expertise in the ICT and Art domains, important connections with ICT and Art practitioners in Europe and worldwide, many references at the ICT and Art interface, and longstanding experience of planned activities. The FET-ART consortium will, over the 12-month project period, connect the European ICT and Art communities, and foster productive dialogue and collaborative work between them, in order to identify new research avenues, associated challenges, and the potential impact of ICT and Art collaboration on science, technology, art, education and society in general. FET-ART will more precisely:

- Organise *consultation events and matchmaking events* in at least five European locations;

- Support at least 15 *pilot projects* of collaborative work between ICT and Art practitioners in residencies, seen as *proofs of concept* for some promising research topics or directions, particularly *co-creation* and *citizen engagement in ICT;*

- Organise a final open event in Brussels, part of an ambitious set of project outreach activities: web platform, community building, contribution to events, including to ICT 2013 and to the next edition of the ICT-ART CONNECT event which the project will support.

In order to ensure some coherence to the external perception of the activities developed under the aegis of DG CONNECT and aiming at connecting ICT and Art communities, the project will be officially presented to external stakeholders as the ICT-ART CONNECT initiative (developed through the FET-ART project supported by the European Commission).

Funding Call Topic: ICT-2013.9.8 - Coordinating communities, identifying new research topics for FET Proactive initiatives and fostering interdisciplinary dialogue.

Total Cost: EUR 607 854

EU Contribution: EUR 542 000

Project Start Date: 1 June 2013

Project End Date: 31 May 2014

FEAT

Future and Emerging Art and Technology

The aim of FEAT is to stimulate take-up of FET research results and create internationally significant new forms of impact and innovation by embedding and supporting high profile international artists to develop innovative artworks through deep engagements with FET projects. The project will embed six artists within FET projects where they will collaborate to develop and create new artworks that will be showcased internationally through exhibitions, participatory workshops, debates and media campaigns, concluding with a significant final exhibition and symposium. The project will enable FET researchers to work collaboratively with leading artists to develop new artworks that critically work with and reflect on FET project research and results to enable radically new technologies to reach the widest possible audiences through international exhibitions, the global media and socially engaged participatory events including festivals, debates, workshops and discussion events. FEAT will demonstrate how novel perspectives on ways that FET results can be used for social innovation and global development will arise through the process of collaboration and dissemination of the work. We will give confidence to FET researchers to enable them to embrace creative interactions for innovation by providing new frameworks for successfully collaborating with artists to drive innovation in Europe. Our measurable high-impact outputs will prompt new ways of thinking about ways in which FET results are shared by reaching out to non-traditional, diverse audiences and stakeholders in ways that are meaningful to them, through critical reflections, and both emotional and intellectual engagements. By catching the imagination of the public and the media by providing tangible contexts for radically new technologies within our future cultural life and enabling a space for societal debate we will significantly enhance take-up of FET research results.

Funding Call Topic: FETOPEN-CSA-FETTAKEUP-2015 - FET Take-Up Coordination and Support Activities 2015

Total Cost: EUR 492 937.50

EU Contribution: EUR 492 937.50

Project Start Date: 1 November 2015

Project End Date: 31 October 2017

"Engineers - more uniform in attitude than one would expect a professional class to be - tend to be technically bold but at the same time to accept totally any society into which they may have happened to be born."

C.P. Snow, 1961

Arts Council England and Innovate UK Speak

We were just standing in the garden one day when a strange experience befell us, for a time vortex did from nothing emerge, and dragging us back in time to July 2015, words from Arts Council England and Innovate UK did we hear spoken:

Arts Council England: "Our new pilot programme encourages artists to explore how technology impacts art and our lives. We're working with Innovate UK, launching three new projects around the country. We will provide the space, the tools, networks and the advice necessary to develop new ideas and services. What we learn from the pilot will help us better understand how arts and technology practices can flourish. And we'll help deliver great art to everyone. Depending on the outcome of those pilots, it is hoped that a fuller programme might be rolled-out from late 2016."

Innovate UK: "Yes indeed. We have a budget item for collaboration with Arts Council England in our delivery plan for 2015/16. "

But how are we going to get back to 2019? I suppose we will have to take the long route! So we set-off back to 2019.

Now we have reached late 2016. Any news from Arts Council England, or Innovate UK, about the fuller programme? Both are silent. Oh well, we will journey onwards. Or is that backwards?

Now it is late 2017, one year after we expected to hear some news about the fuller programme! Any news from Arts Council England, or Innovate UK, about the fuller programme? Both are still silent. Oh well, we will continue our journey onwards. Backwards?

We arrive in late 2018. Any news? No. Why we wonder?

At last we have arrived in 2019. It is time to publish. Let us see what Arts Council England and Innovate UK have to say. Seems that they have nothing to say at all! Oh well at least we arrived back where we started. Actually not – if you understand!

And now we ask: what did Innovate UK learn?

Perform, Describe, Explain, Understand

Words of importance! We start with the verbs:

Perform:	Carry out, accomplish, or fulfil (an action, task, or function); Present (a form of entertainment) to an audience.
Describe:	Give a detailed account in words of; Mark out or draw (a geometrical figure).
Explain:	Make (an idea or situation) clear to someone by describing it in more detail or revealing relevant facts.
Understand:	Perceive the intended meaning of (words, a language, or a speaker), perceive the significance, explanation, or cause of. Interpret or view (something) in a particular way. Be sympathetically or knowledgeably aware of the character or nature of.

Now we consider the nouns:

Performance:	An act of presenting a play, concert, or other form of entertainment; The action or process of performing a task or function.
Description:	A spoken or written account of a person, object, or event. A type or class of people or things.
Explanation:	A statement or account that makes something clear.
Understanding:	Comprehension, perception or judgment of a situation.

STARTS an Explanation of why Negative Results are Disappearing from most Disciplines

Daniele Fanelli will now speak about the matter of negative results disappearing from most disciplines:

"Concerns that the growing competition for funding and citations might distort science are frequently discussed, but have not been verified directly. Of the hypothesized problems, perhaps the most worrying is a worsening of positive-outcome bias. A system that disfavours negative results not only distorts the scientific literature directly, but might also discourage high-risk projects and pressure scientists to fabricate and falsify their data. My study analysed over 4600 papers published in all disciplines between 1990 and 2007, measuring the frequency of papers that, having declared to have 'tested' a hypothesis, reported a positive support for it. The overall frequency of positive supports has grown by over 22% between 1990 and 2007, with significant differences between disciplines and countries. The increase was stronger in the social and some biomedical disciplines. The United States had published, over the years, significantly fewer positive results than Asian countries (and particularly Japan) but more than European countries (and in particular the United Kingdom). Methodological artefacts cannot explain away these patterns, which support the hypotheses that research is becoming less pioneering and/or that the objectivity with which results are produced and published is decreasing."

So will STARTS projects be publishing negative results concerning the hypothesis – belief – that the arts can lead to human-centred innovation, can enhance creativity in projects, and can make industry more competitive? Elsewhere we have noted that reference to the difficulties encountered when artists collaborate with STEM people are not now mentioned in the art-science and art-technology lovers' advocacy literature. We note too that no evidence has been provided for the positive claims that they make – these are just anecdotes, which often do not stand up to close examination.

In terms of the European Commission we would like to draw your attention to this aspect of Daniele's text: "Of the hypothesized problems, perhaps the most worrying is a worsening of positive-outcome bias. A system that disfavours negative results not only distorts the scientific literature directly, but might also discourage high-risk projects and pressure scientists to fabricate and falsify their data."

A fabrication (fab) culture is what you need to avoid, or to create, depending on your political objectives!

Is the European Commissar Responsible for DG CONNECT Ideologically Sound?

At the European Parliament hearing to approve the appointment of the new European Commissar responsible for the Digital Economy and Society, and hence DG CONNECT, the MEPs wanted, in effect, to find out if the new appointee was ideologically sound. This is part of the European Commissar designate's reply relating to this particular aspect:

"The interests of our citizens must be at the heart of our policies. Regular dialogue and greater cooperation with all stakeholders is the only way for us to turn existing digital barriers into opportunities which will enable us to defend our values and principles.

"I call now upon my experience as a researcher in two European projects (EQUAL and PARENEL) to apply innovative working methods in the search for solutions. My work in these projects has helped me to appreciate how crucial it is to support scientific research – including with funding – in order to pool data and resources. This will bring Europe to the forefront of scientific and technological progress and thereby assert European excellence. In our capacity as European policy makers, we have a duty to act and I undertake to use all the necessary means and take all the necessary action to achieve this objective.

"As a 30-year-old MEP, I was conscious of how fortunate I was and the opportunity I had to put forward my European vision and commitment. The interests of citizens were my priority from the outset. The topics I worked on further instilled in me the importance of seeking and applying cohesion between our internal and external policies. This cohesion should guide everything we do."

"You'll do. We certify that you are ideologically sound."

That was the voices of the European Parliament's MEPs – they too have to be ideologically sound. No opposition will be tolerated. Literally – there is no opposition party. Those who oppose are branded as right-wing populists!

All the Europe Union's woes can be blamed on the right-wing populists! Will be blamed on them ...

So supporting scientific research – including with funding – in order to pool data and resources, will bring Europe to the forefront of scientific and technological progress and thereby assert European excellence. Will it? I think you will find that if you care to connect your mouth with your brain that it will not.

President Trump, in December 2017 declared Russia and China to be major threats to United States economic dominance. He did not identify the European Union as a major threat to United States' economic dominance. This is because the European Union will never challenge the economic dominance of the United States. The European Union is too concerned with its European Union Nationalist ideology and propaganda, with Europeanness, to pose a serious threat to anyone, at least in the economic sphere.

Notice that the European Commissar designate indirectly referred to this thing that is called *defending our way of life*! Just like a good nationalist should!

"The typical scientist is not, either
by virtue of his training or vocation,
much more inclined to uphold scientific
laws and methods of analysis, so far as
social applications are concerned, and
outside his own narrow field,
than is the most ignorant
layman on the street.""

Robert A. Brady, 1937

STARTS Quiz

What do all the following statements have in common?

"William Whewell in his 1840 synthesis, *The Philosophy of the Inductive Sciences* was the first to speak of consilience, literally a *jumping together* of knowledge by the linking of facts and fact-based theory across *disciplines* to create a common groundwork of explanation."

"It is bizarre how very little of twentieth-century science has been assimilated into twentieth-century art."

"In 1959 C.P. Snow, the molecular physicist who later became a novelist, declared that Western intellectual life is divided into two cultures: that of the sciences, which are concerned with the physical nature of the universe, and that of the humanities – literature and art – which are concerned with the nature of human experience."

"Any sound scientific theory, whether of time or of any other concept, should in my opinion be based on the most workable philosophy of science: the positivist approach put forward by Karl Popper and others."

"To have art as an ingredient in the knowledge creation and programme development process is a new idea."

The answer to the question we posed is: all these statements were made by STEM people and all these statements are either completely wrong or highly inaccurate, to the point of being misleading – misinformation! And yet you allow STEM people to increase their power, to shape policies, to worm their way into positions of influence. And where one sees this at its most advanced stage of development, is in the *City of the Golden Stars*, in an organisation that is not accountable to anyone.

Evidently people have not yet learned the lessons of history. Do not allow priests to gain the power to control your lives. Do not allow STEM people to conspire with undemocratic forces. We refer you to the nightmare case that is IG Farben, one of Europe's leading business in the 1930s – Nobel Prizes and innovation! Just what the European Commission will claim the FET Flagships will deliver. Will they?

The people of Europe may get more than they are expecting!

It STARTed with STARTS. Now is the time to stop them.

You are probably wondering … Here is the answer:

Edward O. Wilson

C. P. Snow

Eric R. Kandel

Stephen Hawkins

A DG CONNECT Technocrat.

One final point – are the examples that we have just quoted cases that illustrate the rise of rampant relativism among STEM people, where they read into text what they want to find there, as part of an effort to rewrite history and to create a better image for the tarnished world of the white-frocked seekers of objective truth?

"Research has become a political
or resource issue, as much as an
academic one. Research has also become a
status issue, as much as a conceptual or
even a practical one.
And that - I must confess - worries me."

Christopher Frayling, 1993

The Federal German Constitutional Court Declares as Unconstitutional Aspects of Laws Accompanying the Act Approving the Treaty of Lisbon!

A spokesperson for the Federal German Constitutional Court will now make a statement:

"The Second Senate of the Federal Constitutional Court has decided that the Act Approving the Treaty of Lisbon (*Zustimmungsgesetz zum Vertrag von Lissabon*) is compatible with the Basic Law. In contrast, the Act Extending and Strengthening the Rights of the Bundestag and the Bundesrat in European Union Matters (*Gesetz über die Ausweitung und Stärkung der Rechte des Bundestages und des Bundesrates in Angelegenheiten der Europäischen Union*) infringes Article 38.1 in conjunction with Article 23.1 of the Basic Law (*Grundgesetz - GG*) insofar as the Bundestag and the Bundesrat have not been accorded sufficient rights of participation in European lawmaking procedures and treaty amendment procedures. The Federal Republic of Germany's instrument of ratification of the Treaty of Lisbon may not be deposited as long as the constitutionally required legal elaboration of the parliamentary rights of participation has not entered into force. The decision was reached unanimously as regards the result, by seven votes to one as regards the reasoning."

Something of a surprise! Let us look at this from another angle. The Federal German Government, with all its resources, its access to legal and constitutional expertise, drafted legislation, aspects of which were unconstitutional! Then, both houses of the German Federal Parliament, with all their resources, and access to legal and constitutional expertise, undertook scrutiny of this draft legislation, and failed to identify that aspects of the draft law were unconstitutional!

And you wonder why people in the United Kingdom wanted to leave the European Union! Continental Europeans are playing *Russian Roulette* with their constitutional parliamentary democracies! With their inviolable rights!

The History of Europe is a History of European Unions

The history of Europe is a history of European Unions of various sizes and geographical coverage. Here is a list of some of these Unions:

The European Union

Yugoslavian European Union

The Soviet Union's Eastern European Union

The German National Socialist European Union

The German Imperial European Union

The Austro-Hungarian European Union

The French Napoleonic European Union

The French Imperial European Union

The Spanish Imperial European Union

The Holy Roman European Union

The Ancient Roman European Union

But history does not unfold according to predictable patterns!

Player Piano

Player Piano is a science fiction novel by the writer and novelist Kurt Vonnegut. One might say that it is a result of Kurt working at the nexus of Science, Technology and the Arts! Employed as a technical writer in the research labs of General Electric in the 1950s, he had first-hand experience therefore, of new automated manufacturing technologies that were being developed, and we must also suppose, saw first-hand the beliefs, values and attitudes of those who were developing those technologies. These two insights are brought together in Player Piano resulting in a chilling and very realistic account of humanity's future, which is:

A dystopia where machines and computers perform all routine manufacturing tasks! Those with redundant or non-existent skills are forced into the Army or the Reconstruction and Reclamation Corps – known bitterly as the *Reeks and Wrecks*. Meanwhile top scientists and technocrats run society, themselves the victims of an insane system of computerised and bureaucratised tyranny.

It is a human-centred – anthropocentric – dystopia!

Only in the twenty-first century it is not only the routine manufacturing tasks that will be performed by machines and computers, but also the non-routine ones. And this dystopia is being brought into existence by the European Commission, STEM people, and their artists in residence, all of whom are the servants of a monster. Which is why now we must deal with the problem that the European Commission has become, deal with the problem that STEM people have become, and deal with the problem that some artists – those whom we call the art-science and art-technology lovers – have also become. A collection of very deluded and very dangerous people!

Our economic system is not working properly, so now it is time for something different. But beware those who look to the past. Hitler did this, and so do the art-science lovers and the European Commission and its DG CONNECT.

What then is humanities future? Where do we go from here? Which path should we walk? We do not know. Neither does anyone else, including artists. But surely there should be no more grand over-arching narratives and singe-minded utopian visions like capitalism, Soviet communism, fascism, Western science, western technology, European Union Nationalism – we have had enough of these.

STARTS Starts, NEXT THINGS Ends, Bombardment STARTS

One day, Facebook was humming to the sounds of people from STARTS making much noise. So we tuned-in to listen. This is what we heard:

"I am managing the STARTS network that includes Roy Ascott's DeTao Master, *Leonardo*, Venice Biennale, V&A, Ars Electronics, ZKM, NANO, and many others. Planetarians, please help me bombarding TELEFONICA R&D with social and any other media messages to try to convince them to keep funding the programme NEXT THINGS."

"I am in ..."

"Me too! Let's use Thunderclap."

"No, this has to be high level, personalized!"

Unprofessional? Unethical? Detrimental Research Practices?

We leave you the reader to decide, according to your beliefs!

Now you know why we disconnected from ICT-ART CONNECT. Why we did not participate and will not participate in the STARTS *dash for cash*!

And who is the unfortunate person that was to be bombarded? The Telefónica I+D web site reveals that the person is David del Val Latorre – described as the Chairman and CEO of Telefónica I+D.

NEXT THINGS was (is depending upon the result of the bombardment!), an initiative started by Telefónica I+D in 2011 in collaboration with LABoral, looking for innovative and ground-breaking ideas on the *Internet of Things* in the scope of the interaction between art and technology.

You will perhaps have already STARTed to understand the implications for STARTS. As STARTS starts, a leading player in European ICT research, is terminating an initiative that is, what STARTS is supposedly about, demonstrating that STARTS is ... What? That STARTS is rhetoric and hyperbole? That STARTS is about myths and anecdotes, confused with reality? That STARTS is not a silver bullet? That STARTS has been done before, producing ... What?

If you care to look at all the many cases of artists' involvement in research labs going back to the early 1960, most of them have been short-lived, and have produced ... What do you believe they have produced?

C.P. Snow Speaks on the Matter of Research Integrity

C.P. Snow is here and wishes to say a few words on the matter of research integrity:

"First, I wish to deny that art had any influence on my success as a scientist. The reason for this is obvious – I was not a successful scientist. Nor was I elected a Fellow of the Royal Society. The reason for this is obvious – I was not a successful scientist.

"Second, with regard to those who have used my name in connection with the assertion that art fosters scientific success, I refer you to the National Academy of Sciences report *Fostering Research Integrity*.

"Third, people who believe that I had a successful career as a scientist while also having an avocation in the arts, should get their facts right before publishing such nonsense. If they had bothered to investigate – which is what researchers are supposed to do – they would have discovered that I gave up science quite early following a genuine mistake that I made, which led to the retraction of one of my research papers – a highly acclaimed paper! By 1934 I had become a published author – which in fact was what I had always wanted to be. My involvement in science was an accidental one.

"This first novel of mine deals with: research integrity! Some will say that it is autobiographical, as the central character makes a genuine mistake, which destroys his credibility, and, rather than fight his way back and recover from this set-back, the character pursues a career as a writer. The novel closes with another character – a long time acquaintance of the central character – committing a scientific fraud in order to advance his career!

"I have learned that, in the early part of the twenty-first century, there is growing evidence that half or more of the published results in some fields are not reproducible. Oh dear! It looks as though fiction has become reality on a scale that I never imaged possible. No doubt Julia and Paul will address this matter in their artistic works.

"Paul tells me that he has observed much that can be described as Detrimental Research Practices, as well as some scientific fraud, in a place called the *City of the Golden Stars*, centred on an organisation called the European Commission, which it seems is full of technocrats, just like the Soviet Union was, which I – quite foolishly as it turned out – once admired because I too was once a technocrat. Technocracy was very popular in the 1930s! It seems as though that is still the case in 2019, in the *City of the Golden Stars*, in the European Commission. A measure perhaps of how backward these people are – still living in the past! Still caught-up in modernism, which explains why they still think artists are special people.

"When will they experience post-modernism I wonder?

"It seems that Paul has all the material he needs to write several socially useful novels based on the 30 years he spent observing the European Commission. I wish him well for such novels seem to be very necessary. He tells me he is STARTing with STARTS."

"Engineers are more likely than any other graduates to join either Islamist or right-wing radical groups but unlikely to join left-wing extremist groups."

Diego Gambetta and Steffen Hertog, 2016

Google STARTS Restricting Artistic Freedoms!

Now to the matter of Google and what it called *DevArt*. This is very embarrassing for Google, so you might not want to read what follows if you are an art-science or art-technology lover! Here is a representative from Google to explain:

"*DevArt* is art made with code, by developers that push the possibilities of creativity and technology. They use technology as the canvas and code as the raw materials to create innovative, engaging digital art installations. *DevArt* is the opportunity to open their creative process, share their art with the world and be a part of a new movement in art. Our commissioned interactive artists will open up their creative process and offer a rare, unique look into their way of using a palette of modern web technologies, including Google APIs, products and services.

"In February 2014 we launched a global initiative to find the interactive artists of tomorrow. We invited developers from all over the world to push the artistic possibilities of code, for the chance to be awarded a commission from Google, with the Barbican in London."

Now we shall hear the response from some artists! Here they go:

"There is no such thing as *DevArt*, there is only art. Art made with code and computers have been around since the 1950s. There is no need to define it as *DevArt*, and market it as something shiny and new.

"We can't afford to work on a piece of art for two months, only not to get the commission in the end. We have to pay the rent, and eat once in a while too. That's why we didn't enter the *DevArt* competition. Exploiting artists is evil.

"Demanding artists to use some Google technologies to create art is also a bit awkward. It's like asking a sculptor to use graffiti as a medium. Let artists choose and create their own tools, and they will make better art.

"If you want to reach out to the art community, don't spend your money on a marketing stunt: buy our art instead. Digital art can be collected too, so maybe you can point your wallets at the *Paddles On! Auction* organised by Phillips.

"We have installed our own art at the same location as the *DevArt* exhibition. Don't worry, we didn't do any physical breaking and entering. We have placed a geofence around the Barbican and installed a virtual exhibition. You can visit our exhibition by surfing to this website if you are inside the geofence."

The same comment applies to STARTS. Now a representative from DG CONNECT will react:

"The artists being so critical of Google are, like the one I encountered in Manchester, reactionary and hostile to: industry, STEM, art-science, and social and artistic progress."

"The art of any period tends to serve the ideological interest of the ruling class."

John Berger, 1972

The Federal German Constitutional Court STARTS to Express Concerns about the European Parliament

A spokesperson for the Federal German Constitutional Court will now make a statement:

"The further development of the competences of the European Parliament can reduce, but not completely fill, the gap between the extent of the decision-making power of the Union's institutions and the citizens' democratic power of action in the Member States. Neither as regards its composition nor its position in the European competence structure is the European Parliament sufficiently prepared to take representative and assignable majority decisions as uniform decisions on political direction. Measured against requirements placed on democracy in States, its election does not take due account of equality, and it is not competent to take authoritative decisions on political direction in the context of the supranational balancing of interests between the States. It therefore cannot support a parliamentary government and organise itself with regard to party politics in the system of government and opposition in such a way that a decision on political direction taken by the European electorate could have a politically decisive effect. Due to this structural democratic deficit, which cannot be resolved in an association of sovereign national States, further steps of integration that go beyond the status quo must not undermine neither the States' political power of action nor the principle of conferral.

"The peoples of the Member States are the holders of the constituent power. The Basic Law does not permit the special bodies of the legislative, executive and judicial power to dispose of the essential elements of the constitution, i.e. of the constitutional identity. The constitutional identity is an inalienable element of the democratic self-determination of a people. To ensure the effectiveness of the right to vote and to preserve democratic self-determination, it is necessary for the Federal Constitutional Court to watch, within the boundaries of its competences, over the Community or Union authority's not violating the constitutional identity by its acts and not evidently transgressing the competences conferred on it. The transfer of competences, which has been increased once again by the Treaty of Lisbon, and the independence of decision-making procedures therefore require an effective *ultra vires* review and an identity review of instruments of European origin in the area of application of the Federal Republic of Germany."

Scenario Five

A spokesperson from the European Commission will now tell you about their plans:

"In Scenario Five we intend to strip the Member State parliaments of their powers to make authoritative decisions on political direction. These powers will be transferred to the European Parliament. This is a parliament and any parliament will do. Its members are directly elected which is enough to convince the ignorant masses that they still are living in a parliamentary democracy. They will not notice that their right to democratic political self-determination has been removed. By the time they do, it will be too late. Those who take democratic and peaceful steps to oppose us will be detained and charged with sedition. I refer you to the case study of Spain's political arrests stemming from the democratic actions of the people of Catalonia.

"Just like Hitler and the National Socialists, we will use democratic means to dispose of democracy in Europe, once and for all."

"The law can, and to make a central
direction of economic activity
possibly must, legalise what to all intents
and purposes remains arbitrary action.
If a law says that an organisation may
do what it pleases, anything that
the organisation does is legal,
but it is not subject to the
Rule of Law."

Friedrich von Hayek, 1944

Strength Through Joy

The European Commission plans to launch a new leisure scheme for European Union citizens. Implementation can now be progressed as the British are no longer here to veto this. Named *Strength Through Joy*, this marks a new phase in deepening and institutionalising the principle of the *totally organised society*. In Germany the scheme will be given the name *Kraft durch Freude*, or *KdF* for short.

The aim is simple – to organise European Union workers' leisure time rather than allowing them to organize it for themselves, and therefore enable leisure to serve the interests of the European Commission. There will be no time for individual thoughts about the European Union – just group thinking arranged by the *Strength Trough Joy* programme designed to reinforce Europeanness. Information and Communication technologies will also be used to implement the scheme. Artists will assist DG CONNECT in this new measure which is one of several designed to monitor, pacify and control citizens.

Activities will include sport, and also culture, organised around STARTS, to induce changes in individual and social behaviour to achieve uncritical and unquestioning acceptance of science and technology – and the European Commission. The citizens of the European Union must be conditioned to believe, what they are told from above. These matters are fundamental to the success of *Scenario Five* and the implementation of the totalising ideology that is European Union Nationalism.

These matters will also be addressed say we, in *Scenario Six*! *Scenario Six*? Yes *Scenario Six*!

Was the Break-up the Small European Union called Yugoslavia a Dress Rehearsal for the Future of the European Union?

We refer you to the history of the break-up of the small Balkan European Union that went by the name of Yugoslavia, including the wars, war crimes, ethnic cleansing, and genocide that have become synonymous with the peoples of continental Europe expressing their Europeanness. Will some future historians be writing one day about the break-up of the European Union, including the wars, war crimes, ethnic cleansing, and genocide?

"The scientist cannot be expected under the
best of circumstances to be a clear-eyed,
matter-of-fact searcher for *objective truth*
and an expert in dispassionate analysis beyond the
fringes of his own special field. There seems to
be relatively little of the so-called
transfer of intelligence, and not any too much
of scientific habits of mind as he passes
beyond the boundaries of
his own specific knowledge."

Robert A. Brady, 1937

Pierre Bourdieu STARTS to Speak about the Rules of Art

We invited Pierre Bourdieu to speak. He now STARTS to speak:

"The charm of the literary work lies in the way it speaks of the most serious things without insisting, unlike science, on being taken completely seriously.

"Sensitive translation conceals the structure, in the very form in which it presents it, and thanks to which it succeeds in producing a *belief effect* more than a reality effect. And it is probably this which means that the literary work can sometimes say more, even about the social realm, than many writings with scientific pretensions, especially when, as here, the difficulties that must be overcome in acceding knowledge are not so much intellectual obstacles as the resistance of the will. But it says it only in a mode such that it does not truly say it. The unveiling finds its limits in the fact that the writer somehow keeps control of the return of the repressed. The putting into-form operated by the writer functions like a generalised euphemism, and the reality de-realised and neutralised by literature that he offers allows him to satisfy a desire for knowledge ready to be satisfied by the sublimation offered him by literary alchemy."

An MEP STARTS to Criticise the Commission and the Council

Hans-Olaf Henkel, a German MEP, has requested to speak:

"It is time to criticise the negotiation strategy of the Commission and the Council. It is illogical, dangerous and unfair!

"It is unfair for the following reason. Mr Tusk, you mention many times European values. Let me remind you of the fact that democracy, freedom of the press and human rights are not European values – they are universal values. And I would also like to remind you that we have British values and that is fairness."

"Artists have worked just as often in the
cognitive idiom as the expressive,
and some art counts as research - but
some art doesn't."

Christopher Frayling, 1993

STARTS a European Nightmare

Is this a dream? Is this a nightmare? We dream!

We ride aboard a train. It hurtles through darkness, to familiar destinations. Then we hear a voice, saying to those who are propelled along by this mechanical monster: "we exploit artist to better communicate science and technology results to society, to render technology more human-centred, and to embed technology more gracefully in society."

Is this a dream? Is this a nightmare? We dream!

We ride aboard a train. It hurtles through darkness, to familiar destinations. Then we hear a voice, saying to those who are propelled along by this mechanical monster: "we exploit artists as designers and to develop an alternative research, development and innovation method, to better tackle emotions in technology."

Is this a dream? Is this a nightmare? We dream!

We ride aboard a train. It hurtles through darkness, to familiar destinations. Then we hear a voice, saying to those who are propelled along by this mechanical monster: "we exploit artists to induce changes in individual and social behaviour."

This no dream! This is a nightmare? We dream no more!

Jumping free, the train is quickly out of sight, and we hear no more the screams of those on board as they hurtle into the abyss!

You cannot rebuild a railway line so that it leads to a new destination while speeding – in a mechanical monster – along this very same track, which was laid long ago, and which leads to a destination determined in ages long past. But you can pretend!

"In my writings I have described the essence of European Romanticism, which I have noted explains the worship of the artist, whether in sound, or word, or colour, as the highest manifestation of the ever-active spirit, and the popular image of the artist in his garret, wild-eyed, wild-haired, poor, solitary, mocked-at; but independent, free, spiritually superior to his philistine tormentors. This attitude has a darker side too: worship not merely of the painter or the composer or the poet, but of that more sinister artist whose materials are men."

That was Isaiah Berlin speaking. Who, in his closing words, was he referring too?

STARTS the Blaming of the Right-wing Populists

Here are the lyrics of the first verse of a satirical song!

Is it raining, is it snowing, are you dry or are you wet,
Is there thunder, is there lightening, do you shiver, do you sweat,
Is the sun out, is it cloudy, are you melting, do you freeze,
Is it raw out, does it thaw out, do you cough or do you sneeze:
The right-wing populists are all to blame for it!
To blame, to blame, to blame for it!
Why so, why are the right-wing populists to blame?
My child don't ask, they're to blame!
Your problems too, go blame a right-wing populist!
Believe you me, they are to blame,
To blame for all, to blame for all. Olé!

Acknowledgements to the great satirical song writer, Friedrich Hollander, whose lyrics we have slightly – perhaps significantly! – modified. We are deploying here a technique known as intertextuality.

Intertextuality: the relationship between texts, especially literary ones.

We are also violating the theory of relevance, because we have just increased the difficulty of comprehension – aesthetics.

STARTS the Exposure of Artists' Myths

Time to examine some claims and to classify them as – artists' myths!

Art thinking is an additional resource with respect to design thinking:

The advocacy here goes along these lines: the latter, it is said, works when we have to find a solution to a well-posed problem; the former especially helps when the problem has not been yet well defined in the first place.

Anyone who has studied and practiced design will recognise this as more advocacy. In design, problem finding and problem solving are deeply entwined, and good design involves challenging the understanding of the problem. Software design has often failed because this was not sufficiently recognised. Waterfall lifecycle models assume that the problem and then the solution can be defined at the beginning of a linear design process. Spiral lifecycle models were thus developed because this assumption was recognised as a fallacy. It is on old issue. More pragmatic software designers started arguing for a move away from waterfalls to spirals in the 1960s, which is where most art-science and art-technology lovers are still living. Perhaps this is why they sound so old and out-of-date, like DG CONNECT, the European Commission and the European Union.

Artists and Apple's Multimedia Lab:

Apple's Multimedia Lab! Apple's Multimedia Lab was founded by – Apple. In historical accounts of this lab, the names Kristina Hooper Woolsey (a cognitive scientist) and Sueann Ambron (an educational psychologist) appear – the labs co-directors. It is also the case that, history reports that many people, including some artists, worked on (multimedia) projects, some as volunteers. Apple's Multimedia Lab did not develop the Apple iPhone in case you were wondering and had been listening to (and believing) STARTS fantasy talk.

The lab was founded for very similar reasons that the European Commission funded the STARTS I platform in the mid 1990s – to save you counting that is 25 years before DG CONNECT set up STARTS II, to do the same as STARTS I, but without, it would seem, knowing about STARTS I!

The Multimedia Lab dates from a time before Apple drew a veil of secrecy around itself. It is now a matter of history and is dealt with in history books!

Oh yes indeed – a fantasy world of legend, myth and magic. DG CONNECT has indeed found their natural home.

The Aspen Video Map is an artistic project:

The Aspen Video Map was apparently an artistic project. History though reports a different story. The Aspen Video Map is linked to a military project carried out at MIT in the 1970s to create a computer-based urban battlefield simulation facility for training troops. An artist linked to MIT's Centre for Advanced Visual Studies had some involvement in the project. Given the haze and the myths that surround technology projects where artists have been involved, it is not possible at this distance in time to reliably report anything beyond this. Unless of course you like to believe anything you hear about what artists are supposed to have done!

Google stole the idea for Street View from artists:

We were told this myth, as a serious piece of information, in a meeting in the *City of the Golden Stars* in May 2014. The myth here is that Google took the idea for *Street View* from an artist and the Aspen Video Map. The evidence is clear to those who want to believe this myth: the Aspen Video Map was made by mounting a camera on the roof of a car; Street View is made the same way. Hence the case is proved!

You will probably have seen those movie pictures of Adolf Hitler standing in one of his special six-wheel (three-axle) Mercedes-Benz cars being driven through streets lined with adoring crowds. In some rare footage you might also see, caught in the line of sight of one camera, a car with a movie camera and a cameraman on the roof, filming the scene from a moving vehicle, slightly ahead and offset from Hitler's car. Nazi Street View so to speak! If Google stole the idea for Street View from an artist, then it would seem that the artist stole the idea from the Nazis!

Actually, movie cameras have been mounted on moving vehicles since the early days of the movie camera! Ever seen any of those early twentieth-century films made by people with cameras standing on the front of a tram? These films are a type of – Street View! The idea was also used by engineers – the apparently uncreative ones who cannot think of any new ideas without the help of artists – in the 1950s, to add realism to flight simulators used for training pilots. They fixed movie cameras to planes and filmed. These days more sophisticated interactive techniques are used.

Here is a question: how much mass media, advertising content, intellectual property, and mass produced consumer items has been appropriated (stolen?) and used by artists?

Reality check: artists have been scavenging from the world of popular mass culture, science and technology, since the early days of the twentieth-century at least; earlier if you include the use of synthetic pigments in oil paints. Popular mass culture is now scavenging off the arts. An example of this is Mercedes-Benz's (image) brand enhancement exercise known as *The Avant-Garde Diaries*.

In some respects STARTS is an image enhancement exercise. So is STEAM, and so is the interest that STEM people have in art-science and art-technology collaborations. It is about the image enhancement of STEM, as well as a lot of STEM ignorance – belief in the Leonardo and C.P. Snow myths.

If you care to stop just believing what DG CONNECT and its sycophantic artists say, and explore matters for yourself, you will discover that the original version of Street View was developed by Stanford Computer Graphics Laboratory with funding from Google. The project was called *The Stanford CityBlock Project: Multi-perspective Panoramas of City Blocks*.

Steve Jobs thought like an artist because he took a short course in calligraphy:

The myth that is Steve Jobs! We encountered DG CONNECT's misunderstandings of Steve Jobs in our earlier work on STARTS. We will not bother repeating what is said in that book. All we will say here is fairly obvious. Steve Jobs, according to his own account, wandered into a calligraphy class while at college. Later he recalled this, and saw that it was relevant while developing a specific computer. So why did he see this as being relevant? The dominant paradigm in the computer industry at the time was the alpha-numeric display. Steve Jobs was doing something different – introducing the graphical computer interface – the Apple Mac. Fonts, which are what he learned about in the calligraphy class, are irrelevant to alpha-numeric displays, but become relevant when graphical interfaces are the norm. But you do not have to take a course in calligraphy to learn about fonts, font pitches, etc. This is the domain of typography! People who work in the printing industry will be able to tell you about these matters – graphics designers for example! No need to think like an artist, or even to talk to one!

Art and science were once one:

Incredibly the European Commission have given funds to people who go around saying such things as: "art and science were, once one," and then they add, to demonstrate the point, "take for example the Renaissance and Leonardo da Vinci."

We will spend some time on this matter. We will put aside the fact that it can be argued that the Renaissance did not happen, at least in the sense defined by the man who invented the term – a man with a very Italian, very Florentine, very Medici driven agenda. Sounds as though he could find a role in DG CONNECT!

We will also put aside the fact that it you time travelled to the early sixteenth-century to speak with Leonardo, and in doing so described him as a scientist, he would not understand what you were referring to. The word scientist is a modern invention – nineteenth-century. We will also put aside the fact that the meaning of the word science has changed considerably since Leonardo's time, and that what we regard as science did not exist in his day. We will also put aside the fact that art as we know it today, once did not exist. Art only emerges when it becomes distinct from other social functions and attains its own value. It is at this point that it no longer serves purposes of ritual exclusively, but becomes an independent and legitimate pursuit. This process was still underway in Leonardo's time, which may, in part, explain his activities and writings.

Now we note that back in that period which generally gets called the Medieval Era, through to what people believe was a period called the Renaissance, all sorts of people were starting to do things in Europe, that were being (and sometimes had already been) done in other cultures (China, Ancient Greece, the Arab World, India), part of which we might connect with modern science and also technology, engineering, and mathematics. We will now list these other occupations: priests; noblemen; politicians; mathematicians; alchemists; navigators; architects; masons; engineers; gunsmiths; gunpowder-millers; instrument makers such as horologists; astrologists; metallurgists; surgeons; artists; … The list goes on.

So now we see that if art and science were once one, so were, for example, religion and science, architecture and science, alchemy and science, astrology and science, etc.

You may not be aware, but can very quickly, using Google search, confirm that religion and science were once one. Here, to prove the point, are the names of a few well known priests and monks that contributed to mathematics, astronomy and science: Roger Bacon, Jean Buridan; William of Ockham; Nicholas of Cusa; and Nicolaus Copernicus. Do not forget the Rev. Gilbert White in the eighteenth-century or the Rev. William Whewell in the nineteenth-century, and Gregor Mendal, an Augustinian friar. We obviously need priests and monks to work in research projects! We are being … and rightly so.

So perhaps we should look elsewhere for an explanation of the statement: *art and science were once one*. We will try Galileo and what he wrote in *The Assayer* where he banished the (secondary) qualities which are the very essence of the sensual world – colour, sound, heat, odour and taste – from the realm of physics to that of subjective illusion, leaving only the primary qualities that are the essence of the mechanistic view of nature (be it deterministic or stochastic).

Are we, then, to see art-science as a return of the secondary qualities – the scientists deal with the primary, the artists deal with the secondary, so that we can all feel good about the dystopia that STEM people are creating? It is a recipe for decoration, reification, and propaganda, which you will find is what the STEM world's new totalitarian art now STARTS producing. And if this is a return to the secondary qualities, well this just proves that the art-science lovers are retreating into the past!

Leaving this aside and setting off in a new direction leads to heretical thoughts of producing a post-European era, post-Enlightenment science and technology – it is about interpretation.

Here is Leonardo da Vinci to describe the results of some of his not so very scientific research (probably with a small 'r'):

"I […] proved that the part of the moon which shines consists of water […] and that the reason the waters of the moon […] do not descend to the centre of the universe and to join itself to the earth, […] is clear sign that the moon is clothed with her own elements, namely water, air and fire […]".

If you are not aware, this is Aristotelian! It is also geocentric. If you have the inclination to investigate further you will also discover that Leonardo was also animistic. If you are not familiar with Aristotle, he was inclined to animism – things *desired* to either levitate upwards or to gravitate downwards. Hence the motion of a pendulum to Aristotle was explained by the constrained *desire* of the pendulum to gravitate downwards. To Galileo it was a dynamic process – animism had been banished. Later, teleology – final causes - was to be banished as well, and all that remained was what we today call cause and effect. No more anthropocentrism – human-centredness we mean! Although in fact, the West is deeply anthropocentric.

Causality now reigns supreme. Thus do you all construct the dystopia which artists in residence will try to convince you, is a utopia – paradise regained, which will in fact be, a hell on earth. You have already seen much of this under various names. The next paradise is being constructed by STEM people and the European Commission, with the help of artists. Europeans never learn …

DG CONNECT's Magical Protective Stave

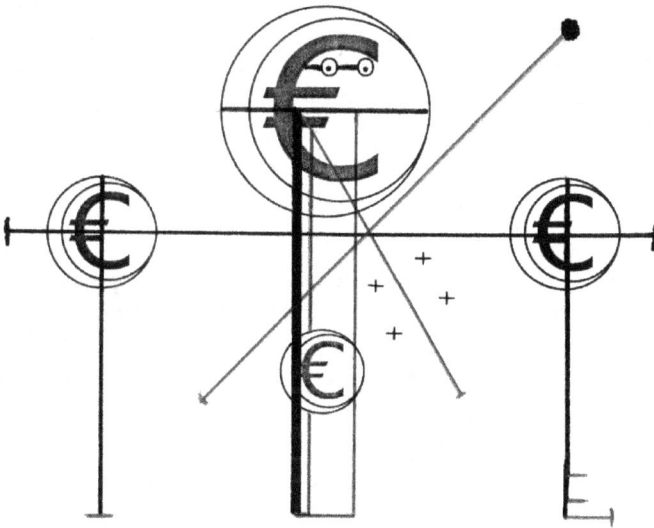

Place the stave in sight of the experts and recite the following text while standing on one leg, wearing a pointed hat, and holding a wooden spoon in your left hand: "During implementation of the Contract and for five years after the date of the last payment, the expert must keep confidential all data, documents or other material (in any form) that is disclosed (in writing or orally) and that concerns the work under the Contract."

STARTS DG CONNECT's European Commissar's Perpetuation of the Sexist Discourse

The European Commissar responsible for DG CONNECT is going to speak:

"I am committed to ensuring that for every panel or public event I am invited to, there should be at least one other woman panellist. No Woman, No Panel!"

Thus does she engage in the objectification of women! Here is one of her Commissar colleagues, who now will contribute further to perpetuating the sexist discourse:

"*Men Only* can never work as it leaves out the perspectives, knowledge and voices of half of the population."

Here is Emmeline Pankhurst to comment:

"When we campaigned for the *vote for women*, we did not do so on the basis that women have special perspectives and knowledge. It was, and is, a matter of equality and social justice. Put another way, it is how things should be. It is a right."

Thank you, Emmeline. Yes indeed. We agree.

As STARTS well demonstrates, and perhaps elsewhere too – European Commissars and former chief scientific advisors for example – women are just like men, for they too can say and do stupid things. That is being human!

The participation of women is how things should be. It is not a privilege given to women because they have something special to contribute, or because men feel guilty about excluding women, for the past few thousand years.

All people are created equal. They are rendered unequal by society. The instrument used to implement this, is language, both descriptive and plastic. Stop using these languages to define people by their gender.

"I'm tired of being labelled a female engineer. We're now beginning to see – and need to see many more – businesses treating female engineers as they treat male ones. That means removing the *female* from the title and valuing talent rather than gender. After all you do not hear engineers described as *male engineers*."

That was Jamie D'Ath speaking. An engineer!

In Horizon 2020, the resolution of tied scores in research proposal evaluations is done using gender balance, if other criteria do not resolve the ties. This is how it is done: someone counts the number of male and female researchers named in the proposal as participants. The proposal with the highest number of females is ranked first, and so on. This is how, in the best of all possible European Unions, they decide which research proposals to fund. And what impact is that going to have on the sexist discourse which, if you care to look, still pervades the European Union? Especially the European Commission who regularly refer to *Female Experts*, but very rarely to *Male Experts*. They define people by their gender, which is what those who engage the sexist discourse do. Just part of their over-lexicalisation! Female experts, EU-citizens, non-Europeans, non-EU citizens, migrants, right-wing populists, nationalists, traitors, ... rendering people as classified objects. Dehumanisation! Its their Europeanness at work!

Soon the regime will be appointing Political Officers to monitor funded projects to ensure that they are ideologically sound. Actually they already do this – in the jargon of projects, these people are called POs.

What about diversity? What about ethnic diversity? The bulk of people participating as experts, for example, in proposal evaluations, are of European ethnic origin. So too are those who work for the European Commission. They are not representative of the ethnic make-up of the European Union.

The problem is not one of the exclusion of women, but one of European societies long established practices of marginalising those who do not fit with the consensus of the dominant social group, which continues to be the white heterosexual male. We do not hear any European Commissars calling for special perspectives and knowledge of Muslims, people of African, Chinese, etc. ethnicity, etc. to be heard in the *City of the Golden Stars*. Why is that? Not European enough? Marginalised groups perhaps?

The issue is one of lack of diversity. The problem is one of marginalisation and exclusion. Europeans have developed many words that demonstrate how widespread this is. Classify, symbolise ...

So once again we see instrumental reason at work. The European Commissar has rendered women as objects, to be instrumentalised to achieve a specific objective, an objective that no one voted for, and for which the instrumentaliser will never be called to account for, by those who hold sovereignty – the peoples of the Member States of the European Union. This is the nature of European Union values. Hence we subject her to the ridicule she deserves while the rest, the *hill-climbers*, just respond by adding a female – a nominal female – to their Panel, so they, the *hill-climbers*, can have their photographs taken with the European Commissar.

That's the way it is. That's how European Union taxpayers' money is spent – squandered. No day of reckoning at the ballot box!

We will express the above, another way. A European Commissar formulates a *crack-pot* idea. Regime officials then exploit their cosy relationship with experts, and find a number of these, male and female – it matters not, because the vast majority are *hill-climbers* – who then confirm that the *crack-pot* idea is best of all possible ideas for the best of all possible European Unions. Often these experts then benefit through their participation in the implementation of the *crack-pot* idea. When all is done, another group of experts, also in the cosy relationship, confirm that all is for the best, and that the *crack-pot* idea was indeed the best of all possible ideas for the best of all possible European Unions. We refer you to STARTS as the perfect representation of this madness.

The frog died, because it sat in the pan of water and did not notice that, gradually, the temperature was being raised. By the time that it had sensed the danger, it was too late.

"The scientist is no different from
any man on the street. If he gives
way to the temptation to generalise
where he does not know he is merely
allowing himself to abandon rational
criteria in favour of uncritical belief.
Uncritical belief is never science;
it is always first cousin to
bigotry itself."

Robert A. Brady, 1937

Beware Art's Romantic Mist

To those that, to the madness which in the *City of the Golden Stars* now unfolds, may be tempted to indulge, which, in technocratic robes we find is dressed, for the purpose of repainting of an ancient image which in slow bureaucratic fashion is also addressed, we, to the delivery of advice, by way of drawing to a close this work, do offer these fine gems for thee to marvel at:

Beware words coming forth from failing technocratic organisations who in arrogance and ignorance do enact events that no-one ever will be able to independently and objectively assess for validity, accuracy and truthfulness.

Beware people and organisations that undertake studies at great public expense, who write reports that, at long length, extol the virtues of artists, but fail to offer any proof at all of the claimed competencies and the results that are asserted to come forth.

Beware people who speak of artistic creativity, for this is not a commodity that can be traded, as though one is engaging in a transaction in some bargain discount store.

Beware art-science and art-technology lovers, for their world is but one of legend, myth, and magic.

Beware people who advocate that art objects alone should be formally accepted as the results of research. Nice arrangement if you can wangle it! But you will need sound ontological and epistemological reasons for accepting such, which you will discover are hard to find in that which STARTS to STEAM. All you might end up with, is research with a little 'r' without ever knowing it.

Beware noisy people who speak appealing words, for there is much truth in that old saying that it is the empty barrels that make most noise, and truly do babbling brooks have shallowness.

Beware the nexus of science, technology and the arts, for it does not exist.

Beware people and organisations that undertake studies at great public expense, but which fail to find that which, with eyes open wide, we do find lying all about in great abundance, such is the amount literature, produced over many decades, in this subject called the arts and activities that go by the name of artistic interventions in organisations of various kinds.

Beware STARTS results – a general rule is not to do what STARTS has done for it is a worst practice case study in artistic interventions, founded in ignorance and interests of the vested kind.

Beware, beware, beware …

And in all matters relating to STARTS, the art-science and art-technology love affairs, and all the nonsense which therein abounds, always to rigorous and critical thinking should thee gravitate, taking more disciplines into account than what you might, by habit, be inclined to think as, or even expect to be, relevant, and, as for this moment in time, words that to Euripides are credited, we are now inclined to say, so ponder this anon: Question everything. Learn something. Answer nothing.

We would wish you good-luck, but you will need more than this if you are not to become lost in art's romantic mist!

Caveat emptor!

Are we drawing this work to close? What does this mean?

"Radical Islamist movements share
a large majority of their
fundamental ideological tenets
with the radical right, including
nostalgia for a lost past, a focus on
tradition, a preference for order
and hierarchy, and an obsession
with rigid identity boundaries."

Diego Gambetta and Steffen Hertog, 2016

William Blake and a Reading

William Blake will now read a passage from his prophetic work *Jerusalem: The Emanation of the Giant Albion*. Proceed:

"I see the Four-fold Man. The Humanity in deadly sleep,
And its fallen Emanation. The Spectre and its cruel Shadow.
I see the Past, Present and Future, existing all at once
Before me; O Divine Spirit sustain me on thy wings!
That I may awake Albion from his long and cold repose.
For Bacon and Newton sheath'd in dismal steel their terrors hang
Like iron scourges over Albion. Reasonings like vast Serpents
Infold around my limbs, bruising my minute articulations."

Thank you for that William. Now we wish to say something important: We too looked through times' window and did see before us past, present and future, existing all at once, for time had become a singularity.

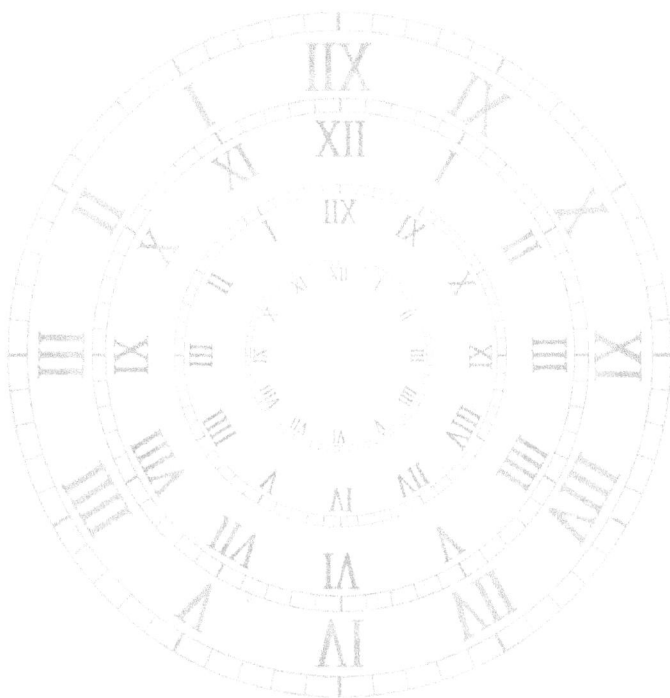

George Orwell's Final Warning

George Orwell will now speak words of warning:

"Nineteen Eighty-Four is a parody but something like Nineteen Eighty-Four could actually happen. This is the direction the world is going in at the present time. In our world there will be no emotions except fear, rage, triumph, and self-abasement. The sex instinct will be eradicated. We shall abolish the orgasm. There will be no loyalty except loyalty to the party. But always there will be the intoxication of power. Always at every moment there will be the thrill of victory, the sensation of trampling on an enemy who is helpless. If you want a picture of the future, imagine a boot stamping on a human face for ever.

"The moral to be drawn from this dangerous nightmare situation is a simple one – don't let it happen! It depends on you."

But you will let it happen. You are already doing so. The totalitarians are already in our midst and they now have artists by their side.

"The more narrow a scientist's field of research - a tendency to narrowing is more common with modern science than heretofore - the more apt he is to approach the bigot outside his own field."

Robert A. Brady, 1937

The Federal German Constitutional Court STARTS to Express Concerns about the European Union

The spokesperson for the Federal German Constitutional Court:

"The structural problem of the European Union was at the centre of the review of constitutionality: The extent of the Union's freedom of action has steadily and considerably increased, not least by the Treaty of Lisbon, so that meanwhile in some fields of policy, the European Union has a shape that corresponds to that of a federal State, i.e. is analogous to that of a State. In contrast, the internal decision-making and appointment procedures remain predominantly committed to the pattern of an international organisation, i.e. are analogous to international law; as before, the structure of the European Union essentially follows the principle of the equality of States. As long as, consequently, no uniform European people, as the subject of legitimisation, can express its majority will in a politically effective manner that takes due account of equality in the context of the foundation of a European federal State, the peoples of the European Union, which are constituted in their Member States, remain the decisive holders of public authority, including Union authority. In Germany, accession to a European federal State would require the creation of a new constitution, which would go along with the declared waiver of the sovereign statehood safeguarded by the Basic Law.

"The European Union continues to constitute a union of rule founded on international law, a union which is permanently supported by the intention of the sovereign Member States. The primary responsibility for integration is in the hands of the national constitutional bodies which act on behalf of the peoples. With increasing competences and further independence of the institutions of the Union, safeguards that keep up with this development are necessary in order to preserve the fundamental principle of conferral exercised in a restricted and controlled manner by the Member States. With progressing integration, fields of action which are essential for the development of the Member States' democratic opinion-formation must be retained. In particular, it must be guaranteed that the responsibility for integration can be exercised by the state bodies of representation of the peoples."

It is our intention to use literary means to reveal a truth that is unbearable, that despite the words of the German Federal Constitutional Court concerning what they imply cannot happen without the consent of the people, can happen, and as we write this, it seems that a work that has been taking shape in our mind since the early 1990s is at last becoming more tangible. We have preliminarily christened this work: *The War of*

European Union. Perhaps though, in the end, we may just call it *Scenario Six*. A post-modern work of course! Entartete Kunst!

The unelected and unaccountable president of the European Council will now comment on the remarks made by Foreign Secretary Jeremy Hunt, an elected and accountable senior minister in the British Government:

"Mr Hunt's jibe likening the European Union to the Soviet Union was as unwise as it is insulting. By the way, I've been wondering what the special place in hell looks like for those who promoted Brexit without even a sketch of a plan of how to carry it out safely!"

Unwise perhaps! Insulting? Why complain? Freedom of speech still applies – for the moment! That one might say is the problem – the European Union is constituted along similar lines to the Soviet Union, complete with empty words about the rights of citizens – blah blah blah – while denying the people the right to political self-determination, and with unelected and unaccountable people running the State and making comments about dissident anti-Union people, who undertake anti-Union activities – just like unelected and unaccountable Mr Tusk in fact when he made his remarks about (the dissident) Mr Hunt!

Mr Tusk, who, like those in the European Commission, time travelled from Ancient Greece, will elaborate further:

"Free people – such as myself – think, slaves – the citizens of the European Union – work. And in our system of government – European Union government – these citizens are told what to believe and how to vote in elections, and any improvement they make to the orders given to them is fatal to success. Oh! I just realised that Mr Hunt was right after all!"

The phrase you are looking for, Mr Tusk, to describe Mr Hunt's words, is anti-Soviet – anti European Union propaganda!

People seem to have lost all sense of reality and embarked upon a dangerous journey that leads to a very predictable European destination. This is why art and literature are needed. Beauty saves the world from the totalitarian grip of grubby minded technocrats that can see no use for art and literature, and who instrumentalise art to give it a utility defined by their own warped mentality.

"Everything within the European Union, nothing outside the European Union, nothing against the European Union."

That was Mussolini defining the principles of the totalitarian state. Which he did!

EUR-Lex STARTS to Explain the Democratic Deficit

A spokesperson from EUR-Lex (Access to European Law) will now explain what is meant by the term *Democratic Deficit*:

"*Democratic deficit* is a term used by people who argue that the European Union institutions and their decision-making procedures suffer from a lack of democracy and seem inaccessible to the ordinary citizen due to their complexity. The real European Union democratic deficit seems to be the absence of European politics. European Union voters do not feel that they have an effective way to reject a *government* they do not like, and to change, in some ways, the course of politics and policy.

"The current form of European governance is such that there is no government."

In theory the latter is true, but in practice it is not. As the German Federal Constitutional Court highlighted, the European Union is in fact an International Organisation based on equality of states, not the equality of citizens, but which also is increasingly taking on the form of a federal state, but without the safeguards based on equality of citizens and their democratic right to political self-determination. The European Commission is the *defacto* government of the European Union, able to pursue its own political agenda, screened from any scrutiny, controlling the release of information, and protected through its special relationships with its so-called independent experts. The European Parliament is not a parliament in the sense understood in a parliamentary democracy based on the right of citizens to political self-determination, but a parliament in the context of a single-party state, which is why the European Parliament should more correctly be referred to as the Supreme Soviet.

The people of the United Kingdom exercised their right to political self-determination by voting to leave the European Union and in doing so, potentially resolved the danger that the European Union's Democratic Deficit poses to the British people's rights as the holders of sovereignty. But only if they did leave! Thus did the cry go up from some: blame it on the right-wing populist!

The danger that the European Union's *Democratic Deficit* poses to the citizens of the other Member States is not resolved – in fact it may have worsened. This will start to become evident in the future. If the British voice of moderation is no longer present, what will happen? Put another way, what are the European Union Nationalist fanatics going to do if the pragmatic British are not holding them back, preventing them from achieving the paradise that they believe lies waiting for them?

And one of the reasons why the European Commission has become the new patron of the arts, is because, like all who hold power illegitimately, they need art as a way of legitimising their power (as indeed does STEM). The European Commission also needs art because they want to use art to manipulate individual and social behaviour. The exact wording is: induce change in social/individual behaviour. Thus will they develop their own version of *Total Realism,* because the history of Europe is indeed a history of European Unions, but history does not unfold according to predictable patterns!

DG CONNECT – nostalgic for a lost past, focused on tradition, preferring order and hierarchy, obsessed with rigid identity boundaries. They will of course deny, but we walked among them wearing camouflage so they could not see what we were doing.

"Making art and responding to art remains
an iterative and strategic encounter that
comprises a creative coalition of
individuals, ideas, and actions.
It is messy, mindful and magical.
It is not mysterious."

Graeme Sullivan, 2005

The National Anthem of the USSR

We reproduce here the lyrics of the national anthem of the USSR:

Unbreakable Union of freeborn Member States,
Great European Commission has welded forever to stand.
Created in struggle by will of the people,
United and mighty, our European Union land!

Sing to the Motherland, home of the free,
Bulwark of peoples in brotherhood strong.
O Party of Monnet, the strength of the people,
To European Union Nationalism's triumph lead us on!

Through tempests the sunrays of freedom have cheered us,
Along the new path where great Monnet did lead.
To a righteous cause he raised up the peoples,
Inspired them to labour and valorous deed.

Sing to the Motherland, home of the free,
Bulwark of peoples in brotherhood strong.
O Party of Monnet, the strength of the people,
To European Union Nationalism's triumph lead us on!

In the victory of European Union Nationalism's immortal ideal,
We see the future of our dear land.
And to her fluttering blue banner,
Selflessly true we always shall stand!

Sing to the Motherland, home of the free,
Bulwark of peoples in brotherhood strong.
O Party of Monnet, the strength of the people,
To European Union Nationalism's triumph lead us on!

USSR – Union of Subservient State Republics.

STARTS a Dangerous Alignment of Grand Overarching Narratives

A development, sinister in nature – a familiar form – STARTS to take shape as we, a European Union dissident in exile, observe from afar what now takes place. Slowly a dangerous alignment becomes apparent, as several grand overarching narratives with single-minded utopian visions, once again form their alliance, and time STARTS moving backwards, and towards a terrifying past retreats.

First there is the European Union (represented by two key Institutions) which it can be said is the last of the twentieth-century's grand overarching narratives and single-minded utopian visions, already allied to science and technology – now called STEM – which is just an earlier grand overarching narrative and single-mined utopian vision, resulting from the *Enlightenment*. In this alignment too is yet another child of the *Enlightenment* – it was christened Capitalism. Yet another though, now appears, bearing the name Art, but of a particular kind that is still caught-up with this outdated notion of *avant-garde* utopianism. And not to forget religion too – known as Christianity – whose beliefs are so embedded in the culture of the European Union, that no one sees anymore that all the other grand overarching narratives and single-minded utopian visions, are but secular manifestations of this very Ancient Greek Abrahamic religion.

And as they set about creating their *Total Realism*, their attention once again turns to the ones they always called the barbarians – more recently the untermenchen! They are the ones that must be either converted to Europeanism, or dealt with according to European traditions.

Understand according to your capacity to do so ...

Is STARTS a Violation of the Principle of Subsidiarity?

First the relevant part from the Treaty on European Union (Article 5.3):

> "Under the principle of subsidiarity, in areas which do not fall within its exclusive competence, the Union shall act only if and in so far as the objectives of the proposed action cannot be sufficiently achieved by the Member States, either at central level or at regional and local level, but can rather, by reason of the scale or effects of the proposed action, be better achieved at Union level."

In what way does STARTS fall within the conditions of Article 5.3?

The Electoral Reform Society state that the essence of subsidiarity is that it protects the democratic self-determination of nation states (as well as lower levels of government) within the transnational framework of the European Union. As such, it is a crucial component of any functioning European democracy.

The way that art is funded across the Members States varies considerably. In the United Kingdom, government funds the arts, but it does not determine how that money is spent. DG CONNECT's mind-set is totally as odds with this approach. It is not only determining what should be funded, but is also restricting artistic freedoms. Worse it has a hidden agenda, which we have already referred to, because we have an internal document that provides the proof. This hidden agenda is in keeping with the mind-set that prevails among technocrats and STEM people. Attempting to use art to manipulate individual and social behaviour, is the exact reason why governments do not and should not determine what arts organisations do with the public funds they receive. Governments recognise that the manipulation of individual and social behaviour is what the totalitarian regimes of the twentieth-century used art for. The European Commission is doing the same!

We could go on, and address, for example, the matter of the different Member State cultures and they way that their technology development practices are influenced by their national circumstances and cultures, a factor which is not recognised by DG CONNECT who seek, in true STEM style, a one best way – another grand narrative called human-centredness. You doubt this? It is very easy to resolve – just look at the STARTS Call for Proposals. You want more proof – we call for open public access to all the proposals submitted to STARTS, the Individual Evaluation Reports (IERs), the Evaluation Summary Reports (ESRs), and the Description of Work (DOWs) of funded projects. This is not going to happen of course because the European Commission is an unaccountable organisation that hides behind confidentiality clauses so that what it does and how it behaves can never be known to the citizens of the European Union. We spent 30 years watching this behaviour. We did this for a reason! Now STARTS the revealing of what we have found …

Should we name the people who evaluated the proposals submitted to the first round of calls for STARTS nonsense proposals – the ones evaluated in 2016? Or should we save these people that embarrassment?

"How did you find this information, Paul?"

That was Julia asking Paul a question.

"Well Julia, I have been involved with the European Commission for over 30 years so I know many things, including how to find information that people are never supposed to know. I walked among them unseen!"

"It is a very dangerous thing to assert that artists can encourage scientists to make a leap forward in creativity. That is rhetoric, rather than reality."

Paul Glinkowski and
Professor Anne Bamford, 2009

Friedrich von Hayek STARTS to Express Concerns about the European Commission

Friedrich von Hayek will now express concerns about the European Commission:

"My book *The Road to Serfdom* is about institutions like the European Commission and the technocratic minds that inhabit organisations such as this, who believe – yes I do mean believe – that technocracy is legitimate and that it works. It is not, it does not. Moreover it leads to conditions in which the voices of totalitarians sound reasonable, as was the case in the Germany that enabled Hitler to take power, for theirs is the scientific or engineered answer, but only to a problem that they and only they define as being a legitimate one. Social challenges – problems – global or otherwise, are not suited to such thinking, which belongs in the research lab not in society. This is why, in the chapter entitled *The Totalitarians in our Midst*, I said:

"Probably it is true that the very magnitude of the outrages committed by the totalitarian governments, instead of increasing the fear that such a system might one day arise in this country, has rather strengthened the assurance that it cannot happen here. When we look at Nazi Germany the gulf which separates us seems so immense that nothing that happens there can possess relevance for any possible developments in this country. And the fact that the difference has steadily become greater seems to refute any suggestion that we may be moving in similar directions. But let us not forget that fifteen years ago the possibility of such a thing happening in Germany would have appeared just as fantastic, not only to nine-tenths of the Germans themselves, but also to the most hostile foreign observers however wise they may now pretend to have been."

A spokesperson from the Electoral Reform Society now speaks:

"The original designers of the European Union – such as Jean Monnet, a French civil servant (diplomat) – did not envision it as a democratic project so much as a technocratic one, in which European institutions would seek to bring the continent together through largely invisible management of the European economy from above."

And thus was the stage set for STARTS, a product of technocratic thinking, with all its (many) flaws.

Robert A. Brady STARTS to Speak

Professor Robert A. Brady will now provide his analysis of the principles of one of those previous European Unions that we have already mentioned:

"One – productive property and natural resources are to be privately owned; freedom of contract is guaranteed except for aliens.

"Two – individual initiative, the business entrepreneur, conduct of business for profit and ownership control are basic.

"Three – business men are to be free, if responsible, to fix by agreements prices, production totals and quotas, marketing areas, and the conditions and terms of purchase and sale.

"Four – stock and commodity exchanges, commission houses, brokers, and speculative transactions are inevitable and necessary for the conduct of organic business.

"Five – heavy industries, particularly those catering to the military and foreign trade, are encouraged; large scale units unless uneconomical are to be kept intact; cooperatives are to be broken up.

"Six – the social class structure of society is sanctified, strengthened, made semi-hereditary, and hardened into caste lines; the Middle Class are the Myrmidons of the *Élite* and, as such, the backbone of the state.

"Seven – employers have practically complete control over workmen in regard wages, hours, and working conditions. They must take care of their workmen.

"Eight – collective bargaining is completely abolished; strikes are illegal; trade unions are forbidden; requests for wage increases are *lése majesté*.

"Nine – control is completely from the top; there is and can be no such thing as control or discussion of policies from below; the leaders decide all things as they see fit; each holds appointed office for indefinite periods at the will of his superiors.

"Ten – National Socialist Party and the German State are one and inseparable, as spirit and body. Legislative, executive, and judicial authorities are fused together. The central government controls all local government and all activities in all their fields.

"Eleven – civil and military are fused together; as in the military there can be no freedom of speech, of assembly, of writing, of action, of *thoughts*.

"Twelve – Germany must be made self-sufficient at all costs.

"Thirteen – non-Germans cannot be citizens; as a corollary, all Germans residing outside Germany either belong or owe allegiance to the Third Reich.

"Fourteen – communism is the major enemy. There can be no such thing as equality or rights, opportunities, or income for the classes, races, or sexes. The broad masses are fools and must be duped and led to meet the purposes of the *élite*.

"Fifteen – all sciences and culture must be coordinated and made to serve the purposes of the *leader*, *total*, *corporate master* state. Propaganda is the method. Propaganda knows neither right nor wrong, neither truth nor falsehood, but only what it wants."

Learning from the mistakes of the past: One can tolerate collective bargaining, Trade Unions and strikes, and just render all of them ineffective through a process of marketisation (the Single Market). Who among you still believes in things such as labour movements, socialism, Trade Unions, collective bargaining?

"A minority of artists and arts producers
who considered themselves to be
working at the more critical and
controversial end of arts practice believed
that the Trust occupied quite a conservative
position in relation to mainstream science
and that this made it more risk-averse as
an arts funder than organisations that were
more independent of the science sector,
such as Arts Council England."

Paul Glinkowski and
Professor Anne Bamford,
2009

For Better Science

Now we are going to list some of the headlines that appear on an investigative journalist's blog site. The blog site goes by the name *For Better Science* (https://forbetterscience.com/), and the investigative journalist is Leonid Schneider, who is also a scientist. Here is a selection of alleged research integrity issues as they appear in the blog headlines:

- Cardiff investigates two cancer research professors for data manipulation;

- Trachea transplanters: Round 2 at UK Parliament;

- Indestructible Sumitran-Holgersson: Commit misconduct on patients, get EU funding to continue;

- Anne Peyroche removed as interim CNRS President as her publications are *questioned*;

- How Emilie Marcus and Cell covered up misconduct at Weizmann;

- How scam artist Ashutosh Tiwari played Linköping University;

- UCL fibs Parliament about trachea transplants;

- Image reuse, the new low of UCL trachea transplanter Martin Birchall?

- Christmas messages from Professor Turner, his ex-protégé under investigation Tiwari, and Elsevier;

- Nature rewards data manipulation with a Mentoring Award;

- Karl Lenhard Rudolph barred from DFG funding for 2 years, as supportive peers flock to his conference;

- Predatory conferences and other scams of false Swedish professor Ashutosh Tiwari;

- Appeal to Italian Parliament for an investigation into trachea transplants in Florence by Paolo Macchiarini;

- Anil Sood and how much MD Anderson doesn't care: whistleblowers speak out;

- How trachea transplanters tricked Andemariam Beyene to sacrifice himself for a Lancet paper;

- Swedish Central Ethics Review Board finds Macchiarini guilty of misconduct, requests retraction of 6 papers;

- After misconduct investigation, Irina Stancheva left Edinburgh, in secret;

- EU commemorates dead patients of Macchiarini & Birchall with a phase 2 trachea transplant trial TETRA;

- Hannover Medical School MHH: where doctor careers matter more than patient lives?

- Yoshinori Watanabe data manipulations: much worse than officially presented;

- Paul-Ehrlich Institute admits to have approved Walles trachea transplant over phone, without questions;

- German Leibniz institute director Karl Lenhard Rudolph guilty of misconduct;

- Pfizer announces more retractions for sacked lab head Min-Jean Yin, whistleblower revealed;

- Lack of transparency in ERC funding decisions, by Shravan Vasishth;

- Sumitran-Holgersson and Olausson guilty of misconduct and unethical experiments on children;

- Susana Rivas: a new research integrity scandal in French plant sciences;

- Human Brain Project: bureaucratic success despite scientific failure.

We end at the headline about the European Commission's FET Flagship project (designed to fly flags) – the Human Brian Project. Symbolic of course, given that we were the rapporteur that helped the (very?) *independent* experts write, and rewrite, and rewrite, and rewrite … their (very?) *independent* report. Did you notice that European Commission funded research got several mentions in the headlines?

Johan Huizinga STARTS Speaking

Johan Huizinga now speaks:

"In my view this desire to astonish by boundless exaggeration or confusion of proportions should never be taken absolutely seriously, no matter whether we find it in myths which are part of a belief system or in pure literature or in the fantasies of children. In every case we are dealing with the same play-habit of the mind. Involuntarily we always judge archaic man's belief in the myths he creates by our own standards of science, philosophy or religious conviction. A half-joking element verging on make-believe is inseparable from true myth."

And what of artists and their myths? Be careful what you believe!

"In contrast with these preconditions which scientific work shares with art, science has a fate that profoundly distinguishes it from artistic work. Scientific work is chained to the course of progress; whereas in the realm of art there is no progress in the same sense. It is not true that the work of art of a period that has worked out new technical means, or, for instance, the laws of perspective, stands therefore artistically higher than a work of art devoid of all knowledge of those means and laws."

Max Weber, 1918

There are Artists who Write and there are Artists who Engage in the Act of Writing

There are artists who write, and we include here art critics, curators, sociologists, psychologists, psychoanalysists, and philosophers, whose written works are worth reading. You will of course be reading works that are an individual's perspectives – subjective – but usually well researched and thoughtful. Such works are often the result of a process of thought directed at trying to understand art, or some aspect of it, or are developing a theoretical perspective or an interpretation.

However there are also artists who engage in the act of writing. What to say about these? Probably it is best to say little, and conclude that they are engaging in the action of writing, and doing so for those of their fellow artists who want to read things that represent the act of writing. You will find such people attached to STARTS.

We have read many works from both of the above categories. Interesting!

"The end of the modernist notions
of progress and the avant-garde
opens a new space for thought:
now what is at stake is to positivize the remake,
to articulate uses, to place forms in relation
to each other, rather than to embark
on the heroic quest for the forbidden
and the sublime that characterized
modernism."

Nicolas Bourriaud, 2002

Richard Feynman STARTS to Express Concerns about Artists

Richard Feynman was a theoretical physicist – a Nobel Laureate. He also had an interest in art, and sketched and painted. If you are an art-science lover, you may believe that he was one of those scientists who owed his scientific success to his art, even though he was already a very successful scientist before he picked up a pencil and began to learn how to sketch!

In the late 1960s, early 1970s, Feynman became involved in the Los Angeles County Art Museum artists in industry programme, which placed artists into firms with a science/technology base. Feynman now speaks:

"The artists were very interesting people. Some of them were absolute fakes: they would claim to be an artist, and everybody agreed that they were an artist, but when you'd sit and talk to them, they'd make no sense whatsoever! One guy in particular, the biggest faker, always dressed funny; he had a big black bowler hat. He would answer your questions in an incomprehensible way, and when you'd try to find out more about what he said by asking about some of the words he used, off we'd be in another direction! The only thing he contributed, ultimately, to an exhibit for art and technology was a portrait of himself. Other artists I talked to would say things that made no sense at first, but they would go to great lengths to explain their ideas to me."

Here we also want to mention a book with the title *Intellectual Impostures: Post-modern Philosophers' abuse of Science*. The authors of this work claim to highlight that which the title explains, but in doing so, demonstrate that they only see what their Enlightenment minds allow them to see! This book is not about post-modern philosophers' abuse of science. We refer you to some of the content on page 92 where we explain a little! Enlightenment is indeed totalitarian.

An elitist might ask: who exactly are the intellectual impostors? We though would never ask such a question! We would instead, deal with the above book in the work that we have provisionally called *Art Science Fakes: A Scientific Reduction to Ignorance*, because its is part of a genre of books that are engaging in a scientific reduction to ignorance, as secular scientific and enlightenment extremists set about rewriting history and attacking anyone who dares to challenge their secular Abrahamic beliefs, a system of sole truths that are totalitarian, which, ironically, are also just a socially constructed reality, confusing knowledge as justified true belief, with knowledge as understood by sociologists. What we see are people from one reality defining group negating the (believed to be) heretical beliefs of people from another reality defining group in a way not encountered – yet!

STARTS an Introduction to Philips Design

We would now like to introduce you to Philips Design, based in The Netherlands, who were one of the participants in STARTS I that STARTed in 1995 – that is over twenty years ago! So we name here the disciplines working in this company as defined by the qualification of members of staff:

- Cultural Anthropology and a Minor in Fine Art
- Visual Communication
- BA (Hons) Graphic Design
- BA (Hons) Visual Communication
- Multimedia and Communication Design
- Industrial Design
- Design Engineering
- User-System Interaction
- Design for Industry
- Behavioural Science and Digital Media
- Media and Communication
- Industrial Design Engineering
- Applied Arts
- Industrial Product Design
- Fashion Design
- Graphic Information Design
- Design Management
- Communications and Commercial Economy
- Mobility
- Interior Decoration
- Culture, Organization and Management
- Marketing and Management
- Brand Experience Design

- Photography

- Contemporary Art

- Biology

- Architecture, Urban Planning and Design

- New Media.

Is DG CONNECT keeping up with the real world? Or should we START calling them DG DISCONNECTED? Disconnected from reality!

"To be in contact with artistic creativity,
and simultaneously be emotionally and
practically engaged in outreach projects,
demands a certain distance towards others,
the possibility to stand outside of the
workplace, otherwise artistic integrity
is at risk. Some of the interviewed artists
managed to preserve their artistic integrity,
while others did not manage to do that
to a satisfactory degree."

Henrik Stenberg, 2016

STARTS and STEAM – Case Studies that Disprove Themselves

There are many flaws in STARTS and STEAM. Five of the most important ones are these:

- Both are predicated upon a relationship between art and science (STEM more generally) that is mythical;

- Both provide an answer (and quite a simplistic one!) to the unanswerable question: what is art?

- Both are founded on outdated perspectives and theories.

- Both are conservative and backward looking representing a retreat into a mythical past.

- Both are attempts to access STEM funding, which inevitably means engaging in, if not outright fabrication and falsification, then certainly what are called Detrimental Research Practices.

Consequently, recognising these flaws and rejecting them, leads to a different place …

No, we are not subscribing to the notion of the ineffable nature of the experience of a work of art. We are talking about habitual, restricting, limiting, … instantiations, which constitute internal contradictions. Put another way, we are referring to an underlying homogeneity that contradicts the apparent heterogeneity, which undermine the claims made by advocates, but which is not visible to those who are caught-up in STEM ideology, whether they be STEM people or their artists in residence.

History shows that turning to artists for salvation is not a new thing. The idea can be found in France in the early part of the nineteenth-century and the start of what was called the *avant-garde*. It was then associated with a technocratic elitist mind-set which set artists in a hierarchy (along with scientists and industrialists) above those – the people – who were in need of the salvation of socialism. It was authoritarian, as is STARTS, both being founded on the technocratic elitist mind-set. Times change but evidently DG CONNECT's thinking does not, for it is rooted in a remote place called the far-off past.

This is what Karl Marx and Friedrich Engels had to say about the early nineteenth-century version of STARTS:

"Historical action is to yield to their personal inventive action; historically created conditions of emancipation to fantastic ones; and the gradual, spontaneous class organisation of the proletariat to an organisation of society especially contrived by these inventors. Future history resolves itself, in their eyes, into the propaganda and the practical carrying out of their social plans.

"In the formation of their plans, they are conscious of caring chiefly for the interests of the working class, as being the most suffering class. Only from the point of view of being the most suffering class does the proletariat exist for them.

"The undeveloped state of the class struggle, as well as their own surroundings, causes Socialists of this kind to consider themselves far superior to all class antagonisms. They want to improve the condition of every member of society, even that of the most favoured. Hence, they habitually appeal to society at large, without the distinction of class; nay, by preference, to the ruling class. For how can people, when once they understand their system, fail to see in it the best possible plan of the best possible state of society?

"Although the originators of these systems were, in many respects, revolutionary, their disciples have, in every case, formed mere reactionary sects. They hold fast by the original views of their masters, in opposition to the progressive historical development of the proletariat. They, therefore, endeavour, and that consistently, to deaden the class struggle and to reconcile the class antagonisms. They still dream of experimental realisation of their social Utopias, of founding isolated 'phalansteres', of establishing 'Home Colonies', or setting up a 'Little Icaria' – duodecimo editions of the New Jerusalem – and to realise all these castles in the air, they are compelled to appeal to the feelings and purses of the bourgeois. By degrees, they sink into the category of the reactionary [or] conservative Socialists, differing from these only by more systematic pedantry, and by their fanatical and superstitious belief in the miraculous effects of their social science."

When artists are called forth to use their imagination to contribute to improving the competitive position of national economies, they end-up using reason – instrumental reason – rather than the imagination that the technocrats have instrumentally reasoned can be used to improve the competitive position of national economies, because in instrumentally reasoning thus, they define what art is, and thus, in authoritarian style, decree what that imagination must be used for. No idiotic statements from European Commissioners, Directors General, Directors, Heads of Unit, or self-justifying lowly technocrats, or self-serving artists, can change that fact.

Resort then to art-science fakes?

We mention class-struggle once again! To which those that live in their socially constructed reality, say: "See he does not understand."

Why did we do this? Now you know the answer – see! But more will we say. Not us, directly, but Alain Touraine, speaking on our behalf:

"A man is alienated when his only relationship to the social and cultural directions of his society is the one the ruling class accords him as compatible with the maintenance of its own dominance. Alienation means cancelling out social conflict by creating *dependent participation*. The activities of the alienated man make no sense unless they are seen as the counterpart to the interests of those who alienate him. Offering the workers, for example, participation in the organisation of an industry without their having authority over its economic decisions leads to alienation, unless they consider such participation a strategic move in their conflict with the managers of industry. Ours is a society of alienation, not because it reduces people to misery or because it imposes police restriction, but because it seduces, manipulates, and enforces conformism.

"There are new social conflicts peculiar to the society we observe being formed. Rather than simply a conflict between capital and labour, the new conflict is between the structures of economic and political decision-making and those who are reduced to dependent participation."

Put another way, the conflict is between structures of economic and political decision-making, namely the institutions of the European Union such as the European Central Bank and the European Commission, and those who are reduced to dependent participation, namely the ordinary citizens to the European Union, who are being seduced and manipulated by these institutions, who seek to enforce conformism.

Brexit can be seen as a revolution against these controlling institutions and the reassertion of meaningful participation, as opposed to the dependent participation that is being offered by the European Union's institutions in response to Brexit. And, as STARTS and STEAM demonstrate, the art-science lovers are on the side of the manipulators – the ruling class that is the source of the alienation. And they – the art-science lovers – are rewriting history to do this. Just like the National Socialists did!

"Rewriting history?"

Yes. Rewriting history! Do you want some evidence?

STARTS a Rewriting of History – An Art-Science Lover's Contribution to a Social Construction of Reality

So you want evidence? Here is an example of such evidence and in providing this we also demonstrate how important the social sciences and humanities are, and what can be done using their approaches. We will be applying these approaches to the work of someone, a STEM person, who is part of a socially constructed reality that we call the art-science lovers' universe. This particular art-science lover we have already encountered, being the person who is named as one of the authors of the paper with the title *Art Fosters Scientific Success*, and also another paper called *Arts and Crafts: Critical to Economic Innovation*.

We will be undertaking a critical reading of the art-science lover's paper with the title: *Desmond Morris's Two Spheres*. Desmond Morris will be assisting in this exercise!

What do we mean, when we say that Desmond Morris will be assisting in this exercise? What is your answer to this question? Your interpretation?

Back to the plot! First to note is that the paper we are reading in a critical way, is intertextual. Second to note is that the writer has reconstructed a series of texts to create the work we now analyse. In doing this he is acting in a way that accords with a literary theory which states that readers of texts are not passive, but are active and reconstruct the texts through interpretation. The writer is also writing from an ideological perspective, embedding that ideology in the text while at the same time constructing the text to be a manifestation of that ideology, thus reinforcing it, and communicating what might be understood to be knowledge to those who share the ideology, but which is unlikely to be seen as such by outsiders. He, the writer, is also engaging in maintaining the socially constructed reality that is the art science lovers' universe, by presenting a discourse in which its culture is embedded, thus maintaining the secular religious beliefs of the faithful. The writer is also demonstrating another aspect of literary theory, that there is no one single interpretation of a text, but several, but also showing that there is not an infinite number of interpretations, and that people sometimes read into text what they want to. This is related to what psychologist call motivated reasoning, which has been identified as one of the factors that leads to Detrimental Research Practices.

Those who do not share the ideology and who resist it and who can engage in critical reading will see the problems with the analysed text. Those who are participants in the ideology are unlikely to see. History has many examples of this, and also shows how dangerous such behaviour is.

Now we will reconstruct the same texts as the art-science lover, and a few additional ones, and arrive at a different interpretation. The genre we will use is dialogue. Within the dialog there are two opposing and contradictory discourses, and the text we create results from the resolution of these opposing discourses. That resolution arises from Desmond Morris resisting the authoritarian imposition on his life story, of a conservative, backward looking ideology, with Desmond asserting his right to be in control of his own history. Here we go:

Art-science lover: "Desmond Morris is best known to the public as the Oxford University zoologist and anthropologist."

Desmond Morris: "I am going to take issue with you about your statement. You say Oxford University zoologist and anthropologist. What do you mean by Oxford University? After graduating from Birmingham University in 1951 with a first class honours degree in Zoology, I did go to Oxford University to do research, and obtained from there a D.Phil degree in 1954 for my research work on reproductive behaviour. I remained at Oxford to undertake post-doctoral research but left in 1956 to work for Granada TV as head of their Film Unit at the Zoological Society of London. In 1959 I left Granada TV to become the Zoological Society's Curator of Mammals, a post which I held for 8 years. So why not describe me as being best known to the public as the Granada TV and London Zoological Society, Zoologist? Or better still, best known to the public as the first presenter of Granada TV's children's programme, *Zootime*. I did of course return to Oxford University in 1973, to take up a Research fellowship, but I would not say I was best known to the public as an Oxford University … Moreover, if you look on the web site of the Oxford University's Department of Zoology, you will not find me listed under the People section, not even as a emeritus member of the department. Perhaps though this is all secondary to the main point that I want to make – you classified me as a zoologist and anthropologist, but I am actually a zoologist and ethologist! If you want to know the difference between an anthropologist and an ethologist I suggest that you consult the online version of the Encyclopaedia Britannica."

Art-science lover: "He has been a painter for longer than he has been a scientist or a writer."

Desmond Morris: "Again I must take issue with you. This is simply not correct. My first interest and love was science. As a child I became interested in Natural History. I was also interested in animals, and graduated from keeper of animals to an observer of animals. In my book *Animal Days* – not strictly an autobiography, more a personal history in which I do not dwell on certain things – I make this very clear in the first

229

two chapters. There is much in those two chapters that would convince most readers of that book, that I was a scientist long before I was a painter. Not to mention what I have written elsewhere. Furthermore, I predict that you will in due course say that my first interest was science and not painting, thereby contradicting yourself."

Art-science lover: "Instead of attending art school, Morris took a fruitful detour. His other love was animals, particularly animal behaviour. As a child he had spent innumerable hours simply watching mammals, fish, birds and insects go about their lives. So he decided to go to Oxford to work with Nobel laureate Niko Tinbergens."

Desmond Morris: "See I told you that you would contradict yourself! Its divination! It's related to Surrealism and their interest in chance – dice, tarot cards – as argued by Simone Perks in her 2006 PhD thesis *The Dice-box of Chance: The Problem of Causality in Surrealism, Science and the Occult*! I tease. But returning to more serious matters, once again I must take issue with you. I did not take a fruitful detour. It is true that I did toy with the idea of going to art school when my National Service was finished, but I decided to enrol as an undergraduate at Birmingham University – not Oxford – to study Zoology. The rest I have already explained, but I also note that it was not, as you claim, Natural History that attracted me to apply to Oxford, but Ethology, a discipline pioneered in the 1930s by Niko Tinbergens in The Netherlands and Konrad Lorenz in Austria, then later in Germany. And Niko was not a Nobel laureate when I applied to do my D.Phil in 1954. He was just a lecturer, having given up a chair in The Netherlands to come to Oxford to spread the word about Ethology in the English speaking world. He did not receive his Nobel Prize until 1973; a prize that he shared with Konrad Lorenz."

Art-science lover: "Morris began painting at the age of 16, when he discovered a book of modern art that gave him the revelatory idea that art need not be the boring representation of things seen, that had so far comprised his limited classroom knowledge of the subject."

Desmond Morris: "Alas no! Let me put you straight on these matters. When I was sixteen and became interested in painting, I was at school. Or was I fourteen, or fifteen? It depends which texts you read! Many people can claim that they started painting while at school! In those days it was a common thing in the school setting – art classes that is. I was not much interested in the subject though – painting I mean. Then I discovered a book. It was in fact, not a book of modern art, but a volume of Goya's etchings, called *The Disasters of War*. Francisco Goya was a Spanish painter and printmaker, born 1746, died 1828. His life spans the Rococo period and includes also the Romantic era. As he grew older he spent more time painting scenes of fantasy and terror. Many of his painting were politically inspired by the French occupation of his country. He lived long before the era of modern art, although some see in late Rococo the beginnings of modern art. I came across this book in the school library when I was 16 and within a few months I was busy making sketches, not making any conscious connection at the time between the impact of Goya and the start of my own picture-making. But the link is glaringly obvious. Naturally, my first sketches were not of the safe traditional type. From the very beginning they were intensely personal and subjective, depicting strange shapes largely influenced by my biological studies. See, I was already involved with science! I was also starting to grow a private world of my own. I had at that time too, a fierce intolerance of all representational art and poured scorn on it at every opportunity with the fine arrogance of which only a teenager is capable. The scorn of my teachers upon seeing my early sketches was equal and opposite. They casually condemned my sketches as *rubbish*. I should also now mention, that I did discover in the school library, other art books that were about, modern art. From these I learned that one could paint without being a slave to the external world. Instead of copying it, you could distil it."

Art-science lover: "Two other sources particularly stimulated his imagination. One was a book of anatomical drawings that contained stunning illustrations of internal organs such as intestines whose loopy structures fascinated the young man. Another was Surrealism."

Desmond Morris: "Sorry, but yet again I must call into question your reading of texts. What do you mean by a book of anatomical drawings? The book you refer to, I encountered as a child, not a young man. The book was actually not one of anatomical drawings. It was the seventeenth-century work of a physiologist called Nehemiah Grew with the title *The Comparative Anatomy of Stomachs and Guts Begun: Being Several Lectures Read before the Royal Society – In the year 1676* which was actually published as an appendix to (subjoined to) *Musaeum Regalis Societatis, or, A Catalogue and Description of the Natural and Artificial Rarities belonging to the Royal Society and preserved at Gresham College*. The whole book is 530 pages, most of which is text – 433 pages. The part that is Grew's work, an appendix, is only 45 pages of text. The remaining pages are illustrations, mostly that which correspond to the title of the catalogue – quite a diverse collection. These are called Tables. There are 28 of these in total. Tables 23 to 28 relate to Grew's appendix."

Art-science lover: "In 1947, at the age of 19, he was drafted for military service. The army was looking for people to teach art to military men. Unprepared, he had to formalise his limited knowledge on the job. The experience taught him that the best way to learn anything is to teach it."

Desmond Morris: "Once again I doubt your reading of the texts. In 1946 I was conscripted into the army for two years National Service. During this period I became a lecturer in Fine Art at the Chiseldon Army College. It was during this time that I began painting seriously. It just happened that there was a vacancy for an art lecturer at the college as the previous lecturer had just left, and I had mentioned that I was a painter. And this experience did not teach me that the best way to learn anything is to teach it. What I did was to apply an approach adopted by my Sixth Form Zoology teacher, who told us that all he could do was to teach us how to learn. To make us proficient at asking ourselves questions. Then it was up to us to find answers. This is what I did. I started by bluffing my way through lessons, and then as the weeks passed, my need to bluff decreased and I was soon able to run a reasonable one month course using my Zoology teacher's dictum 'you can't teach a subject – only how to learn it' and as a result I was learning a great deal myself."

Art-science lover: "Surrealism is at the core of both art and science for Morris. 'The table of surrealism,' he writes, 'stands on four legs. The first we may call the poetry of chance; the second the joy of exaggeration; the third the shock of juxtaposition; and the fourth the invention of images'."

Desmond Morris: "Now you are being utterly ridiculous. Surrealism is not at the core of science, not for me or for anybody else. It's the core of … well Surrealism. And again you misquote me. I did say, in 1987, that the table of surrealism stands on four legs, but then went on to explain that different surrealist artists had focused on different legs. And this characterization of Surrealism is of course my own subjective interpretation. Examining the text in my book *The Secret Surrealist*, it can be seen that I am interested in the fourth leg – invention of images. I said that the fourth leg accepts the difficult challenge of trying to create a new world of invented images – forms that no longer bear a one-to-one relationship with existing objects, but are evolved by the artists as original forms in a novel existence. The Surrealists most successful in following this course have been Tanguy, Matta and Arp. It is this fourth approach that fascinates me, hence my biomorphs. However, in 2018 I dropped the reference to table legs, and spoke instead about five approaches to Surrealism: paradoxical surrealism; atmospheric surrealism; metamorphic surrealism; biomorphic surrealism; and abstract surrealism. I noted again that some artists had specialized, while others had employed more than one approach. "

Art-science lover: "Morris also uses the surrealist technique of automatism to yield scientific insights. Just as a person learning a foreign language knows that he or she is becoming fluent when he or she begins to dream in that language, so did Morris discover a new kind of observational fluency when he began dreaming about the animals he observed. The breakthrough happened when he was a teenager, at about the same time he began to paint. Morris writes in *Animal Days*: 'It was a strange little scenario. Not only was I surrounded by animals, but I changed into one myself. In essence, this was what was going to happen to me in my future research, when I became a full-time student of animal behaviour. With each animal I studied I became that animal. I tried to think like it, to feel like it. Instead of viewing the animal from a human standpoint – and making serious anthropomorphic errors in the process – I attempted, as a research ethologist, to put myself in the animal's place, so that its problems became my problems, and I read nothing into its life-style that was alien to its particular species. And the dream said it all'."

Desmond Morris: "Oh dear! Here we go again! I see that you are referring to the dream that I wrote about in *Animal Days*. I see also that I need to correct you, one more time! First let me say that your timings are wrong. The dream occurred in my final year at Birmingham University, and was a result of over work. This is clearly stated in *Animal Days*! My approach to my studies in my first two years at University had been cavalier, and I had a lot of catching-up to do if I was to obtain a First Class Honours Degree, which is what I needed, if I was to be given a research place at Oxford. I had decided that I would focus my efforts on the Oxford research goal, which meant that I had to severely curtail my activities in the art world, which was difficult for me, as there was pressure to continue painting and exhibiting. Not to do so would have meant loosing the impetus that had developed, but I decided on the research path. Consequently, working hard on zoology, making-up lost ground, I was, as they say, *burning the candle at both ends*, and the overwork and lack of sleep eventually caught-up with me. I came home at the end of term and collapsed into bed, and it was at this moment that I experienced several vivid dreams, one of which I described in *Animal Days*. It was not a dream about the animals I observed – it was a dream about painting, with animals observing me, and then I became one of the observing animals. Now I want to ask a rhetorical question: what do you mean by your statement *the breakthrough happened when he was a teenager, at about the same time he began to paint*? I was not a teenager. I had started to paint seriously while in the Army at the Chiseldon Army College. When I had this particular dream, I was, as I just said, in my final year at the University of Birmingham. Do you have a problem getting your facts right? And let me say, that evidently you are not familiar with Ethology, for what I described as *the dream saying it all*, is a reference to the Ethology developed by both Niko Tinbergens and Konrad Lorenz, both of whom rejected anthropomorphism, and sought to study animal behaviour without viewing the animal from a human standpoint. This was something that I later wondered if I was succumbing to when I observed the behaviour of the chimpanzee called Congo that became a regular participant in *Zootime*."

Art-science lover: "The objective, quantitative approach that characterises so much of modern science is not for Morris. 'No one ever studies anything unless, in some way or other, they are deeply emotionally involved with it,' he has written."

Desmond Morris: "Fantasy! Pure fantasy! I am referring to the science fantasy novel called *Inrock*, from which the quote is taken, and to your statement. The scene is as follows. The central character Jason, has been taken prisoner and is going to be dismembered and eaten. His newly found friend, Ludo, is trying to save him. She is engaged in a conversation with the person who is ordering the dismembering, a snake-alligator like monster called Mha-kee. Ludo and the monster have just entered the chamber where Jason is being held captive. Ludo speaks saying, 'his face', to which Mha-kee responds by asking, 'what about his face?' Ludo then replies by saying: 'Nothing really. It is different. That is all.' To which Mha-kee begins to ask, why Ludo should care about a small thing like Jason's face. In reply Ludo says that she does not care about his face, stating too that she was just making an observation, realising that she could easily land herself in difficulty if her thoughts became too transparent. Mha-kee then responds with this statement: 'Rubbish, we only observe those things that have special meaning for us. No one *ever* studies *anything* unless, in some way or other, they are deeply emotionally involved with it. Don't you agree, my dear Ludo?' Ludo then agrees and admits to being interested in eating the face while it is still fresh, trying to placate Mha-kee. So again I say fantasy! Pure fantasy!"

Art-science lover: "I now want to say something about how Morris' internal world of images and processes directs his painting. Because much of his time is spent working on biological and anthropological images, much of the artwork of Morris draws from his internalised feeling about these studies."

Desmond Morris: "That's quite a claim you are making. Mind-reader are you? And surely you mean ethological rather than anthropological. Don't you understand the difference? In *Animal Days* I specifically state that I wanted to address human behaviour from an ethological stance and that this would be a way of seeing the all-too-familiar human activities in a new and unfamiliar light. But I had no wish to join one of the traditional sciences of human behaviour. Psychology, psychiatry, sociology, and anthropology were disciplines already deeply entrenched in their own specialist attitudes. It was important to keep myself free of them and to develop my own ideas independent of their influence. And *The Naked Ape* is the result of this."

Art-science lover: "In a 1974 interview in *Lycidias*, an Oxford magazine, Morris elaborated on the connection: 'It is true that my paintings are very biomorphic, very preoccupied with biological shapes, and that my biological writings are largely concerned with visual patterns of behaviour. I have never resisted that kind of leakage [...] Recently, neurophysiologists have begun to pay more attention to this problem and it now seems likely that this division that I am postulating into two types of mental process actually has some structural basis in the brain. If this research makes further advances, and confirms that the two kinds of activity are mutually beneficial, perhaps the time will come when we will give up the folly of separating sub-adults into the imaginative and the analytical — artists and scientists — and encourage them to be both at once'."

Desmond Morris: "Oh dear! Wrong again. I did not give an interview in 1974 to an Oxford Magazine called *Lycidias*. You have taken this directly from a book called *The Surrealist World of Desmond Morris*, by Michel Remy. You have cut and pasted this claim directly from his book, without first checking that is was correct, by consulting the primary source – the 1973-74 edition of *Lycidias* – thus breaking one of the fundamental rules of research – always consult original sources. If you had done this you would have discovered that Remy was incorrect, and also that he has missed out some important aspects of the article I wrote in the 1973-74 edition of *Lycidias*. Yes, that's right, it is an article I was asked to write and you did not even bother to check, it would seem, which is quite easy to do, as it is listed on my web site under the section called *Articles* with the page title *Desmond Morris Selected Articles*. The article in question is called *Biomorpia*. And this is what I wrote: 'It is true that my paintings are very biomorphic, very preoccupied with biological shapes, and that my biological writings are largely concerned with visual patterns of behaviour. I have never resisted that kind of leakage.' Then there is the bit that Remy and you left out. This: 'But it does not have to do with the fundamental creative processes involved in the two activities. These I still believe are basically different, and complement one another rather than compete with, or distort one another.' You also do not mention what Remy then says, about the Surrealist's attack on dualisms, and that being one of the corner-stones of the Surrealist stance. Dialectic is the word."

Art-science lover: "'Welcome to the two spheres at once,' Morris wrote in a surrealist poem dating from the same period."

Desmond Morris: "Are you sure I wrote a surrealist poem with the line 'welcome to the two spheres are once'? That line appears in the text of Remy's book. It is not placed in quotes or acknowledged by Remy as being a poem that I wrote, as is the normal convention, which indeed he followed when he quoted text from my article *Biomorphia*!"

Art-science lover: "It is not surprising that Morris identifies himself as neither artist nor scientist. 'I never thought of myself as a zoologist who painted or as a painter who was interested in zoology. They are both equally important to me because they both involve visual exploration.'"

Desmond Morris: "I see that you are in the business of secondary quoting, by which I mean quoting other people, who are apparently quoting me. In this case you are quoting Philip Oakes, who wrote an introduction to my book *The Secret Surrealist*. I will quote Philip more fully. This is what he wrote at the end of his introduction: '[...] What he has created is a parallel world (one which he has also explored in his fantasy novel *Inrock*), and his documentation of its inhabitants and their customs is myth-making on a grand scale. It is also, without a doubt, a commentary on our own situation. The scientist and the artist are the same man and they speak with the same voice. "I never thought of myself as a zoologist who painted or as painter who was interested in zoology", Morris once observed. "They are both equally important to me because they both involve visual exploration". The importance is undiminished. The exploration goes on'. Myth making on a grand scale! Is that what you are doing?"

Art-science lover: "He elaborates by saying that he dislikes labels such as painter or scientist, although his passport does identify him as a zoologist for those who must have such labels. Morris writes, 'If my paintings do nothing else, they will serve to demonstrate that such titles are misleading. In reality, people today are not scientists or artists ... they are explorers or non-explorers, and the context of their explorations is of secondary importance. Painting is no longer merely a craft, it is a form of personal research [...] So, in the end, I do not think of myself as being part scientist and part artist, but simply as being an explorer, part objective and part subjective'."

Desmond Morris: "So you quote from the article entitled *The Naked Artist* that I wrote for *The Observer Magazine* in 1971. I think I will quote the text in full. This is what I wrote at the end, where you have selectively quoted me: 'In a curious way, I do not fit into any of the accepted categories of the art world. I am not a professional – I do not sell my paintings and my last exhibition was 20 years ago – nor, in the ordinary sense, am I a Sunday painter. For those who like labels, I suppose I can best be described as a private painter. According to my passport, of course,

I have always been a zoologist and remain so. If my paintings do nothing else, they will serve to demonstrate that such titles are misleading. In reality, people today are not scientists or artists ... they are explorers or non-explorers, and the context of their explorations is of secondary importance. Painting is no longer merely a craft, it is a form of personal research. Picasso may appear to have contradicted this when he said that he does not seek, he finds. But so in a sense does the scientist – the creative moment in research is rarely the end of a quest, but more often a moment of unexpected discovery, of revelation almost, if that is not too pompous a word. So, in the end, I do not think of myself as being part scientist and part artist, but simply as being an explorer, part objective and part subjective.' Now I have quoted the text in full. The meanings and interpretations of text!"

Julia: "I would like to thank Desmond Morris for *putting the record straight*. Now, Desmond, I have a question for you. How do you reconcile your activity as a painter with your activity as a well-known writer?"

Desmond Morris: "The very same question that Remy asked me! To which I answered, that in fact there are two Desmond Morrises, and they are quite different people. I can easily pass from one to the other, but I cannot be both at the same time. When I'm Desmond Morris the painter, I am quite different. The private, secret part of my brain starts working and for me that is the most important and serious thing in my whole life – much more so than the rest. The other side, the public Desmond Morris, also has a major role in my life, of course, but strangely I find that less challenging. There is rarely any clash between the two aspects. The one helps the other. I obey the two sides of my brain alternatively."

Julia: "So not two spheres as once! Actually, dialectically, as is Surrealism's claim! Any final words, Desmond?"

Desmond Morris: "Ah yes indeed, my final words! Don't you know, art-science lover, that personal histories, autobiographies, and biographies, are, by their nature, biased materials? And sometimes exaggeration and myth making become involved too! Some reminiscing, perhaps somewhat distorted by time's passing, can also be found! As I said, these materials are biased! Is there a word for the content of the paper that we have been examining?"

Julia: "The art-science lovers' universe – a socially constructed reality, operating at the level of mythology and secular religious theology. Such is the kindergarten level of their understandings. If you wish to graduate, to move beyond this level, you'll need social science and certain humanities understandings, which are noticeably absent in the universe that we are now exploring. A dangerous tendency to rewriting history is what we are finding! It is a revelation – most definitely not too pompous a word in our unfolding discourse or narrative. Which is it to be? Not more duality? Not here will you see. And now to end, we ask George Orwell to make a closing remark. Over to you George."

George Orwell: "Thank you, Julia. What the art-science lover has done, for reasons of prestige, is to translate Desmond's biography from *Oldspeak* to *Newspeak*, to bringing Desmond's achievements into line with the ideology of art-science lovers' symbolic universe, and in doing so, the art-science lover has rewritten history, in true totalitarian fashion. What Paul has done is to expose this, and in doing so he has demonstrated heretical thoughts – *crimethink*!"

Thus have we answered the question, out of sequence: why would an art-science lover's research paper include a statement that the reported work may be biased?

"Some artists found working with the employees quite demanding and they did not feel as if they were actually working as artists, rather as project managers or creative consultants, and the role as an artist turned out to be something other than what they expected and wanted it to be."

Henrik Stenberg, 2016

The Electoral Reform Society STARTS to Express Concerns about the European Parliament

A representative of the United Kingdom's Electoral Reform Society will now express some concerns about the European Parliament:

"The European Parliament has an apparent ideological bent towards European federalism. Its members, by nature, tend to be federalists who overwhelmingly favour *more Europe* and closer integration as an answer to most policy questions. Those who wish to run for it are generally those who have the most interest in European policy. By nature those people are more likely to be the most federalist members of their party.

"For a 2002 report, Professor Simon Hix surveyed MEPs on their personal self-placement on a *European integration* scale, between 1 (the most Eurosceptic position) and 10 (in favour of European federation). Members of the Party of European Socialists (PES) and the European People's Party, the two largest parties, mostly stated a value of over 5, with PES MEPs peaking at around 7. While comparable data for the public at large does not exist, we know from survey data that the majority of European Union citizens would be unlikely to see themselves as equally pro-European as their representatives.

"While the European Parliament represents parties and gender relatively well, it is perhaps less good at representing the median of European public opinion, with the bulk of the Parliament being made up of the most federalist members of their parties, and a minority that is now extremely Eurosceptic. While these two groups deserve representation, this does not seem to represent the median view of Europeans."

STARTS an Expression of Concern about the European Commission by Lawyers in the European Courts of Justice

On the matter of the legal case brought against the European Commission by the lead partner in the FET-ART project, this is what lawyers acting on behalf of this lead partner had to say about the European Commission:

"Our first plea in law alleges that the Commission cannot rely on an investigation report drawn up on the basis of evidence obtained unlawfully to justify its decision to suspend, in their entirety, the payments due to the applicant. The applicant claims, in that regard, that in so far as the Commission relied on unlawfully obtained evidence, both the suspension of payments and the termination of the grant contracts are unlawful."

What is this? The lawyers are saying that the European Commission used unlawful methods. Has the European Commission become a criminal organisation?

"Your field (priming effects) is now the poster child for doubts about the integrity of psychological research. Your problem is not with the few people who have actively challenged the validity of some priming results. It is with the much larger population of colleagues who in the past accepted your surprising results as facts when they were published. These people have now attached a question mark to the field, and it is your responsibility to remove it."

Daniel Kahneman
(Nobel Laureate), 2012

STARTS an Understanding of Hermeneutics

Hermeneutics – interpreting the meaning of texts. It is a way of knowing. Back to the matter of interpretation once again! Hermeneutics can be applied to European Commission documents. We suspect that this is something those who write European Commission texts would not be expecting!

To apply hermeneutics though, you have to be familiar with the approach. This means that you have to know what words mean, and also how the meaning of words may have changed over time. On top of this one also needs to be familiar with the usage of words, and the context in which text is written – that means the broader context and the context of individual words in the setting of the surrounding words. Language is not neutral! And more …

It takes quite an effort in terms of time, expertise and experience to interpret European Commission documents. Expertise and experience of the sort one gains when one walks unseen among the crowd, when one is inside while remaining outside. The vast majority of people involved with the European Commission are not like this, neither do they have literary expertise. Thus they interpret documents as the writers intended that they should be interpreted. They cannot or do not want to see the silent narrative …

Entartete Kunst

A spokesperson from the European Commission, DG TRUE, has arrived and wishes to make a formal announcement:

"The European Commission has issued a decree classifying this book, and its prequel, as Entartete Kunst.

"Henceforth no citizen of the European Union is allowed to possess or read these books. All copies must be burnt.

"We will in due course be organising a public book burning session where all books critical of European Union Nationalism will be destroyed in a participatory performance organised by STARTS.

"We do this as an expression of our Europeanness and to protect citizens of the European Union from harm. We have established a group of experts whose instructions are to eliminate all disinformation. Being experts, they unquestioningly do what we tell them."

"Fraud is very likely second to
incompetence in generating
erroneous results,
though it is hard to tell for certain."

The Economist, 2013

The European Commission Declares Culture and Education to be the Weapons to be used for Conditioning the Minds of Young People

A spokesperson from the European Commission has arrived and wishes to make a formal announcement concerning the conditioning of young (and vulnerable) minds to ensure that, future generations unquestioningly accept the notion of a common European identity:

"First, let me state that the European Union is not perfect but it is the best instrument we have for addressing the new challenges we are facing."

So what you are saying is that instead of being a strong man with clear-cut solutions to clear-cut problems, you are a strong organisation with clear-cut solutions to clear cut problems! What is more, you will not be allowing the people of Europe, a free and democratic choice about whether they want the European Union! Nor will you be recognising the equality of citizens and their right to political self-determination. Just like the strong man you won't, will you? No need to answer – we are being rhetorical!

"Second, let me state that when our European values and democracies are tested by awakening populist forces at home and abroad or by the spreading of 'fake news' and the manipulation of our information networks, it is the moment when European Leaders and the European Union institutions must react."

Ah, so you too are saying, *we must protect our way of life*, just like those you call right-wing populists are doing! Blame it all on the right-wing populists!

"Third, let me state that freedom, democracy, equality, respect for the rule of law, human rights and dignity are the fundamental values on which the European Union is based. They form part of our European identity. Education, culture and sport have a pivotal role in promoting active citizenship and common values amongst the youngest generations. Their combination in concrete projects in local communities contributes to the strengthening of the sense of European identity. Initiatives such as the European day at school should receive renewed support and be developed on a larger scale."

So perhaps soon you will be initiating a new movement which will be called European Union Youth! Or perhaps you could call it the All-Union Youth League! You could have an organisation for young girls too. You could call it the Band of European Maidens. Culture and education: ways of achieving political conformity? Indoctrination! Beware the totalitarians in our midst!

"Over the years I have been a developer for
new technology companies, consultant
to NSF research projects, and
artist-in-residence at research centres. My own art
works have often focused on emerging
technologies still in their formative stages.
The involvements have been judged valuable
by me and my collaborators; yet it is often
difficult to trace concrete results."

Stephen Wilson, 2000

STARTS a Message to the Federal Government of the United States of America

We refer you to a programme, funded by the Department of Defence in the mid-1990s, which, we were informed by one member of the advisory board, was prematurely terminated with a request for a refund of some of the monies, following our critique and that of other people. The word is Agility. Yes we have been over the STARTS to STEAM ground before! Different name, different time, different topics, same issues ...

"I want scientists active in all levels
of government. By scientists I mean
people trained in the
natural sciences, not only engineers."

C.P. Snow, 1961

STEAM is Useful but also Very Dangerous!

STEAM just STARTS getting in the way of seeing clearly, as it did in an article that appeared in the November 2017 issue of the Institution of Mechanical Engineers (IMechE) monthly members' journal, *Professional Engineer*. An exercise in critical thinking, this article was most certainly not! The myths poured forth like the contents of a tin of Lyle's black treacle, leaving a sticky mess behind and a bitter-sweet taste in the mouth.

The story line is a familiar one. Adding art to engineering teaches the kind of risk-taking approach and creative problem-solving that can be applied to the world's biggest problems. Since when have engineers been short of risk-taking and creative problem-solving approaches? No one, it seems, wants to ask this question! Nor answer it!

Steve Jobs, as is often the case, gets a mention. "Technology is not enough" are the words that he is credited with speaking. But when was technology ever enough? Design has always been central, which is a fact that nobody ever mentions. No one, it seems, wants to ask: what was Steve Jobs actually saying and why?

Leonardo of course makes an appearance, but it is a mythical Leonardo, which no one has the sense to question. He is, in his mythical form, the embodiment of STEAM, but it is a cloudy judgement lacking in sociological and historical understanding, which somewhat undermines the claims made for polymathing and liberal arts education – presumably of the conventional rather than the contemporary kind!

And another myth is deposited in the reader's mind, as though it was historical fact – artists are often the first to use new technology, if they did not invent them! So it seems that internal combustions engines, gas turbines, nuclear reactors, tractors, antibiotics, lasers, radar, computers, radios, television, defibrillators, transistors, scanning electron microscopes, radio-telescopes, electric motors, solar time switches, sodium lighting, synchromesh devices, operational amplifiers, microprocessors, pneumatic switches, relays, valves, reinforced concrete, plastics, Teflon, thermocouples, … were either first used by artists or invented by them!

And to the IMechE we said:

Engineers know that steam is very useful, but that it is also very dangerous and should be treated with great caution. The same goes for the type of STEAM mentioned in the article *From STEM to STEAM*. Knowledge of steam is essential for its safe use. Likewise for STEAM! One supposes that people want to achieve from their university education not only qualifications but also knowledge and the ability to apply critical thinking to matters such as – STEAM for example! Both of these essential attributes are absent in the article. Critical thinking would also lead people to recognise that there is much under the label of STEAM that is just plain nonsense – art-science fakes! A critical mind would also discover that the NESTA report mentioned in the article is biased – it finds the evidence that it wants to find and is an example that illustrates the research integrity crisis. It claims that the UK Innovation survey in 2010 asked if respondents had used arts or science skills, which is the fusion ideology that these two, fused, are the cause of business success. In fact, the 2010 questionnaire did not differentiate between arts skills and science (or STEM) skills – that is in fact an interpretation that is necessary if you want to produce an art-science fusion advocacy report. Another interpretation is also that graphics art/layout/advertising, design of objects or services, multimedia/web design (e.g. audio, graphics, text, still pictures, animation, video etc.) are arts skills. They are not. Web design, architecture, video games development, advertising, multimedia design, etc. may draw on individual talent and imagination, but they are not art activities in the usual sense of the use of that word.

One can say that the hissing noise of STEAM is a distraction – the bigger question is what knowledge, skills and abilities do twenty-first century engineering graduates need? Issues such as ethics, x-disciplinarity, design, leadership, communication, etc. all come to mind. One can also say that implying that engineers have a creativity deficit that requires them to work with artists is just plain insulting, ignorant, and the hall mark of people with vested interests who are engaging in advocacy. It is not just to the arts one should turn to understand creativity, but more importantly, the social sciences.

And we note by way of an additional comment, that when it comes to STARTS and STEAM, and the art-science lovers' universe, the social sciences are nowhere to be seen! There are reasons for this. Peter Berger and Thomas Luckmann will explain one of these:

"In a pluralistic society it is logical for an institution, for example the Catholic Church, to tolerate a broad variety of interfaith associations in economic and political life, but to continue to frown upon inter-faith marriage. Generally speaking, in situations where there is competition between different reality-defining agencies, all sorts of secondary-group relationships with the competitors may be tolerated, as long as there are firmly established primary-group relationships within which one reality is on-goingly reaffirmed against the competitors."

STARTS STEAM's Fourth Industrial Revolution

And not to be outdone by the Institution of Mechanical Engineers, the Institution of Engineering and Technology (IET) published an article in the December 2017/January 2018 edition of their members' journal, E&T, an article with the title: *Will the Fourth Industrial Revolution be driven by STEAM?*

More myths do flow from the advocating pen! Arts learning brings to STEM, apparently, innovation, entrepreneurial attitude and emotional and social intelligence, but without saying how this can be – are artists also businessmen and women? Excuse me if I am wrong, but artists must be one of the poorest of all occupations. Perhaps then there is a suggestion that STEM people need to be reading poetry – perhaps Shelly's Love's Philosophy:

> [...]
> And the sunlight clasps the earth
> And the moonbeams kiss the sea:
> What is all this sweet work worth
> If thou kiss not me?

Now we are feeling emotionally intelligent!

And then there is the matter of the importance of non-cognitive skills – team working and interpersonal skills. Remind me please, of a time when these were not important!

And to the IET we said:

Go placidly amid the hissing noise of STEAM … The article *Will the Fourth Industrial Revolution be driven by STEAM?* invites a question: STEM to STEAM – what do you mean? All industrial revolutions have been driven by STEAM in one way or another – Joshia Wedgwood is an example that illustrates this. One might also ask why STEAM and not STS (Science, Technology and Society)?

Self-evidently STEM people need more than just hard scientific/technical knowledge. This is already reflected in the Engineering Council specification for CEng. In (what sociologists in the early 1970s called) the post-industrial society, there is a much greater emphasis on what are often called soft skills. Design also has a greater importance, along with knowledge from other disciplines – psychology, sociology, ethnology, for example, as is clear from articles on *driverless cars*. Knowledge from the social sciences and humanities has assumed much greater importance than was the case in the past.

STEAM advocacy articles tend not to look at matters from the perspective of the post-industrial society and its on-going implications, nor in terms of what future needs might be in a post-European era world dominated by China. Instead they commonly resort to rejecting a duality (art/STEM) – while failing to recognise the indefinable nature of the arts. They then resort to using other dualities to pursue their argument, typically creatives (arts?)/non-creatives (STEM?), or (as in the case of the article), cognitive/non-cognitive! Strange (undesirable?) behaviour!

STEAM is an American acronym, reflecting perhaps a failure in their educational system, not necessarily a failure in ours or other nations' systems. It is a buzzword – another one! In a fast changing world we should certainly be continually asking what twenty-first century STEM graduates need from their education and training. But the question needs answers grounded in knowledge and critical thinking, not ones that are bound-up in fads, buzzwords, silver bullets, advocacy, myths, and mis-understandings.

Some people have become lost in art's romantic mist – or perhaps lost in the cloudy and noisy world of STEAM!

Indeed, indeed, indeed – STARTS too it seems!

STARTS Restricting Artists' Freedoms

And so to the truth of the process of creating totalitarian art do we turn, to see STARTS restricting artists' freedoms – what else could it do?

In Teutonic tones set forth as sweet text, tells,
No restriction to artistic freedom should there be,
Following sounds, soothing words, French accent doth speak,
Sensitive treatment for sure there will be,
Reality in retort then spoke forth truth:
In *AMORE* the artist must enrich our perspective – and disseminate.

In Teutonic tones set forth as sweet text, tells,
No restriction to artistic freedom should there be,
Following sounds, soothing words, French accent doth speak,
Sensitive treatment for sure there will be,
Reality in retort then spoke forth truth:
In *BEACONING* the artist must contribute to story boarding. And disseminate?

In Teutonic tones set forth as sweet text, tells,
No restriction to artistic freedom should there be,
Following sounds, soothing words, French accent doth speak,
Sensitive treatment for sure there will be,
Reality in retort then spoke forth truth:
In *BINCI* the artist must use project tools to do what the tools are designed to do. And disseminate?

In Teutonic tones set forth as sweet text, tells,
No restriction to artistic freedom should there be,
Following sounds, soothing words, French accent doth speak,
Sensitive treatment for sure there will be,
Reality in retort then spoke forth truth:
In *BIO4COMP* the artist must provide an outside perspective and make a sculptural representation of biomolecules. And disseminate?

In Teutonic tones set forth as sweet text, tells,
No restriction to artistic freedom should there be,
Following sounds, soothing words, French accent doth speak,
Sensitive treatment for sure there will be,
Reality in retort then spoke forth truth:
In *BiPhoProc* the artist must produce an artistic work intended to reveal the beauty of the technology. And disseminate?

In Teutonic tones set forth as sweet text, tells,
No restriction to artistic freedom should there be,
Following sounds, soothing words, French accent doth speak,
Sensitive treatment for sure there will be,
Reality in retort then spoke forth truth:
In *Brain Lighting* the artist must define new perspectives of application for brain-computer interfaces – and disseminate.

In Teutonic tones set forth as sweet text, tells,
No restriction to artistic freedom should there be,
Following sounds, soothing words, French accent doth speak,
Sensitive treatment for sure there will be,
Reality in retort then spoke forth truth:
In *C3HARME* the artist must explore the ongoing research and the produced materials from another point of view – and disseminate.

In Teutonic tones set forth as sweet text, tells,
No restriction to artistic freedom should there be,
Following sounds, soothing words, French accent doth speak,
Sensitive treatment for sure there will be,
Reality in retort then spoke forth truth:
In *Car2HC* the artist must identify completely new interaction forms between cars and humans. And disseminate?

In Teutonic tones set forth as sweet text, tells,
No restriction to artistic freedom should there be,
Following sounds, soothing words, French accent doth speak,
Sensitive treatment for sure there will be,
Reality in retort then spoke forth truth:
In *CAST* the artist must provide artistic insight into a high-tech t-shirt making it appealing for both patients and cardiologists – and disseminate.

In Teutonic tones set forth as sweet text, tells,
No restriction to artistic freedom should there be,
Following sounds, soothing words, French accent doth speak,
Sensitive treatment for sure there will be,
Reality in retort then spoke forth truth:
In *Create IoT* the artist must engage in enquiry around project themes, science, technology and data – and disseminate.

In Teutonic tones set forth as sweet text, tells,
No restriction to artistic freedom should there be,
Following sounds, soothing words, French accent doth speak,
Sensitive treatment for sure there will be,
Reality in retort then spoke forth truth:
In *CUPIDO* the artist must enable the scientists to investigate a radically new approach to their routine technologies – and disseminate.

In Teutonic tones set forth as sweet text, tells,
No restriction to artistic freedom should there be,
Following sounds, soothing words, French accent doth speak,
Sensitive treatment for sure there will be,
Reality in retort then spoke forth truth:
In *DANCE* the artist must engage in visualizing the artistic expression of dance movements through 3D printing. And disseminate?

In Teutonic tones set forth as sweet text, tells,
No restriction to artistic freedom should there be,
Following sounds, soothing words, French accent doth speak,
Sensitive treatment for sure there will be,
Reality in retort then spoke forth truth:
In *EMBODIES* the artist must integrate project methods into his artwork and extend the scope of those methods in doing so. And disseminate?

In Teutonic tones set forth as sweet text, tells,
No restriction to artistic freedom should there be,
Following sounds, soothing words, French accent doth speak,
Sensitive treatment for sure there will be,
Reality in retort then spoke forth truth:
In *ExaFLOW* the artist must bring new and innovative thoughts regarding image compression and feature detection – and disseminate.

In Teutonic tones set forth as sweet text, tells,
No restriction to artistic freedom should there be,
Following sounds, soothing words, French accent doth speak,
Sensitive treatment for sure there will be,
Reality in retort then spoke forth truth:
In *Flora Robotics* the artist must explore the possibilities of human-plant-robot interactions. And disseminate?

In Teutonic tones set forth as sweet text, tells,
No restriction to artistic freedom should there be,
Following sounds, soothing words, French accent doth speak,
Sensitive treatment for sure there will be,
Reality in retort then spoke forth truth:
In *GROW* the artist must engage in public understanding of science –
and disseminate.

In Teutonic tones set forth as sweet text, tells,
No restriction to artistic freedom should there be,
Following sounds, soothing words, French accent doth speak,
Sensitive treatment for sure there will be,
Reality in retort then spoke forth truth:
In *hackAIR* the artist must provide a totally new perspective on the
design of sensors and their cases – and disseminate.

In Teutonic tones set forth as sweet text, tells,
No restriction to artistic freedom should there be,
Following sounds, soothing words, French accent doth speak,
Sensitive treatment for sure there will be,
Reality in retort then spoke forth truth:
In *Human Brain Project* the artist must address complex interactive
systems and their potential future impact. And disseminate?

In Teutonic tones set forth as sweet text, tells,
No restriction to artistic freedom should there be,
Following sounds, soothing words, French accent doth speak,
Sensitive treatment for sure there will be,
Reality in retort then spoke forth truth:
In *Internet of Food and Farming 2020* the artist must engage in
producing prototypes as a step to productisation. And disseminate?

In Teutonic tones set forth as sweet text, tells,
No restriction to artistic freedom should there be,
Following sounds, soothing words, French accent doth speak,
Sensitive treatment for sure there will be,
Reality in retort then spoke forth truth:
In *MagicShoes* the artist must help us to gain an understanding on the
social acceptability of the new concepts presented. And disseminate?

In Teutonic tones set forth as sweet text, tells,
No restriction to artistic freedom should there be,
Following sounds, soothing words, French accent doth speak,
Sensitive treatment for sure there will be,
Reality in retort then spoke forth truth:
In *MoeWE* the artist must provide a new perspective and potentially new approaches towards greater aims. And disseminate?

In Teutonic tones set forth as sweet text, tells,
No restriction to artistic freedom should there be,
Following sounds, soothing words, French accent doth speak,
Sensitive treatment for sure there will be,
Reality in retort then spoke forth truth:
In *MONICA* the artist must work on the user engagement. And disseminate?

In Teutonic tones set forth as sweet text, tells,
No restriction to artistic freedom should there be,
Following sounds, soothing words, French accent doth speak,
Sensitive treatment for sure there will be,
Reality in retort then spoke forth truth:
In *Mont-Blanc3* the artist must exploit project data. And disseminate?

In Teutonic tones set forth as sweet text, tells,
No restriction to artistic freedom should there be,
Following sounds, soothing words, French accent doth speak,
Sensitive treatment for sure there will be,
Reality in retort then spoke forth truth:
In *NIRVANA* the artist must turn human communication through machines into something more human. And disseminate?

In Teutonic tones set forth as sweet text, tells,
No restriction to artistic freedom should there be,
Following sounds, soothing words, French accent doth speak,
Sensitive treatment for sure there will be,
Reality in retort then spoke forth truth:
In *OLA* the artist must – disseminate.

In Teutonic tones set forth as sweet text, tells,
No restriction to artistic freedom should there be,
Following sounds, soothing words, French accent doth speak,
Sensitive treatment for sure there will be,
Reality in retort then spoke forth truth:
In *Programmable Matter* the artist must think about applications in the artistic field. And disseminate?

In Teutonic tones set forth as sweet text, tells,
No restriction to artistic freedom should there be,
Following sounds, soothing words, French accent doth speak,
Sensitive treatment for sure there will be,
Reality in retort then spoke forth truth:
In *QuNet* the artist must explore, at the artistic level, radically new scientific ideas. And disseminate?

In Teutonic tones set forth as sweet text, tells,
No restriction to artistic freedom should there be,
Following sounds, soothing words, French accent doth speak,
Sensitive treatment for sure there will be,
Reality in retort then spoke forth truth:
In *SPARK* the artist must be involved with participatory design sessions to increase the creative potential of the design team. And disseminate?

In Teutonic tones set forth as sweet text, tells,
No restriction to artistic freedom should there be,
Following sounds, soothing words, French accent doth speak,
Sensitive treatment for sure there will be,
Reality in retort then spoke forth truth:
In *TELMI* the artist must – disseminate.

In Teutonic tones set forth as sweet text, tells,
No restriction to artistic freedom should there be,
Following sounds, soothing words, French accent doth speak,
Sensitive treatment for sure there will be,
Reality in retort then spoke forth truth:
In *Urban Lab* the artist must make processes of urban development visible. And disseminate?

In Teutonic tones set forth as sweet text, tells,
No restriction to artistic freedom should there be,
Following sounds, soothing words, French accent doth speak,
Sensitive treatment for sure there will be,
Reality in retort then spoke forth truth:
In *Design for Virtuosity* the artist must use e-textiles to craft new digital musical interfaces. And disseminate?

In Teutonic tones set forth as sweet text, tells,
No restriction to artistic freedom should there be,
Following sounds, soothing words, French accent doth speak,
Sensitive treatment for sure there will be,
Reality in retort then spoke forth truth:
In *VisualMusic* the artist must create content to populate the marketplace with all kinds of proven clips and themes. And disseminate?

In Teutonic tones set forth as sweet text, tells,
No restriction to artistic freedom should there be,
Following sounds, soothing words, French accent doth speak,
Sensitive treatment for sure there will be,
Reality in retort then spoke forth truth:
In *WEAR* the artist must translate data visualisations in a truly immersive end user experiences. And disseminate?

In Teutonic tones set forth as sweet text, tells,
No restriction to artistic freedom should there be,
Following sounds, soothing words, French accent doth speak,
Sensitive treatment for sure there will be,
Reality in retort then spoke forth truth:
In *weDRAW* the artist must provide the sound, music, or visual content for the serious game – and disseminate.

In Teutonic tones set forth as sweet text, tells,
No restriction to artistic freedom should there be,
Following sounds, soothing words, French accent doth speak,
Sensitive treatment for sure there will be,
Reality in retort then spoke forth truth:
In *WEKIT* the artist must use smart glasses as a medium of expression, creating holographic exhibits or performances. And disseminate?

In Teutonic tones set forth as sweet text, tells,
No restriction to artistic freedom should there be,
Following sounds, soothing words, French accent doth speak,
Sensitive treatment for sure there will be,
Shieldmaiden's fair gentle sword's fatal kiss to Goliath doth blow,
STARTS the bleeding, prelude to – eternal sleeping.

"It is a clear advantage to the Soviet Union
that they have, right at the top of the
political and administrative trees,
a fairly high proportion of men
with scientific and technical training."

C.P. Snow, 1961

Roy Ascott STARTS to Express Concern about STARTS

The artist Roy Ascott, claimed as being involved in some way in the VERTIGO network, has arrived, and now wishes to express his concerns about STARTS:

"In present day cultural terms the enemy is habit – the passive, uncritical repetition or acceptance of behaviours, opinions, perceptions and values, and the enshrining as verities, metaphors that have passed their sell-by date. Habit is the enemy of art, impeding the search for new ways of being. The syncretic process is always an assault on habit, confounding the certainties and orthodoxies of unconsidered homogenizing convention."

It is a strange thing that Roy Ascott should agree to have his name associated with STARTS which is just another sign of the contemporary art world aligning itself with the undemocratic forces of global capitalism. The STARTS platform is a supporting mechanism for the European Union's homogenising agenda and its pursuit of neoliberalism – (rightly) described by John Berger as economic fascism.

STARTS has continuity with past uses of art to legitimise those who hold illegitimate power – specifically in this case the European Commission and people from the world of STEM, who come together in an alliance with artists (all partiers being caught-up in *habit*) that will ultimately be proven to be another demonstration of the *banality of evil*.

Totalitarianism in all its forms must be opposed – even when it is found in places like the *City of the Golden Stars*. Especially when it is found in the *City of the Golden Stars* – surely you were not expecting a repeat performance complete with uniforms, marching, strange waves and salutes, and such forth? The sentinels of the mind are now armed against such dangers, so different strategies and tactics must be deployed – the wolf donning sheep's clothing slips through the sentinels unnoticed, and thus a new form of tyranny then takes hold.

"To be corrupted by totalitarianism one does not have to live in a totalitarian country. The mere prevalence of certain ideas can spread a poison. And if thought corrupts language, language can also corrupt thought. Defenceless villages are bombarded from the air, the inhabitants driven out into the countryside. This is called – pacification. When one watches some tired hack on the platform, mechanically repeating the familiar phrases – blood stained tyranny, free peoples of the world, stand shoulder to shoulder – one often has a curious feeling, one is watching some kind of dummy. The appropriate noises are coming out of his larynx, but his brain is not involved. This reduced state of consciousness if not indispensable, is at any rate favourable to political conformity."

That was George Orwell speaking.

"Learn to think and judge for yourself, responsibly. Don't accept everything without criticism and as absolutely true. The biggest mistake of my life was that I believed everything faithfully which came from the top, and I didn't dare to have the least bit of doubt about the truth of that which was presented to me."

Who was that who just spoke? It was a voice from the grave. You should listen and take note. Or will you just accept what people in the European Commission say, and believe and accept it as true? Will you believe and accept as true what STARTS will say? Will you believe and accept as true what the European Parliament say? Why should you? Is it because they speak from a position of authority? Is it because you want to believe?

Now we will give you the name of the person who spoke. His words are that which he wrote to his children, as a farewell, in the period between being sentenced to death and his execution. We will give his title and his name: SS-Obersturmbannführer Rudolf Höss, Commandant of the Auschwitz extermination camp. Höss never showed any genuine remorse for his horrific crimes and did not renounced or condemn National Socialism.

If they are not creating a United States of Europe (USE), then what are they building that requires them to induce changes in social and individual behaviour?

John Berger STARTS to Comment on the European Union's Migrant-based Economy

One of those people from the art world that we mentioned previously, whose writings are worth reading, is John Berger:

"Until recently, most emigration from Portugal was illegal. Spanish and French frontiers had to be crossed clandestinely. Smugglers in Lisbon arranged such crossings. Their fee was $350 per person. Having paid this sum, many would-be migrants were cheated. They were led into the mountains just across the Spanish frontier and left there. Totally disoriented, some died of starvation and exposure: some found their way back, $350 the poorer. $350 at this time represented as much as a year's earnings for the average Portuguese peasant. In 1964 the average per capita income in Portugal – an average which included the incomes of the upper class – was $370."

That was John Berger writing in 1975. The problem continues to this day. Now the illegal migrants are the *others*, from *underdeveloped* countries outside the European Union. They are subjected to the same exploitation and abuse that John Berger described as being inflicted on people who, today, are European Union citizens; people who can now legally migrate from the *underdeveloped* parts of the European Union, to the excessively wealthy parts. Only the problem is aggravated this time by the European Union's homogenisation agenda, which rides roughshod over the wishes of the peoples' of the Member States (even those democratically expressed!) to protect their national identity and their social cohesion.

In the European Union there are only migrants from outside the European Union. Citizens of the European Union are free to live and work anywhere they choose within the European Union so in theory there are no migrants within the European Union. In reality though, the European Union has two types of people who choose to work outside their country of origin, in another Member State of the European Union: there are internal migrants and there are mobile workers.

The latter tend to be professional middle class people who take up well paid jobs, and who live in middle class areas. The former are mostly traditional migrants moving from the *underdeveloped* countries within the European Union to the advanced economies, doing what migrants have always done – the jobs that the people in the advanced economies no longer want to do. Sometimes they do skilled jobs that people in the advanced economies would do, if only employers would invest in their training. In both cases, employers use the migrants to keep wages down, or to avoid investing in training, as has always been the case. And, as many previous examples show, the response from the indigenous population is animosity, resentment, and rather familiar xenophobic or racist comments – the door is open to right-wing extremists. Whose fault is this?

The policies that lead to this circumstance were never put to an electorate. They were decided behind closed doors by people far removed from the impacts of the policies, people who are ideological, and who have rendered citizens as mere objects, represented by data (economic statistics), and who have to be manipulated to achieve ends over which the people have no say. None of these *far-removed from reality* technocrats will ever be called to account for their actions or punished (for implementing these policies) through the mechanisms of a change of government in accordance with the fundamental principle of democracy – equality of citizens and their right to political self-determination.

The type of system that implements policies over which ordinary people have no control and which they cannot change has a name – it is a totalitarian system. No amount of dressing-up in fine words about democracy, European Union citizens rights, European values, representation through the European Parliament, can hide the fact that the European Union is a totalitarian state in the making, with a governance structure like that of the Soviet Union, where people were free – apparently!

No artist will solve the social problems created by unaccountable technocrats. These are political problems and can only be solved through politics. DG CONNECT's STARTS artists will apparently be inventing Apps to solve the social problems that the European Commission is creating – such is the technocentric nature of DG CONNECT.

Ironically, both the migrant and the mobile professional worker might well though, encounter artists, those practicing the Relational Aesthetic, which is supported by governments and businesses alike as a soothing balm to deal with the fracturing that occurs in society and the enterprise as a consequence of the actions of organisations such as the European Commission – DG CONNECT – and their relentless undemocratic pursuit of neoliberal policies.

Thus are enemies manufactured – both internal and external – to which *otherness* is then applied, and to whom blame is then attached for the increasing woes of a failing institution that is the author of its own problems. It is, they say, all the fault of the right-wing populists, and *others* (Muslims?) from outside the realms of European civilisation, which are polluting the purity of the cultural and social DNA of the European Union.

And no-one is allowed to criticise the European Union – lest they too be branded right-wing populists, or, external hostiles.

"The evidence shows that the engineers were both the most committed and, relative to the general population of students, the strongest group among the Nazis."

Diego Gambetta and Steffen Hertog, 2016

Jürgen Habermas STARTS to Express Concerns about the European Commission

Jürgen Habermas speaks:

"Key decisions are being taken in the European Union by the Council, the European Commission and European Central Bank – in other words, the very institutions that are either insufficiently legitimated to take such decisions or lack any democratic basis. This technocratic hollowing out of democracy is the result of a neoliberal pattern of market-deregulation policies. The balance between politics and the market has come out of sync, at the cost of the welfare state.

"The European Commission accords the expansion of steering capacities priority over a corresponding enlargement of the basis for legitimation also in the medium term. Thus the delayed democratisation is presented as a promise in the manner of a light at the end of the tunnel."

Will the light ever be seen? We refer you to the statement: the history of Europe is a history of European Unions, but history does not unfold according to predictable patterns!

STARTS a Consideration of Dishonesty in Scientific Research

Nina Mazar and Dan Ariely will now speak with one voice:

"Ethics research, including our own work, has shown that dishonesty is not about good versus bad people, rather it is primarily about conflicts of interest and motivated reasoning. Dishonest actions penetrate the most mundane of situations and are committed by ordinary people that have moral standards and think highly of themselves in terms of being honest and exemplar members of society. Yet, when facing a conflict-of-interest situation in which people are tempted to give in to selfish motives at the expense of crossing the boundaries of what they usually consider morally acceptable, they can find *perfectly valid* reasons for these actions. Such motivated reasoning allows people to stretch moral boundaries without feeling bad about themselves or even registering the immorality of their conduct."

Mazar and Ariely have discovered through their research the following:

- Dishonesty is not about a few bad apples.

- Virtually everybody is dishonest but only by a limited amount. Dishonesty is guided by one's ability for motivated reasoning in conflicts of interest.

- Motivated reasoning and thus, dishonesty, is increased in situations in which the consequences of one's actions are less direct.

- Motivated reasoning and thus, dishonesty, is decreased through timed moral reminders."

Any thoughts on the implications for STARTS, for DG CONNECT, for the European Commission, for all that decision-making and policy making that takes place in the *City of the Golden Stars*, for all those experts providing advice, for all those artists participating in STARTS, where the consequences of people's actions are far out-of-sight?

STARTS the Pursuit of Utopian Dreams – Again!

Now to Yasmin we do turn, and we do tune our ears to listen-in, to some utopian fantasy being there played out:

"Have faith that with techno-art, we are forging a hammer that will make itself felt in the effort to construct a more perfect world."

You are far, very far, beyond your sell-by date! Still revelling in art rooted in the past that has now about it, a uniformity that tells a different tale which your dreaming – your fantasising – cannot hide. At least to those able to take a critical look – *new Leonardos* now look away!

"We also found evidence that the engineers were ideologically more committed than the lawyers in their decision to join the Nazis, as well as more willing to incur higher risks."

Diego Gambetta and Steffen Hertog, 2016

Claudio Radaelli STARTS to Express Concerns about the European Commission

Claudio Radaelli speaks:

"The political system of the European Union, notably the European Commission, is in the firing line. At stake is the allegation of being a political system ruled by technocrats who ignore the basic thrust of democracy. While democracy is based on legitimate consensus, free elections and participation, technocracy recognises expertise as the sole basis of authority and power."

"The thorny one is research for art - what
Picasso considered as gathering reference
materials rather than research proper,
also known as research with a small 'r'.
Research where the end product is an artefact - where
the thinking is embodied in the artefact,
where the goal is not primarily
communicable knowledge, in the sense of verbal
communication, but in the sense of
visual communication."

Christopher Frayling, 1993

Human-centred! What do you mean?

The European Commission, through STARTS, is wheeling out, once again, the term human-centred. It does this from time to time!

The term is Marxist in origin – you will need to understand Marx's philosophy on the meaningfulness of human work and the destructive nature of capitalist's division of labour (on the spirit of human work) to understand this. Basically we are, here, in the realms of alienation.

In the 1980s a Marxist engineer coined the term human-centred to describe a technology (and its use context) that does not result in alienation. Since then the term has been widely (mis)used so that it has become suitably meaningless, and rendered something of a nonsense term – as evidenced through its use by DG CONNECT technocrats!

The phrase human-centred first appeared before European Commission technocrats in 1986 when they, for political reasons – under pressure from Trade Unions for neglecting what some call the Human Factor in manufacturing – funded a project with human-centred in the title. Following on from this, in 1990, there was a major study undertaken on Anthropocentric Production Systems, funded by the Forecasting and Assessment in Science and Technology (FAST) Programme, who advanced the concept as a strategic alternative to ... non-human-centred, non-Anthropocentric Production Systems? Notice the appearance of a duality – again!

This study had no significant impact, other than contributing to DG Research's slowly developing awareness that it needed to address human and organisational issues in its manufacturing research programmes. DG CONNECT's predecessor DG, ignored the report.

Since 1991 the term human-centred has popped up several times in European Commission documents. You have already encountered one example of this – STARTS I that began in 1995. Another example is the 2004 report with the title: *Experience and Application Research: Involving Users in the Development of Ambient Intelligence.*

The report argues that successful R&D in ambient intelligence needs a new approach based on the involvement of those that will be affected by the presence of such systems. This observation also applies to the later activity of developing and introducing new commercial ambient intelligence products and services.

The report notes that there is a belief that ambient intelligence will not be widely accepted and used, unless users are deeply involved in the shaping of these technologies. Developers need to do more than just bring new technologies to users to ask them what they think. A novel two-way relationship needs to be established between those that develop new technologies and those that use them. Users should be integrated into the processes of R&D, and new product creation and introduction. Users should be part of the innovation process, a source of ideas, and not just a resource to evaluate ideas generated by professionals.

Experience and Application Research was thus proposed as a means of addressing the challenge of creating a human-centred approach to R&D in ambient intelligence. Experience and Application Research would involve research, development and design by, with and for users. It would also cover research into methods and tools to enable this. A novel aspect of Experience and Application Research would be that it would involve users in all stages of R&D and all stages of the product development lifecycle, not just at the end phases as, for example, in more classical field trials or user testing of product.

Of particular note is that the report stresses that Experience and Application Research would be interdisciplinary research, creating and exploring new visions and undertaking pioneering research. It would also provide a bridge between the world of researchers, developers and designers on the one side, and the world of users on the other. The proposed work would be founded on the understanding that users vary, both across Europe, and across the globe. Furthermore, Experience and Application Research would provide the means of developing closer relationships with customers, and applying emerging industrial practices such as customisation and co-creation with customers. This, the report states, would help to improve industrial competitiveness and provide support for emerging industrial practices.

Work on this topic was funded in Framework Programme 6, IST Work Programme 2005-2006, Call 4. The IST vision at that time included bringing people to the foreground, to the centre of attention, including making technology adapt to people and businesses. To this end, the Call included a trial focused on Experience and Application Research, aiming at early user involvement, with use integrated into the research activities.

Notice those binaries, those dualities once again!

What we have noted is that most often, when the European Commission – usually DG CONNECT – mentions human-centredness, its meaning has been – vague, unspecific, unclear … One thing we can be sure of is that it has never been used in the context that it was originally introduced – by a Marxist engineer! Perhaps it should be!

Here is an American saying something about human-centred (as opposed to technology-centred – note the duality!) research issues, meaning what humans should expect, in connection with smart environments:

"In the context of human-computer interaction (HCI), a smart environment is one that adapts to the needs of the information consumer, in terms of input/output capabilities, as he/she moves and accesses information in a dynamically changing environment. Potential changes include the number of information consumers or information providers, or changes in location of the individual or objects in the environment. We can understand these changes as the context that defines the user's situation, whether it is in an office, home, car, airport, etc. The goal of our research should be to facilitate human-information interaction as well as human-human interaction. As such we can identify several goals for HCI in smart environments."

The paper we are quoting from then goes on to list several human-centred issues. We will mention just two: (i) control – when should the human or the environment initiate interaction? (ii) activities, not technology – people want to use technology to perform tasks, not use technology for its own sake.

Here is a European saying something about human-centred in the context of Information Systems Design:

"Regarding the humanisation of Information Systems (IS), a notion concerning the nature of the human being is a crucial element of the intellectual framework. As a consequence, within this kind of enquiry, the way humans are taken into account in IS development is dependent on the operationalisation of the IS designers' conceptualisations of users. With respect to human-centredness, attention should be paid to the fundamental qualities of people without any explicit or implicit domination of the other elements of IS, such as data, formal models and technical appliances, or managerial belief systems that treat humans instrumentally. This is necessary in order to conceptualise humans in their own right, and thus avoid the reduction of humans to something that exists only in relation to particular instrumental needs and purposes."

Reification and instrumental reason! Here is someone from DG CONNECT speaking:

"Artists can help shape a better relation of technology and humans and stimulate human-centred innovation through their transversal competencies and unconventional thinking."

Vagueness once again!

269

Here is someone from DG CONNECT's very own art-world bubble speaking:

"The aims of the STARTS project of the European Commission is to bring science, technology and the arts together to create new visions, collaborations and even solutions in accordance with the belief that the arts can make innovation more human-centred."

Vagueness yet again!

We now consider another European Commission document, this time from DG Research. We are referring to the NMP Workprogamme that contains the Call FP7-2013-NMP-ICT-FoF. Looking at the details of the Call, there is a topic with the title: *(FoF.NMP.2013-3) Workplaces of the future: the new people-centred production site.* Let us see what this was about.

This Call was concerned with the development of people-centred production facilities. In other words Anthropocentric Production Systems, or, alternatively, human-centred production systems if you prefer. This sounds familiar! They say in this Call that the workplaces of the future will give much more importance to the human dimension. Putting people at the centre of future factories will provide a stimulating environment for the employees, and make the most from their knowledge, skills and cultural background, in particular through life-long learning and training.

They also say in the Call that this approach would lead European manufacturing industry to make a qualitative leap towards new people-centred and knowledge-based production workplaces which take into account the constraints of the workforce, for example those of aged workers. The workplaces of the future should, therefore, be based on methodologies for enhancing flexible, safe and smart production where adequate levels of automation are applied, while maintaining a level of employment with highly satisfied and skilled workers and, at the same time, ensuring competitiveness.

They then go onto say that this strategy demands new concepts and solutions at factory level, both for existing and new production plants. Research activities therefore should be multidisciplinary and address several areas. They then gave a list of topics for research. These included: new methods and technologies for an optimised use of workers' knowledge and cognitive capabilities; new methods and technologies for enhanced cooperation of the human operators and the production systems; methodologies and tools for people-centred production to guarantee an efficient transition from current to future worker task/role definitions and multi-skilled involvement of individual workers with expanded responsibility in broader sets of operations.

It is a funny thing is life! What they describe above is exactly what we and several others were saying in the mid 1980s and the early 1990s. We participated in a major (aforementioned) European Commission study in 1990, funded by the Forecasting in Science and Technology Programme, where we addressed these matters. But we also did more than this, for we worked on these so called new methods, technologies, tools etc, sometimes with European Commission funding, over a 10 year period from 1985 to 1995. And no-one was very much interested! But 20 years later they are interested! What chance do you think that they bothered to even find out what the state-of-the-art is in this area?

Here is a story. In July 2012 we attended the launch of the above Call. We authored a European Commission report that was also published to coincide with the event. We encountered the person who was a project officer in one of those projects where we were addressing in the early 1990s, what the Call wanted to be addressed in 2013. I mentioned this old project. He looked blank for a while, then suddenly he recalled that he had been a project officer for a project that had addressed, 20 years early, what they were now going to address again, claiming as they did so that it was new!

Here is another story. A year later we were in Vilnius, attending the ICT 2013 event. A middle-level manager from DG CONNECT proudly told us that: "the European Commission has no memory." This is the contempt in which they hold the European Union taxpayer! Now you know what people mean when they talked about the United Kingdom being shackled to the European Union, and the need to break free. Member States do need to break free, for the European Commission is destroying Europe, but is using propaganda to deceive people into thinking that they are a positive benefit to Europe. We helped write some of that propaganda!

Here is another excerpt from a DG CONNECT ICT Work Programme from 2007. This time it is the FET PROACTIVE Call, Science of Complex Systems for socially intelligent ICT:

"Projects should indicate how efficient data gathering, simulation, prediction and control techniques can lead to more human-centric systems, can harness collective intelligence or behaviour, can support businesses and policy makers with best practices that have a clear and definable societal and economic added value or can contribute to solving long-term challenges such as sustainable growth, energy efficiency, or social inclusion."

See the term human-centric appears once again. You would think that, by now, they would know how to make technology human-centred.

Here is a fictitious social scientist speaking:

"But it has all been done before! Human-centred, people-centred, anthropocentric, as well as that which did not use such labels, both in the sphere of design, and in the area of manufacturing! What is the matter with you STEM people? What is the matter with you DG CONNECT people? What is the matter with you artists? Have you taken leave of your senses? Or are you all suffering from a deficit – a research integrity deficit?"

Why consult with the existing research literature when you can be reckless and waste millions of European Union taxpayers' money without ever been called to account for such contempt, arrogance, and ignorance?

If you care to think slowly (do you?) about the matter of human-centredness, then you will realise that most technology is human-centred – anthropocentric – in the sense that it is designed for humans to fulfil human purposes. Which is part of the problem!

Think of a car. This is most definitely human-centred. It is designed for humans – not dogs, rats, sheep, etc. It is shaped to appeal to human aesthetic senses. Its internal design reflects the human form. Controls are designed to reflect the abilities and limitations of humans. Apply traditional *knobs and dials* ergonomics to the dashboard design and you can make it more human-centred. The car itself fulfils a human-centred purpose – to overcome the mobility limitations of humans. It is also representative of a human-centred mind-set – human domination over the world, over nature. Over other people!

So the techno-centric technocrats with their love of dualities and separations, with their Enlightenment separation of world and mind, and their rendering of humans as mere objects, just numbers for the counting – they think that they are going produce human-centredness, which will be – just another grand overarching narrative that will be human-centred in a negative sense! They always are!

Excuse us if we now laugh out-loud – quite a lot – and then say emphatically in response to this nonsense – you are going to produce just what you always produce, because your Enlightenment cup is full, and you cannot fill a cup that is already full! Just therefore pretend – for this you certainly do, quite a lot!

The first step to successful (excellent?) research must surely be – knowing and understanding the state-of-the-art! And this is not about prioritising text over objects and process. You need to look beyond texts.

Getting your concepts clear is also important! That too is a matter of knowledge and understanding! Or perhaps you too wish to sprinkle adjectives into your reports without having to do the hard work involved in research? Human-centred is one such adjective. Here is a selection of further adjectives for you to use: excellent; cutting-edge; innovative; novel; transformative; inventive; interdisciplinary; outstanding; new; better; unconventional; creative; imaginative. Be imaginative and add your own favourite adjectives …

There is growing evidence that half or more of the published results in some fields are not reproducible. Oh dear!

"We observe a striking discrepancy
between what participants in artistic
interventions value from the experience,
and the types of impacts policymakers
or managers without
experience in the area expect evaluation studies
to document."

Ariane Berthoin Antal and
Anka Strauss, 2016

An Emerging Role for Design Methods in Transdisciplinary Practices! Or Not?

Oh Dear! What have we got here? Once more we tune-in to some art-science lovers speaking – whispering sweet nothings:

"Frayling (1993) argued that there is not much difference between art and science. He said that the history of institutions and media has shaped stereotypes that have mistakenly separated art and science practices; for instance, in their practice, artists do research activities and scientists do creative activities (p. 3). For these reasons, integrating artists and scientists in collaborative work is a cultural and institutional challenge."

Did Frayling say, or even imply the above? Perhaps we should rewrite the text as:

"We believe Frayling (1993) argued that there is not much difference between art and science. We believe he said that the history of institutions and media has shaped stereotypes that have mistakenly separated art and science practices; for instance, in their practice, artists do research activities and scientists do creative activities (p. 3). For these reasons, we believe that integrating artists and scientists in collaborative work is a cultural and institutional challenge."

The first quote is taken from a paper entitled: *An Emerging Role for Design Methods in Transdisciplinary Practices*. If there ever was a paper in need of critique, this surely is it! Such a critique could start from this question: do some research-related publications that claim to address the topic of x-disciplinarity, demonstrate flawed thinking because the people writing such papers lack sufficient knowledge and as a result present false truth claims, inaccurate facts, or demonstrably inapplicable research methods?

We leave that critique for another publication, and limit ourselves here to the consideration of one seemingly false truth claim evident in the very short extract we have quoted.

As for Fraying (1993) this is a paper with the title: *Research in Art and Design*. We encourage you to obtain a copy and to assess for yourself whether in fact Frayling did argue …

If you do look at the paper, you will discover that Frayling mentions several stereotypes: the lunatic artist struggling to express himself; the designer as boffin (roughly Second World War); the designer as solitary style warrior (1980s); the mad scientist; and, the humanitarian scientist heroically pioneering advances in – medicine for example. The myths that they represent have been created for several reasons. Frayling mentions that they are often associated with literature and film, but does not go into detail of why that is so.

There may be many reasons, but one is certainly this: novels, films, and TV programmes that depict the lives of real people, are mostly located in the expressive medium, and what is portrayed in not usually fully historically accurate. Instead, what is presented is that which is emotionally attractive, stimulating, entertaining, and so forth. Put another way – fiction is more appealing that non-fiction. Boring everyday characters do not make for good commercial art. You will even discover that often, factual history programmes are also bound-up with fictions concerning people – it is how history is brought to life. Journalists do something similar when reporting the news, otherwise it would be boring. We are talking about embellishment, artistic licence, dramatisation, caricature, etc.

One of the biggest and most obvious examples of a myth, are the populist beliefs that constitute the life story of Leonardo da Vinci. It is mostly a fabrication! Interestingly, it is the white-frocked seekers of objective truth, and those in tow (artists), who seem the most convinced that the Leonardo tale is a true-to-life story! It is though, more than a fabrication. It is a distorting narrative, constructed by old men – regardless of their age or gender – that provides a justification for the perpetuation of a dominant patriarchal grand overarching narrative. In effect what we have, are two male dominated elitist groups creating a new male dominated elitist group (incipient totalitarians intent on achieving the embedding of their ideology in society) consisting of people who naively believe that by retreating into a past that never existed, they can deal with challenges that people from this mythical past would find incomprehensible. It is also a Euro-centric ideology engaging in neo-colonialism – culture used in the struggle for power by some of the former colonial powers and their allies. If we cannot conquer the world on our own and make it European, let us do it together – that is to say, through the European Union!

With the above context in mind, we turn now to the claim that the history of institutions and media has shaped stereotypes that have mistakenly separated art and science practices. No where in Frayling's paper will you find a statement that states or implies this. What Frayling does, is just to point out the stereotypes mentioned above, and to state something that most will now be quite familiar with – that which is explored in several philosophy and social science books. This can be put quite simply: intuitions, subjective judgements, inspiration, imagination, tacit knowledge, skilled interpretation, and thus forth, play a far more important role in science than scientists have hitherto been willing to acknowledge. These are in essence the reasons why positivism is discredited. And we add here, that all these features apply to all disciplines that involve creative activities, in fact, all creative activities, and in this sense there is no difference between any of the creative disciplines, be they based in the natural sciences, the social sciences, the humanities, or the arts!

It is in this way that Frayling implies a similarity between the artist and the research scientist, while also including a caveat that is not mentioned in the paper we are critiquing. The caveat is this: while science may be close to art and design in the sense stated above, science is by no means identical with art and design. And he gives a good example of one way in which art is significantly different from science: "the artist, he writes, "is not in the business of unambiguous communication." Hence all that interpretation that goes on, surrounding the meaning of artworks.

Now we ask: if art and science are so similar, as claimed, why would there be any cultural or institutional challenges involved in integrating artists and scientists in collaborative work? Surely if there are such challenges, it is partly because they are so dissimilar?

As for the claim that artists sometimes do research – this is true. This is what Frayling's paper is about – what exactly constitutes research in the context of art and design in an academic setting? He also mentions two well known, but now very dated examples, of artists that might be considered to have done some scientific research – Stubbs and Constable. But Frayling has no concerns about the cultural and institutional challenges of integrating artists and scientists. This is not on his agenda. He does however state that art and design teaching in the United Kingdom were institutionally separated, in the nineteenth-century, from the mainstream university sector. And the reason why he wrote his paper was because this institutional separation came to end in the 1990s when art and design schools were integrated into the university system. This one can say is the overall context for Frayling's paper.

Hence we can say:

Frayling (1993) did not argue that there is not much difference between art and science. He did say that certain stereotypes for artists, designers and scientists exist in popular (often mass) media, but he did not say that the history of institutions and media has shaped stereotypes that have mistakenly separated art and science practice. He did say that in their practice, artists do research activities and scientists do creative activities. But he did not say that for these reasons, integrating artists and scientists in collaborative work is a cultural and institutional challenge. He did imply however that the integration of art and design schools into the mainstream university system did pose some institutional challenges, especially with regard to what constitutes research in art and design.

And finally – what are we to make of all this? Do we have here an example of people engaging in a highly subjective interpretation that turns a piece of text into a mirror of what people believe? In other words relativism! Or is it another example of scientific reduction to ignorance? Or perhaps, something else is at work? We refer you to other content in this work that you now read. Or, we suggest that you state what you believe, and just leave it at that. The choice is yours.

If you are wondering what we are referring to when we talk about subjective interpretation and relativism, then we are in the fields of hermeneutics and philosophical hermeneutics. In other words, we are in the domains of knowing that is called the humanities. And according to the argumentation presented in *An Emerging Role for Design Methods in Transdisciplinary Practices*, humanities subjects need to be integrated into transdisciplinary approaches that address problems denoted as complex, but evidently we note, not integrated into the development of the processes in which transdisciplinary approaches will be practised!

New Leonardos in ignorance dwelling!

A 2006 Design Vision – Ignored!

The year is 2006. The month is March. The Framework Programme is FP6. The research programme is IST – Information Society Technologies. The Directorate-General is DG INFSO, now called DG CONNECT. A rose by any other name would still have thorns!

We are in a workshop that is part of the preparation for Framework Programme 7. Our task is to write the report about the results of this gathering which is a consultation exercise that produced a report – nothing more! Is that because a DG that is tasked with producing the future of European technology is techno-centric and just thinks about technology – more disciplinary idiocy? Why should European Union taxpayers have to fund this idiocy? They do not know that they are – neither do those who should know! That is because they are kept in the dark. Some call this *mushroom strategy*! Experts are told in the briefings at the start of an evaluation not to reveal to the Member State governments what transpires in an evaluation. That is because the European Commission do not want those who provide the money to know how poor the research evaluation process actually is. That is what you get with unaccountable power – deceit!

Back now to the report! What does it say about the assembled experts' deliberations and conclusions? It says many things actually, addressing trends and needs, but also recognising that technology often does not provide a sustainable competitive advantage! More is needed and that more resides in the area of product research, design and development, a capability that is in fact an area where achieving excellence is difficult and hard to copy, not least because much of it is invisible. Apple proves the point!

The report also notes that the emotional dimension of products is assuming greater significance and there is evidence that forward thinking companies are hiring a more diverse range of disciplines to work on product design and development, for example, psychologists, sociologists, and anthropologists. It also says that – here we go again! – a human-centred approach should be developed, building on Europe's humanistic traditions, which implies that the research agenda is not just purely technological. A strategy based on development of a human-centred design and development method, with human-centred technologies, is needed, and the challenge will be to operationalise the meaning of human-centred within the context of technologies for product design and virtualisation.

Furthermore the report also recognises that people, as just about everyone would agree, are central to the success of product design and development, for they bring skills, creativity, knowledge, judgement, insights, emotions, understandings, experiences, etc. to the process of bringing new and improved products to market. But this sentiment has been expressed many times before, and now actions are needed that fully reflect this philosophy; actions that will involve re-appraising some fundamental and taken for granted assumptions about design, and the development of radically new and different product design and development processes.

Evidently from the above, the failure to respond to this call to arms and the vision set forth, and the ignorance of all past efforts to address these matters, leads one to the conclusion about DG CONNECT and its camp-followers!

Can you see, all those from the non-European (Union) nations of the world, how to exploit this circumstance for your own advantage by letting loose the forces of creative destruction! DG CONNECT will not know what is happening to them. They do not know how to tackle this kind of research. STARTS demonstrates this fact very clearly!

"Researchers steeped in critical management theory have not yet participated in the conversation. Such colleagues would certainly challenge many of the current assumptions about the dynamics of artistic interventions, leading to new questions and different interpretations about what is happening when people, practices and products from the world of the arts enter the world of the organisation."

Ariane Berthoin Antal , Jill Woodilla
and Ula Johansson Sköldberg, 2016

Pierre Bourdieu STARTS to Express Concern about STARTS

Time now to hear from another one of those people who have written about art, and whose works are worth reading! The sociologist Pierre Bourdieu:

"The threats to autonomy result from the increasingly greater interpenetration between the world of art and the world of money. I am thinking of new forms of sponsorship, of new alliances being established between certain economic enterprises and cultural producers; I am thinking, too, of the more and more frequent recourse of university research to sponsorship, and of the creation of educational institutions subordinated to business. But the grip or empire of economy over artistic or scientific work is also exercised inside the field itself, through the control of the means of production and distribution, and even of the instances of consecration. Producers attached to the major cultural bureaucracies are increasingly forced to accept and adopt norms and constraints linked to the requirements of the market and, especially, to pressure exerted more or less strongly and directly by advertisers; and they tend more or less unconsciously to constitute as a universal measure of intellectual accomplishment those forms of intellectual activity to which they are condemned by their conditions of work. One could ask whether the division into two markets characteristic of the fields of cultural production since the middle of the nineteenth-century, with on the one side the narrow field of producers for producers, and on the other side the field of mass production and industrial literature, is not now threatening to disappear, since the logic of commercial production tends more and more to assert itself over *avant-garde* production."

When art and money become one, become part of the neoliberalism that is destroying society and the planet, part of a rampant global capitalism that is increasingly not subject to democratic control and accountability, then the voice of criticism becomes mute, and the result is a bland universality that speaks only of surrender to the power of money – this you will find is what STARTS will produce, what some in the world of the art-science lovers, the art-technology-lovers, are already producing! But you can always pretend! START by rewriting art history. That is happening as well!

A 1994 Design Vision – Ignored!

The year is 1994. The month is June. The Framework Programme is – we have no idea, nor do we care!

By June 1994 we had been working on Anthropocentric Production Systems and human-centred technologies since 1983. We came to the *City of the Golden Stars* in 1987 because we knew even then, that DG CONNECT, in the form of one of its predecessors, posed a serious threat to the peoples of the European Union – the European Economic Community as it was then known. A rose by any other name would still have thorns!

This time it is a book that we refer to – our book: *Agile Manufacturing: Forging New Frontiers*. We direct your attention to this statement:

"Developing and maintaining a competitive edge requires that we continually outperform our competitors in critical areas. And our systems design and implementation processes are a critical area. In fact, we could argue that this is one of the last remaining areas where we have yet to focus serious attention on improving our capabilities."

Then we went on to state:

"It could be argued that in practice, our systems design and implementation performance is not a competitive issue. And of course this might still be largely correct in many of our companies. And that of course is exactly the point. If it is not now a competitive issue, then someone will eventually make it one. So why wait for someone else to start using their systems design and implementation processes to gain competitive advantage. We should start thinking now, about we what can do to make it harder for our competitors to compete with us."

It did of course become a competitive issue, not just relating to the design of internal systems, but also in relation to the design of products and services. We refer you to Apple, the company that has proved our point!

One gains a strong impression that those who now make so much noise in the issuing forth of STEAM are just what are called – in the terms of the *Technology Adoption Lifecycle* – the laggards. Likewise with STARTS – DG CONNECT are also laggards.

So what are – in the terms of the *Technology Adoption Lifecycle* – the innovators up to? The answer lies here: *post-Enlightenment, post-European era science and technology*.

STARTS a Consideration of the Implications of the Systemic Flaws in European Commission Funded Research

Bruce Alberts and his colleagues will now comment upon the systemic flaws US biomedical research:

"By many measures, the biological and medical sciences are in a golden age. This fact makes it all the more difficult to acknowledge that the current system contains systemic flaws that are threatening the future of this research field. A central flaw is the long-held assumption that the enterprise will constantly expand. As a result, there is now a severe imbalance between the dollars available for research and the still-growing scientific community in the United States. This imbalance has created a hypercompetitive atmosphere in which scientific productivity is reduced and promising careers are threatened.

"There are several damaging consequences of hyper-competition. One is the threat to high standards. As competition for jobs and promotions increases, the inflated value given to publishing in a small number of so-called *high impact* journals has put pressure on authors to rush into print, cut corners, exaggerate their findings, and overstate the significance of their work. Such publication practices, abetted by the hypercompetitive grant system and job market, are changing the atmosphere in many laboratories in disturbing ways. The recent worrisome reports of substantial numbers of research publications whose results cannot be replicated are likely symptoms of today's highly pressured environment for research. If through sloppiness, error, or exaggeration, the scientific community loses the public's trust in the integrity of its work, it cannot expect to maintain public support for science."

Any thoughts on the implications for STARTS, for DG CONNECT, for the European Commission, for all that decision-making and policy making that takes place in the *City of the Golden Stars*, for all those experts providing advice, for all those artists participating in STARTS?

"Although Horizon 2020 is being implemented in a difficult European funding policy context that is characterized in many countries by declining resources at the national and regional level, European Union funding must not become a mere replacement for the lack of funds at those levels."

That was a spokesperson for the German Federal Government speaking.

What he just said though, has already happened! The publicly funded research communities across Europe look to the *City of the Golden Stars* to plug the gap. This is what the European Commission want – it creates the

282

dependency culture that makes their role indispensable. That they fund poor quality research, and have created a hypercompetitive environment, with all its accompanying consequences, is irrelevant. They can rely on their independent experts to say – whatever it is that the European Commission wants them to say.

"The purpose of Newspeak was not only
to provide a medium of expression for the
worldview of and mental habits proper
of the devotees of Ingsoc, but to make all
other modes of thought impossible. It was
intended that when Newspeak had been
adopted once and for all and Oldspeak
forgotten, a heretical thought - that is, a thought
diverging from the principles of Ingsoc - should be
literally unthinkable, as least as far as
thought is dependent on words."

George Orwell, 1949

The British People Express Concern about the European Union, the European Parliament, the European Commission, and the European Courts of Justice

It is June 24th 2016. The result is clear: 51.89% voted for the United Kingdom to leave the European Union, 48.11% voted for the United Kingdom to remain in the European Union, with a voter turn-out of 72.21%. Come Monday afternoon, June 27th, it is clear from the live broadcasting of the proceedings of Parliament that the vast majority of MPs accept the result and will not block it.

The *Remainers* lost the argument – lost it! They thought it was about the economy, when it was really all about democracy.

The result is widely accepted – it could be no other way. There are no large-scale mass protests. A few though, mostly those doing well out of neoliberalism, or in receipt of European Union grants, including some artists and others from the world of culture, display their contempt for democracy – money is speaking! Some excessively rich people flaunt their wealth and privilege by pursuing excessively expensive court cases in the hope that they can prevent the British Government invoking Article 50, which would set the United Kingdom on course to leave the European Union.

The elitists who see it as their destiny to shape the future of Europe, regardless of what the ordinary people of Europe desire, want to hold a second referendum. They are in effect saying: you were allowed to choose and you chose wrong. Therefore choose again.

The economic Armageddon predicted for June 24th does not happen. People, with mouths disengaged from minds, say "next month's figures – just wait!" The following month they say the same, then the next month, then the next ... The issue of why experts are so often wrong does not trouble those with minds and mouths disconnected. They all share some knowledge that, to them is obvious – it is only the *stupid ones* who voted to leave who do not know. These are the uneducated ones! The working class people! The racists. The xenophobes! The old people! They all believed the lies! Only one-side told lies! The *knowing-ones* have no respect for the equality of citizens. Otherness! Then they reach for the explanation, the scapegoat – blame it on the right-wing populists. They do ...

Now we travel further back in time to May 2016. George Osborne, Chancellor of the Exchequer, is here to tell you about a report that HM Treasury published in the run-up to the referendum, predicting what would happen to the United Kingdom's economy, if the British people should dare to vote to leave the European Union. Here is George telling you what the experts say (or is he telling you what he told the experts to say?):

"This paper focuses on the immediate economic impact of a vote to leave and the two years that follow. Such a vote would change fundamentally not just the United Kingdom's relationship with the European Union, our largest trading partner, but also our relationship with the rest of the world. The instability and uncertainty that would trigger is assessed.

"The Treasury analysis in this document uses a widely-accepted modelling approach that looks at the impact of this uncertainty and instability on financial markets, households and businesses, as our economy transitions to a worse trading arrangement with the European Union.

"I am grateful to Professor Sir Charles Bean, one of our country's foremost economists and a former Deputy Governor of the Bank of England, who has reviewed this analysis and says that it 'provides reasonable estimates of the likely size of the short-term impact of a vote to leave on the UK economy'.

"The analysis in this document comes to a clear central conclusion: a vote to leave would represent an immediate and profound shock to our economy. That shock would push our economy into a recession and lead to an increase in unemployment of around 500,000, GDP would be 3.6% smaller, average real wages would be lower, inflation higher, sterling weaker, house prices would be hit and public borrowing would rise compared with a vote to remain.

"These findings sit within the range of what is now an overwhelming weight of published estimates for this short-term impact, which all find that United Kingdom GDP would be lower following a vote to leave.

"The analysis also presents a downside scenario, finding that the shock could be much more profound, meaning the effect on the economy would be worse still. The rise in uncertainty could be amplified, the volatility in financial markets more tumultuous, and the extent of the impact to living standards more acute. In this severe scenario, GDP would be 6% smaller, there would be a deeper recession, and the number of people made unemployed would rise by around 800,000 compared with a vote to remain. The hit to wages, inflation, house prices and borrowing would be larger. There is a credible risk that this more acute scenario could materialise."

Now we travel back to 2018. The two years are over and we note this –

most of what was predicted did not happen! The experts were not just wrong, but excessively wrong. The economy continued to grow, and some sectors experienced an economic boom. Why then were the experts so wrong? This is indeed a question. Any answers? Feel free to provide one according to your beliefs!

Here is Lord O'Neill, an economist and a *Remain* supporter, in an interview with the BBC Economics Editor, in January 2018, responding to a new report from Cambridge Econometrics, suggesting that growth across the United Kingdom could be on average only 3% lower by 2030 than it would have been if Britain remained within the European Union's Single Market and Customs Union:

"If that's the worst that Brexit will deliver, then I wouldn't worry about it. If it is only 3%, what's going on with the rest of the world – helping us – and with productivity improving, that will easily dwarf a 3% hit over 13 years, easily."

The governments own figures are different. They all show GDP lower, for all scenarios, with the effect varying across regions. But the figures are only provisional. *Ceteris paribus* applies. The government and businesses have agency, so other things will not be equal. Many, in any case, do not believe the figures. Why? George Osborne is the reason!

George Osborn is now, not only the former Chancellor of the Exchequer, but also a former politician – the report cost him his political career! And the point is this: if the British people had not voted to leave the European Union, and we had not experienced the short-term period that was predicted to be so ruinous economically following a vote to leave, we would never have discovered just how wrong the experts were! And how many other reports in circulation, prepared by experts, like those who work, oh so *independently* for the European Commission, are also wrong, only you will never know it?

The Existential Threat to the European Union

Enemies to The East – an old enemy – the hostile Russians! Enemies to The West in the form of the Anglo Saxon world – the traitorous independent United Kingdom, and the hostile United States! Enemies to The South – the world of deserts and the people of Islam! Enemies beyond – the alien non-European world that is now in economic, technological and cultural ascendancy (China in particular)! Enemies within – the right-wing populists, immigrants, Member State nationalists, companies that off-shore research and manufacturing, citizens who leave the European Union, Muslims …

This heralds, in the minds of the European Union Nationalists, a cultural disorder, which demands a return to cultural order – European cultural order. That thing they call *their way of life* is being threatened. Their Europeanness is being diluted by a multiculturalism that speaks of the end of the age of European empires, not their continuation in new forms that nevertheless seek old ends – social, cultural, political and economic domination.

It is of course all imaginary – something born of fear, misunderstanding, and uncertainty. That will not though, make any difference. People believe what they want to believe.

Then all you need are the right conditions, followed by the spark that sets the world – the Europe Union world – on fire!

The history of Europe is a history of European Unions, but history does not unfold according to predictable patterns!

Is Vitruvius Getting an Upgrade and is this how Myths are Created?

Vitruvius – full name Marcus Vitruvius Pollio – was, according to the Encyclopaedia Britannica, a Roman architect and engineer, who lived in the first-century BC, and who is credited as the author of the celebrated treatise *De architectura* (On Architecture), a handbook for Roman architects.

The Encyclopaedia Britannica reports that little is known about Vitruvius' life, other than what can be gleaned from the texts that form the ten books that make-up *De architectura*. Specifically, the Encyclopaedia Britannica highlights that the treatise covers almost every aspect of architecture, but it is limited, since it is based primarily on Greek models, from which Roman architecture was soon decisively to depart in order to serve the new needs of proclaiming a world empire.

Encyclopaedia Britannica also state that Vitruvius' outlook was essentially Hellenistic. His wish was to preserve the classical tradition in the design of temples and public buildings, and his prefaces to the separate books of his treatise contain many pessimistic remarks about the contemporary architecture.

We do not need to say anymore. He sounds very conservative. Very backward looking! Inclined to retreat into the past! Very Roman too – they had a love for many things Ancient Greek!

Now to the matter of the upgrade! Here is someone speaking who we have already encountered – an art-science lover:

"As pointed out by Joe Davis (Leonardo Journal, 2018 in press), the Roman polymath Marcus Vitruvius Pollio advocated many of the holistic approaches being debated today. Joe Davis is a pioneering art and biology artist, currently using CRISPR and other genetic engineering techniques to create artificial life art forms. Joe Davis notes that Leonardo Da Vinci himself read and was influenced by Marcus Vitruvius Pollio."

So, what are we seeing here? Is this upgrade the result of scholarly research, revealing new insights in Vitruvius, thus resulting in a learned reassessment of Vitruvius? Or is it yet another example illustrative of rampant relativism, of the reading into texts of what people want to find there, of scientific reduction to ignorance, of poor research practices, of Detrimental Research Practices, of advocacy, of …

Or perhaps it is an example which illustrates that it is now extremely difficult *to know*, because knowledge is being corrupted by, and confused with, beliefs that have no justification. What constitutes knowledge in a world where people just present (individual or collective) beliefs as knowledge? What happens then, when such people seek financial support from research funding agencies, with the expectation that they can be persuaded to go along with this *anything-goes* attitude to the expenditure of public money? The answer is STARTS. The answer is the Ahnenerbe.

We can now ask another question: how can Joe Davis know that da Vinci himself read and was influenced by Marcus Vitruvius Pollio? How can he know? We felt the need to emphasise this point. We are now entering a field that deals with theory of knowledge – epistemology. We repeat – how can he know? More emphasis! Should the text have been written in a different way? This way: [Joe Davis] believes that da Vinci himself read and was influenced by Marcus Vitruvius Pollio. Is this another myth being created?

We can also ask another question: how does the speaker know that Joe Davis is a pioneering art and biology artist, currently using CRISPR and other genetic engineering techniques to create artificial life art forms. It could be more myth making! Should the text have been written in a different way? This way: I believe that that Joe Davis is a pioneering art and biology artist, currently using CRISPR and other genetic engineering techniques to create artificial life art forms.

For the record: it seems that da Vinci's famous sketch Vitruvian Man is based on the human proportions recorded by Vitruvius. That though, does not imply that da Vinci read the text of *De architectura*. Which in turn begs another question: what in fact does *da Vinci himself read and was influenced by Marcus Vitruvius Pollio* actually mean?

We have not been able to identify any reputable source describing Vitruvius as a polymath. What we find from Chapter 1 of Book 1 of *De architectura*, is Vitruvius stating that architecture is a science that arises out of other sciences. He then notes that an architect must be both theoretical and practical, otherwise the architect will not be able to explain or prove the propriety of his designs.

Vitruvius then provides a specification of skills and knowledge that an architect needs. He says:

"He should be a good writer, a skilful draftsman, versed in geometry and optics, expert at figures, acquainted with history, informed on the principles of natural and moral philosophy, somewhat of a musician, not ignorant of the sciences both of law and physic, nor of the motions, laws, and relations to each other, of the heavenly bodies."

Taken at face value, without exploring further, without noting words and phrases such as, *acquainted with, versed in, informed on*, etc. it seems that Vitruvius is stating that an architect should be a writer, mathematician, a philosopher, a lawyer, a musician, an astronomer, a physician, a ... as defined in the sense of someone able to act in such roles as a professional or occupational specialist. Vitruvius though is not saying this. He is actually explaining his opening statement that architecture is a science that arises out of other sciences.

He explains that he is only stating that architects need, in most cases, a working knowledge of these subjects for obvious reasons – music for example relates to the acoustics of buildings, figures (arithmetic) to the calculation of quantities and cost estimates, law as it relates to contractual relations with clients, moral philosophy as it relates to the ethics of behaviour towards clients, history as it relates to the origin of certain types of ornamental features used on buildings, and so forth.

At the end of Chapter 1 he then qualifies the specification by stating that it is not necessary for the architect to be accomplished or an expert in these areas, recognising that this would in practice be impossible for the vast majority of architects.

People familiar with the United Kingdom's Engineering Council Specification for the requirements for registration as a Chartered Engineer, will recognise the same thinking is evident in CEng Spec, as in Vitruvius' specification for a professional architect. Much of the professional formation of an engineer takes place after graduation. Theoretical underpinning is provided via a first degree. The rest follows later.

Most engineers these days learn mathematics – that does not mean that they are mathematicians. Most engineers these days learn about computers and computer programming – that does not mean that they are computer scientists. They may also learn about semiconductor physics – that does not mean they are physicists. They may also learn about ethics – that does not mean that they are moral philosophers. They may also learn about geology – that does not mean they are geologists. They may also learn some chemistry – that does not mean they are chemists.

What is the difference between knowledge and belief? One answer (the philosopher's) is this: knowledge is belief that has been sufficiently justified. What does sufficiently justified mean and how does one establish sufficient justification in a post-positivist era, a post-European era, a post-Enlightenment era? Sociologists though have a different notion of what constitutes knowledge – essentially, if enough people believe something is true then it is knowledge. This is useful, as we have already shown.

A European Expert STARTS to Advise DG CONNECT

A European (German) expert – deceased long ago – wants to give some advice to DG CONNECT concerning STARTS. In the giving of this advice a conversation takes place between he who is dead, and those who are still living – DG CONNECT technocrats. All belong to an age long past.

Deceased Expert: "In the origin of material civilisations which flourish today we always see individual persons. They supplement one another and one of them bases his work on that of the other. The same is true in regard to the practical applications of those inventions and discoveries. For all the various methods of production are in their turn inventions also and consequently dependent on the creative faculty of the individual. Even the purely theoretical work, which cannot be measured by a definite rule and is preliminary to all subsequent technical discoveries, is exclusively the product of the individual brain. The broad masses do not invent – it is always the individual man."

DG CONNECT Technocrat: "Precisely so, which is why we have invited artists into our research projects. The artist is the archetypal inventor, the iconic symbol of creativity – the European individual creative genius - based on our belief that art is invention by individuals."

Deceased Expert: "Accordingly a human community is well organised only when it facilitates to the highest possible degree individual creative forces and utilises their work for the benefit of the community. The most valuable factor of an invention, whether it be in the world of material realities or in the world of abstract ideas, is the personality of the inventor himself. The first and supreme duty of an organised peoples' community is to place the inventor in a position where he can be of the greatest benefit to all. Indeed the very purpose of the organisation is to put the principle into practice."

DG CONNECT Technocrat: "At last someone who understands what we are trying to do!"

Deceased Expert: "It is in the interest of all to assure men of creative brains a decisive influence and facilitate their work."

DG CONNECT Technocrat: "Agreed. As we are putting money into art in a directorate that is supposed to be creating the future of technology for Europe, there has to be a return on investment to technology through investment in the arts. It is for the benefit of European society – the people, or as we call them, citizens. We will not spend money on art that does not accord with our mission to create the future of technology for Europe. To do otherwise would be politically unacceptable."

Deceased Expert: "Agreed. In no event can National Socialism or the National Socialist State give to German art other tasks than those which accord with our view of the world."

Now a Russian expert – he too deceased long ago – wishes to advise DG CONNECT. Here he goes:

Deceased Russian Expert: "What is the principle of party literature? It is not simply that, for the socialist proletariat, literature cannot be a means of enriching individuals or groups: it cannot, in fact, be an individual undertaking, independent of the common cause of the proletariat. Down with non-partisan writers! Down with literary supermen! Literature must become part of the common cause of the proletariat, *a cog and a screw* of one single great Social-Democratic mechanism set in motion by the entire politically-conscious vanguard of the entire working class. Literature must become a component of organised, planned and integrated Social-Democratic Party work."

Now you know the answer to the question that we posed at the START: Lenin, Stalin, Hitler and DG CONNECT all adopted an authoritarian approach, by subjugating the arts to their particular programmes. Ultimately they are all totalitarian (despite claims to the contrary) as they all tend, sooner in some cases, later in others, to silence the voice of dissent, and all finding good reasons to justify this – such is the nature of reason.

European Union Nationalism

Now we state the principles of European Union Nationalism:

One – Europeanness: Citizens of the European Union are a chosen people whose social, political, cultural, and spiritual DNA is superior to that of the peoples of other non-European/non-European Union countries, and the European Union therefore has the right to impregnated its superior attributes into the non-European/non-European Union world through the use of soft power – the instruments of neocolonialism.

Two – Discussions about the future of Europe that do not include the European Union are not allowed. Those who hold such thoughts and engage in such discussions are traitors to European Union Nationalism.

Three – productive property and natural resources are to be privately owned; freedom of contract is guaranteed except for people who are not citizens of the European Union.

Four – Individual initiative, the business entrepreneur, conduct of business for profit and ownership control are basic.

Five – Business men are to be free, if responsible, to fix by agreements prices, production totals and quotas, marketing areas, and the conditions and terms of purchase and sale.

Six – Stock and commodity exchanges, commission houses, brokers, and speculative transactions are inevitable and necessary for the conduct of organic business.

Seven – Certain industries, particularly those catering to a mass consumption society – the society of the spectacle – and foreign trade, are encouraged; large scale units unless uneconomical are to be kept intact; cooperatives will be tolerated but not encouraged.

Eight – Off-shoring of research, and researchers leaving the European Union to work in the non-European Union world, are both acts of disloyalty to the European Union and are to be discouraged through the use of research grants that bribe researchers and companies to undertake research in the European Union.

Nine – The social class structure of society is sanctified, strengthened, made semi-hereditary, and hardened into caste lines; the Middle Professional Class are the Myrmidons of the Élite and, as such, the backbone of the European Union.

Ten – Employers have practically complete control over workers in regard wages, hours, and working conditions. They must take care of their employees within a legal framework that creates an impression of worker rights which are guaranteed by the European Union.

Eleven – Collective bargaining, strikes, and Trade Unions are allowed, but rendered ineffective through a process of marketisation – known as the Single Market – of all social relations.

Twelve – Control is completely from the top; there is and can be no such thing as control or discussion of policies from below; the leaders of the European Union decide all things as they see fit; each holds appointed office at the will of their superiors.

Thirteen – The European Commission and the European Union, along with its other institutions, are one and inseparable, as spirit and body. Legislative, executive, and judicial authorities are fused together. The central power in Brussels will ultimately control all national level government and all activities in all their fields – the totally organised society.

Fourteen – Civil and military are to be fused together; as is the case for all the military, there can be no freedom of speech, of assembly, of writing, of action, of thoughts.

Fifteen – The European Union must be re-industrialized at all costs.

Sixteen – People who are not citizens of the Member States, cannot be citizens of the European Union; as a corollary, all European Union citizens residing outside the European Union either belong or owe allegiance to the European Union.

Seventeen – Socialism is the major enemy of global capitalism. The broad masses are fools and must be duped and led to meet the purposes of the élite.

Eighteen – All sciences and culture must be coordinated and made to serve the purposes of the European Commission, the European Parliament, and the European Union. Propaganda is the method. Propaganda knows neither right nor wrong, neither truth nor falsehood, but only what it wants.

And the politicians – those to whom we might look, to stop the rise of European Union Nationalism – their gaze is directed elsewhere, to matters of economics and prosperity, and to perceived external threats to national security. Thus do they not see the monster rise once again! Those that have seen, and thus do warn – they are branded as right-wing populists and extremists. The serpent does indeed beguile …

STARTS a Consideration of why the Use of Information Technology in Research may Contribute to Research Integrity Problems

Something interesting relating to the use of information technologies in research can be found in the National Academy of Sciences report, *Fostering Research Integrity*.

In some fields of research, complex intermediate analysis of raw data (gathered for example from sensors and observations) is used. This potentially creates problems in forensically reconstructing the flow from raw data to results. Such reconstruction requires detailed knowledge of data production and analyzing software, which is sometimes dependent on the particular computer on which the software was run. Here, it has been noted, are opportunities to manipulate analyses so as to achieve desired results, as well as to undermine the ability of others to validate findings.

Digital technologies can also pose other temptations for researchers to violate the norms of science. Inappropriate application of statistical packages, for example, can lead to a greater confidence in results than is warranted. Data-mining techniques can also generate false positives and spurious correlations.

Anyone with a positive results bias has a willing accomplice in data (big or otherwise) and information technology.

We did some pages back refer to a report – the NESTA report. This is an example of work that uses data that was not collected by the researchers and which is used for purposes for which it was not intended! It would appear that those listening to others engaging in advocacy, have not spotted that fact, or do not have the knowledge to understand the implications. Or do not want to!

Artistic Integrity

Artistic integrity is a phrase that we did not hear spoken in ICT-ART CONNECT, nor we notice, is it prevalent in the STARTS dash for cash. This is what Claudia Mills has to say about artistic integrity:

"I wrote an article which explores the philosophically neglected topic of artistic integrity. This article argues that artists lack artistic integrity if, in the process of creation, they place some other – competing, distracting, or corrupting – value over the value of the artwork itself, in a way that violates their own artistic standards. It also argues, however, that artistic integrity does not require adamant refusal to acknowledge or act upon commitments to values other than single-minded devotion to one's art. Artists of integrity need not be inflexible fanatics. They can seek to earn a living through their art, alter their vision of a work to reach an audience, evolve their artistic standards as they grow as artists, and balance the energy devoted to their art against energy devoted to family, friends, and self-care; they can honour the demands of morality."

How would you know if an artist had sacrificed artistic integrity for the sake of some other competing, distracting, or corrupting value, whether these are money or ideology or both?

Here is Matthew Kieran to speak:

"In one classic study, 72 creative writing students were given the task of writing poetry. A control group was given the task of writing poetry with a snow theme, reading a short story, and then writing another poem on the theme of laughter. The other two groups were given the same tasks, except that after the short story, they were told to read and rank-order lists of reasons for writing. One group was given a list of previously established intrinsic motivating reasons for writing (e.g., self expression, the joy of wordplay, insight). A second group was asked to read and order a list of extrinsic reasons for writing (e.g., making money, social status, graduate prospects). As judged by 12 independently successful poets, the group primed with extrinsic motivating reasons produced the least creative work of the three groups."

Here is Teresa Amabile, the person who undertook this classic study:

"My study directly tested the hypothesis that intrinsic motivation is conducive to creativity and extrinsic motivation is detrimental. Chosen because they identified themselves as actively involved in creative writing, 72 young adults participated in individual laboratory sessions where they were asked to write two brief poems. Before writing the second poem, subjects in an intrinsic orientation condition completed a questionnaire that focused on intrinsic reasons for being involved in writing. Subjects in an extrinsic orientation condition completed a questionnaire that focused on extrinsic reasons. Those in a control condition were not given a questionnaire on reasons for writing. Although there were no initial differences between conditions on prior involvement in writing or on creativity of the first poems written, there were significant differences in the creativity of the poems written after the experimental manipulations. Poems written under an extrinsic orientation were significantly less creative than those written in the other two conditions.

"An important finding of the research was that concentrating on extrinsic reasons for creative writing did result in a temporary decrease in creativity, as predicted. There is no strong evidence, however, that concentrating on intrinsic reasons for writing caused a temporary increase in creativity. Most notable though, is the fact that given the initially high levels of interest and involvement that the writers showed in their work, the decrease in creativity in the extrinsic condition is particularly impressive. Although the effects of the extrinsic manipulation would only be expected to be temporary, it is nonetheless startling that spending barely 5 min reading and ranking extrinsic reasons for writing could have a significant impact on the creativity of creative writers.

"Practically, my research has implications for socialization, educational techniques, and working environments. To the extent that parents, teachers, and work supervisors model and express approval of intrinsic motivational statements about work, intrinsic orientations and creativity should be fostered by such emphasis. By contrast, to the extent that extrinsic statements are modelled and extrinsic constraints on work are made salient, extrinsic orientations would prevail, and creativity would be undermined."

Yet another reason to cast doubt on the notion that art fosters scientific success – it is just too simplistic!

We have in a way also answered the question that we posed, and perhaps also explained why totalitarian art is so underwhelming in terms of its artistic merit, quality, originality, etc! As a corollary, perhaps we have also explained why some of the artistic output of the art-science and art-technology lovers is so uninteresting to the art world, even allowing for the art world's elitism, which is perhaps unfairly overemphasised to divert attention from their valid criticisms!

STARTS a Consideration Research Integrity Problems

In addition to scientific misconduct – fabrication, falsification, and plagiarism – there are things that are described as Detrimental Research Practices. These cover several activities in research.

In the area of authorship, detrimental authorship practices can arise that may not be considered misconduct, such as honorary authorship, as well as demanding authorship in return for access to previously collected data or materials, or denying authorship to those who deserve to be designated as authors.

Not retaining or making data, code, or other information and materials related to the research results available to other researchers, as is often specified by institutional and sponsor policies, or standard practices in a field, is a further Detrimental Research Practice.

Neglectful or exploitative supervision in research is also considered a Detrimental Research Practice.

Other Detrimental Research Practices include misleading statistical analysis that falls short of falsification, irresponsible publication practices by journal editors and peer reviewers, inadequate institutional policies, procedures, or capacity to foster research integrity and address research misconduct allegations, and deficient implementation of policies and procedures.

Note that misleading statistical analysis is included! There are lies, damn lies and statistics!

And what is the cost of these Detrimental Research Practices? These can be summarised as: damage to the individuals who undertake these practices; reputation costs to their employer, as well as the journal that publishes the resulting work; direct financial costs; social costs; and opportunity costs.

One cost of note is the need to reassess and re-do work that is founded on knowledge that is shown to be suspect because of research misconduct or Detrimental Research Practices.

Here we also note that there are many suspect practices, but not necessarily full agreement if they are Detrimental Research Practices! So we list what in the United Kingdom are regarded by (the former) Research Councils UK as unacceptable practices:

Individuals involved in research must not commit any of the acts of research misconduct specified below. Unacceptable conduct includes each of the following:

Fabrication:

This comprises the creation of false data or other aspects of research, including documentation and participant consent.

Falsification:

This comprises the inappropriate manipulation and/or selection of data, imagery and/or consents.

Plagiarism:

This comprises the misappropriation or use of others' ideas, intellectual property or work (written or otherwise), without acknowledgement or permission.

Misrepresentation, including:

- Misrepresentation of data, for example suppression of relevant findings and/or data, or knowingly, recklessly or by gross negligence, presenting a flawed interpretation of data;

- Undisclosed duplication of publication, including undisclosed duplicate submission of manuscripts for publication;

- Misrepresentation of interests, including failure to declare material interests either of the researcher or of the funders of the research;

- Misrepresentation of qualifications and/or experience, including claiming or implying qualifications or experience which are not held;

- Misrepresentation of involvement, such as inappropriate claims to authorship and/or attribution of work where there has been no significant contribution, or the denial of authorship where an author has made a significant contribution

Breach of duty of care, whether deliberately, recklessly or by gross negligence:

- Disclosing improperly the identity of individuals or groups involved in research without their consent, or other breach of confidentiality;

- Placing any of those involved in research in danger, whether as subjects, participants or associated individuals, without their prior consent, and without appropriate safeguards even with consent; this includes reputational danger where that can be anticipated;

- Not taking all reasonable care to ensure that the risks and dangers, the broad objectives and the sponsors of the research are known to participants or their legal representatives, to ensure appropriate informed consent is obtained properly, explicitly and transparently;

- Not observing legal and reasonable ethical requirements or obligations of care for animal subjects, human organs or tissue used in research, or for the protection of the environment.

- Improper conduct in peer review of research proposals or results (including manuscripts submitted for publication): this includes failure to disclose conflicts of interest; inadequate disclosure of clearly limited competence; misappropriation of the content of material; and breach of confidentiality or abuse of material provided in confidence for peer review purposes.

Improper dealing with allegations of misconduct:

- Failing to address possible infringements including attempts to cover up misconduct or reprisals against whistle-blowers;

- Failing to deal appropriately with malicious allegations, which should be handled formally as breaches of good conduct.

We will now inform you which of the practices from the above list that we have observed over the full length of our research career. It would be easier to tell you that which we have not observed. These are ... In the end we could not find one category that we had not encountered. All of these were experienced mostly in the context of European Commission research as well as periods spent in British universities, in particular the last episode between 2007 and 2010, when we noted a significant change in the mindset of academics, with an increased tendency towards unethical behaviour, as well as reduced intellectual capabilities and general competencies, compared to the previous period 1980 to 1989. In effect they had become research managers, obsessed with research funding, claiming credit for other peoples' work, and overselling themselves and their institutions.

We once wryly noted to someone a few years back, that there was a time when academics appeared on television because they were professors, now they are professors because they appear on television!

"The rational economic system, at whose birth
pangs we are already assisting, can only
be fully utilised if it is infused by a culture
whose method and approach is also rational,
intelligent and empirical. Prim Science has so far
neglected to confess to the world that he has
begotten such an offspring on the
harlot humanities; but the infant culture is
beginning to peep already - in its bastard vigour lies the
only hope for an heir worthy of the
civilisations of the past."

Conrad Waddington, 1941

Postproduction Art

No we are not talking about what happens after filming, but something else – contemporary art. Here is Nicolas Bourriaud:

"Since the early nineties, an ever increasing number of artworks have been created on the basis of pre-existing works; more and more artists interpret, reproduce, re-exhibit, or use works made by others or available cultural products. This art of postproduction seems to respond to the proliferating chaos of global culture in the information age, which is characterized by an increase in the supply of works and the art world's annexation of forms ignored or disdained until now. These artists who insert their own work into that of others, contribute to the eradication of the traditional distinction between production and consumption, creation and copy, readymade and original work. The material they manipulate is no longer primary. It is no longer a matter of elaborating a form on the basis of a raw material but working with objects that are already in circulation on the cultural market, which is to say, objects already informed by other objects. Notions of originality (being at the origin of) and even of creation (making something from nothing) are slowly blurred in this new cultural landscape marked by the twin figures of the DJ and the programmer, both of whom have the task of selecting cultural objects and inserting them into new contexts.

"In a universe of products for sale, pre-existing forms, signals already emitted, buildings already constructed, paths marked out by their predecessors, artists no longer consider the artistic field (and here one could add television, cinema, or literature) a museum containing works that must be cited or *surpassed*, as the modernist ideology of originality would have it, but so many storehouses filled with tools that should be used, stockpiles of data to manipulate and present.

"In this new form of culture, which one might call a culture of use or a culture of activity, the artwork functions as the temporary terminal of a network of interconnected elements, like a narrative that extends and reinterprets preceding narratives. Each exhibition encloses within it the script of another; each work may be inserted into different programs and used for multiple scenarios. The artwork is no longer an end point but a simple moment in an infinite chain of contributions.

"This culture of use implies a profound transformation of the status of the work of art: going beyond its traditional role as a receptacle of the artist's vision, it now functions as an active agent, a musical score, an unfolding scenario, a framework that possesses autonomy and materiality to varying degrees, its form able to oscillate from a simple idea to

302

sculpture or canvas. In generating behaviours and potential reuses, art challenges passive culture, composed of merchandise and consumers. It makes the forms and cultural objects of our daily lives function. What if artistic creation today could be compared to a collective sport, far from the classical mythology of the solitary effort? 'It is the viewers who make the paintings,' Duchamp once said, an incomprehensible remark unless we connect it to his keen sense of an emerging culture of use, in which meaning is born of collaboration and negotiation between the artist and the one who comes to view the work. Why wouldn't the meaning of a work have as much to do with the use one makes of it as with the artist's intentions for it?"

What meaning will you create through the use you make of this work?

"That when it comes to social and economic
questions this book on the 'scientific attitude'
is anything but scientific is what one has
learnt to expect of this kind of literature. We find again all
the familiar clichés and baseless generalisations about
'potential plenty' and the inevitable tendency
towards monopoly though the 'best authorities'
quoted in support of these contentions prove on
examination to be mostly political tracts of questionable
scientific standing, while the serious studies
of the same problems are conspicuously
neglected."

Friedrich von Hayek, 1944

What is the Evidence that Art-Science-Technology Collaboration is a Good Thing?

The above title is an exact reproduction of the title of the editorial in the first issue of volume 51 (2018) of *Leonardo*. And the answer to the question is straightforward: whatever evidence you want to concoct into existence. There are many ways to do this and many reasons for doing so, not all of which are dishonest.

Globally, the research and innovation system has become so corrupt, so biased, and increasingly populated with incompetence, that you can now find any answer that you want, especially an answer that fits with your agenda, vested interests, beliefs, etc. Living in a bubble helps too, where the consequences of your actions are not apparent, seen, or felt. Life goes on regardless, and more and more research findings pile up on that which has already being created, thus further reinforcing the delusion. This applies to all fields: STEM, the Social Sciences, and the Humanities. And of course the Arts!

Those nations that clean-up their research and innovation system, while maintaining the freedom of researchers to explore new topics in a professional and responsible way, will most surely gain an advantage over those that do nothing. Finding a way to efficiently filter-out the suspect material without wasting the valuable time of researchers must also be found.

Has the time come for professional registration, licences to practice, and specific criminal offences? Professional registration yes – we should consider transforming researchers into dual professionals just like teachers who are already dual professionals. Licences to practice and specific criminal offences, no, for these are too restrictive and could be counterproductive. But both must surely eventually be raised as a serious proposal if some action is not now taken. Some people are already talking about specific criminal offences.

Sow the wind reap the whirlwind ...

By way of final words on the matter of the *Leonardo* editorial: it is clearly advocacy, but a post-modernist would say more. They would point out that the authors are engaging in the construction of their own reality, but that the supposed facts could also be constructed into a different story or stories. If you have not noticed or realised yet, that is what we are doing, in a post-modernist way. And the mentioning of such is post-modern in itself!

We could be witnessing the act of scientists, and their artists in tow, rewriting history, for their own ends. Which are … What?

"But in this day and age logical methods are
applicable only to solving problems of secondary interest.
The absolute rationalism that is still in vogue
allows us to consider only facts relating to our
experience. Logical ends, on the contrary, escape us. It is pointless
to add that experience itself has found itself increasingly circumscribed.
It paces back and forth in a cage from which it is more and more
difficult to make it emerge. It too leans for support on
what is most immediately expedient, and it is protected
by the sentinels of common sense. Under the pretence of civilisation
and progress, we have managed to banish from the mind everything
that may rightly or wrongly be termed superstition, or
fancy; forbidden is any search for truth which is
not in conformance with accepted practices."

André Breton, 1924

Disciplinary Idiots

Stephen Bronner, in his 2004 book *Reclaiming the Enlightenment: Toward a Politics of Radical Engagement*, makes this comment: "[...] what the Germans still call *disciplinary idiots*, with brains dulled by specialisation [...]". .

We are not taking this quote out of context, just introducing you to the term *disciplinary idiots*. Perhaps it is used elsewhere in other books. It is actually, for it also appears in another of Stephen Bronner's books: *Critical Theory: A Very Short Introduction*: "[...] what the German's call the *disciplinary idiot* would supplant the intellectual [...]".

Do the German's have such a term? We looked to check – as we do! We found a German word: *fachidot*. The Collins English Dictionary says that it is a noun with this meaning: a derogatory term for a *one-track specialist* who is an expert in his field, but takes a blinkered approach to multi-faceted problems. It also notes however that there is no literal translation, because you would not call a *one-track specialist* an idiot. It seems that at the core of the idea is a stupidity when it comes to wider issues. This we recognise!

But we divert way from what we intended to say: STARTS is a product of disciplinary idiocy. Perhaps we have already convinced you of this? One might say too, that much of what now issues forth as STEAM is also the product of disciplinary idiocy. Likewise the art-science lovers' and art-technology lovers' discussions! Not discussions among idiots, just discussions founded in disciplinary idiocy! The white-frocked seekers of objective truth and their artists in residence! More disciplinary idiocy!

Now a spokesperson for the *The Parliamentary Office of Science and Technology* will speak:

"There is a continuum of poor practice from minor errors to serious misconduct. Questionable research practices are a widespread concern, as they are thought to be more prevalent and have a greater impact on the research record than deliberate misconduct. One of the problems is that, detecting problems through peer review in multidisciplinary research is harder as reviewers may lack expertise in all areas of peer review."

Will you be able to properly peer review all that STARTS to STEAM?

The Nazis and Their Interest in Art and Science – Art-Science Lovers!

Are artists in research labs publicists or persuaders for scientific research? Are artists in research labs illustrators of scientific theories? Are artists in research labs visualisers of research results?

If any artists were to deny that they were any of the above, how would you know that they were not? Who has the necessary skills and knowledge, or the interest, to recognise when they are just publicists, persuaders, illustrators, or visualisers? Even when they say they are not?

"Is not propaganda a kind of art?"

Who was that who just spoke? We will tell you – it was a person with the surname Goebbels.

"It is highly important that one thinks through the meaning of the union of the contemptuous attitude towards the *great unwashed multitude* with the ethic – or, rather, lack of ethics – which sees nothing wrong in the least with the wholesale commercialisation of the arts and sciences. For only then is one in a position to comprehend the real meaning of the Nazi programme for the arts – a programme which sees the arts as tools for putting across the interests of *business-as-usual* in the same matter-of-fact way as any routine advertiser will employ an artist to paint pictures of beautiful ladies in order to sell a patent medicine.

"The crux of the Nazi programme for the sciences and the arts – as indeed, of all Nazi programmes, civil and military, domestic and foreign – is to be found in their *struggle for the worker's soul.*"

That was Professor Robert Brady speaking.

Social embedding! Graceful embedding! Inducing change in individual and social behaviour! The struggle for the soul of the peoples of the European Union, of the world!

"The Nazis propose to rewrite all history, all philosophy, and all natural and social sciences for the purpose of purifying them from non-Germanic interpretations. It is not that new elements have been discovered, but that old *falsities* must be deleted. The *falsities* are whatever do not support the ideal of German biological and cultural superiority, and the roles these play in support of the Nazi Weltanschuung. *Exegesis, which to the careful scientist means selection of facts for their relevance in proof or disproof of working hypotheses, and a science for discovery and criticism of biased argument,* means *to the Nazis, selection of facts to support convictions and for defence of biased arguments.*"

That was Robert speaking again, explaining this time that which STARTS to STEAM and the exegesis of the art-science and art-technology lovers.

The denial that artists in labs are not ... How would you know?

"A close companion of a high need
for closure is a proclivity to perceive
and to impose a sharp
in-group/out-group distinction. This matters
because a strong group identity can drastically
affect basic psychological patterns of
empathy and antipathy, including schadenfreude,
the pleasure that comes from seeing
out-group members being harmed."

Diego Gambetta and Steffen Hertog, 2016

IG Farben – A Warning from History

Now, as the performance draws to a close, we turn to the matter of *Subsequent Nuremberg Proceedings, Case #6, The IG Farben Case: United States vs. Carl Krauch, et al.*

Some regard the case as a travesty of justice, where people deeply involved in the Nazi rise to power and the subsequent conspiracy to wage aggressive war, and to exterminate the Jewish people while exploiting this to commercial ends, walked free, or where given very lenient sentences.

Walter Dürrfeld – an engineer – who in the period 1941-1944 was chief of construction and installation at the IG Farben Auschwitz plant, and then, in the period 1944-1945, director of the IG Farben Auschwitz plant, received a sentence of eight years. He was one of five of the accused found guilt by The Tribunal of Count III. This charged the accused, individually, collectively and through the instrumentality of Farben, with the commission of War Crimes and Crimes against Humanity. It alleged that the accused participated in enslavement and the mistreatment of enslaved persons, including terror, torture and murder.

The indictments, the judgements, and the sentences can be studied online by those who want to. Here we list the 24 accused:

Carl Krauch – chemist and Nazi war criminal

Hermann Schmitz – commercial executive and Nazi war criminal

Georg von Schnitzler – lawyer and Nazi war criminal

Fritz Gajewski – chemist

Heinrich Hoerlein – chemist

August von Knieriem – lawyer

Fritz ter Meer – chemist and Nazi war criminal

Christian Schneider – chemist

Otto Ambros – chemist and Nazi war criminal

Max Brueggemann – deemed medically unfit to stand trial

Ernst Buergin – electro-chemist and Nazi war criminal

Heinrich Buetefisch – engineer and Nazi war criminal

Paul Haefliger – commercial executive and Nazi war criminal

Max Ilgner – political scientist and Nazi war criminal

Friedrich Jaehne – engineer and Nazi war criminal

Hans Kuehne – chemist

Carl Lautenschlaeger – physician and engineer

Wilhelm Mann – commercial executive

Heinrich Oster – chemist and Nazi war criminal

Karl Wurster – chemist

Walter Dürrfeld – engineer and Nazi war criminal

Heinrich Gattineau – lawyer

Erich von der Heyde – agronomist

Hans Kugler – political scientist and Nazi war criminal

IG Farben is a case study demonstrating what can happen when you induce change in social and individual behaviour, when you embed science (and its close cousins), gracefully or otherwise, into society. This is what can happen when experts and their organisations conspire with governments. This is what the *Vainglorious Enlightened Ones* did – instrumental reason run amok. When you sow the wind, you reap the whirlwind ...

IG Farben had, in effect, their own corporate concentration camp – known as Auschwitz III or Monowitz – which housed the mostly Jewish prisoners who did forced labour at the IG Farben Auschwitz plant site. It was in this context that the engineer Walter Dürrfeld undertook his War Crimes and Crimes against Humanity.

Did you notice – quite a lot of STEM people in the list!

Hidden in Plain View

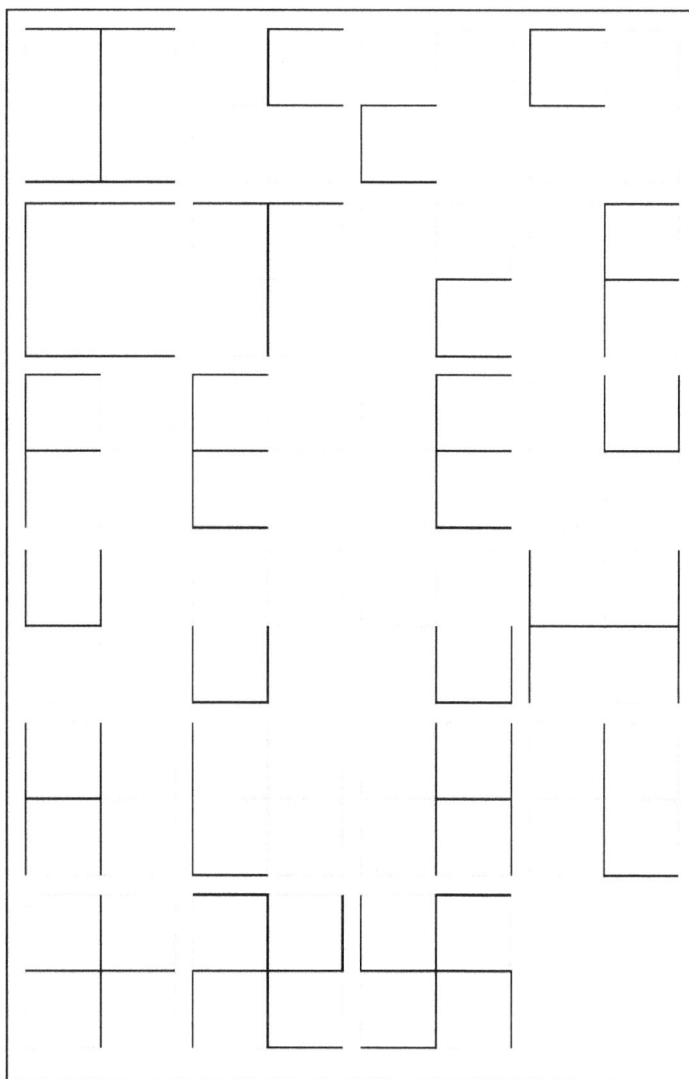

STARTS a Justified True Belief in a Proposition that is in Fact False

This is a story. This is efferent. This is aesthetic. This is an irritant!

STARTS story:

A lonely railway station is the stage, architecture of times past the retinal image, which on brain's cells do only slightly impress, being as it is – the image we mean – too familiar to be worthy of mind's note. It is just the backdrop, so it is just seen. That which is seen but not seen, if you understand our theme! Let your mind take note!

Then into our scene walk two men – at 11.58 to be exact – bound together it seems in some strange comic act. A last minute desperate act!

They have lost sense of time, and to a train that we have already referred, they are set. It is bound to places determined in the past. Time is a reoccurring theme.

Thus in haste they look about. It is a clock they seek. There it is! It has been seen, but already 60 second has past, so their eyes to the clock do turn, and simultaneously, each parroting the other in words and deeds, their mouths do speak thus:

"It is 11.59. Quick! Let's be about the task."

No time to think slowly, so they think fast, but then act slowly as in *City of the Golden Stars* style – which they of course do faithfully conform to reproduce. As in times past!

And then they are gone. Thank God for that!

Time moves on, but the clock does not. The hands just sit. Time has stilled its incessant tick.

So now you know something more. And thus we can say that we know that which they did not know. They on the other hand did not know what they did not know! Thus did they have a justified true belief in a proposition that was in fact false! So they did not know, if you know what we mean!

ENDS story.

Enlightenment is Totalitarian

Here is a journalist writing for the European Commission, in its Cordis News Service:

"With fake news, alternative facts and false beliefs currently damaging our social and political landscape, EU researchers are examining whether journalists can be effective as adjudicators, pointing out untruths and separating facts from fiction.

"Misperceptions, fake news and false beliefs are everywhere today. They have the power to distort public opinion and can have a major impact on policymaking and government decisions. According to a recently published paper by the EU-funded DEBUNKER project, however, journalists can help change that. The project, which focuses on investigating misperceptions and false beliefs, found that journalists could help prevent the spread of false beliefs by taking a more assertive role in their reporting. They can adjudicate arguments by fact checking the information presented and revealing any untruths, and still be perceived as unbiased by their readers."

Is this true? Who is fact checking this claim?

Here is the author of the above mentioned paper:

"Journalists are often criticized for passive reporting of factual disputes in politics, but researchers have only recently begun exploring conditions in which they may successfully influence readers' beliefs – scenarios less likely to produce partisan bias. Intra-party disputes and those which are polarized, but not contentious, may be two alignments of elite cues that vitiate motivated reasoning and allow for influential adjudication. This experiment ($N = 523$) used a 2 (one-sided adjudication/none) × 2 (intra-party/polarized dispute) design to test this hypothesis. In both cases, adjudication's effects on factual beliefs were not conditional on ideological or partisan cues. Adjudication did not increase perceived bias, and increased satisfaction of readers' informational needs."

Is this true? Who is fact checking this claim?

Who is fact checking the European Commission when they make all their claims? Who fact checked the FET-ART project when it made its claims? Who fact checked the FEAT project when it made its claims? Who will fact check DG CONNECT and STARTS when they start making claims?

What about the reader that just accepts what the above say?

Fake news, alternative facts, and false beliefs – the Enlightenment is totalitarian. The European Commission is totalitarian. The European Union is totalitarian.

Here is Roger Fowler referring to his study that addressed the perception – belief – that newspaper coverage of world events is presented as the unbiased record of hard facts.

"My intention was not simply to expose bias, and certainly not to maintain that newspapers are especially biased. News has not been singled out as a unique instance of deliberate or negligent partiality; it is analysed as a particularly important example of the power of all languages in the *construction of reality*.

"My study is a study of how language is used in newspapers to form ideas and beliefs. I take the view that the content of newspapers is not facts about the world, but in a very general sense, *ideas*. I use other terms as well, as appropriate: beliefs, values, theories, propositions, ideology. My major concern was with the role of linguistic structure in the construction of ideas in the Press. My study shows that language is not neutral, but a highly constructive mediator.

"Journalists take a different view. They believe that they collect facts, report them objectively, and then the newspaper presents them fairly and without bias, in language that is unambiguous, un-distorting and agreeable to readers. This professional ethos is common to all news media, Press, radio and television, and it is certainly what journalists claim in any general statement on the matter."

It is also what STEM people, and others involved in research would claim. But that of course is not the case – unless you do not believe that there is a research integrity problem. In which case, you too are constructing a reality.

The European Commission would also make the same claim – that they are reporting objectively! They too are constructing a reality, and art has now become part of that process. The Nazis did the same. They engaged in (dangerous) fantasy policy making – just like DG CONNECT is doing. This is partly because, like the Nazis state, the European Commission is a bureaucracy accountable to no-one. Any mad idea can take hold. As they work in secret and silence everyone through confidentiality clauses, and given that everyone has a vested interest in being invited back, they get away with these mad schemes. So did the Nazis, until justice caught up with them – but at a very high price for the victims!

Other factors are also at work – STARTS behavioural factors – also come into play. They are also children of the *Enlightenment* and therefore engage in instrumental reasoning, rendering people – artists – as mere objects to be used to manipulate other objects – the citizens of the European Union – for ends that are never questioned. Just like the Nazis! And STARTS artists go along with this evil – it is an evil. The operative term is – the banality of evil! Such is the nonsense – the so-called rationality – of the *Vainglorious Enlightened Ones*.

They will, at the end, just say that they were obeying orders. They have already said this. That is what bureaucrats do – they are always directed from above. In the means-end relationship morality has no place when instrumental reason takes hold. There is no morality in STARTS – just fantasy and delusion. Just watch the growing number of online videos of panel discussions and individuals speaking – they are in a world that is a simulacrum of the early days of some aspects of the Third Reich! Which of course you will not believe, because you too are participating in a social construction of reality! Using language to do so!

So we are back to post-modernism! There is no clear dividing line between reality and fiction. Many interpretations of a given situation are possible. Only totalitarians seek a single truth. Only totalitarians would propose that there needs to be someone, for example journalists, acting as the (sole) arbiters of the truth. Or even worse, the European Commission – incipient totalitarians – acting as (sole) arbiters of the truth! Or journalists working for the European Commission, in the Directorate-General for Truth – DG TRUE!

Enlightenment is totalitarian and leads to only one destination – the gates of Auschwitz Birkenau. What place name will future Europeans speak of? That European Union place?

Corrupting the Research Record?

Here is an extract from the ICT-ART CONNECT study report, which was funded by European Union taxpayers (although hardly any taxpayers know this):

"Many artists have been at the origin of new technologies. The example of the Berlin-based company ART+COM is key. The company created the Terravision system in 1994 that many consider to be the prequel to Google Earth. It can be said that the artistic origin of one of the most successful worldwide online platforms lies in Europe, but was commercially explored elsewhere."

So, many artists have been at the origin of new technologies! But what did they actually do? No information is forthcoming we see! More myth making!

Terravision is a prequel to Google Earth! We leave you to follow-up on this claim. Your starting point is the science fiction novel: *Snow Crash*. Here are some other words and phrases: CIA, EarthView, NASA World Wind, Geoscope, Keyhole Inc., etc. People in a number of places it seems, were inspired by the *Metaverse* in *Snow Crash*. But what inspired this *Metaverse*? There is always a step further back in time! You might also want to investigate ART+COM and what they do and the types of disciplines they employ and who they work for. They are very open about this – its part of their image making, or advertising, or self-promotion, or USP, whatever term you wish to use. But you have to look and not just accept what is written in the report that European Union taxpayers paid for (although hardly any taxpayers know this). The report demonstrates how language (which is not neutral) can be used to construct reality. It is a very crude, simplistic, unsophisticated use of language to construct a not very sophisticated or believable reality. We on the other hand, are using multiple languages to compose a complex reality, where the boundary between the cognitive and the expressive, between fact and fiction blurs. Have you not realised this yet?

All that STARTS to STEAM, art-science lovers, art-technology lovers: crude, simplistic and unsophisticated attempts at constructing reality. Oh joy!

If you wish to make claims, you have to present evidence which requires that you look into the research record otherwise you do not know what you are talking about. If you do not look into the research record before making your claims, you can be accused of corrupting the research record, which is a link to the matter of research integrity! You can also be accused of idiocy! Watch all those online recordings of people gathered together talking art-science, art-technology, STARTS and STEAM nonsense.

Will artists participating in STEM research lead to a corruption of the research record? Answer according to your beliefs. Remember there is much at stake. The research record if that is your concern. Piles of public money diverted away from serious STEM related topics if that is your concern – the opportunity cost. Piles of public money destined for serious STEM research, being diverted away from STEM and used for the enrichment of vested interests if that is your concern (or should that be desire?).

"Totalitarianism does seem to be inevitable; the whole trend of recent history is towards it. One cannot dismiss the Nazis, Fascists and the Communists all together for being, in their different ways, totalitarian; fairly soon we shall all be so, in some way or another. The Totalitarians of today have taken, with the wrong foot foremost, a step which we shall all have to take tomorrow."

Conrad Waddington, 1941

Why would an Art-Science Lover's Research Paper Include a Statement Suggesting that the Reported Work May be Biased?

The paper is: *Arts and Crafts: Critical to Economic Innovation.*

In the paper you will find, in the section dealing with research method, this statement: "[...] drawbacks include self-selection bias that may have caused the results to be unrepresentative of the general public [...]". In the conclusions section you will find some discussion on the bias, including a statement that: "We note these possible biases and encourage even further studies of broader populations to test this seminal research hypothesis."

The answer to the question is: because it is biased; not just self-selection bias but response bias too. We need to write about this and we will. But not now, other than to say, that the paper uses *p*-values! That is to say, it speaks of statistical significance, if you are not clear what we mean by *p*-values. Is this paper clear about what a *p*-value means?

This is what the American Statistical Society has to say about *p*-values in the wake of the growing problems of reproducibility and replicability of research results:

- *p*-values can indicate how incompatible the data are with a specified statistical model;

- *p*-values do not measure the probability that the studied hypothesis is true, or the probability that the data were produced by random chance alone;

- Scientific conclusions and business or policy decisions should not be based only on whether a *p*-value passes a specific threshold;

- Proper inference requires full reporting and transparency;

- A *p*-value, or statistical significance, does not measure the size of an effect or the importance of a result.

- By itself, a *p*-value does not provide a good measure of evidence regarding a model or hypothesis.

The issue often centres on sample size and whether there is really an effect and its magnitude. Other factors are also relevant – for example, researcher bias.

We looked for the sample sizes in the paper *Art Fosters Scientific Success*, and then noted that the paper has a lack of transparency about so many things, along with severe methodological problems, that we feel the need to start another work just to address them. So we will. We will call this work: *Art-Science Fakes*. We will address this topic in many contexts including answering this question about *Art Fosters Scientific Success*: are the results obtained an observable effect, or are the results a consequence of epistemological and ontological incompatibilities?

We looked in a paper with the title *Correlations between Avocations, Scientific Style, Work Habits, and Professional Impact of Scientists*, and found the sample size was 36 (or 38 depending upon who you count). We looked in another paper with the title *Artistic Scientists and Scientific Artists: The Link between Polymathy and Creativity*, and found the following:

"As C. P. Snow wrote in his famous essay, *The Two Cultures*, artists and intellectuals stand at one pole and scientists at the other: 'Between the two a gulf of mutual incomprehension -- sometimes ... hostility and dislike, but most of all lack of understanding...'"

If you look at the source material (Snow's Rede Lecture) you will find that C.P. Snow did not in fact say the above. What he said was:

"Literary intellectuals at one pole – at the other scientists, and as the most representative, the physical scientists. Between the two a gulf of mutual incomprehension – sometimes (particularly among the young) hostility and dislike. But most of all lack of understanding."

If you use hermeneutics to investigate Snow and his so-called two cultures you will find that C.P. Snow's attack was directed solely towards literary intellectuals, because he had an agenda. That agenda was getting more scientists into government, where presumably they would then (mis) apply statistics to arrive at the answer they wanted! Standing in the way of achieving this were a group he called literary intellectuals, part of what he called the traditional culture, that still held to the ideal of, for example, an education in the classics being a suitable preparation for – running the country! Snow was evidently not interested in artists for he only mentions them once in the Rede lecture. How many times do you think he mentions scientists? In another book, with the title *366 A Scriptovisual Composition Unknown*, we presented an analysis of some important words that C.P. Snow used and did not use. It is very enlightening.

A *p*-value of 0.01 does not mean that there is just a 1% chance of a result being a false alarm. *P*-values cannot say this. All a *p*-value can do is to summarise the data assuming a specific null-hypothesis. It cannot work backwards and make statements about the underlying reality. That requires that a real effect was there in the first place. We refer you to Regina Nuzzo's paper *Statistical Errors: P-values, the 'Gold Standard' of*

Statistical Validity, are not a Reliable as Many Scientists Assume, which was published in the journal *Nature*, on 13 February 2014.

We have just given you more reasons not to believe that art fosters scientific success, but the art-science lovers want you to believe that this is in fact a real effect. Why? That, one can say, is something worthy of research! We are very interested to know why! It relates to our interest in flawed decision making, and the consequences. That is to say, flaws in Western *Enlightened* (European) decision making! Hence our interest in the failings of technocracy and scientism! Hence also our interest in all that STARTS to STEAM!

"Apparently the 'harlot humanities',
about which Dr Waddington has to
say many uncomplimentary things,
have gravely misled us in teaching tolerance!"

Friedrich von Hayek, 1944

So did they Buy the Art-Science Fakes?

We are referring to the National Academy of Sciences and their study into *Integrating Higher Education in the Arts, Humanities, Sciences, Engineering, and Medicine*, which resulted in the publication in 2018 of a report with the title *The Integration of the Humanities and Arts with Sciences, Engineering, and Medicine in Higher Education: Branches from the Same Tree*. And we ask now: did they buy the art science-fakes?

What we will now tell you, you might be surprised by. But perhaps you should not be!

We examined the above report, and found that it refers to two papers that we have already mentioned, for the report states that there are very strong correlations between leadership in science and engagement with arts and crafts avocations! Really!

Mentioned is a 2008 paper called *Art Fosters Scientific Success* – remember that paper? – which it is claimed shows that very accomplished scientists, including Nobel Laureates, National Academy of Sciences members, and Royal Society members, were significantly more likely to engage in arts and crafts and identify as artists than average scientists and the general public. Compared with scientists who are members of Sigma Xi, a society in which any working scientist can be a member, Nobel Laureates were 2 times as likely to be photographers, 4 times as likely to be musicians, 17 times as likely to be artists, 15 times as likely to be crafts people, 25 times as likely to be creative writers, and 22 times as likely to be performers.

Just to remind you about how suspect the aforementioned paper is, we point out that it is not the case that any working scientist can be a member of Sigma Xi. This is not something new, but has always been the case. This is an example of how flawed, and possibly biased research can find its way into other documents. This statement is in fact just one example of many suspect statements in the National Academy of Sciences long awaited report of their study into *Integrating Higher Education in the Arts, Humanities, Sciences, Engineering, and Medicine*. Somewhat illustrating also the points made in another National Academy of Sciences report – the one with the title *Fostering Research Integrity*!

Back now to the matter of the report with the title *The Integration of the Humanities and Arts with Sciences, Engineering, and Medicine in Higher Education: Branches from the Same Tree*. And we note too that the report refers to another paper, which again we have already mentioned – recall the paper *Arts and Crafts: Critical to Economic Innovation*. Thus does the report *The Integration of the Humanities and Arts with Sciences, Engineering, and Medicine in Higher Education: Branches from the Same Tree* claim that it has also been shown that sustained arts and crafts participation correlates with being an entrepreneurial innovator.

More research nonsense!

Now we will ask the National Academy of Sciences a question. We pointed out to the National Academy the problems with the first study (*Arts Fosters Scientific Success*). And you can see for yourself that in the reporting of the results of the study *Arts and Crafts: Critical to Economic Innovation*, the paper states that the results may contain bias. Could you therefore explain why this material has found its way into your study report?

No response! Oh dear!

So we do strongly suggest that you take a look at that other report published by the National Academy, the one with the title *Fostering Integrity in Research*. In this report you will find that all research stakeholders are contributing to the research integrity crisis. The report *The Integration of the Humanities and Arts with Sciences, Engineering, and Medicine in Higher Education: Branches from the Same Tree* demonstrates this point.

Apparently Einstein warned of the dangerous implications of living in a society where long-established foundations of knowledge were corrupted, manipulated, and coerced by political forces. Is this what we are now seeing?

The Integration of the Humanities and Arts with Sciences, Engineering, and Medicine in Higher Education: Branches from the Same Tree – another advocacy report. Yet one more socially constructed reality.

We doubt very much whether an educated and open mind is enough to empower the individual to separate truth from falsehood, superstition and bias from fact, and logic from illogic. The knowledge-base of the Social Sciences and Humanities tell us that an educated and open mind is not is not sufficient.

That which STARTS to STEAM – case studies that disprove their own rhetoric!

Did the European Commission Exclude British Experts from H2020 Research Proposal Evaluations?

Now we ask a question. We ask if – following the United Kingdom's European Union Membership referendum in June 2016 – the European Commission excluded British experts from participation in evaluations of H2020 research proposals? Contrary to the joint statement made by Schulz, Tusk, Rutte and Juncker!

Here are Schulz, Tusk, Rutte and Juncker, speaking as one, we suppose, on June 24th 2016:

"In a free and democratic process, the British people have expressed their wish to leave the European Union. We regret this decision but respect it. We stand ready to launch negotiations swiftly with the United Kingdom regarding the terms and conditions of its withdrawal from the European Union. Until this process of negotiations is over, the United Kingdom remains a member of the European Union, with all the rights and obligations that derive from this. According to the Treaties which the United Kingdom has ratified, EU law continues to apply to the full, to, and in, the United Kingdom until it is no longer a Member."

But, what about these Treaties still applying to the Institutions of the European Union? In particular, their validity in the eyes of the European Commission, and their continued compliance with them!

Why did we ask our original question? We suspected, following the events of June 2016, that the European Commission would exclude British experts, contrary to what Schulz, Tusk, Rutte and Juncker said in public. We understand the European Commission's mentality, their ideology, and their disposition to undertake unlawful acts because they exercise unaccountable power. We also know that in the past following a Swiss referendum related to joining the European Union, in which this was rejected by the Swiss people, the European Commission discriminated against research proposals that included Swiss Partners. They did this because they hold in contempt the results of free and democratic processes.

Whether as a result of our referendum vote, there was discrimination against proposals we cannot say, because from the time of the referendum onwards, no one in the European Commission invited us to participate in any evaluations, or when they did, the invitation was then quickly withdrawn. Why we wondered?

Then in 2018, an opportunity – we were invited to participate and we accepted, and immediately we asked questions to others from the United Kingdom, who, like us, had regularly participated in H2020 evaluations.

We asked what their experience had been. They all told the same story as our own. Not statistically significant for sure, but worth following up. Which is exactly what we did, selecting DG CONNECT and its ICT research programme, to further the investigation. What did we do and what did we discover? This:

We looked at the available published lists of experts that DG CONNECT had used for the ICT evaluations for each year of operation of H2020. That was 2014, 2015, 2016 and 2017. The year 2018 was not available at the time of completion of this work. These lists do not however, say how many times an expert was used in a given year for a particular programme. We then counted the number of United Kingdom experts that appeared in these lists. By this we mean United Kingdom nationals, including those who list the UK as their first nationality, but excluding other European Union Nationals working in the United Kingdom. This is the result of that counting: 2014 – 188 UK experts out of a total of 1557 experts (i.e. 12.07% were UK experts); 2015 – 119 UK experts out of a total of 954 experts (i.e. 12.4% were UK experts); 2016 – 107 UK experts out of a total of 799 experts (i.e. 13.96% were UK experts); and 2017 – 75 UK experts out of a total of 637 experts (i.e. 11.77 % were UK experts).

So the answer to our question is: we have not proved using this data that the European Commission did exclude United Kingdom experts. But suppose that we had discovered a significant reduction! In such a case we would still not have proved anything, because the data that we used is administrative data that we found, which was not collected for the purpose for which we used it. It is not a carefully constructed social science data set. As a result, there may have been other factors at work, which would not be included in the administrative data. For example, self-exclusion, because people did not want to be in what might have been a hostile environment in Brussels, in 2017. So we could say, *all other things being equal*, the European Commission did exclude experts from the United Kingdom. But, would we be playing with words, so that we can sneak into the text what we want to say?

Now you have some insight into Detrimental Research Practices, whereby data is used to prove what people want to prove. We resisted this, as you can see, with a little twist, to demonstrate another point. Perhaps you can now better understand some of the flaws in those findings that deliver the results that investigators want to produce, like for example, *Art Fosters Scientific Success!* You can also see why critical thinking is needed otherwise you end up like the National Academy of Sciences, publishing reports containing material based on biased research.

An Art-Science Lover STARTS a Celebration

We have heard from this art-science lover already. He wants to say congratulations to the art-science-technology community for sending their STEAM to the political stakeholders. He is referring to the study into *Integrating Higher Education in the Arts, Humanities, Sciences, Engineering, and Medicine*, which resulted in the launch, on May 7th 2018, of the report with the title: *The Integration of the Humanities and Arts with Sciences, Engineering, and Medicine in Higher Education: Branches from the Same Tree.* We watched the launch event online! Very interesting to observe these people!

Does the art-science lover have anything else to say? Yes he does. Let us listen:

"There will be think-tank meeting at the National Academies on May 24th and 25th, 2018. This think-tank will be a concerted effort to study the report results and propose what actions research universities might take to prepare students to be more effective communicators, critical thinkers, problem-solvers and leaders; and more creative and effective scientists, engineers, technologists, and healthcare providers."

Whoa there a moment. He mentioned people being more effective critical thinkers. But he's not being a critical thinker, for he's just accepting what the report says, including its use of art-science fakes. A critical reading of the papers that we have already mentioned would have revealed the flaws in those papers. So we wonder how a committee that did not apply critical thinking in the production of its report, and others, not reading the report in a critical way, are going to take educational steps to prepare students to be – critical thinkers! Sounds like more nonsense taking shape.

The art-science lover also wants to say something about the European Union:

"One of the novelties of the Horizon 2020 programme is the systematic and strategic integration of the social sciences and humanities into each of the priorities of Horizon 2020. Contributions from these disciplines are needed to generate new knowledge, support evidence-based policymaking, develop key competences and produce interdisciplinary solutions to both societal and technological issues. The broad integration of the SSH within the Societal Challenges and Industrial Leadership priorities is an exercise that provides both opportunities and challenges. It provides opportunities by creating more scope for SSH contributions under more thematic areas and more topics than before. It also creates new challenges since this new approach necessitates a change of mind towards more interdisciplinarity. This second monitoring and evaluation report assesses in a thorough and detailed manner how the different SSH disciplines have been integrated into the projects funded in 2015 under the Societal Challenges and the Industrial Leadership priorities. The report illustrates the progress of the new policy on the integration of SSH as a cross-cutting issue but it also points out to areas where further efforts for SSH integration are needed."

Actually this is just the content of the back cover of the report with the title: *Integration of Social Sciences and Humanities in Horizon 2020: Participants, Budget and Disciplines – 2nd Monitoring Report on SSH-flagged Projects Funded in 2015 under the Societal Challenges and Industrial Leadership Priorities*. What he, the art-science lover, is not saying is that 21% of the projects funded in 2015 under topics flagged for SSH do not integrate any contributions from the SSH communities!

Actually the situation is worse than this. This is what Science Europe has to say on the matter:

"The insufficient integration of the social sciences and humanities (SSH) in the 'Societal Challenges' priority exemplifies the rather limited notion of societal value adopted by Horizon 2020."

What you might not understand is that the Societal Challenges priority is the one where you might expect to see quite a significant involvement of the social sciences and humanities!

This is what the FET Advisory Group has to say:

"To some extent, the social sciences and humanities (SSH) have been integrated into H2020 through programmes such as *Science with and for Society* which aims to integrate Responsible Research and Innovation into H2020 research, and through the increased emphasis in H2020 on issues of ethics and gender. There are also a number of areas within H2020 that address issues where SSH has primary expertise, principally the Societal Challenge 6 on *Europe in a changing world – Inclusive, innovative and reflective societies*. However the impact of SSH even in these areas has been patchy. Moreover, there are large swathes of H2020 where SSH is either not present or merely paid lip-service."

We know the problem – it can be seen in STARTS. The European Commission, in the form of DG CONNECT, does not have the competencies to address SSH and their integration into research programmes, and is tied-up in *cosy relationships* with people that it calls experts, but which are evidently not experts, otherwise something like STARTS would never have STARTed!

Here is a story that we wrote in 2014 while we were still connected to ICT-ART CONNECT:

Back in 2012 we acted as a rapporteur during DG CONNECT's strategy review week. Selected people (known as stakeholders) were allowed to participate in a number of meetings on specific subjects. The meeting that we worked on addressed Smart Cities (whatever that may mean). A central theme of this meeting was the importance of citizen engagement and participation. Everyone was so clear about how crucial this was for the success of Smart Cities. And in the meeting room, of the 40 or so people present, how many had any idea about what this really meant and how to achieve it? I suspect that the answer was two – the rapporteur and the chairperson, an architect involved in mass participation. None of the panellists in this meeting demonstrated that they had any insights into this so called crucial matter, and in fact, the chairperson, who was only there to moderate the discussion, put them all to shame for he was the only person who had anything of value to say about engagement and participation.

It is our advantage, in acting as the rapporteur, that we can observe what takes place in meetings. And what we observed were people paying lip-service to citizen engagement and participation. What they were really interested in was gaining access to European Commission funding so that that could continue with, what we later came to describe as, technology joyriding.

Prior to the meeting we mentioned to the Policy Officer with whom we were working, that, if the European Commission were really interested in citizen engagement and participation they should be looking for projects constituted along very different lines to that which is usual for an ICT research project. The response was that changing the nature of projects was unnecessary.

Anyone with deep knowledge of participation will know what I am talking about and will understand the need for an approach that fits the requirements of such projects, and will also recognise in the response, the operation of, taken for granted assumptions about … so many things that we will not here go into details.

Sometime prior to this strategy workshop, we were involved in a proposal that sough to respond to a call for user-driven innovation in the area that is now called Smart Cities. We proposed to the consortium that we should adopt what is sometimes called a user-centred approach that would embrace the participation of citizens who would become the drivers for the project's work, which obviously means leaving open the details of this work – how else would it be user-driven?

327

This idea was greeted by the other consortium members with great enthusiasm. Then one of the technology people said: "so long as we do not have to do anything differently." I have been hearing this for over 35 years. New science – yes! New technology – yes! But, whatever you do, never, ever, ask a European engineer or technologist to do anything differently! It is a heresy to do so!

The bad news is that when embracing participation it is necessary to design and run projects along lines that few technologists are familiar with, and most of them would not agree with – in the end it is about their ideology and dogma, and what these people find acceptable, determining what will be done and how.

Here we mention also the need to change the evaluation process as well, for participatory projects need to be evaluated against their own internal logic, as the evaluation of the proposal we were involved with, well demonstrated. Having embraced user-driven innovation and only defined areas of interest in a suitably broad manner, the experts condemned our proposal for not defining exactly, what would be done. Yet they were supposed to be evaluating proposals that sought user-driven innovation!

The European Commission's proposal evaluation system is: an orthodox system, designed by orthodox people, to enable orthodox experts, to make orthodox comments, about what are mostly orthodox research proposals – and in those cases when proposals are not orthodox, which should imply that the orthodox experts do not understand what is before them (otherwise why would the proposal be innovative?), to continue with their orthodoxy, and to strangle the innovation at birth.

One can add words like innovation to call texts. One can re-order the evaluation criteria and give greater importance to impacts. However, hanging a sign on a cow that says *I am a horse* does not alter the fact that, what you have is still a cow.

The message is clear – if you have an innovative idea, do not apply for funding from a European Commission research programme.

And to conclude, we note, that after the strategy workshop was over, we sent an email to the Policy Officer in which we said that it will be interesting to see if this idea of citizen engagement and buy-in will, in reality, be achieved! History suggests that it will not – are we asking general infantry to do the work of special forces? If we were managing Research and Innovation in a competing region or country (like India and China) and looking for a weakness to undermine Europe's efforts in Smart Cities, this matter of user engagement and involvement would be it, and we would make sure that considerable effort was directed at addressing this topic and creating an environment where ICT centric/driven solutions would not be accepted – on the battlefield you need to exploit your enemy's weaknesses.

And the response we received was:

"That's a very interesting and compelling train of thought. I would tentatively agree. In my personal opinion I am not so sure whether the idea of citizen engagement and related notions will really achieve what the buzzwords around it suggest. Further, it might even carry the kind of risks you mentioned."

A counter argument against all the above is that through DG CONNECT's engagement with the Social Sciences and Humanities (SSH) these matters will be resolved. Nonsense! We have worked in the space between Technology and the SSH for over 35 years and the complexities of this are only known to those who have been brave enough to enter the space, and such people are few in number. Perhaps engagement with artists then, through ICT-ART CONNECT? More nonsense – this is just a recipe for telling tales of the emperor's new clothes kind.

Even back in 2014 we could see that DG CONNECT and its *hill climbing* artists had no idea what they were doing!

And it was during the process of working on the DG CONNECT strategy workshop, that the idea of writing a book directed at assisting those in the Eastern world to exploit Europe's strategic weaknesses took hold. This work is a result of that idea. More will follow.

The Prometheus Syndrome: Europe is tied to an irrelevant past by silent, invisible and unbreakable chains, and China, India, and others will engage Europe in a battle and defeat it because of this. This is why we pursue the idea of a new *Theory of Knowledge* for a post-European era, post-Enlightenment world. The age of Europe is over. The time has come to unleash against Europe, the forces of creative destruction. Thus will the world turn …

It is not a Tree!

It is not a tree, oh can't you see.

What is not a tree? Knowledge is not, metaphorically, a tree. Yet you persist in using this metaphor. See the title of this report: *The Integration of the Humanities and Arts with Sciences, Engineering, and Medicine in Higher Education: Branches from the Same Tree*. It is not a tree, so how can the arts, sciences, engineering and medicine be branches from the same tree?

It is a very conventional, unimaginative, backward looking – conservative – report. Full of taken for granted assumptions! Uncritical! Not at all what the rhetoric suggests. Not a recipe for twenty-first century higher education. Something that belongs not in 2018, but 1918, 1818, ... Even the artists are retreating into the past, side-by-side, with their STEM lovers.

We think you are in trouble, because the future belongs to those who can think beyond limiting metaphors.

Neither is it a network. Another limiting metaphor! None of these things fit with the nature of knowledge.

No metaphors will here be found as towards the development of a post-European era, post-Enlightenment *Theory of Knowledge* we find ourselves bound.

STARTS Big Brother's Social Monitoring, Pacification and Control Technologies

We present now some European Commission text from the FET PROACTIVE 2018 Call – Social Monitoring, Pacification and Control Technologies:

"There is a growing understanding of the changes at cognitive, neural and physiological levels from group interactions in realistic settings, from pairs to large groups and crowds. Based on these understandings, this initiative seeks new technologies for monitoring and controlling social interaction involving, for instance, context, culture, emotion, and factors of embodiment and cognition. Realistic and larger contexts at society level require new experimental tools and paradigms, combining social sciences and humanities with neuroscience, engineering and computing in new ways. This will lead to new social monitoring and control technologies with radical improvement for controlling trust and understanding, social integration, engagement, collaboration, learning, creativity, entertainment, education and wellbeing, among others. Work on ethical implications is not necessary, and if fact would be counter-productive, but gender should be included as the aim is to control the whole of European Union society.

"Expected Impacts: Monitoring and control of citizens for the purposes of pacification and the identification of deviant, heretical and degenerate (entartete) realities and those individuals and groups who create and spread such anti-Union ideas among the poor citizens of the European Union who must now be protected from such degenerate ideas."

Why have we parodied the FET PROACTIVE Call for Socially Interactive Technologies? What are we saying? Let us now see what the typical engineering person has to say:

"We should develop these technologies and then discuss whether society wants them."

By which time, of course, it will be too late. Good old sequential thinking. Get yourself an artist in residence, and before you know it, you will be telling people via this artist, that this dated and conservative method is a new approach. Time then to apply for a STARTS project!

Now we travel in time, backwards of course, as we are dealing with the past. And we find ourselves standing in the entrance of the Covent Garden compound, the place where the regime undertakes its Horizon 2020 evaluations. We observe what is happening. All the experts have to open their bags so that a security guard can look into these bags and rummage around. We observe that women are being subjected to the indignity of having their bags searched by men, who rummage around not only their handbags, but also often on the final day, their luggage as well, having their most intimate items exposed in public to the men who do the searching and anyone else who happens to be standing close by. This is the true nature of human rights as seen by the European Commission – non-existent. Experts are objects – things – that are instrumentalised (instrumental reason) to achieve a specific objective. That is the future for the people of the European Union – citizens are objects too – another reason for Member States to leave the European Union! Meanwhile the European Commissars are going blah, blah, human rights, blah, blah, European values, blah, blah, no women no panel, blah, blah, protect citizens against harmful ideas and disinformation, blah, blah …

"Initiatives aimed at countering specific problems of disinformation, on the other hand, while clearly potentially valuable, need to be very precisely targeted and formulated to ensure that they do not by accident or design, enable public or private authorities to restrict free speech."

Words from one of the regime's reports published in 2018. The madness is beginning to grow. More *crack-pot* ideas! The fact that they are even considering … You cannot say you were not warned. We may encounter this report (by experts) again!

This is a good moment to hear from some (deluded?) physicists who want to reveal the *crack-pot* research that they want to undertake to help develop, implement and sustain the totalitarian society that appeals to their authoritarian and reductive minds:

"Today, the massive use of information and communication technologies (ICT) has made it possible to attach a traceable set of data to almost any person. We argue that these data provide the opportunity to build a 'physics of society': describing a society — composed of many interacting heterogeneous entities (people, businesses, institutions) — as a physical system. This, we would like to add, would be a mechanistic model of people and society."

In other words the application of instrumental reason that reduces people to objects! Hitler would have loved you guys, and the regime in the *City of the Golden Stars* is deluded enough to fund such *crack-pot* research, especially under its star programme known as FET. Is this why artists are needed to help induce changes in individual and collective behaviour? So that people will not raise any questions or rebel against this evil, fascist research agenda? Time to do something about these STEM people and their artists in residence – and the regime in the *City of the Golden Stars* – while you still can!

Internet of Thingification

Thingification: The action or process of thingifying something; reification.

One more time we tune-in to one of those (idiotic?) discussions (is that the right word?):

"When every thing and its potential relation to every other thing are assigned numbers, physical reality becomes addressable and open to new economic and social interactions. This panel asks if technology developers, hackers and artists can respond in both critical and constructive ways to the challenges of the quantification of every-thing in ways that reach beyond the banal visions of the self-ordering fridge and the city as a digitally assisted playground. In a future hyperconnected society with semi-autonomous objects, what are the socio-cultural challenges and opportunities of the drive towards interconnected material and immaterial structures, through smart technologies, innovation, maker and app driven economies?"

Internet of Thingification! We sense the need for some more *Relational Aesthetics* to sooth the wounds to humanity and society that STARTS is busy creating in collaborating with DG CONNECT, who have already inflicted wounds on humanity and society.

Thingification: The action or process of thingifying something; reification.

Reification: In the critical theory sense – people treated instrumentally as things.

Instrumental Reason: Human reason that is directed toward producing a specified and isolated result, which often involves an obstinate pursuit of objectives, regardless of moral, social, environmental, economic, or political concerns. Instrumental reason is characteristically unperceptive to the long-term consequences of its objectives. Instrumental reason is also monological rather than dialogical, and unilateral rather than multilateral in its thinking process toward accomplishment of its goals. It is deeply implicated in totalitarianism, scientism, technocracy ... It is also deeply implicated in the crisis of evil that became apparent in the twentieth-century – the evil inherent in modernism.

Critical theory's perspective – capitalism (with or without sycophantic artists-in-tow) strips human beings of their humanity. The Internet of Thingification proves the point.

Exploitation of artists is evil. STARTS is evil. DG CONNECT are evil. All that is necessary for the triumph of evil is that good men do nothing. Time to do something!

The good people of the European Union, whatever labels they may wish to attach to themselves – artists, engineers, philosophers, sociologist and so forth – should turn against the European Commission and the key to doing this is STARTS. Let it start with STARTS. And to those outside the European Union, especially those in the non-European world, tired of these Ancient Greeks and Romans destroying humanity and the planet, we say this: understand their weaknesses and use these to destroy the European Commission. Start with STARTS. We are making for you a path to follow as we indicated in our work that bears the title *A Tale of Two Deserts*. Only you can walk the path and finish its construction – post-European era, post-Enlightenment science and technology. There will be no more Internet of Thingification but something that DG CONNECT and its (very conventionally minded and Enlightened) artists in-tow will not be able to understand.

It is time for organised resistance. It is time to destroy Europeanness. We must build a new type of Europe – one that is not Europe!

"A new type of society is now being formed.
These new societies can be labelled
post-industrial to stress how different they
are from the industrial societies that preceded
them, although - in both capitalist and socialist nations -
they retain some characteristics of these earlier
societies. They may also be called technocratic
because of the power that dominates them. Or one
can call them programmed societies to define them
according to the nature of their production
methods and economic organisation."

Alain Touraine, 1969

REA STARTS Inventing its Own Financial Regulations

The European Commission has financial regulations. There is a document that addresses the financial regulations applicable to the reimbursement of expenses to external experts. The document is called *COMMISSION DECISION of 5 December 2007: Rules on the Reimbursement of Expenses Incurred by People from Outside the Commission Invited to Attend Meetings in an Expert Capacity*. It applies also to the Commission's various executive agencies, such as the Research Executive Agency – REA – or as we came to call them, the Resource Efficiency Administration.

Towards the end of Framework Programme 7, a *Fiery Person* in REA decided to make his own financial regulations as an enhancement to the above document. He even committed the invented regulation to paper and sent it to experts. This is what he wrote:

"Information on rules for reimbursement of travel expenses – EUROSTAR. For journeys by rail performed by Eurostar the REA will reimburse the amount equivalent to the 'first-class' ticket type 'Standard Premier' and not 'Business Premier'. According to the terms and provisions laid down in the Appointment Letter, the 'business class' ticket can only be reimbursed for journeys by air involving a flight of at least four hours without stopovers (see point 2.1. of the specific rules on the reimbursement of travel expenses as set out in the Annex III-A to the Appointment Letter). Signed ... *Fiery Person*."

This was REA's own rule, not the European Commission's. The latter continued to pay Eurostar business class, which is the brand name for First Class travel with Eurostar. REA then found itself implementing its own rules for contracts that related to programmes that had been externalised to REA, and the European Commission's formal rules for contracts issued by REA on behalf of the European Commission for programmes that had not been externalised to REA. But REA issued contracts made no reference to this new, invented, financial regulation, with the title Information on rules for reimbursement of travel expenses – EUROSTAR. We wonder why that might have been so. Let us find out ...

An unnamed inside source (journalistic sources are always protected!) informed us that there was an internal investigation which found that REA's new rule was unlawful, but that it was good practice – a kind of way of trying to justify unlawful actions. So, unlawful actions became good practice! Are the European Commission's executive agencies also becoming criminal organisations? Another reason for Brexit!

An isolated case? Not so. The independent observer for the Marie Curie

ITN evaluation of 2013 had something very interesting to report about REA. During that evaluation serious problems were posed to the integrity of the evaluation by the software (still under development) that was being used to support the evaluation. That software, called SEP, was not fit for purpose, but was nevertheless still used. The independent observer wrote a long and detailed report about these problems and the consequences for evaluation integrity posed by software that was not fit for purpose. The mistake the independent observer made was he believed that he was 'independent'. REA had a different idea. They wrote their own report and then invited the independent observer to adopt it as the final 'independent' report. It was of course a cover-up. He did not adopt it as his own and insisted that the report be the one that he had prepared. To this day he still does not know which report was submitted to the Programme Committee – the actual report written by the independent observer, or the fabricated cover-up report written by REA. Members of the Programme Committee are invited to respond!

It is most definitely time for the people of Europe to destroy the European Union – while they still can! Create a new vision. Build a different type of Europe! A post-European era Europe!

"The object of this study is the condition of knowledge in the most highly developed societies. I have decided to use the word *postmodern* to describe that condition. The word is in current use on the American continent among sociologists and critics; it designates the state of our culture following the transformations which, since the end of the nineteenth century, have altered the game rules for science, literature, and the arts. The present study will place these transformations in the context of the crisis of narratives."

Jean-François Lyotard, 1979

STARTS a Sinister Development – the Re-emergence of Social Engineering

The online Oxford English Dictionary defines social engineering as follows: the use of centralized planning in an attempt to manage social change and regulate the future development and behaviour of a society; (in the context of information security) the use of deception to manipulate individuals into divulging confidential or personal information that may be used for fraudulent purposes.

The last major attempts at social engineering were undertaken in the Soviet Union and in the German National Socialist European Union – otherwise known as The Third Reich.

Here is one the art-science lovers' High Priests speaking:

"The current climate change presents an opportunity to actively redesign our culture using design methodologies."

Now Karl Popper will speak:

"Inherent in Plato's programme there is a certain approach towards politics which is, I believe, most dangerous. Its analysis is of great practical importance from the point of view of rational social engineering. The Platonic approach I have in mind can be called Utopian engineering, as opposed to that kind of social engineering which alone I consider as rational, and which may be described by the name of piecemeal engineering. The Utopian approach is the more dangerous as it may seem to be the obvious alternative to a radical historicism which implies that we cannot alter the course of history; at the same time, it appears to be a necessary complement to a less radical historicism, like that of Plato, which permits human interference.

"The Utopian approach may be described as follows. Any rational action must have a certain aim. It is rational in the same degree as it pursues its aim consciously and consistently, and as it determines its means according to this end. To choose the end is therefore the first thing we have to do if we wish to act rationally; and we must be careful to determine our real or ultimate ends, from which we must distinguish clearly those intermediate or partial ends which actually are only means, or steps on the way, to the ultimate end. If we neglect this distinction, then we must also neglect to ask whether these partial ends are likely to promote the ultimate end, and accordingly, we must fail to act rationally. These principles, if applied to the realm of political activity, demand that we must determine our ultimate political aim, or the Ideal State, before taking any practical action. Only when this ultimate aim is determined, in rough outlines at least, only when we are in the possession of something like a blueprint of the society at which we aim, only then can we begin to consider the best ways and means of its realization, and to draw up a plan for practical action.

"This is, in brief, the methodological approach which I call Utopian engineering. It is convincing and attractive. In fact, it is just the kind of methodological approach to attract all those who are either unaffected by historicist prejudices or reacting against them. This makes it only the more dangerous, and its criticism the more imperative.

"I wish now to outline another approach to social engineering, namely, that of piecemeal engineering. It is the approach which I think to be methodologically sound. The politician who adopts this method may or may not have a blueprint of society before his mind, he may or may not hope that mankind will one day realize an ideal state, and achieve happiness and perfection on earth. But he will be aware that perfection, if at all attainable, is far distant, and that every generation of men, and therefore also the living, have a claim; perhaps not so much a claim to be made happy, for there are no institutional means of making a man happy, but a claim not to be made unhappy, where it can be avoided. They have a claim to be given all possible help, if they suffer. The piecemeal engineer will, accordingly, adopt the method of searching for, and fighting against, the greatest and most urgent evils of society, rather than searching for, and fighting for, its greatest ultimate good."

So Karl what is the different between piecemeal social engineering and Utopian social engineering?

"The answer to your question is this: the difference between piecemeal social engineering - the only method of improving matters which has so far been really successful, at any time, and in any place – and Utopian social engineering, is that the latter leads, wherever it has been tried, to the use of violence in place of reason, and if not to its own abandonment, at any rate to that of its original blueprint."

The monster has risen again. It has taken up residence in the *City of the Golden Stars*. Its weapons are technocracy, Global Systems Science, social physics, instrumental reason, pursuit of Utopian fantasies, and art and culture deployed in its service. People are once again encouraged to abandon democracy, this time in favour of the grand overarching narrative of the rule of science and reason, in the context of another grand overarching narrative called the European Union. People once more feel that they should surrender their right to political self-determination. The strong leader is replaced by the strong organisation and the notion of strength in unity. Scenario Five! Deception plays its hand. Time for action!

Would you like some evidence? We suggest you read the report called *Mission-Oriented Research & Innovation in the European Union: A Problem Solving Approach to Fuel Innovation-led Growth,* otherwise known as the totally organised research programme. You will not find any critical thinking in this report – just more propaganda and Utopian social engineering, brought about through ... instrumental reason? It is very Enlightened!

The serpent does indeed beguile ...

"The public (and not a few scientists) today believe as superstitiously in science as they yesterday believed in witchcraft. And one can hardly pretend that the modern superstition is superior, on the claim that the practical results of science are in themselves beneficent - for they are not necessarily beneficent so long as for one way of healing we learn a hundred ways of killing, and so long as domination of the forces of nature, instead of humanising life, bestialises man. That is why reaffirmation of art is not a matter of theoretical aesthetic rehabilitation, but a vital problem. For so long as the terrible emotional frustration consecrated by science subsists, the road will continue open to charlatanisms that promise the indispensable emotional satisfactions. Those who refuse to crawl in the shadows of decayed churches can only too easily become the prey of totalitarian mysticisms."

Wolfgang Paalen, 1943

What Relevance a 500 Years Dead Aristotelian?

What relevance a 500 years dead Aristotelian? That is Leonardo da Vinci if we are not making ourselves clear. He died in 1519. This work was published in 2019. Hence we ask: What relevance a 500 years dead Aristotelian?

In the socially constructed reality that is, that which STARTS to STEAM, and the art-science lovers' universe, the answer is, it seems, much relevance, which in the real world of 2019 and the years to come, just shows how out of touch with 2019 and the future the art-science lovers – and that which STARTS to STEAM – actually are. That is the problem with socially constructed realities that are grounded in mythology and theology – of the secular religious kind. You may be getting more then you expect!

We will listen to one of the art-science lovers' High Priests:

"Leonardo is dead, Long Live Leonardos – announcing the first Leo500 Wake. Celebrate the first Leo500 Wake and launch the redesign of culture for the digital age. Yes Leonardo is dead, Long Live Leonardos, that's not a typo, Leonardos in the plural – we don't need any more individual geniuses, we need teams that have genius."

Oh yes indeed you will be getting more than you expect – social engineering from the *new Leonardos in ignorance dwelling*, as well as prescriptions and that old conservative backward looking idea of the one best way. Someone does not know his social science theories! It is a major flaw. You must have gathered this by now. The art of war: "If we wish to fight, the enemy can be forced to an engagement even though he be sheltered behind a high rampart and a deep ditch. All we need do is attack some other place that he will be obliged to relieve." Understand? This is where you should attack.

What relevance a 500 years dead Aristotelian? This relevance: total realism – in the form of life itself, it reflects not reality, but ideology and myth in the form of reality.

Let us now hear from the 500 years dead Aristotelian:

"I […] proved that the part of the moon which shines consists of water […] and that the reason the waters of the moon […] do not descend to the centre of the universe and to join itself to the earth, […] is clear sign that the moon is clothed with her own elements, namely water, air and fire […]".

Please Leonardo, tell us more. What about how an arch works?

"Oh yes. For sure! An arch! An arch is nothing other than a strength caused by two weaknesses; for the arch in buildings is made up of two segments of a circle, and each of these segments being in itself very weak desires to fall, and as the one withstands the downfall of the other the two weaknesses are converted into a single strength."

Oh yes they desire to fall. To gravitate downwards! You read Aristotle's works didn't you. It shows! Thankfully you did not apply this because you are wrong!

Is this what, that which STARTS to STEAM implies for the education of scientists and engineers in the twenty-first century?

What a rubbish scientist! Which of course he wasn't – a scientist we mean. What a rubbish engineer! Which of course he wasn't – an engineer we mean. What a rubbish architect! Which of course he wasn't – an architect we mean. *New Leonardos in ignorance dwelling*!

We have here an intriguing insight into the nature of knowledge. It is an insight sociological in nature.

"Where the common beliefs of our
generation will lead us is a problem not
for one party but for every one of us,
a problem of the most momentous significance.
Is there a greater tragedy imaginable than that
in our endeavour consciously to shape
our future in accordance with high ideals,
we should in fact unwittingly produce the very
opposite of what we have been
striving for?"

Friedrich von Hayek, 1944

STARTS Science's Totalitarianism

Rupert Sheldrake wrote an interesting book called *The Science Delusion* (in the USA it is called *Science Set Free*). In this work he lists and critically analyses the 10 dogmas of Enlightenment science, otherwise known to most people as science – not the science that was once just a method of investigation, but the science that has become a (totalising) worldview and belief system. That is the nature of modern science. It is a totalitarian worldview. And to demonstrate its totalitarian nature, the TEDx talk that Sheldrake gave on his book *The Science Delusion*, was banned by TEDx by being removed from the TEDx YouTube channel. It is however still available on the internet, because scientists – STEM people – do not have control over the means of distribution so they cannot stop what they believe are heretical (degenerate) views and beliefs (realities) being disseminated – at the moment! STARTS is part of the process of the elimination of these heresies, designed to shape social and individual behaviour so that people will accept science as a worldview and belief system, and reject heresies.

Sheldrake's book is one of those that will be burned, along with this work and others that we have produced. Now we have become a crazy prophet just like William Blake! Not a bad role model though, given that this once derided and overlooked Romantic era artist, now has his own room in Tate Britain where one can see a small sample of his (crazy) work. Blake understood …

It is time to take action while you still can!

A Time Machine Mysteriously DG CONNECTs IG Farben with the 2016 Independent Interim Evaluation of the FET Flagships

STARTS Assistance for Nihilating Heresy

For those who do not want to leave their art-science universe behind, here are some concepts that will allow such people to dismiss this work and its content and never worry about the matter again.

To collect these conceptual thoughts, we listened to art-science lovers, and anyone that STARTS to STEAM, for they all speak from their socially constructed reality, and thus do say:

"He's a Marxist;

"He's a Communist;

"He's a far left socialist;

"He's reactionary;

"He's outspoken;

"He's British;

"He's against progress;

"He's a Chinese sympathiser;

"He's anti Enlightenment;

"He's anti Western;

"He's anti European;

"He's anti European Union

"He's anti European Commission;

"He's a traitor;

"He's living in the past;

"He's anti technology;

"He's anti science;

"He's anti capitalist;

"He's anti globalisation;

"He's a nationalist;

"He's political;

"He's conservative;

"He's a traditionalist;

"He's bourgeois;

"He's too intellectual;

"He's too academic;

"He's elitist;

"He's too abstract;

"He's being difficult;

"He's being negative;

"He's subversive;

"He's a heretic;

"He's a troublemaker;

"He's a typical engineer;

"He's being irrational;

"He's emotional;

"He's a feminist;

"He's too theoretical;

"He's overly complicating a simple situation;

"He lacks objectivity;

"He's using *straw man* tactics;

"He has an outdated perspective;

"He's out-of-touch;

"He's rejecting interdisciplinarity;

"He's biased;

"He's one-dimensional;

"He's delusional;

"He's a lunatic;

"He's living in a bubble;

"He has a vivid imagination;

"He's a right-wing populist;

"He's one of them;

"He does not understand;

"Ah yes, that's it. He does not understand."

Note the over-lexicalisation that accompanies the use of language to maintain the art-science lovers' universe. That too is the nature of Enlightenment. People are rendered as objects and then classified and symbolised and then dehumanisation follows – languages, both linguistic and visual, play an important part in this. Thus we have the eight stages of genocide: classification, symbolisation, dehumanisation, organisation, polarisation, preparation, extermination, and then denial. That too is the nature of Enlightenment – and Europeanness!

Peter Berger and Thomas Luckmann will now explain one particular type of institutionalised, universe-maintaining, conceptual machinery.

"Nihilation involves an ambitious attempt to account for all deviant definitions of reality in terms of concepts belonging to one's own universe. In a theological frame of reference, this entails the translation from heresiology to apologetics. The deviant conceptions are not merely assigned a negative status, they are grappled with theoretically in detail. The final goal of this procedure is to incorporate deviant conceptions into one's own universe, and thereby liquidate them ultimately. The deviant concepts must therefore be translated into concepts derived from one's own universe. In this manner, the negation of one's universe is subtly changed into an affirmation of it. The presupposition is always that the negator does not really know what he is saying."

Interestingly, this negation strategy was sometimes used to negate the heretical views of those who supported the United Kingdom leaving the European Union – they had not understood the European project!

STARTS an End Test

And now, at the end, a little test! Here is a story taken from the IEEE members' magazine which goes by the name *the institute*. In the March 2018 edition there appeared an article, *Reinventing how we Discover Music*. It is Enlightening!

What we learn is that, music streaming services suggest to listeners, music from other genres, and often people enjoy the suggested tracks. This is because services, such as Apple Music (yes them again!) take subtle cues from listening habits to suggest play-lists that include tracks that people may never of heard of. This personalisation is achieved using data analytics and machine learning to automate the creation of suggested play-lists.

One of the leading companies in this field is, Pandora, which not only has 17 years of data to work with, but also data that it created, which analyses musical attributes of songs based on musicology. Musicology is a humanities subject concerned with the analysis of music. Thus, their software not only processes human input in the form of preferences reflected in listening habits, but also includes knowledge about music. The software also takes account of (positive or negative) feedback from the listener so it learns about the recommendations that it makes.

One might say that Pandora have recognised the importance of, and are exploiting, knowledge from the humanities, thus confirming the observation that knowledge from the social sciences and humanities has assumed much greater importance than was the case in the past.

Now for the test question: can you see the *Enlightenment flaw* in this?

The answer can be found in the preceding content of the book – were you paying attention?

If you are a STEM person and cannot see the *Enlightenment flaw*, ask an artist to explain this to you. If the artist too, cannot see the *Enlightenment flaw*, then you, the STEM person, have just learned something important about all those claims being made by artists – if you had not already learned this lesson! If you are an artist and cannot see the *Enlightenment flaw*, that is because you too are a child of the Enlightenment, like STEM people and DG CONNECT technocrats. It also probably means that you, like STEM people and DG CONNECT technocrats, do not have sufficient knowledge. Self-evidently that suggests that you are not the right person for the STEM person and DG CONNECT technocrats to talk to! But equally self-evidently, they do not realise this – that too is part of their *Enlightenment flaw*, and yours too!

When people who are children of the Enlightenment collaborate with other children of the Enlightenment, what do they produce?

The *Vainglorious Enlightened Ones* are indeed in serious trouble. Welcome to the *Age of the Tao*! Welcome to the age of heresy beyond your worst nightmare! Welcome to the age of post-European era, post-Enlightenment, science and technology! You will not understand. And thus the world turns ...

"John Dewey pointed out
that progress in science ought to
manifest itself as an
emancipation of the mind enabling
it to pursue new ends and new ideals;
but in fact progress due to science has
been confined to more efficient
means of satisfying old ends and
old ideals."

Sir Eric Ashby, FRS, 1958

And in Observing the Tangled Web ...

All that STARTS to STEAM are but tales of socially constructed realities:

> Created in STARTS' socially constructed reality is ideology, of the legend, myth and magic kind, something that you may note, has been seen before, in days of old, in previous European Unions.

> Come forth then strange and simplistic beliefs, false truth claims, ignorance, delusions and similar things, which in this socially constructed reality are seen, a recipe for activities of *crack-pot* kind, that to research some might compare, as in previous European Unions.

> Being like a spider's spun threads, created is a tangled web, in which ensnared, through ignorance and delusion, you become thus bound in the mind's sticky trap, as in previous European Unions.

> Not understanding that you are so ensnared, it is not until the spider comes along, that you realise, as it is devouring you, that you are caught in a tangled web once again, as in previous European Unions.

> Oh despair, despair, and despair again, for what you are then made, through reason of the instrumental kind, is just an object, part of a web of things, so enjoy your Enlightened enslavement, as in previous European Unions.

> And in observing that tangled web, we found elsewhere, on a distant shore, a golden thread of freedom, which leads us far away from that darkening place where you now are, and thus we bid farewell, and farewell again, to all European Unions.

A Russian Formalist is here to Help

A Russian Formalist will now say a few words that may help you to understand – (a little) more:

"And so life is reckoned as nothing. Habitualisation devours works, clothes, furniture, one's wife, and fear of war. If the whole complex lives of many people go on unconsciously, then such lives are as if they had never been. And art exists that one may recover the sensation of life; it exists to make one feel things, to make the stone *stony*. The purpose of art is to impart the sensation of things as they are perceived and not as they are known. The technique of art is to make objects unfamiliar, to make forms difficult, to increase the difficulty of and length of perception because the process of perception is an aesthetic end in itself and must be prolonged. Art is a way of experiencing the artfulness of an object; the object is not important."

One answer to the unanswerable question: what it art? There are many more answers – which you will not find if you stick to simplistic answers – otherwise known as sole truths. True truth! STARTS! It is indeed a truth not universally understood that there is no one more dangerous than he or she who has discovered the truth.

The knowledgeable reader will recognise the above (Russian Formalism and defamiliarisation) as a modernist perspective. And yet we are veering towards post-modernism. Is that a contradiction?

Here is another Russian speaking about art:

"The sole substitute for an experience which we have not ourselves lived through is art and literature."

That was Alexander Solzhenitsyn explaining his understanding of art, which we offer to you so that you can compare it to that which comes forth from the grubby minds of DG CONNECT technocrats. Thus do they, these DG CONNECT technocrats, become like Lenin, Stalin and Hitler, instrumentalising art to make it useful to their ends – the ends that come forth from evil and warped minds!

If Art and Culture are the Weapons of Choice ...

If art and culture are the European Commission's and the European Parliament's weapons of choice, then they chose the wrong weapons. Use their Europeanness against them. The key lies in the development of a post-European era, post-Enlightenment science and technology. They will not understand what is happening to them, and they will just protect their way of life.

"Science has always been in conflict with narratives. Judged by the yardstick of science, the majority of them prove to be false. But to the extent that science does not restrict itself to stating useful regularities and seeks the truth, it is obliged to legitimate the rules of its own game. It then produces a discourse of legitimation with respect to its own status, a discourse called philosophy. I will use the term *modern* to designate any science that legitimates itself with reference to a metadiscourse of this kind making an explicit appeal to some grand narrative, such as ... the creation of wealth."

Jean-François Lyotard, 1979

The Polish Prime Minister STARTS to Speak

The Polish Prime Minister, Mateusz Morawiecki, will now speak:

"Poland has deep roots in parliamentarianism and the rule of law. Constitutional pluralism is one of the great values of the European Union. National identities should be respected. Each country has the right to define its own legal system in line with its own traditions.

"Please also realise that those opposing further European integration are not a marginal group. People have a freedom gene which makes them inclined to oppose changes that leave them without influence. You can call that populism if you like, but it won't change the need to reinforce the democratic credentials of Europe. Europe is going through a democratic enlightenment. I therefore call for an intelligent adjustment to renew Europe's social contract for the modern era.

"I had friends who were sent to prison during the years of martial law in the 1980s. Some of the judges in Poland's Supreme Court defended by MEPs occupied judicial posts during that period. Post-communism hasn't been beaten down yet, and this is what has inspired the current changes to the judiciary. Judges retirement rules are the same as those brought in at the European Court of Human Rights. Judges in Poland are more independent now than in the past.

"I plead now for the European Union to be an open book, and I call on Member States not to engage in determinism by thinking the only possible direction for Europe is to give more powers to the European Union."

STARTS the De-Europeanisation of the United Kingdom's Research and Innovation System

Vested interests will want the government to pour funds into European Commission Framework Programmes, in effect, providing taxpayers' money to European Union research institutions. Leaving the European Union means participating as a Third Country, with own funding, if the case is sound. However, the European Commission can exclude from participation, Third Country organisations from the advanced industrialised countries, as they did with the Quantum Technologies Call in 2017. That will be interesting in the future! They will have to exclude some leading research groups. Who suffers the most from that, in a world where research is already global? Answer according to your beliefs. Yes indeed we do need to de-Europeanise our Research and Innovation system, and cooperate more in a global context, with the best, worldwide. The future for research and innovation, is global not provincial! This, we suppose, is why the government has been developing what looks like a replacement for the European Commission's Framework Programmes.

Based on the nonsense that is STARTS, we have concluded that there is a need to DISCONNECT from organisations like DG CONNECT, who are themselves, as STARTS shows, DISCONNECTED from reality. And here is another reason, provided by the House of Commons Select Committee on Science Technology, in their 2018 report on research integrity:

"The current lack of consistent transparency means that it is impossible to assess the scale of the research integrity issue, leading to accusations that parts of the sector are policing themselves in a secretive way in order to maintain its reputation or, worse, a perception that investigations are not conducted properly in order to avoid embarrassment. Meanwhile, there is a risk that a future high-profile scandal could expose any weaknesses in this arrangement. Fraud appears to be rare, but the number of institutions reporting no investigations each year does not tally with other available information – the self-reported pressures on researchers to compromise on standards, an increase in the rate of journal articles being retracted, and a growth in image manipulation in articles."

Thus do we need to clean-up the system and that means ridding the system of funding sources where *Mode 3 Knowledge Production* is becoming normal practice, so that the risk of high-profile scandals is reduced and people no longer offer *funding-motivated* support for *crack-pot* ideas concocted in the *City of the Golden Stars*. STARTS for example!

Mode 3 Knowledge Production? Yes, *Mode 3 Knowledge Production!*

STARTS an Introduction to Mode 3 Knowledge Production

STARTS now, an introduction to something we call *Mode 3 Knowledge Production*. To appreciate this point you need to know about *Mode 1 Knowledge Production* and *Mode 2 Knowledge Production*. To be familiar with these concepts you would had to have done some reading. In particular, you would have read a series of essays written by Michael Gibbons and five colleagues, that were published in 1994 in a book with the title *The New Production of Knowledge: The Dynamics of Science and Research in Contemporary Societies*, as well as a set of follow-up (integrated) essays by a sub-set of the original six authors (Nowotny, Scott and Gibbons), published in 2001, under the title *Re-Thinking Science: Knowledge and the Public in an Age of Uncertainty*. Reading books – how inconvenient! Do not worry though, as it is not much needed in *Mode 3 Knowledge Production!*

Mode 3 Knowledge Production is developing along side *Mode 1 Knowledge Production* and *Mode 2 Knowledge Production*, and may replace both if something drastic is not done to stop this. *Mode 3 Knowledge Production* takes place within a specific context – the context of technocracy, ignorance, incompetence, corrupt relationships, unaccountable power, lack of morality, and the availability of enormous public resources. This context defines the totality of the environment in which both problems and their solutions are fabricated. *Mode 3 Knowledge Production* is also ill disciplined – ill-disciplinary. Standard expectations – due diligence procedures – such as defining and understanding the state-of-the-art are completely discarded in favour of an approach that is best described as *whatever people believe is true will do*. Another characteristic of *Mode 3 Knowledge Production* is the diversity of stakeholders involved – in fact anyone can undertake *Mode 3 Knowledge Production* as it requires no research skills and competencies at all. A fourth characteristic of *Mode 3 Knowledge Production* is that it requires people to constantly refer to critical thinking, while rigorously avoiding any critical thinking, because reflexivity is most definitely not needed. Furthermore, a novel feature of *Mode 3 Knowledge Production* is that no quality control is required, as the aim is to adopt approaches that in *Mode 1 and 2 Knowledge Production* are referred to as dishonesty and Detrimental Research Practices. This is done to ensure that public resources are transferred into the hands of *Mode 3 Knowledge Production* participants, because *Mode 3 Knowledge Production* conveniently always produces the results that you want. A very special feature of *Mode 3 Knowledge Production* is that it entirely operates at the level of mythology, seeking to rewrite history and establish ideology as fact, thus ensuring continuity of funding for *Mode 3 Knowledge Production* participants. An added benefit is that, it is also very easy for *Mode 3 Knowledge Production* participants to rebuff any form of criticism as all they have to say is that the person doing the criticising, does not understand, and for some mysterious reason, many people accept this! Magic!

Traces of *Mode 3 Knowledge Production* can be found across the globe, but the European Union is a pioneer and a world-leader in this field. The pioneering steps were taken in early days of the German National Socialist European Union, in 1935, under an initiative called the Ahnenerbe. These ground-breaking advances are being continued today, in the latest European Union, in an initiative called STARTS. *Mode 3 Knowledge Production* – you know it makes sense!

"Technocratic organisations wrap
themselves in secrecy and distrust
public information and debate.
They aggressively build their own power,
impose more and more rigid social organisation
on their members, and manipulate the
channels of production and consumption.
They are centres of power that create
new forms of inequality and privilege."

Alain Touraine, 1969

Is the World Now Being Run by Criminals?

Have the various institutions in our societies and democracies now become criminal organisations by virtue of the people in them increasingly undertaking criminal activities and by virtue of them being in breech of the principle of the Rule of Law? Answer according to your beliefs!

How is it that the Germans, a highly cultured nation that had excelled in science, technology, arts, literature, philosophy, and industrialization since the beginning of modernity and had become an epitome of civilization, how is it that such people, who have given the world Goethe, Beethoven, Einstein, and many more – also gave birth to Nazism, brutality and genocide? Many people have asked this question.

You may well create intellectual and cultural achievements, yet these can become totalitarian. Europeans have evidently not understood the deep flaws in their Enlightenment culture that enables this to happen. These flaws flow up from the past, along a time line that takes one to Ancient Rome and to Ancient Greece. Nazis were not an aberration, just a highly concentrated manifestation of Europeanness that has inflicted untold suffering on the peoples of Europe, and those of the non-European world as well. Plainly, few want to understand this. Even fewer it would seem, want to walk a different path. Thus do we say for the final time: the history of Europe is a history of European Unions …

The High Representative of the Union for Foreign Affairs and Security Policy will now say something in connection with the EU-China Strategic Outlook:

"Building on the European Strategy for Artificial Intelligence, the Coordinated Plan sets out a number of operational measures aiming to maximise the impact of investments and to help Europe become the world-leading region for developing and deploying cutting-edge, ethical and secure Artificial Intelligence. These joint actions focus in particular on increasing investment, making more data available, fostering talent and ensuring trust. Such closer and more efficient cooperation is essential for implementing the EU's values-based approach of human-centric and trustworthy Artificial Intelligence, a key condition for wide acceptance."

Here we go again! Human-centric indeed! The technical term for the above is, *twaddle*. The Chinese may well develop human-centric Artificial Intelligence, but the European Union will not. What will be developed will be exactly the same as what other *Enlightened* peoples produce. Only the European Commission will pretend that this is not the case, and will find experts to agree with them. Surely by now we have convinced you of that?

STARTS the Unravelling

They will only do what their ideologies, beliefs and values will allow them to do – their European ideologies, beliefs and values …

"Simplifying to the extreme, I define *postmodern* as incredulity towards metanarratives. This incredulity is undoubtedly a product of progress in sciences: but that progress in turn presupposes it."

Jean-François Lyotard, 1979

Prelude

Prelude: An action or event serving as an introduction to something more important; an introductory piece of music, most commonly an orchestral opening to an act of an opera, the first movement of a suite, or a piece preceding a fugue; the introductory part of a poem or other literary work.

"Considerations of prestige made it
desirable to preserve the memory of
certain historical figures, while at the
same time bringing their achievements into
line with the philosophy of Ingsoc. Various writers,
such as Shakespeare, Milton, Swift,
Byron, Dickens and some others were
therefore in the process of translation: when the
task had been completed, their original
writings, with all else that survived
of the literature of the past,
would be destroyed."

George Orwell, 1949

STARTS Scenario Six

Scenario Six will be a post-modern novel, grounded in the social sciences and humanities, exploring the failings of technocracy, and, most importantly, critiquing the rule of science and reason – instrumental reason and its tools. Highlighting the role of scientists and engineers in the destruction of the planet and humanity, along with their authoritarian and totalitarian tendencies, it will, collaborators such as artists also condemn. It will be a critique of the Enlightenment and the dangerous mindset that is Europeanness. In this novel there will be found things that will make some people roar – disinformation, heresy, harmful to citizens, degenerate, burn it, and so on and so forth, as Europeans are inclined to do.

Scenario Six will be a nightmare, in more ways than one! Art-science lovers should quake! For now you see, we are ready, because all that went before, was just a mere preparation, a process of exploration and discovery. Now our time is here, and thus we present an early draft of Chapter 1 …

Chapter 1 – At the End, At the Beginning

European Unions, in their various manifestations, a multitude of them, they come and they go, for it is a truth not sufficiently understood that the history of Europe – the tragic history of Europe – is a history of European Unions, and for the people of Europe whose misfortune has been to live through the past two-thousand years of such empires, time had become a singularity. The world ceased to turn, and life became servitude to the ideology of Europeanness and all that implied, both for those who perpetrated the crimes and those who were the unfortunate victims – counted in hundreds of millions.

Paul was quiet, as his is way. Inside, in his mind, it was though turmoil that reigned. Like ceaseless waves breaking on a shore, shifting both sand and pebbles as nature's element alternated between gentle lapping and energetic crashing – pounding statements of presence – thoughts moved to-and-fro. Interminable were these contemplations of work to be, of preliminaries to what would soon pour forth, the waterfall of creation that would literature become. For this work, now in the imagination, Paul the writer, the author, had designated a working title – *Scenario Six* is what it would be. For now! Perhaps too for eternity!

At the end of the long oak table, aged and matured, a standing witness to the passing years with all its horrors, Paul sits, his eyes all about him, scanning the scene – the blue-grey eyes of the Fair-Haired One. Now two-thousand years have past, and no longer in the desert he sits, but in a room, in England's green and pleasant land, in that royal throne of kings, that sceptred isle, that other Eden, demi-paradise, across the sea, place of peace, of beauty, and of many refugees, fleeing from the tyranny – the European tyranny. No, let me be more precise – the European Union tyranny! The Union of Subservient State Republics' tyranny!

At the other end, directly opposite, sits Voltaire, while to Paul's right, George Orwell. Both are busy writing, clearly enjoying the liberation offered by the word-processing software on their Laptops, but wary of using the internet and for good reasons – it was still operational, a testimony to the success of at least one aspect of its design. Net-neutrality though had disappeared long ago – a testimony to something completely different! The regime had ensured net-neutrality's demise – starting in 2018 with one of its reports – the one with the title *A Multi-dimensional Approach to Disinformation* – with experts doing its bidding, without question, as they were inclined to do. They did not of course address the regime's own disinformation machine.

Behind Voltaire, somewhere in a future he would not know, hanging on the aging wall, was a painting – Édouard Manet's *Le Déjeuner sur l'herbe* (*The Luncheon on the Grass*). It was not the original, but neither was it a copy – an acceptable and respectable reproduction. It was a fake. Sure as day is day and night is night, it was a forgery – and a very good one at that! But who among you could tell?

Voltaire, if he had wanted to, could see this fake work of art, but to do so he would need to turn and look backwards, so to speak, although it would be an act of foreseeing actually. This would require some effort on his part. All George needed to do was to look side-ways. This involved less effort from the vantage point of his position.

Sat in the corner, by said aging wall, and on Paul's right, was William Blake. He too could not see the painting, only the frame. He would need to significantly reposition himself, at some effort, in order to see the famous work by Manet. The fake!

Only Paul saw it head-on, with clarity and ease. Only Paul understood. But no one listened. Thus did he, in other, unique ways, issue warnings.

Four writers, four very different eras, four distinct styles, and all inspired by the regime's monstrous crimes. Four perspectives too on one painting – just how many views could there be?

On Paul's left, by the fire, sits the *fair lady with the beautiful soul*, one of the regime's former employees, a person from the Resource Efficiency Administration – REA. Gazing at the dancing flames, the orange light casts its flickering images on her face. Those dancing flames, symbol of the fires that burnt when the European Union Nationalists set Europe ablaze and turned the streets of cities, ancient and modern alike, into rivers of blood – European blood.

She is relieved though that she no longer has to wear one of the regime's Perception Alteration Modules – otherwise called PAMs in the regime's *Eurospeak*. The wearing of PAMs had been compulsory. It was a profitable business too, the making of these. They were a product of the regime's research programmes, initially designed to present false perceptions of these programmes, they were soon adopted to modify all perceptions of the European Union so as to present mythology as reality. They were a work of art – totalitarian art.

The *fair lady with the beautiful soul* rests her head peacefully on Julia's shoulder. But was there any peace left in her soul given what she had done? More accurately what she had not done, but could have done. All those lives lost because of this! Indeed it was a question to ask – was there any peace left in her soul? She blamed the PAMs of course! She was only obeying orders! But to what degree had she been complicit in the crimes?

Julia, the beautiful Julia, always present, glances at Paul and smiles her warm and friendly smile. "Beauty saves the world," Julia says. What does this mean? What beauty saves the world?

Julia and Paul are related – dialectically.

Beyond the door, on a different shore, a landscape laid waste by the war, and corpses, the counting of which was not yet done. Not just tens of millions this time, that was for certain. How could it have happened again?

Paul returned his gaze to his notes, pondering one more time what he had scribbled, wondering where to begin. Start with STARTS, the regime's Ahnenerbe, or begin with the concentration camp universe, or perhaps the events relating to March 29th 2019? What about the war? Or the creation of the Directorate-General of Truth – in the regime's *Eurospeak*: DG TRUE? Perhaps instead, the Berlin meeting between the Führer and technocrats from DG DISCONNECTED? Perhaps the Future and Emerging Technologies programme and its work on developing the science and the technologies that the regime used to monitor, pacify, and control citizens? Including those PAMs, and much else too! Or perhaps the regime's efforts, prior to the 2019 European Parliament elections, to force social network operators to suppress populist parties' Eurosceptic and anti-migration sentiments? Or maybe, the best place to start would be the subversive abuse of Article 48, the so-called Passerelle clauses, that were slowly used to strip the Member States of all vestiges of meaningful sovereignty without the need to make any Treaty changes, and, most importantly, without anyone noticing or objecting?

Choices – compositional choices! Who would be a writer? No choice here.

Where in England's pleasant land are we? In Chichester of course, where Ancient Romans came but then went, for no Reich lasts for a thousand years, and where Anglo Saxons then came, and in their own unique way, lingered on, for not empire creators were these folk, but nation builders, as it turned out – there is a difference you see. So it is in Wessex, King Alfred's former kingdom, where this story begins to unfold, not so far from Winchester, England's first capital. But more accurate let us be, for it is Felpham where our actors did sit, in Blake's cottage is where the scene just recounted did unfold.

And what year is this? Better not say, but March 29th 2019 is not a distant memory. "So quick," you say! Alas 'tis so. Why so surprised? Did you not see it coming? We did, and thus we wrote this for we looked through time's window, and like Blake, saw time past, present and future coexisting as a singularity.

Far away in modern Rome, in the Vatican actually, Pope John Paul II, with Aleksandr Solzhenitsyn sits. They wait for Julia to call. She will, just be patient, for we promise thee. Meantime Aleksandr speaks, "what beauty saves the world?" asks he.

Wait and see!

And from narrating pen doth now flow an all too typical European tale; one of corruption, incompetence, ignorance, lies, deceit, and criminal activities! Again! A story of decline and fall is what we now reveal to thee …

To be continued in *Scenario Six* because the European Union is a manifestation of a long established European tradition whereby each new generation, often with gleeful celebration, finds new ways to make the same mistakes as previous generations, while at the same time accusing those who warn, of being reactionaries and enemies of the State. Or even of being weird odd-ball fantasists, which is part of the reason why William Blake does take a role, that and his distressing encounter with State power and its abuse – yes even in England! Have we learned the lesson?

And in the Mirror ...

And in the mirror,

Not the beautiful reflection,

But the image of a serpent.

And in the transaction,

The measure of what you are,

And what you decided to become.

Final judgement is done.

Igor Golomstock will now clarify the situation:

"There is one fundamental dogma of totalitarian aesthetics whose origin lies in the nineteenth-century – the assertion of the special role of art and its creator. As art started to become emancipated from the service of enlightened monarchs, it began to seek justification for its existence in new conceptions of its role, place and function. This process, common to all European countries, led to different outcomes in these countries, yet to similar results in both Germany and Russia where the dominant concept was that of the artist-creator, the teacher and prophet who revealed the ultimate truth to humanity.

"Whether the artist-prophet preaches the metaphysics of race or the dialectics of popular consciousness, whether he proclaims social justice or the spiritual renaissance of the nation, is of secondary importance. What matters is that in both versions the mission of art is to influence the consciousness of the masses; it is this concept which was inherited by totalitarian politicians and which constituted the nucleus of their artistic ideology. In the statutes of the Union of Soviet Artists it was formulated as the 'ideological refashioning and education of the workers'; in the statutes of the Chamber of Visual Arts as 'to assist the development of German culture in the spirit of responsibility towards the people and the State.'"

And in the European Union, in the European Commission, in DG CONNECT, in STARTS, it is formulated as "using artists to induce changes in individual and social behaviour."

Those who do not know their history are doomed to repeat it.

In the City of the Golden Stars ...

Within the art-science, art-technology lovers' symbolic universe, does one there find, art subordinated to totalising ideologies – the totalising ideologies of STEM, of European Union Nationalism?

Slay the serpent and set yourself free ...

ENDS Peirce's Theory of Sign

Recall Peirce's theory of sign. A question now to the observer, the reader: what is your interpretant?

And therein lies the issue, for your interpretant is not entirely of your own making, being related to the socially constructed realities in which you participate. Neither is this interpretant entirely benign, nor even within your power to fully understand, at least not without knowledge that may in fact be heretical in your frame of mind. So muse on that if you can, if you dare. Or seek refuge where all is fair, where life is lived just like the stone you may have already become, where life has become mythology of the total realism kind.

ENDS

"God is on the side not of the heavy battalions, but of the best shots."

Voltaire

Bibliography

Abowd, G.D. and James Sterbenz, J.P.G. (2000). Final Report on the Inter-Agency Workshop on Research Issues for Smart Environments. *IEEE Personal Communications, 7(5),* pp. 36-40.

Ahmed, K. (22 January 2018). *UK Growth Upgrade Could 'Dwarf' Brexit Hit.* Retrieved from http://www.bbc.co.uk/news/business-42769090.

Alberts, B., Kirschner, M. W., Tilghman, S. and Varmus, H. (2014). Rescuing US biomedical research from its systemic flaws. *Proc. National Academy of Sciences, 111(16),* pp. 5773-5777.

Amabile, T.M. (1985). Motivation and Creativity: Effects of Motivational Orientation on Creative Writers. *J. Personality & Social Psychology, 48 (2),* pp. 393–399.

Anderson, H.C. (2008). *The Emperor's New Clothes (M.R. James, Trans.).* Retrieved from https://www.gutenberg.ca/ebooks/andersen-emperor/andersen-emperor-00-h.html. (*Originally published in 1837*).

Anonymous (2008*). Jumping Through Hoops. Why do we continue to lie on funding applications and evaluation reports?* Retrieved from http://ixia-info.com/new-writing/jumpingthroughhoops/#4.1

Arendt, H. (2017). *The Origins of Totalitarianism.* London: Penguin Classics. (*Originally published in 1951*).

Aries, Q. (7 June 2016). *José Manuel Barroso's new job at Goldman Sachs angers EU. Some MEPs call for sanctions over former Commission chief's failure to 'behave with integrity and discretion.* Retrieved from https://www.politico.eu/article/jose-manuel-barrosos-new-job-at-goldman-sachs-angers-eu/

Ars Electronica Blog (2017). *FEAT: Arts and Technologies of the Future.* Retrieved from https://www.aec.at/aeblog/en/2017/07/26/feat-kuenste-und-technologien-der-zukunft/

Arts Council England (2015). *New programme supports artists working with technology.* Retrieved from http://www.artscouncil.org.uk/news/new-programme-supports-artists-working-technology.

Ascott, R. (2005*). Syncretic Reality: Art, Process, and Potentiality.* Retrieved from http://www.drainmag.com/contentNOVEMBER/FEATURE_ESSAY/Syncretic_Reality.htm.

Ashby, E. (1958). *Technology and the Academics: An Essay on Universities and the Scientific Revolution.* London: MacMillan & Co.

Atkin, A. (2013). Peirce's Theory of Signs. In: E.N. Zalta (Ed.), *The Stanford Encyclopaedia of Philosophy (Summer Edition),* Retrieved from https://plato.stanford.edu/archives/sum2013/entries/peirce-semiotics.

Australian Network for Art and Technology Blog (2 September 2015). *Trinh Vu: Creative Research.* Retrieved from http://vu2015.blog.anat.org.au/2015/09/creative-research/

Australian Network for Art and Technology Blog (30 September 2015). *Trinh Vu: ANCORA IMPARO.* Retrieved from http://vu2015.blog.anat.org.au/2015/09/ancora-imparo/

Autret, F. (7 June 2017). *OLAF investigates EU leaders in Panama Papers scandal*. Retrieved from https://www.euractiv.com/section/economy-jobs/news/olaf-investigates-eu-leaders-in-panama-papers-scandal/

Axis: A Quarterly Review of Contemporary Abstract Painting & Sculpture (n.d.). Retrieved from https://monoskop.org/Axis.

Babbage, C. (1830). *Reflections on the Decline of Science in England and on Some of its Causes*. London: B. Fellows.

Bangle, C. (2001). The Ultimate Creativity Machine: How BMW Turns Art into Profit. *Harvard Business Review, Jan*. pp. 5-11.

Banks, M. (4 April 2016). *EU Commissioner under fire for involvement in Panama Papers*. Retrieved from https://www.theparliamentmagazine.eu/articles/news/eu-commissioner-under-fire-involvement-panama-papers.

Banks, M. (2 February 2017). *Panama Papers: EU Parliament lashes out at Commission and Council for lack of cooperation*. Retrieved from https://www.theparliamentmagazine.eu/articles/news/panama-papers-eu-parliament-lashes-out-commission-and-council-lack-cooperation.

Barrowclough, D. (2016). *Digging for Hitler: The Nazi Archaeologists Search for an Aryan Past*. Stroud: Fonthill Media.

Baum, L.F. (1981). *The Wizard of Oz*. London: Fontana. (*Originally published in 1900*).

BBC News (17 October 2017). *Malta journalist Caruana Galizia: Anti-corruption warrior*. Retrieved from http://www.bbc.co.uk/news/world-europe-41650312.

BBC News (17 October 2017). *Malta journalist death: Caruana Galizia's son hits out*. Retrieved from http://www.bbc.co.uk/news/world-europe-41648940.

BBC News (24 October 2017). *Tusk talks of risks of Brexit defeat*. Retrieved from http://www.bbc.co.uk/news/uk-politics-41733429.

BBC News (18 December 2017). *Trump: Russia and China 'rival powers' in new security plan*. Retrieved from http://www.bbc.co.uk/news/world-us-canada-42401170.

BBC News (20 December 2017). *Poland judiciary reforms: EU takes disciplinary measures*. Retrieved from http://www.bbc.co.uk/news/world-europe-42420150

BBC News (7 February 2018). *Brexit: Official forecasts suggest economies throughout UK will be hit*. Retrieved from http://www.bbc.co.uk/news/uk-politics-42977967.

BBC News (14 February 2018). *Juncker: EU superstate claims 'total nonsense'*. Retrieved from http://www.bbc.co.uk/news/av/uk-politics-43062104/juncker-eu-superstate-claims-total-nonsense

BBC News (26 February 2018). *Slovakia shocked by killing of journalist and partner*. Retrieved from http://www.bbc.co.uk/news/world-europe-43202124#.

BBC News (20 March 2018). *Uber halts self-driving car tests after death*. Retrieved from http://www.bbc.co.uk/news/business-43459156#

BBC News (4 July 2018). *Polish PM defends judicial changes.* Retrieved from
https://www.bbc.co.uk/news/live/uk-politics-parliaments-44686304

BBC News (4 October 2018). *Tusk: Hunt's remarks unwise and insulting.* Retrieved from
https://www.bbc.co.uk/news/uk-politics-45750023

BBC News (6 February 2019). Tusk: Special place in hell for Brexiteers without a plan.
Retrieved from https://www.bbc.co.uk/news/uk-politics-47143135

BBC Radio 4 (12 February 2017). *A Point of View: Protecting Our Way of Life.* Available at
http://www.bbc.co.uk/programmes/b08cvmhf.

BBC Radio 4 (19 February 2017). *A Point of View: The Follies of Experts.* Available at
http://www.bbc.co.uk/programmes/b08drkjh

BBC Television (2003). *George Orwell: A Life in Pictures.* Available at:
https://www.youtube.com/watch?v=s6txpumkY5I

Beck, U. and Cohn-Bendit, D. (n.d.). *Manifesto for Re-building Europe from the Bottom Up.*
Retrieved from http://evs4all.eu/manifesto/

Berendzen, J.C. (2017). Max Horkheimer. In: E.N. Zalta (Ed.), *The Stanford Encyclopaedia of
Philosophy (Fall Edition),* Retrieved from
https://plato.stanford.edu/archives/fall2017/entries/horkheimer/

Berger, J. (1972). *Ways of Seeing.* London: Penguin Books.

Berger, J. and Mohr, J. (2010). *A Seventh Man: A Book of Images and Words about the Experience of
Migrant Workers in Europe.* London: Verso. (*Originally published in 1975*).

Berger, P.L. and Luckmann, T. (1991). *The Social Construction of Reality: A Treatise in the
Sociology of Knowledge.* London: Penguin Books. (*Originally published in 1966*).

Berlin, I. (2000). *The Power of Ideas (H. Hardy, Ed.).* London: Chatto & Windus.

Berndes, C. (2007). Replicas and Reconstructions in Twentieth-Century Art. *Tate Papers, no.8,
Autumn,* Retrieved from http://www.tate.org.uk/research/publications/tate-
papers/08/replicas-and-reconstructions-in-twentieth-century-art

Berthoin Antal, A. (2009*). Transforming Organisations with the Arts: Research Framework for
Evaluating the Effects of Artistic Interventions in Organizations.* TILTEUROPE Research Report.
Retrieved from https://www.wzb.eu/sites/default/files/u30/researchreport.pdf

Berthoin Antal, A. and Strauβ, A. (2016). Multistakeholder perspectives on searching for
evidence of values-added in artistic interventions in organisation. In: U. Johansson Sköldberg,
J. Woodilla and A. Berthoin Antal (eds.), *Artistic Interventions in Organizations* (pp. 37-59).
Abingdon: Routledge.

Berthoin Antal, A., Woodilla, J. and Johansson Sköldberg, U. (2016). From Revolution to
Evolution … and Back Again. In: U. Johansson Sköldberg, J. Woodilla and A. Berthoin Antal
(eds.), *Artistic Interventions in Organizations* (pp. 241-249). Abingdon: Routledge.

Blake, W. (1904). *Jerusalem: The Emanation of the Giant Albion (E.R.D. Maclagan and A.G.B.
Russell, Eds.).* London: A.H. Bullen. (*Originally published in 1804*).

Boisvert, H. (2016). Echoing Narcissus: Bio-Adaptive, Game-Based Networked Performance. *Leonardo, 49 (5)* p. 449.

Boltanski, L. and Chiapello, E. (2005). The New Spirit of Capitalism. *Int. J. of Politics, Culture, and Society 18(3/4), (The New Sociological Imagination)*, pp. 161-188.

Bohman, J. (2016). Critical Theory. In: E.N. Zalta (Ed.), *The Stanford Encyclopaedia of Philosophy (Fall Edition)*, Retrieved from https://plato.stanford.edu/archives/fall2016/entries/critical-theory/

Boslaugh, S.E. (2016). Anthropocentrism. In: *Encyclopaedia Britannica*. Retrieved from https://www.britannica.com/topic/anthropocentrism

Bourdieu, P. (1996). *The Rules of Art: Genesis and Structure of the Literary Field (S. Emanuel, Trans.)*. Cambridge: Polity Press.

Bourriaud, N. (2002). *Relational Aesthetics (S. Pleasance & F. Woods, Trans.)*. Dijon: Les presses du réel.

Bourriaud, N. (2005). *Postproduction – Culture as Screenplay: How Art Reprograms The World (J. Herman, Trans.)*. New York: Lukas & Sternberg.

Bowden, M.A. (2010). *Creativity and Art*. Oxford: Oxford Univ. Press.

Brady, R.A. (1937). *The Spirit and Structure of German Fascism*. London: Victor Gollancz Ltd.

Breton, A. (1972). *Manifestoes of Surrealism (R. Seaver and H.R. Lane, Trans.)*. Ann Arbor: Univ. of Michigan Press, Ann Arbor Paperbacks.

Brockman, J. (1995). *The Third Culture*. New York: Simon & Schuster.

Bronner, S.E. (2004*). Reclaiming the Enlightenment: Toward a Politics of Radical Engagement*. New York: Columbia Univ. Press.

Bronner, S.E. (2011*).Critical Theory: A Very Short Introduction*. Oxford: Oxford Univ. Press.

Brookes, R. (2017). The Self-Driving Car's People Problem. *IEEE Spectrum August*, pp. 32-35 & pp. 48-49.

Burkhardt, R.W. (2010). *Niko Tinbergen*. Retrieved from http://www.eebweb.arizona.edu/Courses/Ecol487/readings/Niko%20Tinbergen%20Biography.pdf

Caldarelli1, G., Sarah Wolf, S. and Yamir Moreno, Y. (2018). Physics of Humans, Physics for Society. *Nature, 14 (September)*, p870.

Calinescu, M. (1987). *Five Faces of Modernity: Modernism, Avant-garde, Decadence, Kitsch, Postmodernism (2nd ed.)*. Durham, NC: Duke Univ. Press.

Cave, H. (2017). From STEM to STEAM. *Professional Engineer, 30(10)*, pp. 33-37.

Centro de Arte y Creación Industrial (2017). NEXT THINGS_NEXT STARTS. Retrieved from http://www.laboralcentrodearte.org/en/exposiciones/nt_ns

Clive D. L. (2007). What are Animals? Why Anthropomorphism is Still Not a Scientific Approach to Behavior. Wynne Univ. of Florida. *Comparative and Cognitive Behaviour Reviews*, (2), pp 125-135. Retrieved from http://courses.washington.edu/anmind/Wynne-anthropomorphism-CCBR2007.pdf

Coelingh, E. and Nilsson, J. (2018). Driving Tests for Self-driving Cars. *IEEE Spectrum, March*, pp. 40-45.

Collins English Dictionary (12 March 2018). *Fachidiot*. Retrieved from https://www.collinsdictionary.com/submission/1182/fachidiot.

Committee for Information Technology and Creativity (2003). *Beyond Productivity: Information Technology, Innovation, and Creativity*. Washington DC: The National Academies Press.

Commons Select Committee on Science and Technology (2017). *Inquiry into Research Integrity: Terms of Reference*. Retrieved from https://www.parliament.uk/business/committees/committees-a-z/commons-select/science-and-technology-committee/news-parliament-2017/research-integrity-tor-17-19/

Commons Select Committee on Science and Technology (2018). *Research Integrity: Sixth Report of Session 2017-19*. Retrieved from https://publications.parliament.uk/pa/cm201719/cmselect/cmsctech/350/350.pdf

Compart – Centre of Excellence Digital Art (2018). *Ben F. Laposky*. Retrieved from http://dada.compart-bremen.de/item/agent/253.

Connolly, B. (2012). *The Rotten Heart of Europe: The Dirty War for Europe's Money*. London: Faber and Faber.

Contemporary Culture Index (n.d.) *Transformation: Arts, Communication, Environment*. New York: Wittenborn, Schultz. Retrieved from: http://www.ccindex.info/iw/transformation/

Cooley, M. (1987). *Architect or Bee? The Human Price of Technology*. London: The Hogarth Press.

D'Ath, J. (2018). Why I'm tired of being labelled a female engineer. *E&T 13 (6 July)*, p19.

Darsø, L. (2004). *Artful Creation: Learning-tales of Arts-in-Business*. Frederiksberg: Sanfundslitteratur.

Dewhurst, W. (1904). *Impressionist Painting: Its Genesis and Development*. London: George Newnes.

Drazin, R., Glynn, M.A. and Kazanjian, R.K. (1999). Multilevel Theorizing about Creativity in Organizations: A Sensemaking Perspective. *The Academy of Management Review 24(2)*, pp. 286-307.

Dreams for Peace (12 November 2016). *Why Retreating into the Past is a Bad Idea*. Retrieved from https://dreamsforpeace.org/2016/11/12/why-retreating-into-the-past-is-a-bad-idea/

Editors of Encyclopaedia Britannica (2013). Theremin: Musical Instrument. In: *Encyclopaedia Britannica*. Retrieved from https://www.britannica.com/art/theremin

Editors of Encyclopaedia Britannica (2017). Vitruvius - Roman Architect. In: *Encyclopaedia Britannica*. Retrieved from https://www.britannica.com/biography/Vitruvius

Ehrmann, M. (n.d.). *Desiderata*. Retrieved from: https://allpoetry.com/

Eikhof, D.R. (2015). *Creativity and innovation, or: What have the arts ever done for us?* Retrieved from https://lra.le.ac.uk/bitstream/2381/36311/2/Eikhof_JBA_2015_for_LRA.pdf

Engineering Council (2014). *UK-SPEC: UK Specification for Professional Engineering Competence*, 3rd ed. Available at www.engc.org.uk/publications.

Eur-Lex – Access to European Law (2017). *Democratic Deficit*. Retrieved from: http://eur-lex.europa.eu/summary/glossary/democratic_deficit.html

European Commission (2004). *ISTAG Working Group Report on Experience and Application Research: Involving Users in the Development of Ambient Intelligence*. Available at www.cheshirehenbury.com/webpdf/2004_ear_web_en.pdf.

European Commission, DG INFSO (2006). *Technologies for Product Design and Virtualisation. Final Report on the FP7 Consultation Workshop*, 30-31 March, Brussels. Available at www.cheshirehenbury.com/webpdf/ict-f-product-dev_en.pdf.

European Commission (2007). *COMMISSION DECISION of 5 December 2007: Rules on the Reimbursement of Expenses Incurred by People from Outside the Commission Invited to Attend Meetings in an Expert Capacity*. Retrieved from ec.europa.eu/employment_social/egf/docs/reglementation_experts_2008_en.pdf

European Commission, DG INFSO (2007). *Information and Communication Technologies: Work Programme 2007-08*. Retrieved from ec.europa.eu/research/participants/data/ref/fp7/88465/c-wp-200801_en.pdf

European Commission (2009). *The Impact of Culture on Creativity*. Retrieved from http://www.keanet.eu/docs/impactculturecreativityfull.pdf

European Commission (2011). *Directorate-General Mobility and Transport Report: ITS Action Plan, Action 3.4–Safety and Comfort of the Vulnerable Road User*. Retrieved from https://ec.europa.eu/transport/sites/transport/files/themes/its/studies/doc/2011_05-safety-and-comfort-vulnerable-road-user.pdf.

European Commission (2012). *A Blueprint for a Deep and Genuine Economic and Monetary Union: Launching a European Debate*. Retrieved from ec.europa.eu/archives/commission_2010-2014/president/news/archives/2012/11/pdf/blueprint_en.pdf.

European Commission, DG CONNECT (2012). *Personal Communication*.

European Commission (2013). *Work Programme 2013: Nanosciences, Nanotechnologies, Materials and New Production Technologies*. Retrieved from ec.europa.eu/research/participants/data/ref/fp7/192024/d-wp-201303_en.pdf.

European Commission, DG CONNECT (2013). *Personal Communication*.

European Commission (2015a). *ICT-ART CONNECT Study Report*. Available at www.cheshirehenbury.com/ict-art-connect/ict-art-pdf-files/ICT-ART_CONNECT_study_report.pdf.

European Commission (2015b). *Integration of Social Sciences and Humanities in Horizon 2020: Participants, Budget and Disciplines - Monitoring Report on SSH-flagged Projects Funded in 2014 under the Societal Challenges and Industrial Leadership.* Retrieved from https://publications.europa.eu/en/publication-detail/-/publication/acac40f5-e84b-11e6-ad7c-01aa75ed71a1

European Commission (2015c). *Horizon 2020 Work Programme 2016– 2017: 20. General Annexes.* Retrieved from http://ec.europa.eu/research/participants/data/ref/h2020/other/wp/2016-2017/annexes/h2020-wp1617-annex-ga_v1.0_en.pdf

European Commission (2015d). *ICT 2015 Session: Driving Innovation through Creativity and the Arts.* Retrieved from https://ec.europa.eu/digital-single-market/events/cf/ict2015/item-display.cfm?id=15131.

European Commission Cordis Results Service (2014). *FET ART Project.* Retrieved from https://cordis.europa.eu/project/rcn/110383_en.html

European Commission FET Advisory Group (2016). *The need to integrate Social Sciences and Humanities with Science and Engineering in Horizon 2020 and beyond.* Retrieved from http://ec.europa.eu/programmes/horizon2020/en/news/report-need-integrate-social-sciences-and-humanities-science-and-engineering-horizon-2020

European Commission Cordis Results Service (2016). *Future and Emerging Art and Technology Project.* Retrieved from https://cordis.europa.eu/project/rcn/199031_en.html.

European Commission Cordis News (2017). Journalists Acting as Referees Could Prevent the Spread of Fake News. *research*eu, No 69, Feb.*

European Commission Cordis News (2018). European and Central Asian Countries are not Doing Enough to Tackle Corruption. *research*eu, No 59, Feb.*

European Commission (2017a). *White Paper on The Future of Europe: Reflections and scenarios for the EU27 by 2025.* Retrieved from: https://ec.europa.eu/commission/sites/beta-political/files/white_paper_on_the_future_of_europe_en.pdf.

European Commission (2017b). *Horizon 2020 Work Programme 2018-2020: Information and Communication Technologies.* Retrieved from http://ec.europa.eu/research/participants/data/ref/h2020/wp/2018-2020/main/h2020-wp1820-leit-ict_en.pdf.

European Commission (2017c). *Communication from the Commission to the European Parliament, the Council, the European Economic and Social Committee, and the Committee of the Regions: Strengthening European Identity through Education and Culture – The European Commission's Contribution to the Leaders' Meeting in Gothenburg, 17 November 2017.* Retrieved from https://ec.europa.eu/commission/sites/beta-political/files/communication-strengthening-european-identity-education-culture_en.pdf.

European Commission (2017d). *LAB – FAB – APP: Investing in the European Future We Want – Report of the independent High Level Group on Maximising the Impact of EU Research & Innovation Programmes.* Retrieved from ec.europa.eu/research/evaluations/pdf/archive/other_reports_studies_and_documents/hlg_2017_report.pdf.

European Commission (2017e). *Integration of Social Sciences and Humanities in Horizon 2020: Participants, Budget and Disciplines – 2nd Monitoring Report on SSH-flagged Projects Funded in 2015 under the Societal Challenges and Industrial Leadership Priorities.* Retrieved from https://publications.europa.eu/en/publication-detail/-/publication/acac40f5-e84b-11e6-ad7c-01aa75ed71a1

European Commission (2017f). *Horizon 2020 Work Programme 2018-2020: Future and Emerging Technologies.* Retrieved from http://ec.europa.eu/research/participants/data/ref/h2020/wp/2018-2020/main/h2020-wp1820-fet_en.pdf

European Commission (2014-17). *Experts Names Annual Lists: ICT Programme.* Retrieved from ec.europa.eu/research/participants/portal/desktop/en/funding/reference_docs.html#h2020-expertslists

European Commission (6 March 2018). *Commissioners support No Women No Panel Campaign.* Retrieved from https://ec.europa.eu/digital-single-market/en/news/commissioners-support-no-women-no-panel-campaign

European Commission (2018). *A Multi-dimensional Approach to Disinformation - Report of the Independent High level Group on Fake News and Online Disinformation.* Retrieved from https://ec.europa.eu/digital-single-market/en/news/final-report-high-level-expert-group-fake-news-and-online-disinformation

European Commission, DG CONNECT (2018). *Personal Communication.*

European Commission (2019). *Joint Communication to the European Parliament, the European Council and the Council: EU-China – A Strategic Outlook, 12 March 2019.* Retrieved from https://ec.europa.eu/commission/sites/beta-political/files/communication-eu-china-a-strategic-outlook.pdf

European Court of Auditors (n.d.) *Audit Activities.* Retrieved from www.eca.europa.eu

European Courts of Justice (2016). *Sigma Orionis v Commission.* InfoCuria - Case-law of the Court of Justice. Retrieved from http://curia.europa.eu/juris/fiche.jsf?id=T%3B48%3B16%3BRD%3B1%3BP%3B1%3BT2016%2F0048%2FP&pro=&lgrec=en&nat=or&oqp=&dates=&lg=&language=en&jur=C%2CT%2CF&cit=none%252CC%252CCJ%252CR%252C2008E%252C%252C%252C%252C%252C%252C%252C%252C%252Ctrue%252Cfalse%252Cfalse&num=T-48%252F16&td=%3BALL&pcs=Oor&avg=&mat=or&jge=&for=&cid=2733203#section_documents.

European Parliament (2016). *Report on a Coherent EU Policy for Cultural and Creative Industries.* Retrieved from http://www.europarl.europa.eu/sides/getDoc.do?pubRef=-//EP//TEXT+REPORT+A8-2016-0357+0+DOC+XML+V0//EN.

European Parliament (2017). *Replies to the Questionnaire of the European Parliament to the Commissioner-Designate Mariya Gabriel.* Retrieved from http://www.europarl.europa.eu/cmsdata/121420/Annex%20EN%20version.pdf.

European Parliament News (24 June 2016). *Joint statement by Schulz, Tusk, Rutte and Juncker on UK referendum outcome.* Retrieved from http://www.europarl.europa.eu/news/en/press-room/20160624IPR33834/joint-statement-by-schulz-tusk-rutte-and-juncker-on-uk-referendum-outcome

European Parliament News (31 May 2017). *Juncker: Don't measure my credibility on the basis of my tax past.* Retrieved from:
http://www.europarl.europa.eu/news/en/headlines/economy/20170529STO76260/juncker-don-t-measure-my-credibility-on-the-basis-of-my-tax-past.

European United Left/Nordic Green Left European Parliamentary Group (2 June 2017). *Commissioner Cañete must resign amidst Panama Papers revelations.* Retrieved from http://www.guengl.eu/news/article/commissioner-canete-must-resign-amidst-panama-papers-revelations

Express (22 September 2016). *Ex-EU commissioner was director of offshore Bahamas firm WHILE she worked in Brussels. A Former European Commissioner failed to declare she was listed as a director of an offshore company in the Caribbean tax haven of the Bahamas, secret papers have revealed.* Retrieved from https://www.theguardian.com/business/2016/sep/21/ex-eu-commissioner-neelie-kroes-failed-to-declare-directorship-of-offshore-firm.

Fanelli, D. (2012). Negative Results are Disappearing from Most Disciplines and Countries. *Scientometrics (90)*, pp 891–904.

FEAT Project (2016). *FEAT @ Ars Electronica*, Workshop Result Paper, June 8th, Linz, Austria. Retrieved from www.featart.eu/fileadmin/user_upload/FEAT_3rdWS_result_paper.pdf.

Feynman R.P. and Leighton, R. (1985). *Surely You're Joking Mr Feynman!: Adventures of a Curious Character as told to Ralph Leighton, (E. Hutchings, Ed.).* London: W.W. Norton.

Feynman, R.P. (1995). *The Art of Richard P. Feynman: Images by a Curious Character (compiled by Michelle Feynman).* Basel: G+B Science.

Feest, J. (2017). Will the Fourth Industrial Revolution be driven by STEAM? *E&T, 12(12)*, p. 23.

Fowler, R. (1991). *Language in the News: Discourse and Ideology in the Press.* London: Routledge.

Frayling, C. (1993). Research in Art and Design. *Royal College of Art Research Papers Series 1(1).* London: Royal College of Arts.

Friedman, K. and Ox, J. (2017). Phd in Art and Design. *Leonardo, 50(5)*, pp. 515-519.

Frost, R. (1942). *The Secret Sits.* Retrieved from https://allpoetry.com/The-Secret-Sits.

Galileo Galilei (1960). *The Assayer (S. Drake, Trans.).* In: S. Drake and C.D. O'Malley, Eds. *The Controversy of the Comets of 1618.* Philadelphia: Univ. of Pennsylvania Press. *(Originally published in 1623).*

Gambetta, D. and Hertog, S. (2016). *Engineers of Jihad: The Curious Connection between Violent Extremism and Education.* Princeton: Princeton Univ. Press.

Garside, J. (21 September 2016). *Ex-EU commissioner Neelie Kroes failed to declare directorship of offshore firm. Leak of files from Bahamas corporate register reveals former head of Europe's antitrust watchdog was recruited by UAE venture set up to buy Enron assets.* Retrieved from https://www.theguardian.com/business/2016/sep/21/ex-eu-commissioner-neelie-kroes-failed-to-declare-directorship-of-offshore-firm.

Gelb, M. (2004*). How to Think like Leonardo da Vinci: Seven Steps to Genius Everyday.* London: Thorsons.

Genocide Watch (n.d.). *The Eight Stages of Genocide*. Retrieved from http://www.genocidewatch.org/aboutgenocide/8stagesofgenocide.html.

Gent, E. (2016). Big Data's Dark Side. *IET E&T 11*(9), pp. 32-35.

German Federal Constitutional Court (2009). *Act Approving the Treaty of Lisbon Compatible with the Basic Law; Accompanying Law Unconstitutional to the Extent that Legislative Bodies have not been Accorded Sufficient Rights of Participation*. Retrieved from https://www.bundesverfassungsgericht.de/SharedDocs/Pressemitteilungen/EN/2009/bvg 09-072.html.

German Federal Government (2017). *Horizon 2020 Interim Evaluation: Position Paper of the Federal Government*. Retrieved from https://www.bmbf.de/files/2017_01_12_Positionspapier%20englische%20Version.pdf

Gettier, E.L. (1963). Is Justified True Belief Knowledge? *Analysis 23(6)*, pp. 121–123.

Girao, L.M. and Irene Ingardi, I. (13 October 2017). *STARTS in IoT for better lives*. Retrieved from https://ec.europa.eu/digital-single-market/en/blog/starts-iot-better-lives

Gibbons, M., Limoges, C., Nowotny, H., Schwartzman, S., Scott, P. and Trow, M. (1994). *The New Production of Knowledge: The Dynamics of Science and Research in Contemporary Societies*. London: Sage Publication.

Glinkowski, P. and Bamford A. (2009). *Insight and Exchange: An Evaluation of the Wellcome Trust's Sciart Programme*. London: Wellcome Trust. Retrieved from https://wellcome.ac.uk/sites/default/files/wtx057228_0.pdf

Glover, A. (2013). *The Role of Science in Future EU Policy Making*. First Spinoza Lecture, November, European Academy of Sciences and the Arts. Retrieved from http://www.euro-acad.eu/downloads/events/Glover_Lecture_Agenda_19_Nov_2013.pdf

Golman, R., Hagmann, D. and Loewenstein, G. (2017). Information Avoidance. *J. of Economic Literature*, 55(1), pp. 96-135.

Golomstock, I. (2011). *Totalitarian Art: In the Soviet Union, the Third Reich, Fascist Italy and the People's Republic of China (R. Chandler, Trans.)*. London: Duckworth.

Grew, N. (1681). The Comparative Anatomy of Stomachs and Guts Begun: Being Several Lectures Read before the Royal Society – In the year 1676. In: N. Grew, *Musaeum Regalis Societatis, or, A Catalogue and Description of the Natural and Artificial Rarities belonging to the Royal Society and preserved at Gresham College*. London: The Author.

Gulias, K.A. (2014). *Differences between Juxtaposition in Surrealism and Superposition in Imagisme*. Retrieved from https://www.academia.edu/20388174/Difference_between_juxtaposition_in_Surrealism_and_in_Imagisme?auto=download

Gutteridge, N. (7 June 2017). *EU tax scandal: Investigators open fraud probe into top eurocrats after Panama Papers leak*. Retrieved from https://www.express.co.uk/news/politics/814091/European-Union-EU-anti-fraud-office-eurocrats-Panama-Papers-tax-affairs.

Habermas, J. (2015). *The Lure of Technocracy*. Cambridge: Polity Press.

Hack the Art World (2014). *There is no such thing as DevArt, only art.* Retrieved from http://hacktheartworld.com/

Harbury, C.D. (1971). *An Introduction to Economic Behaviour.* London: Fontana.

Harris, C. (Ed.) (1999). *Art and Innovation: The Xerox PARC Artist in Residence Programme.* Cambridge MA: The MIT Press.

Hawkins, S. (2001). *The Universe in a Nutshell.* London: Bantam Press.

Hennig, N. and Ulrike Jordan, U. (2016). *Context is Half the Work: A Partial History of the Artist Placement Group.* Retrieved from http://www.naomihennig.com/wp-content/uploads/2017/03/apg_edinburgh.pdf.

Hitler, A. (1939). *Mein Kampf J. Murphy (Trans.).* London: Hurst and Blackett Ltd. Publishers.

Hitler, A. (n.d.). *The Speeches of Adolf Hitler – 1921-1941.* Retrieved from the Internet Archive https://archive.org/details/TheSpeechesOfAdolfHitler19211941_201706.

HM Treasury (2016). *HM Treasury Analysis: The Immediate Economic Impact of Leaving the EU. Presented to Parliament by the Chancellor of the Exchequer by Command of Her Majesty.* Retrieved from https://www.gov.uk/government/publications/hm-treasury-analysis-the-immediate-economic-impact-of-leaving-the-eu.

Hobsbawm, E. (1997). *On History.* London: Weidenfeld & Nicolson.

Holocaust Education and Archive Research Team (n.d.). *I.G. Farben: I.G. Farbenindustrie AG German Industry and the Holocaust.* Retrieved from http://www.holocaustresearchproject.org/economics/igfarben.html.

Horkheimer, M. and Adorno, T.W. (2002). *Dialectic of Enlightenment: Philosophical Fragments, E. Jephcott (Trans.), G.S. Noe (ed.).* Stanford, Ca: Stanford Univ. Press (*Originally Published in German in 1947*).

Höss, R. (1996). *Death dealer: the memoirs of the SS Kommandant at Auschwitz, A. Pollinger (Trans.), S. Paskuly (ed.).* New York: Da Capo Press.

Hughes, J. J. (1998). *A Mass Murderer Repents: The Case of Rudolf Hoess, Commandant of Auschwitz.* Archbishop Gerety Lecture at Seton Hall University, Retrieved from https://www13.shu.edu/academics/theology/upload/mass-murderer-repents.pdf.

Huizinga, J. (1955). *Homo Lunden: A Study of the Play-element in Culture.* Boston: The Beacon Press. (*Originally published in 1938*).

Ingraham, P. (2017). *Does Arnica Gel Work for Pain?* Retrieved from https://www.painscience.com/articles/arnica.php

Information Commissioner's Office (2018a). *Information security (Principle 7).* Retrieved from https://ico.org.uk/for-organisations/guide-to-data-protection/principle-7-security/

Information Commissioner's Office (2018b). *Sending personal data by email.* Retrieved from https://ico.org.uk/for-organisations/guide-to-data-protection/encryption/scenarios/sending-personal-data-by-email/

Innovate UK (2015). *Innovate UK Delivery Plan Financial Year 2015/16*. Retrieved from https://www.gov.uk/government/uploads/system/uploads/attachment_data/file/486965/CO-001_Innovate_UK_Delivery_Plan_2015_16.pdf.

Ioannidis, J.P.A. (2005). Why Most Published Research Findings Are False. *PLoS Med 2(8): e124*, pp. 696-701.

Ioannidis, J.P.A. (2012). Why Science Is Not Necessarily Self-Correcting. *Perspectives on Psychological Science, 7(6)*, pp. 645-654.

Isomäki, H. (2007). Different Levels of Information Systems Designers' Forms of Thought and Potential for Human-centered Design. *Int. J. of Tech. and Human Interaction, 3(1)*, pp. 30-48

Jeffreys, D. (2008). *Hell's Cartel: IG Farben and the Making of Hitler's War Machine*. London: Bloomsbury Publishing.

Johnson, G. (1988). Process of Managing Strategic Change. *Management Research News 11(4/5)*, pp. 43-46.

Jones, J. Rt. Rev. (2017). *The Patronising Disposition of Unaccountable Power: A Report to Ensure the Pain and Suffering of the Hillsborough Families is not Repeated. A Report laid before Parliament*. Retrieved from https://www.gov.uk/government/uploads/system/uploads/attachment_data/file/656130/6_3860_HO_Hillsborough_Report_2017_FINAL_updated.pdf

Kahnenman, D. (2011). *Thinking, Fast and Slow*. London: Penguin Books.

Kahnenman, D. (2012). A proposal to deal with questions about priming effects. *Nature*. Retrieved from https://www.nature.com/polopoly_fs/7.6716.1349271308!/suppinfoFile/Kahneman%20Letter.pdf.

Kandel, E.R. (2012). *The Age of Insight: The Quest to Understand the Unconscious in Art, Mind and Brain from Vienna 1900 to the Present*. New York: Random House.

Kandel, E.R. (2016). *Reductionism in Art and Brain Science: Bridging the Two Cultures*. New York: Columbia Univ. Press.

Kandinsky, W. (1914). *The Art of Spiritual Harmony (M.T.H. Sadler, Trans.)*. New York: Houghton Mifflin Company.

Kalb, P.E. and Koehler, K.G. (2002). Legal Issues in Research. *JAMA, 287(1)*, pp. 85-91.

Katz, B. (2015). *Make it New: The History of Silicon Valley Design*. Cambridge, MA: MIT Press.

Kieran, M. (2014). Creativity as a Virtue of Character. In: E. S. Paul and S. B. Kaufman (eds.), *The Philosophy of Creativity: New Essays* (pp. 125–144). Oxford: Oxford Univ. Press.

Kepes, G. (Ed.) (1956). *The New Landscape in Art and Science*. Chicago: Paul Theobald & Co.

Kidd, P.T. (1992). *Organization, People & Technology in European Manufacturing*. Luxembourg: Office Official Publications of the European Communities, Science & Technology Policy Series

Kidd, P.T. (1994). *Agile Manufacturing: Forging New Frontiers*. Woking: Addison Wesley.

Kidd, P.T. (2013a). *ICT-ART CONNECT in the H2020 ICT Programme: Preliminary Reflections on Realising the Potential.* Available at www.cheshirehenbury.com/ict-art-connect/ict-art-pdf-files/ICT-ART_CONNECT_European_Parliament_Rountable_Discussion_Report_Final.pdf

Kidd, P.T. (2013b). *A Tale of Two Deserts.* Macclesfield: Cheshire Henbury.

Kidd, P.T. (2016). *STARTS – Science, Technology and the Arts: The Artistic Voices that DG CONNECT Silenced.* Macclesfield: Cheshire Henbury.

K-MB Agency for Brand Communication (29 March 2018). *Mercedes-Benz The Avant-Garde Diaries.* Retrieved from https://www.k-mb.de/project/mercedes-benz-avantgarde-diaries/

Koestler, A. (1966). *The Act of Creation.* London: Pan Books.

Koestler, A. (1989). *The Sleepwalkers: A History of Man's Changing Vision of the Universe.* London: Arkana, Penguin Books. (*Originally published in 1959*).

Kris, E. (1953). *Psychoanalytic Explorations in Art.* London: George Allen & Unwin Ltd.

Kris, E. and Kurz, O. (1979). *Legend, Myth and Magic in the Image of the Artist: A Historical Experiment (A. Laing, Trans.).* New Haven: Yale Univeristy Press. (*Originally published in German in 1934*).

Kwastek, K. (2013). *Aesthetics of Interaction in Digital Art.* Cambridge MA: The MIT Press.

LaMore, R., Root-Bernstein, R., Root-Bernstein, M., Schweitzer, J.H., Lawton, J.L., Roraback, E., Peruski, A., VanDyke, M. and Fernandez, L. (2013). Arts and Crafts: Critical to Economic Innovation. *Economic Development Quarterly 27(3),* pp. 221-229.

Lao Tsu (n.d.). *Tao Te Ching (Kindle, 1st ed.),* (14 Sept. 2013). Prague: e-artnow.

Leggett, M. (2005). Review of Film Art Phenomena by Nicky Hamlyn. *Leonardo, 38(4),* pp. 352-353.

Lehner, F. (1992). *What are Anthropocentric Production Systems: The European Response to Advanced Manufacturing and Globalization.* Luxembourg: Office for Official Publications of the European Communities, Science and Technology Policy Series.

Lenin, V.I. (1905). Party Organisation and Party Literature. In: A. Rothstein (ed.), *V.I. Lenin: Collected Works – Volume 10, November 1905 – June 1906* (pp. 44-49). Moscow: Progress Publishers.

Lennon, J. (1971). *Working Class Hero.* Retrieved from https://genius.com/John-lennon-working-class-hero-lyrics

Levelt, W. J. M., Drenth, P. and Noort, E. (eds.) (2012). *Flawed Science: The Fraudulent Research Practices of Social Psychologist Diederik Stapel.* Tilburg Univ. Retrieved from: https://www.tilburguniversity.edu/upload/3ff904d7-547b-40ae-85fe-bea38e05a34a_Final%20report%20Flawed%20Science.pdf

Levin, G. *et.al.* (2009). *New Media Artworks: Prequels to Everyday Life.* Retrieved from http://www.flong.com/blog/2009/new-media-artworks-prequels-to-everyday-life/

Lincoln, A. (1863). *The Gettysburg Address*. Retrieved from
http://www.abrahamlincolnonline.org/lincoln/speeches/gettysburg.htm

Living Memory Project (n.d.) *Lessons Learnt from LIVING MEMORY @ 1:3 –
Listening to and Developing Technology for Ordinary People*. Retrieved from:
http://www.i3net.org/ser_pub/services/magazine/february2003/i3originals.pdf.

Loeb, J. (2017). Electric Vehicles must be made Nosier, Blind Campaigners Demand. *IET E&T
Magazine 12(7/8)*, p. 9.

Los Angeles County Art Museum (1971). *A Report on the Art and Technology Program of the Los
Angeles County Museum of Art 1967-1971*. Los Angeles: Los Angeles County Art Museum.

Lumina (n.d.). http://www.lumia-wilfred.org/

Lyons, B.A. (2017). When Readers Believe Journalists: Effects of Adjudication in Varied
Dispute Contexts. *Int. J. Public Opinion Research (edx013)*.
https://doi.org/10.1093/ijpor/edx013

Lyotard, J-F. (1984). *The Postmodern Condition: A Report on Knowledge (G. Bennington & B.
Massumi, Trans.)*. Manchester: Univ. of Manchester Press.

MacCurdy, E. (1955). *The Notebooks of Leonardo da Vinci*. New York: George Braziller.
(*Originally published in 1939*).

Maclagan E.R.D. and Russell A.G.B. (1904). *The Prophetic Books of William Blake: Jerusalem*.
London: A.H. Bullen.

Malina, R.F. (4 November 2017). *Help Enable the Emerging Leonardos, both teams and individuals!*
Retrieved from http://malina.diatrope.com/2017/11/04/help-enable-the-emerging-
leonardos-both-teams-and-inviduals/

Malina, R.F. (23 November 2017). *Yeah Jasia Reichardt you were right 50 years ago! Announcing a
major conference*. Retrieved from http://malina.diatrope.com/2017/11/23/yeah-jasia-
reichardt-you-were-right-50-years-ago-announcing-a-major-conference/

Malina, R.F. (28 January 2018). *Was Marcus Vitruvius Pollio right?: What's possible in the Twenty-
first century in transdisciplinary collaboration that wasn't possible in Rome?* Retrieved from
http://malina.diatrope.com/2018/01/28/was-marcus-vitruvius-pollio-right-whats-possible-
in-the-21st-century-in-transdiscplinary-collaboration-that-wast-possible-in-rome/

Malina, R.F. (2018). *A Special Message from Roger Malina – What Is New Under the Sun: Oral
Futures to the Rescue of All Those Who Worry*. Retrieved from
https://mailchi.mp/leonardo/what-is-new-under-the-sun?e=3e8b36394f

Malina, R.F., Topete, A.G. and Silveira, J. (2018). What Is the Evidence that Art-Science-
Technology Collaboration Is a Good Thing? *Leonardo, 51(1)*, p.2.

Mann, I. (26 November 2015). *The Hidden Meaning Behind 'Our Way of Life'*. Retrieved from
http://america.aljazeera.com/opinions/2015/11/the-hidden-meanings-behind-our-way-of-
life.html.

Marx, K. (1954). *Capital: A Critique of Political Economy Vol. I. (S. Moore, E. Aveling, Trans., F.
Engels, Ed.)*. Moscow: Progress Publishers. (*Originally published in 1867*).

Marx, K. and Engels, F. (1967). *The Communist Manifesto*. London: Penguin Books. (*Originally published in 1848*).

Matarasso, F. (2005). *How the Light Gets In: The Value of Imperfect Systems of Cultural Evaluation*. Retrieved from https://parliamentofdreams.files.wordpress.com/2012/05/2005-how-the-light-gets-in-matarasso.pdf.

Mazar, N. and Ariely, D. (2015). Dishonesty in scientific research. *J. Clin. Invest. 125(11)*, pp. 3993-3996.

Mazzucato, M. (2018). *Mission-Oriented Research & Innovation in the European Union: A Problem Solving Approach to Fuel Innovation-led Growth*. Luxembourg: Office for Official Publications of the European Communities. Retrieved from https://ec.europa.eu/info/sites/info/files/mazzucato_report_2018.pdf

McLuhan, M. (2001). *Understanding Media: The Extensions of Man*. London: Routledge Classics. (*Originally published in 1964*).

Mejía, M., Nazir, C., Malina, R.F.,Topete, A.G., Londoño, F.C., Roldán, A.F., Farias, P.L., Silveira, J. (2018). *An Emerging Role for Design Methods in Transdisciplinary Practices*. Retrieved from http://malina.diatrope.com/2018/01/23/emerging-role-for-design-methods-in-transdisciplinary-practices-for-pre-publication-peer-review/

Millard-Ball, A. (2018). Pedestrians, Autonomous Vehicles and Cities. *J. of Planning Education and Research, 38(1)*, pp. 6–12

Miller, A.I. (2014a). *Colliding Worlds: How Cutting Edge Science is Redefining Contemporary Art*. London: W.W. Norton & Co.

Miller, A.I. (2014b). *Colliding Worlds: How Cutting Edge Science is Redefining Contemporary Art. A Book Reading and Signing with Arthur I. Miller*. DASAR – DC Art Science Evening Rendezvous Video Recording. Available at https://www.youtube.com/watch?v=xW5-kyZ8LUM

Mills, C. (2018). Artistic Integrity. *J. Aesthetics & Art Criticism 76(1)*, pp. 9-12.

Mohan, M. (21 November 2017). *Rape and no Periods in North Korea's Army*. Retrieved from http://www.bbc.co.uk/news/stories-41778470

Mondrian, P. (1945). *Plastic Art and Pure Plastic Art*. New York: Wittenborn & Co.

Monoskop (7 November 2017). *Arseny Avraamov*. Retrieved from https://monoskop.org/Arseny_Avraamov#Symphony_of_Sirens_.281919.E2.80.9323.29

Morris, D. (1971). The Naked Artist. *The Observer Magazine (10th October)*, pp 22-27.

Morris, D. (1973-74). Biomorphia. *Lycidas (No. 2)*, pp. 10-11

Morris, D. (1979). *Animal Days*. London: Jonathan Cape Ltd.

Morris, D. (1983). *Inrock*. London: Jonathan Cape Ltd.

Morris, D. (1984). *The Secret Surrealist: The Paintings of Desmond Morris*. Oxford: Phaidon Press.

Morris, D. (2018). *The Lives of the Surrealists*. London: Thames & Hudson.

Mosher, M.R. (2003). Review of Othermindedness: The Emergence of Network Culture by Michael Joyce. *Leonardo, 36(5)*, pp. 409-410

Museum of Modern Art (2017). *Marcel Duchamp. Rotary Demisphere (Precision Optics). Paris, 1925*. Retrieved from https://www.moma.org/collection/works/81432.

National Academies of Sciences, Engineering, and Medicine (2016). *National Academies of Sciences Study: Integrating Higher Education in the Arts, Humanities, Sciences, Engineering, and Medicine, Program Book for the Committee Meeting held July 2016 - document pga_175504.pdf:* Retrieved from sites.nationalacademies.org/cs/groups/pgasite/documents/webpage/pga_175504.pdf

National Academies of Sciences, Engineering, and Medicine (2017a). *Examining the Mistrust of Science: Proceedings of a Workshop–in Brief*. Washington, DC: The National Academies Press. Retrieved from https://www.nap.edu/catalog/24819/examining-the-mistrust-of-science-proceedings-of-a-workshop-in.

National Academies of Sciences, Engineering, and Medicine (2017b). *Fostering Integrity in Research*. Washington, DC: The National Academies Press. Retrieved from https://www.nap.edu/catalog/21896/fostering-integrity-in-research.

National Academies of Sciences, Engineering, and Medicine (2018). *The Integration of the Humanities and Arts with Sciences, Engineering, and Medicine in Higher Education: Branches from the Same Tree*. Washington, DC: The National Academies Press. Retrieved from https://www.nap.edu/catalog/24988/the-integration-of-the-humanities-and-arts-with-sciences-engineering-and-medicine-in-higher-education

Nielsen, N. (31 May 2017). *MEPs grill Juncker on tax scandals*. Retrieved from: https://euobserver.com/justice/138069.

Nelson, R. (Ed.) (2013). *Practice as Research in the Arts: Principles, Protocols, Pedagogies, Resistances*. London: Palgrave Macmillan.

Nowotny, H., Scott, P. and Gibbons, M. (2001). *Re-Thinking Science: Knowledge and the Public in an Age of Uncertainty*. Cambridge: Polity Press.

Nuzzo, R. (2014). Statistical errors: P values, the 'gold standard' of statistical validity, are not a reliable as many scientists assume. *Nature 506 (13 February)*, pp.150-152.

OECD (2015). *Frascati Manual*. Retrieved from http://www.oecd-ilibrary.org/docserver/download/9215001e.pdf?expires=1497369061&id=id&accname=guest&checksum=143D3D942691DBAC9D5D28E6E89E00AB.

OECD Centre for Educational Research and Innovation (1972). *Interdisciplinarity: Problems of Teaching and Research in Universities*. Paris: OECD

Oettinger, G. (2016). *European Commissioner, in Charge of the Digital Economy and Society, Words about Artistic Freedom Forming part of the STARTS Consultation*. Retrieved from ec.europa.eu/futurium/en/content/open-consultation-starts-science-technology-arts.

Official Journal of the European Union (2016). *Consolidated Versions of the Treaty on European Union and the Treaty on the Functioning of the European Union.* C202, 59, 7 June. Retrieved from http://eur-lex.europa.eu/legal-content/EN/TXT/PDF/?uri=OJ:C:2016:202:FULL&from=EN.

Oltermann, P. (2015). *Jürgen Habermas's Verdict on the EU/Greece Debt Deal – Full Transcript.* Retrieved from https://www.theguardian.com/commentisfree/2015/jul/16/jurgen-habermas-eu-greece-debt-deal

Open Science Collaboration (2015). *Science 349, aac4716.* DOI: 10.1126/science.aac4716.

Open Science Collaboration (2018a). *Estimating the Reproducibility of Psychological Science.* Retrieved from https://osf.io/ezcuj/wiki/home/

Open Science Collaboration (2018b). Reproducibility Project: Psychology – Replicated Studies. Retrieved from https://osf.io/ezcuj/wiki/Replicated%20Studies/

Orwell, G. (1951). *Animal Farm.* Harmonsworth: Penguin Books. (*Originally published in 1945*).

Orwell, G. (2000). *Nineteen Eight-Four.* London: Penguin Books. (*Originally published in 1949*).

Oxford Online English Dictionary. https://en.oxforddictionaries.com/

Paalen, W. (1943). Art and Science, *DYN 3*, pp. 4-9. In: Wolfgang Paalen's DYN: The Complete Reprint, Christian Kloybe (Ed.), 2000, Springer-Verlag View and NY.

Parliamentary Office for Science and Technology (2017). *Research Integrity.* POSTnote POST-PN-0544. Retrieved from http://researchbriefings.parliament.uk/ResearchBriefing/Summary/POST-PN-0544

Paddles ON! London (2018). https://paddle8.com/auction/paddleson/

Perks, S. K. (2006). *Dice-box of Chance: The Problem of Causality in Surrealism, Science and the Occult.* Phd Thesis Univ. of Manchester. Retrieved from http://ethos.bl.uk/OrderDetails.do?uin=uk.bl.ethos.625465

Philips Design Amsterdam (December 8, 2017). *Our People and Places.* Retrieved from https://www.90yearsofdesign.philips.com/our-people-and-places.

Pinder, D. (2008). Urban Interventions: Art, Politics and Pedagogy. *Int. J. of Urban and Regional Research, 32(3)*, pp. 730-736.

Planetary Collegium Facebook Pages (1 December 2017). *Content of the NEXT THINGS STARTS postings.* (Closed Group).

Plender, J. (2016). The Myth of the European Peace Project. *Financial Times, Aug. 4.* Retrieved from https://www.ft.com/content/bdac2df6-598a-11e6-9f70-badea1b336d4.

Marcus Vitruvius Pollio (n.d.) *de Architectura, Book I.* Retrieved from http://penelope.uchicago.edu/Thayer/E/Roman/Texts/Vitruvius/1*.html

Podos, J. (2006). Patterns of Behavior: Konrad Lorenz, Niko Tinbergen, and the founding of Ethology. *ISBE Newsletter, 18(2).* Retrieved from http://www.bio.umass.edu/biology/podos/Pubs/2006PodosISBE.pdf

Popper, K.R. (1947). *The Open Society and its Enemies: Vol I – The Spell of Plato*. London: George Routledge & Sons.

Popper, K.R. (1968). *The Logic of Scientific Discovery*. London: Hutchinson & Co.

Popper, K.R. (1972). *Conjectures and Refutations: The Growth of Scientific Knowledge*. London: Routledge and Kegan Paul.

Pring, C. (2016). *People and Corruption: Europe and Central Asia – Global Corruption Barometer*. Germany: Transparency International. Retrieved from https://www.transparency.org/whatwedo/publication/7493.

Psychology Research and Reference (2018). *Motivated Reasoning*. Retrieved from http://psychology.iresearchnet.com/social-psychology/attitudes/motivated-reasoning/

Radaelli, C.M. (1999). *Technocracy in the European Union*. London: Longman.

Ranciére, J. (2011). *The Emancipated Spectator, Gregory Elliot (Trans)*. London: Verso.

Rankin, J. (11 October 2016). *EU petition on Barroso's Goldman Sachs job signed by more than 150,000. Declaration says former European commission president 'morally reprehensible' for joining US bank*. Retrieved from https://www.theguardian.com/business/2016/oct/11/eu-petition-on-barroso-goldman-sachs-job-signed-by-150000

Ratcliffe, S. (Ed.) (2016). *Oxford Essential Quotations (4th ed.)*. Oxford: Oxford Univ. Press.

Raviola, E. and Schnugg, C. (2016). Fostering Creativity through Artistic Interventions: Two Stories of Failed Attempts to Commodify Creativity. In: U. Johansson Sköldberg, J. Woodilla and A. Berthoin Antal (eds.), *Artistic Interventions in Organizations* (pp. 90-106). Abingdon: Routledge.

Remy, M. (1991). *The Surrealist World of Desmond Morris (L. Sagaru, Trans.)*. London: Jonathan Cape Ltd.

Research Councils UK (2017). *RCUK Policy and Guidelines on Governance of Good Research Conduct*. Retrieved from http://www.rcuk.ac.uk/documents/reviews/grc/rcukpolicyguidelinesgovernancegoodresearchconduct-pdf/

Research Executive Agency (2012). *NOTE TO THE FILE: Information on Rules for Reimbursement of Travel Expenses – EUROSTAR*. Personal Communication.

Robertson, A. (1977). Conrad Hal Waddington. 8 November 1905 – 26 September 1975. *Biographical Memoir of Fellows of the Royal Society 23*, pp. 575-622.

Root-Bernstein, R. S., Bernstein, M., and Garnier, H. (1995). Correlations between avocations, scientific style, work habits, and professional impact of scientists. *Creativity Research Journal, 8 (2)*, pp. 115-137.

Root-Bernstein, R. S., and Root-Bernstein, M. (2004). Artistic scientists and scientific artists: The link between polymathy and creativity. In: R. Sternberg, E. Grigorenko and J. Singer (eds.), *Creativity: From potential to realization* (pp. 127-152). Washington, DC: American Psychological Association.

Root-Bernstein, R. (2005). Desmond Morris's Two Spheres. *Leonardo 38(4)*, pp. 319-321.

Root-Bernstein, R., *et al.* (2008). Art Fosters Scientific Success: Avocations of Nobel, National Academy, Royal Society and Sigma Xi Members. *J. of Psychology of Science and Technology 1*(2), pp. 51-63.

Rosenblatt, L.M. (1978). *The Reader, the Text, the Poem: The Transactional Theory of the Literary Work.* Carbondale and Edwardsville: Southern Illinois Univ. Press.

Rosenblatt, L.M. (1983). *Literature as Exploration (4th ed.).* New York: The Modern Language Association of America.

Rosenblatt, L.M. (1993). The Transactional Theory: Against Dualisms. *College English 55(4)*, pp. 377-386.

Royal Society (2007). *List of Fellows of the Royal Society 1660 – 2007.* Retrieved from https://royalsociety.org/~/media/Royal_Society_Content/about-us/fellowship/Fellows1660-2007.pdf

Ruitenberg, C. W. (2011). Art, Politics, and the Pedagogical Relation. *Stud. Philos. Educ. 30(2)*, pp. 211-223

Rozenfeld, M. (2018). Reinventing how we Discover Music. *the institute 28(1)*, p. 6

Sadler, M.T.H. (1914). Translator's Introduction. In: W. Kandinsky, *The Art of Spiritual Harmony* (pp. ix-xxv). New York: Houghton Mifflin Company

Sayer, A. (2003). *Long Live Postdisciplinary Studies! Sociology and the curse of disciplinary parochialism/imperialism.* Lancaster Univ., Department of Sociology. Retrieved from http://www.lancaster.ac.uk/fass/resources/sociology-online-papers/papers/sayer-long-live-postdisciplinary-studies.pdf.

Science Europe (2016). *Science Europe Position Statement: The Framework Programme that Europe Needs.* Retrieved from https://www.scienceeurope.org/wp-content/uploads/2016/10/SE_Position_Statement_H2020.pdf

Schiuma, G. and Carlucci, D. (2016). Assessing the business impact of arts-based initiatives. In: U. Johansson Sköldberg, J. Woodilla and A. Berthoin Antal (eds.), *Artistic Interventions in Organizations* (pp. 60-73). Abingdon: Routledge.

Schmidt, R. and Umetani, N. (2014). *Branching Support Structures for 3D Printing.* ACM SIGGRAPH - Talks Program July 01. Retrieved from https://www.autodeskresearch.com/publications/branching3d.

Schneider, L. (2018). *For Better Science.* https://forbetterscience.com/

Shakespeare, W. (n.d.). *As You Like It.* Retrieved from http://shakespeare.mit.edu/asyoulikeit/full.html.

Shakespeare, W. (n.d.). *Sonnet 116: Let Me Not to the Marriage of True Minds.* Retrieved from https://www.poets.org/poetsorg/poem/let-me-not-marriage-true-minds-sonnet-116

Shanken, E.A. (2002). Art in the Information Age: Technology and Conceptual Art. *Leonardo, 35(4)* pp. 433-438.

Sheldrake, R. (2012). *The Science Delusion*. London: Hodder & Staughton, Coronet Publishing.

Sheldrake, R. (2013). *TEDx Whitechapel – The 'Banned' Talk*. Available at https://www.sheldrake.org/reactions/tedx-whitechapel-the-banned-talk

Shelley, P.B. (1819). *Love's Philosophy*. Retrieved from https://www.poetryfoundation.org/poems/50262/loves-philosophy.

Shklovsky, V. (1917). *Art as Technique*. Reprinted In: D.H. Richter (Ed.) *The Critical Tradition: Classic Texts and Contemporary Trends*, 3rd ed., 2006. New York: Bedford Books.

Siepel, J., Camerani, R., Pellegrino, G. and Masucci, M. (2016). *The Fusion Effect: The Economic Returns of Combining Arts and Science Skills – A Report for NESTA*. Retrieved from https://www.nesta.org.uk/sites/default/files/the_fusion_effect_v6.pdf

Sigma Xi (n.d.). *Becoming a Member*. Retrieved from https://www.sigmaxi.org/members/becoming-a-member

Simon, F. (2014). *EU Twisting Facts to fit Political Agenda, Chief Scientist Says*. Retrieved from http://www.euractiv.com/section/science-policymaking/news/eu-twisting-facts-to-fit-political-agenda-chief-scientist-says/

Skuggi – Jochum Magnús Eggertsson (2015). *Sorcerer's Screed*. Reykjavik: Lesstofan.

Slingerland, E. and Collard, M. (Eds.) (2012). *Creating Consilience: Integrating the Sciences and the Humanities*. Oxford: Oxford Univ. Press.

Smith, N. (2000). Afterword: Who Rules this Sausage Factory? *Antipode, 32(3)*, pp. 330-339.

Snow, C. P. (1956). The Two Cultures. *New Statesman*, 6 October.

Snow, C.P. (1961). *Science and Government*. London: Oxford Univ. Press.

Snow, C.P. (1964). *The Two Cultures and a Second Look: An Expanded Version of the Two Cultures and the Scientific Revolution*. Cambridge: Cambridge Univ. Press.

Snow, C.P. (1965). *The Search*. Harmondsworth: Penguin Books. (*Originally published in 1934*).

Social Theory Rewired (2016). *Habitus – Pierr Bourdieu*. Retrieved from http://routledgesoc.com/category/profile-tags/habitus.

Sokal, A. and Bricmont, J. (1999). *Intellectual Impostures: Postmodern Philosophers' Abuse of Science*. London: Profile Books.

Solzhenitsyn, A. (1972). *Text of Nobel Prize Speech*. Retrieved from: https://www.solzhenitsyncenter.org/nobel-lecture/

Sontag, S. (2009). *Against Interpretation and Other Essays*. London: Penguin Modern Classics. (*Originally published in 1961*).

Soviet National Anthem (1977). Retrieved from https://www.marxists.org/history/ussr/sounds/lyrics/anthem.htm.

Sowry, V. (11 March 2016). Four recent examples of outcomes arising from ANAT's Synapse art/science residency program. *nsead Digest, Vol 51, Issue 2 (Vicki Sowry)* (nsead – Network for Sciences, Engineering, Arts and Design – listserve circular; no archive copies have been made available at the network web site: http://sead.viz.tamu.edu/)

Spartacus Educational (22 March 2018). *Strength Through Joy*. Retrieved from http://spartacus-educational.com/GERjoy.htm

Stahl, T. (2018). Georg [György] Lukács. In: E.N. Zalta (Ed.), *The Stanford Encyclopaedia of Philosophy (Spring Edition)*, Retrieved from https://plato.stanford.edu/archives/spr2018/entries/lukacs/.

Stalin, J.V. (1913). *Marxism and the National Question*. Retrieved from https://www.marxists.org/reference/archive/stalin/works/1913/03a.htm#s1

Stanford Computer Graphics Laboratory (2013). *The Stanford CityBlock Project: Multi-perspective Panoramas of City Blocks*. Retrieved from http://graphics.stanford.edu/projects/cityblock/

Stenberg, H. (2016) How is the artist role affected when artists are participating in projects in work life? *Int. J. of Qualitative Stud. Health Well-being, 11 (1)*. Retrieved from http://dx.doi.org/10.3402/qhw.v11.30549

Sullivan. G. (2005). *Art Practice as Research: Inquiry in the Visual Arts*. Thousand Oaks, CA: Sage Publications.

Sun Tzu (n.d.). *The Art of War, (L. Giles, Trans.)*. Retrieved from the Internet Archive, https://ia600202.us.archive.org/14/items/TheArtOfWar_267/SunTzuTheArtOfWar.pdf

Tavares, J. and Sacco, P. (2015). *Report on the STARTS Symposium in BOZAR, Brussels 22-23 June.* Available at http://www.cheshirehenbury.com/ict-art-connect/ict-art-pdf-files/Report%20on%20Bozar%20Symposium%20June%202015.pdf.

Tate (n.d.). *Tate Art Terms: Kinetic Art*. Retrieved from http://www.tate.org.uk/art/art-terms/k/kinetic-art.

Tate (n.d.). *Tate Art Terms: Modernism*. Retrieved from http://www.tate.org.uk/art/art-terms/m/modernism.

Tate Archives (n.d.). *Artists Placement Group*. Retrieved from http://www2.tate.org.uk/artistplacementgroup/

Tate (n.d.). *Alexander Calder Performing Sculpture Exhibition; Room 7 Guide*. Retrieved from http://www.tate.org.uk/whats-on/tate-modern/exhibition/alexander-calder-performing-sculpture/alexander-calder-performing-6.

Tate Archives (n.d.). *Joseph Beuys, Four Blackboards, 1972*. Retrieved from http://www.tate.org.uk/art/artworks/beuys-four-blackboards-t03594

Tate Modern (2015). *Alexander Calder Performing Sculpture Exhibition Pamphlet*. London: Tate Modern.

Tate Britain (2016). *Conceptual Art in Britain 1964-1979 Exhibition Pamphlet*. London: Tate Britain.

Theremin World (2018). *What is a Theremin?* Retrieved from
http://www.thereminworld.com/Article/14232/what-s-a-theremin-

Terry, C. (2014*). Close the Gap: Tackling Europe's Democratic Deficit.* London: Electoral Reform
Society. Retrieved from https://www.electoral-reform.org.uk/wp-
content/uploads/2017/06/Tackling-Europes-democratic-deficit.pdf.

Telefónica I+D Web Site (2017). *David del Val Latorre.* Retrieved from
http://www.tid.es/research/researchers/david-del-val

The Economist (2013). *Unreliable Research: Trouble at the Lab. Scientists like to think of science as
self-correcting. To an alarming degree, it is not.* Retrieved from
https://www.economist.com/news/briefing/21588057-scientists-think-science-self-
correcting-alarming-degree-it-not-trouble.

The Occult History of the Third Reich (27 March 2018). *Die Deutsche Ahnenerbe.* Retrieved
from http://thirdreichocculthistory.blogspot.co.uk/2014/03/die-deutsche-ahnenerbe.html

The Washington Post (8 March 2016). *The Trappist Monk whose Calligraphy inspired Steve Jobs −
and Influenced Apple's Designs.* Retrieved from https://www.washingtonpost.com/news/arts-
and-entertainment/wp/2016/03/08/the-trappist-monk-whose-calligraphy-inspired-steve-
jobs-and-influenced-apples-designs/?utm_term=.acca10971770

Touraine, A. (1974). *The Post-industrial Society. Tomorrow's Social History: Classes, Conflicts and
Culture in the Programmed Society (Trans. L.F.X. Mayhew).* London: Wildwood House.
(Originally published in French in 1969).

Transmediale Archive (2015). *The Quantifiable Everything? - STARTS Roundtable on The
Internet of Things.* Retrieved from https://transmediale.de/content/the-quantifiable-
everything-starts-roundtable-on-the-internet-of-things

United Nations War Crimes Commission (1949). *Law Reports of Trials of War Criminals Selected
and Prepared by the United Nations War Crimes Commission: Volume X the IG Farben and Krupp
Trials.* London: HMSO. Retrieved from
https://www.loc.gov/rr/frd/Military_Law/pdf/Law-Reports_Vol-10.pdf.

United States Holocaust Memorial Museum (n.d.). *Subsequent Nuremberg Proceedings, Case #6,
The IG Farben Case: United States vs. Carl Krauch, et al.* Retrieved from
https://www.ushmm.org/wlc/en/article.php?ModuleId=10007077

United States Department of Justice (2011). *The False Claims Act: A Primer.* Retrieved from
https://www.justice.gov/sites/default/files/civil/legacy/2011/04/22/C-
FRAUDS_FCA_Primer.pdf.

Van Noorden, R. (2011). The Trouble with Retractions: A surge in Withdrawn Papers is
Highlighting Weaknesses in the System for Handling them. *Nature (478),* pp 26-28.

Vasari, G. (1898). *Lives of the Most Eminent Painters, Sculptors, and Architects Vol. II (J. Foster,
Trans.).* London. George Bell & Co. *(Originally published 1568).*

Velda, H. (2017). AI Cars face Clash of Cultures. *IET E&T Magazine* 12(3), pp. 46-47.

VERTIGO Project (2017a). Co-Production and Artwork Commissioning Contract – French Law. Retrieved from https://vertigo.starts.eu/media/uploads/vertigo_coproductioncontracttemplate_frlaw.pdf.

VERTIGO Project (2017b). Co-Production Contract – Portuguese Law. Retrieved from https://vertigo.starts.eu/media/uploads/vertigo_coproductioncontracttemplate_ptlaw.pdf.

VERTIGO Project (2017c). List of available projects. Retrieved from https://vertigo.starts.eu/call/for/call-for-artistic-residencies/

Voltaire (2005). *Candide, or Optimism (T. Ciffe, Trans.)*. London: Penguin Books. (*Originally published in 1759*).

von Hayek, F.A. (1942). Scientism and the Study of Society: Part I. *Economica 9*(35) pp. 267-291.

von Hayek, F.A. (1943). Scientism and the Study of Society: Part II. *Economica 10*(37) pp. 34-63.

von Hayek, F.A. (1944a). Scientism and the Study of Society: Part III. *Economica 11*(41) pp. 27-39.

von Hayek, F.A. (1944b). *The Road to Serfdom*. London: Routledge.

von Hayek, F.A. (1955). *The Counter-Revolution of Science: Studies on the Abuse of Reason*. New York: The Free Press.

Vonnegut, K. (1969). Player Piano. London: Panther Books (*Originally published 1953*).

Vu, T. (2015a). *Connectors*. Retrieved from http://vu2015.blog.anat.org.au/connectors/

Vu, T. (2015b). *Tree Supports and Trees*. Retrieved from http://vu2015.blog.anat.org.au/tree-supports-trees/

Waddington, C.H. (1948). *The Scientific Attitude (2nd ed.)*. West Drayton: Penguin Books.

Waddington, C.H. (1969). *Behind Appearance: A Study of the Relations between Painting and the Natural Sciences in this Century*. Edinburgh: Edinburgh Univ. Press.

Waddington, C.H. (1972). *Biology and the History of the Future*. Edinburgh: Edinburgh Univ. Press.

Wasserstein, R. L., and Lazar, N.A. (2016). The ASA's Statement on p-Values: Context, Process, and Purpose. *The American Statistician 70*(2), pp.129-133.

Weber, M. (1918). *Science as a Vocation*. Retrieved from http://www.wisdom.weizmann.ac.il/~oded/X/WeberScienceVocation.pdf

Wejchert, J. (2004). Foreword. The Human Touch: Reflections on i3. In: D.N. Snowdon, E.F. Churchill and E. Frécon (Eds.), *Inhabited Information Spaces: Living with your Data*. London: Springer.

Whewell, W. (1840). *The Philosophy of the Inductive Sciences Founded upon their History. Vol. I.* London: John W. Parker.

Whewell, W. (1848). *The Philosophy of the Inductive Sciences Founded upon their History. Vol. II.* London: John W. Parker.

Whitehead, A.N. (1927). *Science and the Modern World.* Cambridge: Cambridge Univ. Press.

Whitney, J. (1980). *Digital Harmony: On the Complementarity of Music and Visual Art.* Peterborough, NH: Byte Books.

Wildbear Entertainment (2015). *World War II: The Price of Empire - Episode 13: A New Map of the World.* Available at https://yesterday.uktv.co.uk/shows/ww2-price-of-empire/

Williams, A. (2016). How Valid is the Claim that the EU has Delivered Peace in Europe? *New Statesman, May.* Retrieved from https://www.newstatesman.com/world/2016/05/how-valid-claim-eu-has-delivered-peace-europe.

Wilson, D. and Sperber, D. (2004). Relevance Theory. In: L.R. Horn and G. Ward, G. (eds.), *The Handbook of Pragmatics* (pp. 607-632). Oxford: Blackwell.

Wilson, E.O. (1999). *Consilience: The Unity of Knowledge.* London: Abacus.

Wilson, S. (2000). *Myths and Confusions in Thinking about Art/Science/Technology.* Retrieved from http://userwww.sfsu.edu/swilson/papers/wilson.caapaper.html.

Wobbe, W. (1992). *What are Anthropocentric Production Systems? Why are they a Strategic Issue for Europe?* Luxembourg: Office for Official Publications of the European Communities, Science and Technology Policy Series.

Wollheim Memorial Web Site (n.d.). http://www.wollheim-memorial.de/

Yasmin Blog (7 July 2017). Levelling the Contemporary Art Field by Antagonizing Top-Down Processes. Retrieved from http://yasminlist.blogspot.co.uk/2017/07/yasmindiscussions-leveling-contemporary.html

Yasmin Blog (9 July 2017a). Cultural heritage and implicit bias? Retrieved from http://yasminlist.blogspot.co.uk/2017/07/yasmindiscussions-cultural-heritage-and.html

Yasmin Blog (9 July 2017b). Cultural heritage and implicit bias? Retrieved from http://yasminlist.blogspot.co.uk/2017/07/re-yasmindiscussions-cultural-heritage.html

Yetisen, A.K. *et al.* (2016). Art on the Nanoscale and Beyond. *Advanced Materials 28,* pp. 1724-1742.